The Versailles Treaty and Its Legacy
The Failure of the Wilsonian Vision

The Versailles Treaty and Its Legacy, a realist interpretation of the long diplomatic record that produced the coming of World War II in 1939, is a critique of the Paris Peace Conference of 1919 and reflects the judgment shared by many who left the Conference in disgust amid predictions of future war. The critique is a rejection of the idea of collective security, which Woodrow Wilson and many others believed was a panacea, but which was also condemned as early as 1915.

This volume delivers a powerful lesson in treaty-making and rejects the supposition that treaties, once made, are unchangeable, whatever their faults.

Norman A. Graebner was the author, co-author, editor, and co-editor of twenty-six books. He joined the University of Virginia faculty in 1967 as the Edward R. Stettinius Professor of Modern American History, and in 1982 became the Randolph P. Compton Professor. In 1978, he was Harmsworth Professor at Oxford University; he was also one of the founders and early presidents of the Society for Historians of American Foreign Relations (SHAFR). *The New York Review of Books* identified Graebner, along with Gaddis Smith at Yale, as a national leader in diplomatic history. Graebner served as an officer in the major national historical associations, and he received the highest award given to a civilian from the U.S. Military Academy for a program he developed and led at West Point. He died in May 2010 at the age of ninety-four.

Edward M. Bennett is Emeritus Professor of history at Washington State University. The recipient of several outstanding teaching awards, he has written, co-authored, edited, and co-edited ten books dealing with U.S. foreign relations. He is a past member of the executive committee of the Pacific Coast Branch of the American Historical Association. He has been a member of the SHAFR Graebner Prize Committee, as well as its chair. He was also one of ten American historians selected by the American Historical Association and the American Council of Learned Societies to participate in the colloquia authorized by Presidents Reagan and Gorbachev to assess the Soviet–American relationship in World War II.

The Versailles Treaty and Its Legacy

The Failure of the Wilsonian Vision

NORMAN A. GRAEBNER

EDWARD M. BENNETT
Washington State University, Pullman

CAMBRIDGE
UNIVERSITY PRESS

CAMBRIDGE
UNIVERSITY PRESS

32 Avenue of the Americas, New York NY 10013-2473, USA

Cambridge University Press is part of the University of Cambridge.

It furthers the University's mission by disseminating knowledge in the pursuit of education, learning and research at the highest international levels of excellence.

www.cambridge.org
Information on this title: www.cambridge.org/9781107647480

© Norman A. Graebner and Edward M. Bennett 2011

First published 2011
Reprinted 2012 (twice)
First paperback edition 2014

A catalogue record for this publication is available from the British Library

Library of Congress Cataloguing in Publication data

Graebner, Norman A.
    The Versailles Treaty and its legacy : the failure of the Wilsonian vision / Norman A. Graebner, Edward M. Bennett.
        p.   cm.
    Includes bibliographical references and index.
    ISBN 978-1-107-00821-2 (hardback)
    1. League of Nations – History.   2. Security, International.   3. International relations.
    4. World politics – 1919–1932.   I. Bennett, Edward M. (Edward Moore), 1927–
    II. Title.
    D588.G7   2011
    940.3′141–dc22   2010050095

ISBN 978-1-107-00821-2 Hardback
ISBN 978-1-107-64748-0 Paperback

This book is dedicated to Mary Moon Graebner and Margery Harder Bennett.

Without the many things they did to make its completion possible, there would be no book.

Contents

Preface

This volume seeks to explain why the world required two massive world wars, with combined casualties reaching 65 million, to come to terms with Germany. The rise of the German Empire in 1870–1871 did not rest on external aggression; rather it emerged from the willing unification of several dozen historic German states under Prussian leadership. For centuries, these German principalities, amid their disunity, were vulnerable to the external encroachments of Austria and France, the Continent's two major powers. German unification required the symbolic elimination of the powerful external influences of Austria in the Austro-Prussian War of 1866 and of France in the Franco-Prussian War of 1870–1871. Both wars, each lasting only six weeks and ending in the total annihilation of both the Austrian and French armies, ended the old European order and revealed Germany, with its powerful army, as the Continent's dominant state.

Germany's sudden acquisition of continental dominance required some adjustment of attitudes and roles in regional politics, especially in Britain and France. Such needed adjustments were not impossible. Germany's dominance did not rest on conquest, although Germany annexed France's Alsace-Lorraine along the German border in the 1871 treaty that ended the war. Germany's dominance was largely endemic, resting on its location, size, resources, industries, and the qualities of its large population. None of these assets was based on conquest. The issue of 1871 was whether Europe would willingly coexist with these realities or seek to eliminate them with war – which was impossible.

Recognizing the insecurities that Germany's unification created, German Chancellor Prince Otto von Bismarck sought, with considerable success, to assure Europe that Germany did not threaten the established interests of the European states. Bismarck understood that the immediate danger for Europe's peace lay in Austro-Russian rivalry. To control these two rivals, Bismarck brought them into the Three Emperors' League. Such levels of statesmanship established the new Germany as a valuable member of Europe's international structure. That statesmanship evaporated suddenly in 1890 when the German

Kaiser, Wilhelm II, dismissed Bismarck, terminated the Three Emperors' League, established an alliance with Austria, and cast Russia adrift. France, diplomatically isolated and determined to regain Alsace-Lorraine, quickly negotiated an alliance with discarded Russia. This divided Europe into two heavily armed alliance systems – with Britain joining France – that sought in 1914 to settle Europe's burgeoning rivalries with war.

At the Great War's end in 1918, Germany, although defeated, remained Europe's most powerful nation. Because of the extreme wartime hatreds, the Allied powers barred Germany from sending a delegation to the Paris Conference of 1919. Without a voice in the Paris deliberations, German leaders rejected the Versailles Treaty, with its territorial and military impositions, and signed it only under duress. Sustaining the Paris decisions against German (and Japanese) opposition required the perpetuation of the alliance that had produced them. President Woodrow Wilson discounted this requirement through his advocacy of collective security, as embodied in the new League of Nations. This eliminated, for the victors, the necessity and responsibility for sustaining the provisions of the Versailles Treaty. Critics warned at the outset that collective security would never function unless the League, in any crisis, had the power to coerce collective action.

In the absence of that power, the League stood helpless when Hitler, after 1933, unleashed his long successful assault on the military and territorial provisions of the Versailles Treaty. Franklin Roosevelt's Washington, supported by the other Allied victors, discovered the defense of the Versailles territorial provisions in the status quo doctrines of non-recognition and peaceful change. Unfortunately, such defenses of the Versailles arrangements proved ineffective. Eventually, Hitler, along with Italy and Japan, gained their territorial objectives in China and Western, Central, and Eastern Europe, leaving the victors with the unappetizing choice of the total disintegration of the Versailles order or war. On the unresolved issue of Danzig and Hitler's assault on Poland in September 1939, Britain and France, having refused repeatedly to defend the Versailles Treaty, chose war rather than further retreat. It was a futile gesture. The victors at Versailles had over-reached. Now they, along with the undefended victims of Nazi aggression, would pay the price.

Norman A. Graebner, who received his Ph.D. degree from the University of Chicago, was persuaded to take a realist view of foreign policy partly through the writings of Hans Morgenthau. Edward M. Bennett was a Graebner student at the University of Illinois, Urbana, who absorbed the same realist perspective in the classes and seminars of Professor Graebner. That viewpoint followed the simple formula for effective foreign policy presented by Professor Morgenthau – success rests on a balance between commitments and power, and between power and diplomacy, and if either is out of balance, failure of policy will follow.

Both authors came to see that Woodrow Wilson failed to understand these requirements for effective foreign policy, and that it was his overweening confidence in his perception of the world he dealt with that led to the defeat of the very instruments he had formulated to protect the world from a future major war. Ironically, it was a similar failure of perception on the part of Neville Chamberlain, and overwhelming confidence in his (Chamberlain's) singular direction of policy, that led to an equal failure in Britain at the crucial juncture in the late 1930s.

To understand the failures of the period following World War I, it is necessary to examine how the world managed to avoid disastrous consequences by means of the balance-of-power system that prevailed in the nineteenth century, and then study what forces prevailed to upset this most successful system of balances. Professors Graebner and Bennett both delved deeply into the rich British archival source material. Graebner had a full year to look at various archives when he was Harmsworth Professor at Oxford University. He knew that Bennett had spent part of two professional leaves – first at the old Public Records Office near the British Museum and later at the new state-of-the-art facility at Kew Gardens – looking at the diplomatic archives that led to his book on the Chamberlain–Roosevelt rivalry. Therefore, Professor Graebner proposed in 2005 that he and Professor Bennett co-author a volume examining the failure of the Versailles Treaty to accomplish the task intended for it by its signatories. This book is the result of that collaboration.

Unhappily, Professor Graebner died in May 2010. It is therefore left to me [Bennett] to thank everyone at Cambridge University Press for the roles they have played in accepting this volume for publication and getting it into production. In particular, I would like to thank Lew Bateman, Senior Political Science Editor, for urging its acceptance in the first place and for his encouragement, and Senior Editorial Assistant Anne Lovering Rounds, who shepherded the book along the publication trail, acting with all due speed to get it off the ground. My thanks also to Ronald Cohen for his excellent editorial work on the manuscript and for imparting a smooth, vital quality to the text. Finally, special thanks to my wife and fellow historian, Margery Harder Bennett, who has been my research assistant in searching the archives and my typist and in-house editor for this and every book I have ever written.

I

The International Order on Trial

I

In the modern world, nations have existed as members of an international community that offered security and enhanced the possibilities of national existence. What held the separate entities in a stable relationship with one another was the freedom of every nation to respond, alone or with others, to any threat to the established order. This balancing system required the existence of a preponderance of power that was prepared, under duress, to confront any unwanted assaults on the established order. In recent centuries, the European balance of power had always triumphed over any assaults on the status quo that became too ambitious. France under Louis XIV, and later Napoleon, sought drastic changes in the map of Europe; in both endeavors, France went down in total defeat. If the balance of power failed to prevent wars, it limited their consequences, and thereby preserved the existing order of power, encouraging restraint and accommodation. With good reason, America's Founding Fathers and those who followed them placed their faith in the balancing system as the surest guarantee of the nation's well-being and security.[1]

The first mammoth assaults on Europe's long-established equilibrium were Germany's easy six-week triumphs over Austria and France in 1866 and 1871. Prussia thereby terminated the historic involvement of Austria and France in Germanic affairs. Berlin used the latter victory to proclaim the new German Empire in the Hall of Mirrors at Versailles, impose an indemnity on Paris, and annex the French province of Alsace-Lorraine. In less than a decade, Germany had emerged from a congeries of Germanic states to become Europe's most powerful nation. Facing a vengeful France, Germany sought security in its pre-eminent military establishment, as well as in the incitement of nationalistic emotions – all certain to disquiet other European powers and

[1] For superb evaluations of the balance of power system, see Hans J. Morgenthau, *Politics Among Nations* (New York, 1949), 125–66; Hedley Bull, *The Anarchical Society: A Study of Order in World Politics* (London, 1977).

I

prod them into countermeasures of defense. Prince Otto von Bismarck, the German Chancellor, moved quickly to quiet Europe's reaction. As early as 1873, he negotiated the Three Emperors' League to govern the behavior of Austria and Russia, Europe's primary and most vengeful antagonists. Later he added Italy to his alliance system. By 1875, France had reorganized its army and appeared prosperous and strong. Yet that year, U.S. minister J. C. Bancroft Davis could write from Berlin, "On my own judgment peace will be preserved so long as there continues to be a good understanding between Russia, Austria, and Germany."[2] As late as 1890, when the German Kaiser, Wilhelm II, dismissed Bismarck, Europe, having accepted the new German Empire, and with the Continent's chief antagonists under control, appeared stable and secure.

Suddenly, Bismarck's peace structure faced disintegration. The new Kaiser terminated the Three Emperors' League, strengthening ties with Austria and dismissing Russia. Russia, now isolated, sought security in the arms of France. The burgeoning Franco-Russian relationship, resulting in the 1894 alliance, created the linchpin of what George Kennan termed "the decline of Bismarck's European order."[3] Europe's division into two alliance systems placed future peace on the altar of diplomatic inflexibility and the deterrent power of the alliance structure. U.S. Minister Bartlett Tripp, in Vienna, predicted a troubled future for Europe, explaining on January 4, 1894: "I see no possibility of the great nations of Russia and Germany at present submitting to a peaceful solution of the questions of international differences now impending.... Nothing but wise statesmanship and the existing fear on the part of the nations of the terrible result of such a contest can avert the impending conflict...."[4]

Many observers regarded Russia, with its immense territories, huge population, expansive tradition, and known designs on Eastern Europe and the Balkans, as the ultimate danger to Western security. British diplomat Cecil Spring-Rice reminded Theodore Roosevelt in September 1896:

> It looks like the gathering of great forces for a struggle, not in the immediate (that would be better) but in the far future.... Russia is self sufficient. She is also practically invulnerable to attack. She is growing and has room to grow.... Owing to Alsace and Lorraine, Europe is hopelessly divided.... Taking all these things together, it is not at all improbable that Europe may be in a given period at the mercy of a power really barbarous but with a high

---

[2] J. C. Bancroft Davis to Hamilton Fish, dispatch no. 164, August 23, 1875, Diplomatic Dispatches, Germany, RG59, National Archives. For a superb discussion of Germany's effort to maintain peace between Russia and Austria, see Paul W. Schroeder, "The 'Balance of Power' System in Europe, 1815–1871," *Naval War College Review*, 27 (March-April 1975), 29–31.

[3] For the French-Russian alliance's threat to Europe's peace, see George F. Kennan, *The Fateful Alliance: France, Russia, and the Coming of the First World War* (New York, 1984).

[4] Tripp to Walter Q. Gresham, Secretary of State, dispatch no. 62, January 4, 1894, Diplomatic Dispatches, Austria, RG59.

military organization.... [N]o power will attack Russia – no one can afford to. Russia therefore has simply to bide her time.[5]

For Theodore Roosevelt, Russia was an appalling problem that Germany alone had the power to crush. He wrote in August 1896: "Even if in the dim future Russia should take India and become the preponderant power of Asia, England would merely be injured in one great dependency; but when Russia grows so as to crush Germany, the crushing will be once for all."[6]

French *revanche*, emboldened by the alliance with Russia, appeared equally menacing to European peace and stability. It was the Franco-Russian alliance that lent credibility to France's determination to recover Alsace-Lorraine.[7] But for French *revanche*, Europe might have faced the Eastern Question with comparative ease. What gave the impending crisis its dreadful character was the fear of a simultaneous Franco-Russian assault on Central Europe. No American saw the essentially tragic nature of the Franco-Russian alliance more clearly than did William R. Thayer, an acute observer of the European scene, who wrote in November 1891:

> Russia is ... the center of the warlike storm-area to-day. Eliminate her from European politics, and the other powers would have no plausible excuse for keeping up their armaments, because France, in spite of her grievances and wrath, would see the hopelessness of dashing her head against Germany, supported by Austria and Italy. The possibility of winning Russia as an ally ... has forced Germany to stand by her guns. But the Russian monster threatens not only Germany; as Napoleon discerned eighty years ago, he endangers all western Europe.

One day, Thayer predicted, France and Germany – indeed, all Western Europe – would stand together against the Cossack invader.[8]

Tragically, Europe's burgeoning insecurities had transformed the Continent into an armed camp. Never had its leading nations embarked on such an insatiable quest for weapons. "Every city," wrote Thayer, "has its barracks and parade-ground; every frontier frowns with a double row of fortifications.... Europe from the Douro to the Don, is a camp whereon ten times three hundred thousand of her able-bodied men are bivouacking, ready at a sign to spring to arms and slay each other."[9] Tripp reported from Vienna: "Europe is one armed camp, and every lightning flash from diplomatic wires is like the firing of a sentry gun – a call to arms."[10]

[5] Spring-Rice to Theodore Roosevelt, September 14, 1896, in Stephen Gwynn, ed., *The Letters and Friendships of Sir Cecil Spring-Rice: A Record* (London, 1929), 1: 210–11.

[6] Roosevelt to Spring-Rice, August 5, 1896, in Elting E. Morison, ed., *The Letters of Theodore Roosevelt* (Cambridge, MA, 1951), 1: 555.

[7] Edward A. Freeman, "Dangers to the Peace of Europe," *Forum*, 12 (November 1891), 301; W. J. Stillman, "Italy and the Triple Alliance," *Nation*, 51 (October 30, 1890), 340.

[8] Charles W. Thayer, "The Armed Truce of the Powers," *Diplomat* (Westport, 1974), 322, 323.

[9] Ibid., 312.

[10] Tripp to Secretary of State Richard Olney, dispatch no. 175, January 18, 1896, Diplomatic Dispatches, Austria, RG59.

II

By 1900, Germany had supplanted Russia as the focus of Europe's insecurities. Germany's military primacy was obvious enough, and Bismarck's
assurances of German acceptance of the post-1871 status quo had evaporated. German power was moving onto the high seas with the Kaiser's
widely proclaimed naval-building program, designed to challenge Britain's
dominance of the oceans. Germany's rapidly expanding naval power rendered Berlin's known interests in the Middle East, its possible ambitions to
build a colonial empire, a rising threat to Europe's established order. In 1898,
the Kaiser proclaimed that Germany had "great tasks ... outside the narrow
boundaries of Old Europe."[11] Had Germany, in its expansiveness, concentrated on specific, limited goals, other nations might have better judged their
interests in questioning German ambition. But Berlin, by pursuing general,
ill-defined, unknown but suspected, changes in the status quo, aroused universal apprehension.

What rendered Germany's suspected quest for primacy in world affairs even
more unsettling was the burgeoning rhetoric of German nationalism. German
spokesmen resented the superior prestige that Britain and France enjoyed as
traditional world powers. The Kaiser complained that British nobility, when
touring the Continent, visited Paris but never Berlin. He issued a veiled warning to the King of Italy: "All the long years of my reign my colleagues, the
Monarchs of Europe, have paid no attention to what I have to say. Soon, with
my great Navy to endorse my words, they will be more respectful." Germans
felt cheated by Europe's refusal to recognize their rightful position in world
affairs. Friedrich von Bernhardi, the noted spokesman of German nationalism, expressed his country's ambitions when he wrote: "We must secure to
German nationality and German spirit throughout the globe that high esteem
which is due them."[12]

As early as 1894, France and Russia sought security in their alliance against
Germany and Austria. Isolationist Britain had long resisted membership in
any formal alignment against Germany, but in 1904 the London government
signed the Entente Cordiale with France. So dominant and threatening had
Germany become that Britain, France, and Russia, to right the European balance, formed the Triple Entente (1907), with its detailed military preparations,
to convince Germany that any aggression would fail. Britain now assumed
the lead in confronting German ambition. The Entente represented Europe's
ultimate massing of power in defense of the old order.

---

[11] The Kaiser, quoted in *Newsweek*, November 25, 1991, 57.

[12] Fritz Fischer's *Griff nach der Weltmacht* (1961) and James Joll's translation, *Germany's Aims
in the First World War* (1967), based on a deeper examination of the German record, revealed
the extent of German ambitions before and during the Great War of 1914, but those revela-
tions did not determine the pre-war doubts and insecurities unleashed by German behavior
prior to 1914.

Still, the Entente contained a serious flaw. It was only the organizational deficiencies of the Tsarist regime that clouded Russian expansionism. In the diplomacy that led to the Triple Entente, Russia demanded and received concessions to its historic aspirations in the Balkans. To sustain the credibility of their alliance, Britain and France encouraged Russian firmness against Austria, even as they knew that any Allied victory over Germany would weaken German and Austrian influence in Eastern Europe and open wide the gates to Russian expansion. Thus the faltering balance of power eliminated British and French primacy on two fronts. The potential European giants, Germany and Russia, had emerged as the new poles in the European equilibrium.

III

The murder of the Austrian Archduke, Franz Ferdinand at Sarajevo, the capital of Bosnia, on June 28, 1914, lit the slow fuse that five weeks later exploded into catastrophe. For a decade, the Balkans had been the scene of plots and conspiracies, but the rivalry that mattered on that June day was the burning determination of Serbian nationalists to recapture the former Serbian province of Bosnia, annexed by Austria in 1908. The assassination of the Archduke, quickly linked to Serbian officialdom, provided Vienna the occasion to resolve its Serbian question permanently.[13] This was the moment that Bismarck's alliance system had sought to avoid. Emperor Franz Joseph's Vienna was replete with pomp, externally grandiose but internally sterile.[14] Austria lacked the power to wage a successful war, but Vienna's imperial command, led by General Conrad von Hötzendorf, had entrusted its ambitions to a war against Serbia.

Germany issued its "blank check" to Austria, knowing that Austria's warlike mood against Serbia might bring Russia into the field.[15] Berlin placed the burden of decision on the Tsarist government.[16] Serbia responded to Austria's demands with moderation, but ordered mobilization. Austria rejected Serbia's concessions and also ordered mobilization. Europe knew that it was in deep trouble. Imaginative diplomacy might have prevented the impending crisis, but in the test of wills, time and inflexibility became the determinants of national action, eliminating any possibility of diplomatic compromise.[17]

---

[13] Serbian officials knew of the plot, but failed to warn the Austrian government. For a detailed account of the crisis, see Sidney Bradshaw Fay, *The Origins of the World War* (New York, 1928), II, 157–66.

[14] For a description of Vienna in the 1914 crisis, see Frederick Morton, *Thunder at Twilight: Vienna 1913/1914* (New York, 2001).

[15] Quoted in Sir Horace Rumbold, *The War Crisis in Berlin: July-August 1914* (London, 1940), 339.

[16] Prince von Bülow, *Memoirs: 1903–1909* (New York, 1930), 318.

[17] Sir John Keegan stresses this inflexibility in his *The First World War* (New York, 1999), 60–70.

What elevated the time factor to a controlling role in the crisis was not only the credibility of each alliance, but also the existence, in all the major powers, of detailed military plans and timetables for mobilization and attack. Because of the known readiness of the opposing armies, each nation's hopes for victory were anchored to a first strike. Germany, requiring an immediate resolution of the Austro-Serbian confrontation, pressed Vienna for a quick showdown with Serbia before France and Russia had time to mobilize. By late July, Austria's ultimatum, with its 48-hour deadline, had brought all of Europe to the verge of war. Austria and Serbia had already mobilized. Assured that Russia would not move, Austria declared war on July 28.

Only the postponement of military operations could have provided time for calm reflection and negotiation, but the need for a time advantage overwhelmed the more illusive hope of averting war. Russia mobilized on July 30 in the face of a direct German warning. The Kaiser ordered German mobilization on August 1; within minutes, France made that same fateful decision. Britain waited an additional day. As late as July 25, Serbia and Austria had mobilized 400,000 men; a week later, Europe stood poised for a gigantic struggle, with almost 12 million men under arms. Every mobilization order had been issued in the name of defense.[18] Seldom had the world experienced such a failure of diplomacy. No nation, other than Serbia, was in danger of attack, and that was preventable. None possessed clear and reasonable objectives commensurate with the predictable costs. Again and again, the five-week drive toward war could have been halted. Because the war had no rationale that could direct or limit its objectives, it could only become one of attrition, with the single goal of victory.

IV

The war's euphoric inception revealed the emotional state of preparedness. British students rushed to the colors, cheered on by families and friends. German soldiers left Berlin on August 3, 1914, with the jubilant pledge, "We'll be back by Christmas." Within weeks, the massive clash of arms became more immense and costly than those responsible had anticipated; instead of short and promising, it evolved into a four-year struggle of unprecedented death and destruction. Some 13 million died, mostly young men under conditions of almost unimaginable terror. The limited wars of the nineteenth century engaged several hundred thousand men at most; the Great War of 1914 trapped millions of soldiers in battles that lasted not days, but months.

Military plans anticipated quick and decisive victories. For no nation was this more true than for Germany. Count Alfred von Schliefen, Chief of the

---

[18] For the time factor in the rapid expansion of the war, see Ole R. Holsti, "The 1914 Case," *The American Political Science Review*, LIX (June 1965), 365–73; Gilbert C. Fite and Norman A. Graebner, *Recent United States History* (New York, 1972), 13–15; John Keegan, *The First World War* (New York, 1999), 60–70.

German General Staff, had perfected the German strategy as early as 1905. It called for a wheeling movement of the German army, with its major force massed on the right, driving through Luxembourg, Belgium, and northern France. As the huge German army advanced toward Paris during August, the French staged their counteroffensive against the German middle to shatter the weaker German lines and force a German retreat. Both offensives failed. The French could not dislodge the German center; the Germans, approaching Paris, failed to penetrate the French defenses at the Marne.[19] That victory brought the Western Front to a standstill, as the opposing forces soon faced one another from long lines of trenches that ultimately stretched from the sand dunes of the Belgian coast to end within view of the Swiss mountains.

Rendering the positions virtually impregnable were the well-placed, death-dealing machine guns, backed by mortars and accurate rifle fire. Only four months separated mobilization from the stabilization of the Western Front. The meticulously planned war was over before it began. The generals now faced challenges they had not anticipated and for which there were no promising responses. The machine gun had forced the war into the trenches, where there was nothing but attrition, misery, hopelessness, and unprecedented human and physical destruction.[20] Amid the futility and human cost of trench warfare, ultimate success would come to those who could best tolerate the losses.[21] On the Eastern Front, Russia was already approaching the limits of its military capacity for modern warfare. As early as late August 1914, Russian forces had advanced to Tannenberg in East Prussia, only to suffer a devastating German assault, with casualties so immense that Russia ceased to be a major factor in the war."[22]

As 1916 dawned, the contestants on the Western Front remained mired in a costly stalemate reaching from Switzerland to the North Sea. Already the German and Allied casualties had become horrendous, with hundreds of thousands killed, and even more wounded. It was clear that neither side could withstand the frightful casualties of 1914 and 1915 indefinitely, and must press hard for the needed victory. General Erich von Falkenhayn, the German commander, planned an offensive that would chew up the French army and at last open the road to Paris. Convinced that the French would defend their historic and

---

[19] For the critical battle of the Marne, see Keegan, *The First World War*, 100–09.

[20] For a history of the machine gun, beginning with the Maxim in 1884, see Steve Featherstone, "The Line Is Hot: A History of the Machine Gun, Shot," *Harper's Magazine*, 311 (December 2005), 59–66. The British and the Germans found it useful in killing hordes of African natives at the turn of the twentieth century. Initially, the British hesitated to use it against fellow Europeans, whereas the Germans proceeded to perfect a strategy for its use in a possible European war.

[21] For the evolution and horrors of trench warfare, see Lyn Macdonald, *1915: The Death of Innocence* (New York, 2004).

[22] Keegan, *The First World War*, 148–50. Tannenberg inaugurated the long wartime Russian agony that culminated in revolution.

semi-sacred fortress, Verdun, to the last man, Falkenhayn massed German artillery and manpower in the Verdun sector to overwhelm and destroy the French forces that, he hoped, would refuse to retreat.[23] The German Fifth Army, under German Crown Prince Wilhelm, prepared to conduct this victorious operation. By February, the Germans had brought 1,200 guns of all sizes into position.

Ten miles separated Verdun from the German lines – ten miles of intricate defenses, held by determined French troops. So heavy was the initial German bombardment that it obliterated many of the French trenches. Still, the German infantry advances came hard. French artillery positions along the German flanks took a heavy toll and diverted the German attack. Between February and June, 20 million shells reduced forests to splinters and erased whole villages. French soldiers died without seeing the enemy. Verdun was horrible, wrote one French soldier, "because man is fighting material, with the sensation of striking out at empty air...." So pulverized was the terrain before Verdun that many French soldiers were never found. One witness recalled that the shells "disinterred the bodies, then re-interred them, chopped them to pieces, played with them as a cat plays with a mouse." Never had French soldiers revealed such tenacity, but from that disaster the spirit of France would not soon recover.[24] German units came within sight of Verdun, but that was all. Even for the Germans, the losses had become unbearable.

British and French leaders understood that they could not achieve victory before they had driven the Germany army from French soil. Marshal Joseph Joffre, the French commander-in-chief and hero of the Marne, carefully planned a joint French and British offensive along the Somme. In late June 1916, Joffre's powerful assault, in which the British suffered 60,000 casualties on the first day – 20,000 dead and 40,000 wounded – forced Falkenhayn to transfer troops from the Verdun sector. Eventually, Sir Douglas Haig's British forces suffered half a million casualties in their unsuccessful attempt to break the German lines.[25] The Somme demonstrated the raw firepower of machine guns against enemies that possessed no defense against them. No British soldier saw more clearly the terrible futility of the British effort than young Guy Chapman in his sensitive memoir, *A Passionate Prodigality* (1933):

> The next hour, man, will bring you three miles nearer to your death. Your life and your death are nothing to these fields – nothing, no more than it is to the man planning the next attack at G.H.Q. You are not even a pawn. Your death will not prevent future wars, will not make the world safe for your children. Your death means no more than if you died in your bed, full of years and respectability....[26]

[23] For Falkenhayn's strategy of attrition, see Robert T. Foley, *German Strategy and the Path to Verdun: Eric von Falkenhayn and the Development of Attrition, 1870–1916* (New York, 2005).

[24] For the battle of Verdun, ibid., 277–86.

[25] Battle of the Somme, ibid., 286–99.

[26] Guy Chapman, *A Passionate Prodigality* (New York, 1933), 122.

That summer, the combined casualties at Verdun reached 800,000; on the Somme, perhaps 1,200,000.

The absence of specific culpability for the war compelled every European capital to place responsibility for its immeasurable costs on others. That the conflict was fought on French soil lent special credence to Allied accusations that German aggression was the sole cause of the death and devastation. To sustain the morale of weary troops and distraught civilians, as well as to overcome the normal reluctance of soldiers to kill, governments resorted to propaganda designed to demonize the enemy, thereby rendering domestic sacrifices tolerable and the willingness to kill acceptable, even meritorious.[27] The resulting animosity deteriorated to the level of hatred, with appalling quests for revenge.

V

Among that perceptive minority of Europeans who in 1914 recognized the essentially tragic nature of the approaching conflict was the noted French pacifist, Romain Rolland. By September, he had taken refuge in Switzerland to escape the necessity of choosing sides. That month he wrote prophetically:

> Thus the three great peoples of the West, the guardians of civilization, are rushing headlong toward their ruin and are calling to their rescue ... the hordes of the whole universe in order that they might devour one another. Is our civilization so firmly rooted that you do not fear to weaken its pillars? (Fite and Graebner, *Recent History of the United States*. New York, 1972.)

Few Europeans could see as clearly as Rolland that Europe's great civilization had fallen upon itself in one vast suicidal struggle that could only weaken those elements of political and military superiority that underwrote its progress, security, and predominance in world affairs.

Unfortunately, the Great War, both in its coming and its subsequent conduct, challenged not only Europe's centrality in world politics, but also the institutions that assured the apparent grandeur of its civilization. Despite its societal and economic successes, the Europe of the late nineteenth century was beset with astonishing failures. Democracy itself was limited to the few. In England, neither women nor millions of men with low incomes were permitted to vote. The poor of Europe were very poor, and they were legion. Every large city had slums of appalling horror. But men were stirring in their search for a new order that would eliminate the weaknesses of the old. Militant nationalists and socialists promised to reconstruct society through centralized government, directing the power of the state toward the elimination of its iniquities. Both groups were ultimately totalitarian, merely representing different constituencies.

[27] For major studies of Great War propaganda, see Peter Buitenhuis, *The Great War of Words* (Vancouver, 1987); Michael Sanders, *British Propaganda during the First World War* (London, 1982); H. C. Peterson, *Propaganda for War* (Norman, 1939). The Peterson volume dwells largely on the British propaganda campaign against American neutrality.

As late as 1914, neither nationalism nor socialism had effectively challenged the Western ideal of liberal capitalism. Europe appeared capable of assimilating every revolutionary pressure because no program for change was incompatible with its political traditions. Through the late nineteenth century, much of the industrial working class, far from becoming poorer and more miserable, had improved its lot both relatively and absolutely. Between capitalists and proletarians, a new middle class bridged the class distinctions, demonstrating that life under the established order could be better.[28] Long before 1914, liberal capitalism had contributed far more to the general welfare than nationalists and socialists had believed possible. Europe's parliamentary system had muted its revolutionary challenges by making concessions to reasonable demands while protecting personal liberties and constitutional processes.

That Europe's liberal heritage had apparently absorbed its opposition seemed clear to one of Britain's leading intellects, J. B. Bury. This noted historian wrote in 1913: "The struggle of reason against authority has ended in what appears now to be [a] decisive and permanent victory for liberty. In the most civilized and progressive countries freedom of discussion is recognized as a fundamental principle...." Bury believed a reversion to tyranny in Europe improbable. Yet, as an afterthought, he acknowledged one remaining danger to European civilization. Coercion would return, he warned, "if a revolutionary social movement prevail, led by men inspired by faith and formulas (like the men of the French Revolution) and resolved to impose their creed...."[29] The Great War of 1914, by unleashing men of faith and formulas, threatened to exhaust the slow process of adjustment.

Both revolutionary nationalists and socialists gambled on the war to undermine the primacy of the old order. Nationalists saw clearly that every government of Europe, under the pressure of war, would be compelled to mobilize the agencies of political power. If the demands of war endangered Europe's political heritage of liberal democracy, they offered untold opportunities for those who favored the ultimate in blood-and-iron nationalism. Adolf Hitler, the war's chief beneficiary, hailed it ecstatically. In his *Mein Kampf* (1925), he recalled his reaction to the outbreak of war:

> The fight of the year 1914 was certainly not forced upon the masses, ... but desired by the entire people.... To me personally those hours appeared like redemption.... Overwhelmed by impassionate enthusiasm, I had fallen on my knees and thanked Heaven out of my overflowing heart that it granted me the good fortune of being allowed to live in these times.[30]

Russian socialists detected in the war the prospect of revolution. Vladimir Ilyich Lenin, Russia's leading revolutionary, saw that Bolshevism's only hope lay in a major war, but he doubted that it would come. He wrote to his friend

[28] On nationalism's and socialism's limited impact, see "The Strange Case of Karl and Adolf," *The Economist*, 352 (September 11, 1999), 8.
[29] Bury, quoted in Fite and Graebner, *Recent United States History*, 8.
[30] See Adolf Hitler, *Mein Kampf*, trans. Ralph Manheim (Boston, 1971), 161.

Maxim Gorki in 1912, "I am afraid that Francis Joseph and Nicholas will not give us this pleasure." But the two monarchs did, and in the process eliminated their own dynasties. Fascism and communism, the two new forces of the century, arose in Germany and Russia, Europe's most powerful nations.[31]

VI

Long before the United States entered the war as an active participant, President Woodrow Wilson had developed a profound contempt for political and diplomatic traditions that seemed to serve mankind so badly. For Wilson, Europe's rulers had again neglected their obligations to govern wisely; instead, they had plunged much of the globe into the most catastrophic of wars. Europe's long record of war seemed to demonstrate the Continent's profound ineptitude in creating an international order that would advance the cause of peace and answer the needs of a distraught and exploited humanity.

Wilson's conviction that his country's special character gave it a transcendent mission to serve humanity came easily enough. To him, the United States possessed the idealism and integrity necessary for designing a new international community. America was born, he once declared, that men might be free. In accepting the Democratic nomination in 1912, he expressed the hope that the nation had "awakened to the knowledge that she has certain cherished liberties and ... priceless resources ... to hold in trust for posterity and for all mankind."[32] On Independence Day 1914, Wilson again staked out an American claim to world leadership. "My dream," he said, "is that as ... the world knows more and more of America, it ... will turn to America for those moral inspirations which lie at the basis of all freedom, ... and that America will come into the full light of day when ... her flag is the flag not only of America, but of humanity."[33]

In framing that desired American mission for the world, Wilson confronted historic American isolationism, intensified by the horrors of the European war. As the Wabash (Indiana) *Plain Dealer* observed, "We never appreciated as now the foresight exercised by our forefathers in migrating from Europe." Wilson doubted isolationism's viability, but hesitated to drag the country into the jungle of power politics. Wilson found greater promise for the country's active involvement in world affairs in historical American nationalism, based on the supposition that American civilization was superior to that of other continents.[34] Much of America's uniqueness lay in its democratic institutions and the conviction

---

[31] For the impact of the war on German society especially, see Gerhard Weinberg, *Germany, Hitler, and World War II* (New York, 1995).

[32] Wilson's acceptance speech, August 7, 1912, in Ray Stannard Baker and William E. Dodd, eds., *The Public Papers of Woodrow Wilson: College and State* (New York, 1925), II, 453.

[33] Wilson's address at Independence Hall, Philadelphia, July 4, 1914, Baker and Dodd, *The Public Papers of Woodrow Wilson: The New Democracy* (New York, 1927), I, 147.

[34] For the influence of isolationism and nationalism on Wilson's thought, see J. A. Thompson, "Woodrow Wilson and World War I: A Reappraisal," *Journal of American Studies*, 19 (1981), 329–30.

that they were the world's ultimate salvation. Herein lay the foundations of an authentic American foreign policy that would enhance the nation's pride, guarantee the indispensable public support, and establish the basis of an appealing international agenda – even as it defied the creation of any plan of action. The peaceful and humane visions of American nationalism demanded a system of internationalized commitments that would enable the United States to act with a maximum of purpose and support and a minimum of cost, danger, and risk.[35]

Wilson sought a post-war international structure that would translate his preferences for a democratic order into specific programs of action. In this quest he was not alone. One group of distinguished Americans launched the League to Enforce Peace in 1915. At Independence Hall, Philadelphia, in June of that year, the League elected former President William Howard Taft as its president.[36] The heart of the League's proposal was a system of collective security under which all nations would assume the obligation to enforce conciliation and, if necessary, combine to punish an aggressor. "The delinquent who contemplates a break in the peace," declared Harvard president A. Lawrence Lowell, "must know that retribution will be certain, instant, and irresistible."[37]

Similar internationalist pressure came from London, where Sir Edward Grey, the British Foreign Minister, had become convinced that a stable and permanent post-war settlement would require a direct and continued U.S. involvement in European affairs. Grey seized on the League appeal as an indirect method of bringing American influence to bear on world politics. In November 1915, Wilson assured Grey that he favored a concert of nations organized to prevent war.[38] Speaking in Des Moines, Iowa, in early February 1916, the President expressed the hope that the war would produce "some sort of joint guarantee of peace on the part of the great nations of the world."[39]

Then, on May 27, the President addressed a mammoth assembly of the League to Enforce Peace in Washington to reaffirm his interest in an association of nations, one that would, he promised, "prevent any war begun either contrary to treaty covenants or without warning and full submission of the

[35] Inis Claude analyzes the role of collective action as a substitute for isolationism in "The Collectivist Theme in International Relations," *International Journal* (Canadian Institute of International Affairs), 24, No. 4 (Autumn 1969), 639–50. Lloyd Ambrosius argues that Wilson's general commitment to peace without any particular national obligation to act was basically isolationist. See Lloyd Ambrosius, "Wilson's League of Nations," *Maryland Historical Magazine*, 65 (Winter 1970), 370–93.

[36] For the program of the League to Enforce Peace, see Ruhl J. Bartlett, *The League to Enforce Peace* (Chapel Hill, 1944), 39–41; William Howard Taft, *Taft Papers on League of Nations*, eds. Theodore Marburg and Horace E. Flack (New York, 1920), 48–50.

[37] A. Lawrence Lowell, "A League to Enforce Peace," *Independent*, 82 (June 28, 1915), 523; Lowell, "A League to Enforce Peace," *World's Work*, 30 (October 1915), 720.

[38] George M. Trevelyan, *Grey of Fallodon* (Boston, 1937), 356–59; Leon Boothe, "Lord Grey, the United States, and the Political Effort for a League of Nations, 1914–1920," *Maryland Historical Magazine*, 65 (Spring 1970), 36–39.

[39] Address in Des Moines, February 1, 1916, Arthur S. Link, ed., *The Papers of Woodrow Wilson* (69 vols., Princeton, 1966–1994), 36: 80.

causes to the opinion of the world, a virtual guarantee of territorial integrity and political independence." He favored collective power behind a moral judgment of the world against an aggressor.[40] But he assured his audience that such an association would summon coercion, not to selfish ambition, but to the service of peace, order, and justice.[41] Addressing the Senate on January 22, 1917, the President defined the essential elements of his vision for a peaceful international order. It would require, at the outset, that the treaties and agreements terminating the ongoing war assured "a peace that is worth guaranteeing and preserving, ... not merely a peace that will serve the several interests and immediate aims of the nations engaged." Such a peace would rest on the triumph of self-determination. "No peace can last, or ought to last," he warned, "which does not recognize and accept the principle that governments derive all their just powers from the consent of the governed...." To render that post-war settlement permanent, the world would require an international power, based on "the organized major force of mankind, [so dominant that] no nation, no probable combination of nations could face or withstand it." That guarantee of peace eliminated all reliance on the traditional appurtenances of power politics. "There must be," he averred, "not a balance of power, but a community of power; not organized rivalries, but an organized common peace."[42]

Wilson made himself the prophet of a world free of power politics, one in which the old balance of power would recede before a new community of power. The President admonished the European states to avoid entangling alliances "which would draw them into competitions of power, catch them in a net of intrigue and selfish rivalry, and disturb their own affairs with influences intruded from without."[43] Finally, Wilson advocated a "peace without victory," for a victor's peace, accepted in humiliation and under duress, would rest on quicksand.[44]

Wilson's full endorsement of a league of nations brought the national debate over collective security to a high level of intensity. On February 1, 1917, Senator Henry Cabot Lodge answered Wilson in the Senate. The Senator agreed readily that effective counterforce alone could maintain the peace, but he warned that any arrangement that permitted each nation the right "to decide whether its force should be used ... does not advance us at all...." But an organization designed to respond automatically to any threatened aggression, he averred, would require infringements on national sovereignty. No country, Lodge warned, would agree in advance to go to war at the command of others.[45]

[40] See, for example, "Wilson's Great Utterance," *The New Republic*, 17 (June 5, 1916), 103.
[41] Wilson's address to the League to Enforce Peace, Washington, May 27, 1916, in Baker and Dodd, *The New Democracy*, II, 184–88. Quotation on p. 188.
[42] Wilson's address to the Senate, January 22, 1917, ibid., 40: 535–37.
[43] Baker and Dodd, 539.
[44] Ibid., 536. For a major critique of the lack of realism in Wilson's foreign policy statements, including Lansing's response, see Jan Wilhelm Schulte-Nordholt, *A Life for Peace* (Berkeley, 1991).
[45] Lodge's speech in the Senate, February 1, 1917, *Cong. Record*, 64th Cong., 2nd Sess., 2367.

No more than Lodge could spokesmen of the League to Enforce Peace resolve the conflict between sovereignty and collective security. Lowell advanced the pleasant notion that the mere existence of a league would serve as a powerful deterrent inasmuch as no aggressor would test the wrath of so many enemies.[46] Taft assured the nation that the threat of economic and diplomatic isolation "would, except in rare cases, accomplish the purpose of this organization of world force without its use." For Taft, diplomatic pressure, operating through the league and supported by world opinion, would serve as a massive deterrent to war.[47] Unfortunately, the assumption that a league could ultimately prevent war without actual resort to force skirted the issue of collective security – which demanded a relinquishment of national sovereignty that no nation would accept. Despite the widespread adherence to the principle of collective security, neither writers, scholars, nor statesmen could formulate any practical answer to the problem of war.

VII

American observers who had dwelled on the impossibility of a European war looked on with relief when it came. Geography seemed to offer assurance that the war, however dreadful it might become, would remain far from American shores. The *Chicago Herald* responded to the outbreak of war with "a hearty vote of thanks to Columbus for having discovered America." After recounting the Russian, German, French, and English declarations of war in 1914, the *New York World* quipped, "If Europe insists on committing suicide, Europe must furnish the corpses for the funeral." To such sentiments of isolationism, the President responded sympathetically. Like Americans generally, he was convinced that the war would serve no useful purpose. Acknowledging the fact that Americans were drawn from many countries, especially from those now at war, he urged the country to be "impartial in thought as well as in action." Wilson assured the German ambassador: "We definitely have to be neutral, since otherwise our mixed populations would wage war on each other."[48] By maintaining a fine poise and self-control, by refusing to sit in judgment of others, he told the nation, the United States would keep itself "free to do what is honest and disinterested and truly serviceable for the peace of the world."[49]

Wilson's quest for impartiality had no chance of success. For most Americans it mattered who won, and of those, 90 percent favored the Allies. With Britain and France lay the country's chief political, cultural, and economic affinities. What magnified such partiality was the Wilson administration's own

---

[46] A. Lawrence Lowell, "The League to Enforce Peace," *North American Review*, 205 (January 1917), 29.

[47] William Howard Taft, "From Battle and Murder, and From Sudden Death," *The Nation's Business*, V (February 1917), 19.

[48] Quoted in Arthur Link, *The Struggle for Neutrality, 1914–1915* (Princeton, 1960), 65–67.

[49] For Wilson's motives in avoiding war, see John Milton Cooper, *The Warrior and the Priest: Woodrow Wilson and Theodore Roosevelt* (Cambridge, MA, 1983), 273–74.

deep commitment to the Allied cause. Robert Lansing, First Counselor in the State Department and, after June 1915, Secretary of State, along with Wilson's ambassador to London, Walter Hines Page, were convinced that Germany constituted a danger to liberty and democracy everywhere. Some noted that all State Department decisions favored Britain.[50] Such pro-British behavior centered on the President himself. One day in early 1915, Wilson, defending a pro-British decision, reminded the cabinet that "the Allies are standing with their backs to the wall fighting wild beasts." British propaganda and such German decisions as the invasion of Belgium, the execution of nurse Edith Cavell, the shelling of Paris, the bombing from aircraft – all properly reported in the American press – had the effect of outraging an increasingly prejudiced American mind.[51]

What mattered most in Europe's war on American neutrality was Britain's control of the North Atlantic sea lanes, enabling it to command American shipping to Europe's continental ports. Under an Order in Council of August 20, 1914, the London government, to limit the flow of vital goods into Europe for ultimate German use, broadened the traditional definition of contraband, and ordered British warships to stop vessels en route to German ports, often bringing them to British ports for closer examination. In November 1914, the British mined the North Sea so thoroughly that no neutral vessel could proceed without securing directions from British officers in port who, in turn, could examine the ship's cargo before releasing instructions for safe sailing. Finally, in March 1915, another British Order in Council placed all trade to and from Germany under penalty of confiscation.[52] The industrial revolution had outmoded the established practices of maritime warfare.

That such direct and persistent defiance of American rights produced no crisis in U.S.–British relations resulted partially from the character of American attitudes, partially from the nature of the British blockade. Few American officials had any genuine desire to assert U.S. sovereignty on the high seas at the cost of undermining the British war effort. British policy, calculated not to antagonize the American public, enabled U.S. officials to accept the British system without inciting extensive charges of partisanship within the United States itself. The British blockade, always handled by surface vessels, was never capricious or destructive.[53]

---

[50] Hugo Munsterberg to Wilson, November 19, 1914, *Papers Relating to the Foreign Relations of the United States: The Lansing Papers, 1914–1920* (2 vols., Washington, 1939–1940), 1: 161–65. Lansing defended the State Department in Lansing to Wilson, November, 1914, ibid., 167–79. Lansing attributed the apparent partiality in U.S. policy to Britain's control of the seas.

[51] For the important role of British propaganda, see Peterson, *Propaganda for War*, passim.

[52] For a thorough examination of the neutrality issue, see Richard W. Van Alstyne, "Neutrality: The World War of 1914–1918," in *American Diplomacy in Action* (Stanford, 1947), 753–63.

[53] John W. Coogan traces Britain's systematic violation of U.S. neutral rights and Wilson's lack of neutrality in accepting them in *The End of Neutrality: The United States, Britain, and Maritime Rights, 1899–1915* (Ithaca, 1981), 209ff.

Eventually, the successful British effort to monopolize the expanding war-time industrial output of the United States forced Germany to retaliate in the only manner available. On February 4, 1915, the German government declared a war zone around the British Isles within which it would attempt to destroy all enemy ships. Neutral vessels, Germany warned, should remain outside the area. This decision, responding to German requirements, placed Berlin and Washington on a collision course. For six months, the war had raged in Europe without provoking any U.S. response, because nowhere had German action touched any historic American concern. What soon created the direct challenge to U.S. interests on the high seas was the German resort to the submarine, a new and potentially effective weapon. This frail craft, lacking armament and space, was vulnerable to ramming and deck guns. It could not, therefore, practice the traditional rules of visit and search unless merchant vessels forfeited all forms of retaliation. Any general arming of merchant-men – and the British quickly adopted this expedient – would compel U-boats to submerge and run after launching their torpedoes, thereby relieving them of any obligation for the safety and welfare of survivors. Clearly there were no precedents in international law to govern such maritime practices.

Wilson recognized no German right to strike Britain through commerce destruction unless German submarines fulfilled all obligations imposed by established maritime procedures. The President read a warning to Berlin on February 10, 1915, when he declared that if Germany destroyed American lives and property on the high seas, the United States would view it as an "indefensible violation of neutral rights" and would hold that nation to "strict accountability."[54] The United States would defend its interests in the Atlantic in any manner that it pleased, employing expediency in its acceptance of the Allied blockade while demanding nothing less than full German recognition of its technical rights on the high seas.

Within days after the announcement of the German war zone, the submarine demonstrated its effectiveness against Allied merchant shipping. On March 28, 1915, a German U-boat sank the British liner *Calaba* in the Irish Sea with the loss of one American. Then, on May 1, a submarine torpedoed the American tanker *Gulflight*. The vessel reached port, but three Americans lost their lives. That day, the German ambassador in Washington warned Americans, in the New York papers, to avoid travel to Europe on belligerent vessels.[55] Shortly thereafter, the massive British liner, *Lusitania*, laden with munitions, sailed from New York. Among its passengers were some 200 Americans who had ignored the German warning. After a fast, successful crossing, the *Lusitania*, on May 7, was moving slowly long the Irish coast when a German U-boat launched one torpedo at the giant target, and departed. The liner sank in eighteen minutes with the loss of more than 1,000 passengers, including 128 Americans. There

[54] Bryan to James Watson Gerard, February 10, 1915, *Papers of Woodrow Wilson*, 32: 207–10.
[55] See the *New York Sun*, May 1, 1915, quoted in *Lansing Papers*, 1: 382–83.

had been no warning and no rescue. "It is at once a crime and a monumental folly," declared the *New York Nation* on May 13. "[Germany] has affronted the moral sense of the world and sacrificed her standing among the nations."

Members of the administration disagreed on the American response. Secretary of State Bryan argued that Americans should not have traveled on the British vessel. Lansing favored a policy of strict accountability that guaranteed American citizens traveling on belligerent ships full protection under the established rules of maritime warfare. "We must," he wrote, "start our consideration of the course to be taken ... on the proposition that the act of the commander of the submarine was illegal, inhuman, and indefensible." Lansing argued that the U.S. government, having issued no warning against travel on British steamships, could not place responsibility on travelers for the loss of American life.[56]

Wilson accepted Lansing's reasoning. In his first *Lusitania* note, on May 13, he reaffirmed the right of American citizens sailing the high seas to enjoy the right of neutrals. Submarines, he argued, "cannot be used against merchantmen ... without an inevitable violation of many sacred principles of justice and humanity." He demanded that Germany make reparations and take steps to "prevent the recurrence of anything so obviously subversive of the principles of warfare."[57] Wilson reminded a Chicago audience that war did not suspend the principles of international law.

Not until May 29 did the German reply reach Washington. The Berlin government expressed regret over the loss of American lives on the *Lusitania*, but made no effort to defend its actions. It noted that the *Lusitania* carried munitions – whose explosion, it charged, caused the heavy loss of life. The vessel, it added, carried guns and was prepared to defend itself.[58] Lansing, on June 1, reminded Secretary Bryan that the German note acknowledged no German illegality in the *Lusitania*'s destruction, rendering its account totally unsatisfactory.[59]

In his second *Lusitania* note, on June 7, the President assigned the United States the mission of upholding the integrity of international law, denying Washington the freedom to compromise with German practices on the high seas. Whether the *Lusitania* was carrying munitions of war, he wrote, was irrelevant to the central issue – "the legality of the methods used by the German naval authorities in sinking the vessel." The inhumanity of the action alone, he charged, was sufficient to nullify any defense of the weapons employed.[60] The second *Lusitania* note was sufficiently belligerent to prompt Bryan's resignation. For Bryan, the President was leading the country into an unnecessary war.[61]

---

[56] Lansing to Bryan, May 9, 1915, ibid., I: 387–88.
[57] Wilson's first *Lusitania* note, May 13, 1915, *Papers of Woodrow Wilson*, 33: 174–78.
[58] For the German reply, see *Papers Relating to the Foreign Relations of the United States, 1915, Supplement* (Washington, 1928), 419–21.
[59] Lansing to Bryan, June 1, 1915, *Lansing Papers*, 1: 417.
[60] Wilson's second *Lusitania* note, June 7, 1915, *Papers of Woodrow Wilson*, 33: 355–60.
[61] For Bryan's resignation, see *War Memoirs of Robert Lansing* (Indianapolis, 1935), 29–30.

Clearly the sinking of the *Lusitania*, with its heavy death toll, shook the country. For those who favored full American membership in the club of great powers, the sinking of the *Lusitania*, as historian John Milton Cooper suggests, made the submarine a commanding political issue. Still, the *Lusitania's* sinking did not diminish the country's overwhelming reluctance to enter the European conflict. Both Republican and Democratic leaders warned the President that they would oppose any warlike moves. Wilson confided his dilemma to Bryan shortly before the secretary's resignation: "I wish with all my heart that I saw a way to carry out the double wish of our people, to maintain a firm front in respect of what we demand of Germany and yet do nothing that might by any possibility involve us in the war."[62]

VIII

For the moment, it mattered little. German officials had no interest in antagonizing the United States, and instructed German U-boat commanders to spare Allied and neutral passenger liners. Then suddenly, on August 19, a submarine sank the British liner *Arabic*, with the loss of two Americans. Lansing, Bryan's successor, warned the German government that another such incident would bring war. Berlin assured Washington that new orders to German commanders were so stringent that such an incident was "now considered out of the question."[63] In January 1916, Germany offered an indemnity as an act of grace, but again avoided an admission that it had engaged in illegal action. Germany agreed only to reduce its submarine warfare.[64]

Disaster struck again on March 24, 1916, when a German submarine torpedoed the French steamer *Sussex* while it was crossing the English Channel. The vessel reached port with eighty casualties, including several injured Americans. Lansing advised the President that the time for writing notes had ended; German submarine attacks could no longer be tolerated. Several days later, Lansing advocated the severing of diplomatic relations unless Germany terminated its submarine warfare.[65] Wilson's *Sussex* note of mid-April contained the ultimatum that unless Germany immediately declared its intention to "abandon its present practices of submarine warfare and return to a scrupulous observance of the practices clearly prescribed by the law of nations, the Government of the United States can have no choice but to sever diplomatic relations with the German Empire altogether."[66] Again Germany relented,

---

[62] John Milton Cooper, "The Shock of Recognition: The Impact of World War I on America," *The Virginia Quarterly Review*, 79 (Autumn 2000), 577; Wilson to Bryan, June 7, 1915, *Lansing Papers*, 1: 439.

[63] For the *Arabic* case and the German response, see *War Memoirs of Robert Lansing*, 43–53.

[64] Wilson's conversation with the German ambassador, January 10, 1916, *Papers of Woodrow Wilson*, 35: 463–64.

[65] Lansing to Wilson, March 27, 1916, *Lansing Papers*, 1: 538; Lansing to Wilson, April 12, 1916, *Papers of Woodrow Wilson*, 36: 466.

[66] Wilson's *Sussex* note, April 10, 1916, *Papers of Woodrow Wilson*, 36: 456. The note went through several revisions.

but with the proviso that ships not attempt to escape or offer resistance, and that the United States demand of all nations the same regard for international law.[67] Wilson accepted the pledge, but not the conditions.

Temporarily, the *Sussex* pledge removed the submarine issue.[68] The relative quiet in U.S.-German relations continued until January 1917, when German military commanders launched a campaign to unleash the submarine. Only by isolating Britain completely from its sources of supply, they warned, could Germany retain any chance of victory. On January 8, Field Marshal Paul von Hindenburg demanded unrestricted submarine warfare, to begin February 1. One day later, the German government made that fateful decision. On January 31, the German ambassador brought the announcement that unrestricted submarine warfare would begin the following day. After February 1, every vessel afloat in British waters, Allied or neutral, was subject to attack without warning.[69]

Wilson's choices were limited. His *Sussex* note had committed him to sever diplomatic relations with Berlin. On February 3, he carried out his threat, informing Congress of his decision. He still hoped that the United States might avoid the horrors of Europe's stalemated war, but the pressures for involvement were unrelenting. Gradually the enormity of German determination to cripple Britain forced the President's hand. U.S. Ambassador Page in London informed Washington on February 25 of an intercepted message from Alfred Zimmerman of the German Foreign Office to the German minister in Mexico. Zimmerman instructed the minister, in the event of an American declaration of war, to negotiate a German–Mexican alliance, promising Mexico the return of Texas, New Mexico, and California.[70] Several days later, the Zimmerman note captured the nation's headlines and created a profound anti-German sensation. Meanwhile, on February 26, Wilson recommended a policy of armed neutrality and asked Congress for authority to mount guns on American merchantmen. In openly defying the German blockade, Wilson had reached the point of no return. No longer could there be any recourse to notes to protect American life. The decision for war or peace lay in the hands of German U-boat commanders. On March 12, a submarine torpedoed and sank an unarmed merchant vessel without warning; on March 18, three unarmed American merchant vessels went down with heavy casualties. Wilson's cabinet, without a dissenting vote, advocated war.

On April 2, 1917, the President went before Congress to ask that body to accept the status of war then existing with Germany. The cost would be high. "It is a fearful thing," he acknowledged, "to lead this great, peaceful people into war, into the most terrible and disastrous of wars." But the right, he added, had become more precious than peace. As an active participant, the United States

---

[67] For the German response of May 4, 1916, ibid., 621–25; *Lansing Papers*, 1: 564–65.
[68] Lansing Memorandum, December 1, 1916, *Lansing Papers*, 1: 227–37.
[69] For the German decision on unrestricted submarine warfare and the coming of war, see Ernest R. May, *The World War and American Isolation, 1914–1917* (Chicago, 1966), 416–37; *War Memoirs of Robert Lansing*, 219–37.
[70] See Barbara W. Tuchman, *The Zimmerman Telegram* (New York, 1958).

would fight for the standards of right conduct; it would use force "without stint or limit," but in the service of humanity.[71] Wilson closed with the assurance that the country's entry into the war would, at last, render the world free. After a moment of silence, his listeners erupted with deafening applause.[72] Congress acted quickly on the war resolution. The Senate vote, on April 4, was 82 to 6. The House, two days later, added its approval, 373–50. The dissenters pointed to two pressures that drove the nation to war: the partiality of U.S. practices on the high seas, and the successful pro-British demands of American financial interests. As historian H. C. Peterson concluded: "To some the history of the 'neutrality' period demonstrates that the United States cannot keep out of war.... What it does prove is that it is impossible to be unneutral and keep out of war."[73] What, in essence, denied the United States an easy escape from its ultimate decision for war was the German threat to the world balance of power. For a century, America's privileged position in world politics favored a British-dominated European equilibrium. Wilson dictated rules of maritime warfare to Germany, based on appeals to legality and morality. But those rules assigned the full weight of America's huge productive power to the Allies. With or without war, Wilson barred Germany from every apparent avenue to victory. In 1917, the historic relationship between American security and the British-led European balance of power seemed to demand no less. But the nation went to war, not because of historic, recognizable objectives in Europe worth pursuing, but because Germany claimed the right to kill Americans on the high seas, where the President declared they had a right to be.

Wilson responded to the challenges unleashed by the Great War, not by recalling the well-established and guiding principles of international politics, but by advocating their elimination. The international system that he sought to destroy had not always served humanity well, but in its slow evolution across four centuries it had reflected the reality of competing national sovereignties suspended in an anarchical world. Recurrent warfare was the price of living in an unfinished world. Despite all its strife, the existing international order had permitted the emergence of a civilization of immense complexity, marked by incredible human progress. The long-established system failed markedly in the Great War, inviting condemnation, not because of its inherent weaknesses but because of a profound failure of statesmanship. Wilson offered a vision of a more peaceful and cost-free successor, but his denigration of the long-established international system would neither eliminate it nor assure its improved performance.

---

[71] Address to Joint Session of Congress, April 2, 1917, *Papers of Woodrow Wilson*, 41: 519–27.
[72] *War Memoirs of Robert Lansing*, 242.
[73] Peterson, *Propaganda for War*, 330.

2

The Road to Paris: 1917–1918

I

America's total commitment to an Allied victory in Europe assured President Woodrow Wilson a commanding position in global affairs. Never had Europe been as much in need of external leadership and rescue. The horrors of previous years seemed to reach their culmination in the disasters of 1917. As submarines levied their toll on the high seas, the war on the Western Front reached new levels of disaster. Early in 1917, Britain and France, independently, planned massive assaults to break through the German lines. In April, French General Robert Georges Nivelle launched his "unlimited offensive" at Chemin des Dames. Unfortunately, Nivelle's plans, widely distributed, reached the German high command. Nivelle knew this, but insisted that it changed nothing. The superbly prepared German line was a defendant's dream. So suicidal were the casualties that French soldiers refused to leave the trenches and face the withering fire of well-placed German machine guns. To quell the mutiny, French officers shot their own troops to enforce the orders to attack.[1] French casualties during ten days of April approached 200,000.[2]

---

[1] Pierre van Paassen, the noted foreign correspondent, witnessed many of the trials, conducted in Paris during the mid-1920s, in which families sought recompense for the execution of French soldiers on the Western Front. If the French mutiny at Chemin des Dames attracted the greatest attention from historians, the trials covered executions at other battles, such as Verdun. Individuals and units often resisted orders to attack, or dropped into shell holes until nightfall, because of the intensity of the machine gun fire. Others argued that it was not their turn to leave the trenches. Accused of disobeying orders, they were often selected capriciously to face firing squads, and thereby set an example that orders were to be obeyed. The trials, covering specific events, revealed the full horrors of the war on the Western Front. These trials received no coverage in the French press, and when van Paassen reported them to his editors in the United States, they also refused to publish them. See Pierre van Paassen, *Days of Our Years* (New York, 1939), 150–61.
[2] For the key battles of 1917, see Sir James E. Edwards, *A Short History of World War I* (New York, 1968), 218–23; William Manchester, *The Arms of Krupp, 1587–1968* (Boston, 1968), 300.

In desperation, the Allies turned to Douglas Haig's British forces. Haig responded with his well-planned Flanders offensive at Passchendaele. Unfortunately, the preliminary bombing destroyed the Flemish drainage system. The water, with nowhere to go, flooded the trenches. The accompanying rains were the heaviest in thirty years. The fighting in that massive sinkhole began in July, then resumed in October and November. Haig lost 350,000 men, tens of thousands of them Canadians, New Zealanders, and Australians. Many soldiers simply drowned.[3] The Italian collapse at Caporetto in October was of a lesser scale, but sufficient to effectively eliminate Italy from the war. Highly skilled German troops, reinforcing the Austrian sector, attacked in a heavy fog. The Italian defense collapsed as thousands of Italian troops fled the battlefield.[4] The British suffered 20,000 deaths in one day at the Somme; thereafter, the war's death toll reached 20,000 every four days. Clearly, the costs were reaching the outer limits of human endurance. Erich Maria Remarque, in his *All Quiet on the Western Front*, captured the war's impact on many who survived: "[I]f we go back we will be weary, broken, burnt out, rootless, and without hope.... We will grow older, a few will adapt themselves, some others will merely submit...."[5]

By April 1917, the Great War had become, for Woodrow Wilson, a struggle to the death between Allied democracy and German autocracy. If the ongoing war comprised temporary and irrational resorts to violence, perpetrated by wicked, undemocratic governments, then permanent peace rested on the combined endeavor of "the really free and self-governed people of the world." Only free peoples, said Wilson, "can hold their purposes and their honor steady to a common end and prefer the interests of mankind to any interest of their own." In concluding his war message, Wilson placed his crusade for democracy in its final form:

> [W]e shall fight for the things which we have always carried nearest our hearts, – for democracy, for the right of those who submit to authority to have a voice in their own Governments, for the rights and liberties of small nations, for a universal dominion of right by such a concert of free peoples as shall bring peace and safety to all nations and make the world itself at last free.[6]

When the President failed to obtain any statement of specific war aims from London or Paris, he proceeded to frame his own program and thereby establish his leadership in the quest for lasting peace. During September 1917, at his suggestion, Colonel Edward House, his representative in Paris, assembled a group of experts, known as The Inquiry, to study the problems that would

[3] B. H. Liddell Hart, *The Real War 1914–1918* (Boston, 1930), 337–43; Manchester, *The Arms of Krupp*, 300; Keegan, *The First World War*, 355–69.

[4] Manchester, *The Arms of Krupp*, 300.

[5] Erich Maria Remarque, *All Quiet on the Western Front* (Greenwich, 1967), 174–75.

[6] Wilson's war message, April 2, 1917, Arthur S. Link, ed., *Papers of Woodrow Wilson* (69 vols., Princeton, 1966–1994), 41: 523–24, 527.

face the post-war world.[7] Late in December, when The Inquiry's studies were already well advanced, House returned to Washington and urged the President to take up the question of war aims. Wilson responded by requesting The Inquiry to prepare a body of specific recommendations for incorporation into a public statement.

Having pondered a long memorandum from The Inquiry, Wilson delivered his famous Fourteen Points address to a joint session of Congress on January 8, 1918. His statement of American ideals and aspirations served as a warning to Allied leaders who remained committed to national rather than international objectives. The President's general propositions included open diplomacy, freedom of the seas, the reduction of armaments, and self-determination among the alien peoples within the German and Turkish empires. For Wilson, it was the fourteenth point that underwrote his design for a new era of peace: a general association of nations, operating under specific covenants for the "mutual guarantees of political independence and territorial integrity to great and small states alike."[8]

Self-determination for the peoples of the Austro-Hungarian Empire constituted a special challenge. In his January 1917 address to the Senate, the President reaffirmed his conviction that no peace could last that did not recognize the principle "that governments derive all their just powers from the consent of the governed." He hoped, however, to involve the Austrian government in a final effort to end the war quickly by seeking agreement among the Allied powers that the Austro-Hungarian Empire would not be dismembered. In his Annual Message of December 4, 1917, he declared that "we do not wish in any way to impair or to re-arrange the Austro-Hungarian Empire."[9] His Fourteen Points speech again assured the peoples of Austria-Hungary that they would have their place among the nations preserved, and would "be accorded the freest opportunity of autonomous development." Vienna chose to waive the promise of favored treatment by refusing to leave the war.[10]

II

Unfortunately, Wilson's ideal, principled, peace program confronted a world at war, driven by territorial ambitions and a quest for revenge. Every combatant anticipated territorial gains as the emoluments of victory. German imperial ambitions were real, if imprecise, but that country's special challenge to Wilson's vision of a peaceful future lay not in its threat to the world's

---

[7] For the organization's history and contributions, see Lawrence E. Gelfand, *The Inquiry: American Preparations for Peace, 1917–1919* (New Haven, 1963).

[8] Wilson's address to Joint Session of Congress, January 8, 1918, *Papers of Woodrow Wilson*, 45: 536–39.

[9] Annual Message on the State of the Union, December 4, 1917, ibid., 45: 197.

[10] On Austria's decision to remain in the war, see House to A. J. Balfour, March 1, 1918, Charles Seymour, ed., *The Intimate Papers of Colonel House* (4 vols., Boston, 1928), 3: 378–81.

treaty structure but to the future of democracy. Secretary of State Robert Lansing defined Washington's unfolding crusade against Germany as early as January 9, 1916:

> It is my opinion that the military oligarchy which rules Germany is a bitter enemy to democracy in every form; that, if that oligarchy triumphs over the liberal governments of Great Britain and France, it will then turn upon us as its next obstacle to imperial rule over the world.
>
> Lansing observed again on January 28: "The Allies must not be beaten. It would mean the triumph of Autocracy over Democracy.... I hate the horrors of war but I hate worse the horrors of German mastery."[11]

In his war message, the President declared that, without Germany's destruction, there could be no security for any of the world's democracies.[12]

To rally the nation behind his crusade against Germany, the President, on April 13, 1917, created the Committee on Public Information under publicist George Creel. Creel set out to educate the public with a propaganda campaign totally unprecedented in American history. The committee began publication of the *Official Bulletin*, a daily press release that reached 100,000 creators of the news. It commissioned filmmakers as well as noted historians to assemble anti-German material.[13] To further eliminate opposition to the war, Congress, on July 15, passed the Espionage Act, which imposed heavy fines and imprisonment on anyone who encouraged disloyalty in the armed forces or obstructed recruitment. This act launched a domestic crusade against socialists and other radicals, typified by Jane Addams and Eugene V. Debs, who had been in the vanguard of Wilson's early progressive internationalist supporters, with their emphasis on reform of the international system. But they opposed the war, and in their continued opposition, many fell victim to the Espionage Act. Debs and other key leaders of progressive internationalism went to prison.[14] German-Americans, despite their overwhelming loyalty, were harassed and abused by local vigilantes. Super-patriots demanded the eradication of all evidence of German culture; some communities outlawed the German language in schools.[15]

---

[11] *War Memoirs of Robert Lansing* (Indianapolis, 1935), 208–09.

[12] War message of April 2, 1917, *Papers of Woodrow Wilson*, 41: 524–25.

[13] Many noted historians who entertained strong anti-German sentiments willingly wrote anti-German pamphlets for the Creel Committee; others of equal reputation refused to do so. For the role played by those who devoted their scholarship to supporting the war, see George T. Blakey, *Historians on the Homefront: American Propagandists for the Great War* (Lexington, 1970). For a similar examination of the role of historians in the war, with emphasis on the environment in which they acted, see Carol S. Gruber, *Mars and Minerva: World War I and the Uses of Higher Learning in America* (Baton Rouge, 1975).

[14] For the feminists, liberals, pacifists, socialists, and social reformers who comprised the ranks of the progressive internationalists, but who deserted him when he chose war, see Thomas J. Knock, *To End All Wars: Woodrow Wilson and the Quest for a New World Order* (New York, 1992), 50–55.

[15] Frederick C. Luebke, *Bonds of Loyalty* (DeKalb, 1974), passim.

Meanwhile, members of the administration continued their assault on Germany as the enemy of democracy, reminding the American people that their security, economic welfare, and individual freedoms were at stake. In increasingly intemperate language, Lansing told a Princeton audience on June 16, 1917, that Germany was the "wild beast" of the world, led by "assassins and butchers." When, in August, Pope Benedict XV appealed to Wilson for the restoration of the *status quo ante bellum*, Lansing reminded him of the need to deliver the "free peoples of the world from the menace and the actual power of a vast military establishment controlled by an irresponsible government [which had] secretly planned to dominate the world....[16] At Columbia University on June 6, 1918, the secretary continued his verbal assault: "Prussianism has appealed to the sword, and by the sword Prussianism must fall. It is the divine law of retribution which we as the instruments of justice must enforce so that the world may be forever rid of this abomination."[17] It was left for the *North American Review* of February 1918 to reveal the full impact of Washington's anti-German crusade:

> Peace, a perdurable peace, will come only when the fangs of the mad beast of Europe have been drawn, when the military power of Germany is broken, when the German people are under the harrow, sweating to pay the indemnity that is the price of their crime, in their poverty and suffering made to realize the suffering they have brought to the world.[18]

Clearly the anti-German crusade had gone too far. When Lansing, in September 1918, submitted a speech, prepared for delivery at New York University, for review, Wilson's adviser, Edward House, objected. "I do not," he commented, "like Lansing's speech. It is intemperate and, in my opinion, is one that should not be made by a Foreign Secretary." Already, House argued, the established levels of anti-German sentiment would cause trouble enough when the fighting stopped. Ironically, as the war approached its end several weeks later, Lansing himself bemoaned the vindictive temper of the American people that he had so assiduously helped to arouse.[19] That temper eliminated any possibility that the President would have the intent, capacity, or freedom to deal forthrightly with German representatives at any post-war peace conference.

III

Japan's challenge to Wilson's new world order lay in its known rejection of the American commitment to China's commercial, territorial, and administrative

[16] Lansing to Pope Benedict XV, August 27, 1917, *Papers of Woodrow Wilson*, 44 (Princeton, 1983), 58.

[17] For Lansing's assault on Germany, see Joseph M. Siracusa, "Wilson's Image of the Prussian Menace: *Ideology and Realpolitik*," in John A. Moses and Christopher Pugsley, eds., *The German Empire and Britain's Pacific Dominions, 1871–1919: Essays on the Role of Australia and New Zealand in World Politics in the Age of Imperialism* (Claremont, 2000), 87–88.

[18] "We Must Kill to Save," *North American Review*, 207 (February 1918), 165.

[19] Siracusa, "Wilson's Image of the Prussian Menace," 88.

integrity, as embodied in the American Open Door declarations of 1899–1900. This popular national commitment presumed that the United States could defend Chinese interests without the necessity of force or any precise definition of American interests in China. Lansing reminded Paul S. Reinsch, the U.S. minister in China, that "it would be quixotic in the extreme to allow the question [of the Open Door] to entangle the United States in international difficulties."[20] It required only Britain's request of August 7, 1914, for Japanese naval support in the Pacific, under the recent Anglo-Japanese treaty, to unleash a renewal of Japan's expansionist ambitions in China. One week later, Japan issued an ultimatum to Germany, demanding the surrender of all its holdings in China. The German government refused to comply with the ultimatum.[21] Japan, on August 23, declared war on Germany and proceeded to take over the German leaseholds of Tsingtao, in Kiaochow Bay, as well as the German holdings on the Shantung Peninsula in north China. In the Pacific, the Japanese took possession of the German Mariana, Caroline, and Marshall Islands, including the cable center of Yap.[22] China admonished American officials that it expected Japan to respect China's territorial integrity.[23] Count Okuna, the Japanese premier, assured Washington that Japan had "no thought of depriving China or other peoples of anything which they now possess."[24]

Japan required Chinese and international recognition of its new possessions. To that end, Japan, in January 1915, confronted a weak China with twenty-one demands, listed in five groups. In the first four, China would recognize Japan's special economic interests in south Manchuria, east Mongolia, and north China, as well as Japan's retention of Shantung. The Japanese demanded the right to build a railroad from Lungkow to a junction with the Tsingtao–Tsinan Railroad, as well as to open additional cities and ports in the province for foreign residence and commerce.[25] When U.S. newspapers published these demands, Japan labeled the Group V demands as "requests," inasmuch as they infringed on Chinese administrative integrity.[26] Washington responded to the twenty-one demands on March 13 in a note drafted by Lansing at Secretary Bryan's request. The note charged Japan with violating U.S. treaty rights in Shantung, south Manchuria, and east Mongolia. Nevertheless, the

[20] Lansing to Reinsch, November 4, 1914, U.S. Department of State, *Papers Relating to the Foreign Relations of the United States* (hereafter *FRUS*), *1914, Supplement* (Washington, 1928), 190.

[21] George W. Guthrie, U.S. Ambassador to Japan, to Bryan, August 16, 1914, ibid., 170–71.

[22] A. L. P. Dennis, *The Anglo-Japanese Alliance* (Berkeley, 1923), 44–45; *War Memoirs of Robert Lansing*, 281; Baron Masuo Kato, Japanese Foreign Minister, to Viscount Sutemi Chinda, Japanese Ambassador to the United States, August 23, 1914, *FRUS*, *1914, Supplement*, 174–75.

[23] Chinese Minister of Foreign Affairs to John MacMurray, Secretary of U.S. Legation in China, September 3, 1914, ibid., 188–89.

[24] See Baron Chinda to Bryan, October 1, 1914, ibid., 183.

[25] Carnegie Endowment for International Peace, *The Sino-Japanese Negotiations of 1915: Japanese and Chinese Documents* (Washington, 1921), 3.

[26] Reinsch to Bryan, March 6, 1915, *FRUS*, *1915*, 99–103.

note continued, "the United States frankly recognizes that territorial contiguity creates special relations between Japan and these districts."[27]

Washington, powerless to respond with threats of force, resorted to a largely untried form of diplomatic pressure, that of non-recognition. Secretary of State Bryan, on May 11, 1915, informed the Chinese and Japanese governments that the United States "cannot recognize any agreement or understanding which has been entered into between the Governments of Japan and China, impairing the treaty rights of the United States and its citizens in China, the political or territorial integrity of the Republic of China, or the international policy relative to China commonly known as the Open Door policy."[28] China succeeded in eliminating the six most stringent of the Japanese demands, but on May 25 accepted the fifteen that remained. These included the Japanese retention of Shantung in any post-war peace treaty. What Japanese policy lacked in legitimacy, it gained in diplomatic advantage. In October 1915, Japan joined the European alliance fighting Germany, and through secret treaties with Britain, France, Italy, and Russia, gained recognition of its claims to Shantung and the German islands in the Pacific north of the equator.[29] Clearly, Wilson's defense of Chinese territorial integrity was in trouble. He refused to relent, but with no military clash over the Open Door.

It required only the U.S. declaration of war in April 1917 to renew the Japanese–American conflict over China. As allies, the two nations faced the obligation to frame a post-war Far Eastern settlement. In June, Lansing reminded the Japanese ambassador in Washington that the U.S. commitment to the Open Door policy remained firm. Bryan's earlier recognition of Japan's special interests in China, he said, applied only to Shantung, south Manchuria, and east Mongolia.[30] Undaunted, the Tokyo government, in August, dispatched Viscount Kikujiro Ishii to the United States, ostensibly to coordinate U.S. and Japanese war efforts, but actually to gain Washington's recognition of Japan's "paramount interests" in China.[31] Colonel House urged the President to grant the Japanese request. He reminded the President that Japan "is barred from all the under-developed places of the earth, and if her influence in the East is not recognized as in some degree superior to that of the Western powers, there will be a reckoning."[32] Wilson rejected House's advice; the United States, he averred, expected no less than Japan's full observance of the Open Door principle.

Formal talks began in September. Wilson assured Ishii that the United States desired nothing but Japan's faithful observance of the Open Door and

[27] Bryan to Baron Chinda, March 13, 1915, ibid., 105–11. Quotation on page 108.
[28] Bryan to Guthrie and Reinsch, May 11, 1915, ibid., 146.
[29] Tatsuji Takeuchi, *War and Diplomacy in the Japanese Empire* (New York, 1935), 197–98.
[30] Lansing to the Japanese ambassador, June 22, 1917, *FRUS, 1917* (Washington, 1926), 260–62.
[31] Carnegie Endowment for International Peace, *The Imperial Japanese Mission, 1917* (Washington, 1918). This volume deals largely with Ishii's public activities in Washington during the negotiations.
[32] House to Wilson, September 18, 1917, Seymour, *Papers of House*, 3: 25.

the principle of equal opportunity for all nations in China. The President questioned the spheres of influence in China, leading Ishii to request Tokyo's permission to abolish them. Ishii received no reply, leaving him no choice but to use his own discretion.[33] Ishii's instructions remained firm: to obtain recognition of Japan's superior rights in China.

At Lansing's first meeting with Ishii, on September 6, the Japanese ambassador made clear his quest for U.S. recognition of Japan's special claims on China. Lansing, defending the principle of the Open Door, informed Ishii that Japan's location granted it no superior rights in dealing with China.[34] During subsequent sessions, Lansing and Ishii held to their diplomatic positions, thereby reducing the negotiations to the choice and meaning of words. Facing the necessity of reaching some formal agreement as wartime allies, Lansing and Ishii incorporated both the American and the Japanese demands in the same document. In the first paragraph of the Lansing–Ishii Agreement of November 2, 1917, the United States recognized "that Japan has special interests in China, particularly in the part to which her possessions are contiguous." In succeeding paragraphs, the Japanese agreed that the "territorial integrity of China ... remains unimpaired," and that both countries would "always adhere to the principle of the so-called 'open door' or equal opportunity for commerce and industry in China."[35]

Lansing demanded an additional agreement whereby the United States and Japan would take no advantage of wartime conditions "to seek special rights or privileges in China." Ishii accepted the self-denying clause, but only under the condition that it remain a secret protocol.[36] U.S. minister Reinsch wondered how he could explain to the Chinese government this apparent reversal in American policy.[37] Wilson lauded the Lansing–Ishii Agreement as a triumph for the Open Door principle in China; Tokyo reminded the Chinese government that the United States recognized Japan's paramount interests in China. The key phrases in the agreement could have whatever meaning officials anywhere chose to attribute to them. Lansing and Ishii were not sufficiently free to seek a genuine solution. In resolving nothing, they merely managed the necessary postponement of the inevitable clash over the principle of the Open Door.[38]

Japan sought to prevent China from entering the European struggle on the side of the Allies: that action would grant China a legitimate seat at the peace

---

[33] Kikujiro Ishii, *Diplomatic Commentaries*, trans. William R. Langdon (Baltimore, 1936), 113–15.

[34] Memorandum by the Secretary of State on a Conference with the Japanese Ambassador on a Special Mission, September 6, 1917, *FRUS: Lansing Papers, 1914–1920* (2 vols., Washington, 1939–1940), 2: 432–35.

[35] For the final agreement of November 2, 1917, see *FRUS, 1917,* 264–65.

[36] *Lansing Papers,* 2: 450–51.

[37] Reinsch to Lansing, November 4, 1917, *FRUS, 1917,* 265–66.

[38] Some wartime journalists predicted a future U.S.-Japanese war over China. One observed that the United States and Japan resembled two trains moving relentlessly toward one another on a single track.

conference, where Chinese diplomats could summon the victors to justify the Open Door. Minister Reinsch assured the Chinese that if they entered the war, the United States would assist them in securing a satisfactory post-war settlement with Japan. When China declared war on Germany on August 14, 1917, it no longer mattered. Japan, to meet this anticipated challenge, had reaffirmed its secret treaties with Britain and France. Then, in September, Japan reimposed its fifteen demands on the government of North China in exchange for Japanese aid in railroad construction.

IV

Faced with the challenge of making high policy for war and peace, the European power structure began to crumble. Columnist Walter Lippmann recounted the war's impact on governmental authority. "The existing governments," he wrote, "had exhausted their imperium – their authority to bind and their power to command. With their traditional means they were no longer able to carry on the hyperbolic war; yet they were unable to negotiate peace.... They in effect had lost control of the war."[39] Yet the wartime pressures on the European governments produced revolution only in Russia. The vast conscriptions, casualties, shortages, corruption, and erosion of public morale created a revolutionary environment. The collapse of the Tsarist regime in February 1917 epitomized the failure of the old dynastic-imperial structure to meet the demands of modern warfare.

For Washington and the other Western capitals, Alexander Kerensky's Provisional Government promised not only a liberal parliamentary system, but also a more effective Russian effort on the Eastern Front. For the first time, the Allied prospects for dealing with wartime Russia appeared reassuring. Unfortunately, the Provisional Government's welcome decision to keep Russia in the war assured its undoing. Capitalizing on the unbroken succession of Russian battlefield disasters, the socialists, who commanded the support of both the industrial workers and the rank and file of Russian soldiers, overthrew the Provisional Government. Lenin, who engineered the Bolshevik triumph of November 1917, had in April returned from exile in Switzerland under a general amnesty offered by the Provisional Government. Lenin confronted the Allied war effort with an unforeseen challenge. He regarded the European war as little but an effort of the capitalist-imperialist nations to divide up the underdeveloped areas of the world. It was Lenin's total rejection of liberal values as well as the war itself that placed him at odds with Wilson's program for a liberal-democratic world order that included Russia.

During November 1917, the Bolshevik regime created a crisis by suggesting that the nations fighting Germany seek a negotiated peace. The Bolsheviks had no choice but to come to terms with Germany, and only a general peace movement would rescue them from the necessity of negotiating

[39] Walter Lippmann, *The Public Philosophy* (Boston, 1955), 12.

with a victorious Germany alone. Failing to institute peace negotiations, the Bolsheviks attempted to force a statement of war aims from the Allies. They published the documents of the Russian Foreign Office regarding the secret treaties of 1915 by which the hard-pressed Allies promised one another compensation in the form of long-standing territorial objectives. They also charged the Allies with cynical and imperialistic war aims. It was, in part, to meet this Bolshevik challenge that House advised Wilson to take up the issue of war aims and offer aid and sympathy to the Russian people and their leaders. Wilson rejected House's recommendation, convinced that by withholding aid and recognition from the Bolsheviks, he could channel Russian radicalism into more liberal and responsible behavior.

Lansing shared the President's total rejection of the Bolsheviks. He inaugurated his attack on the new Russian leaders in a memorandum of December 4, advising the President to ignore their regime. There existed, he argued, no evidence that it represented the will of the Russian people.[40] Again, on January 2, 1918, he reminded the President that the Bolsheviks had seized power through force and had no authority to speak for the country.[41] Lansing regarded the Bolsheviks, no less than German leaders, as dangerous to Western civilization. For him, the Bolsheviks acknowledged no respect for national sovereignty and appeared determined to replace all governments with proletarian despotisms. Lansing doubted, moreover, that the Bolsheviks would ever bring all of Russia under their control, for the revolution continued to face widespread resistance. But any open criticism, he advised, might drive Russia's radical regime into a bargain with Germany. Thus Lansing advised the President that the United States "must continue for the present [to be] a silent witness of the internal confusion which prevails in Russia...."

Wilson turned to the problem of Russia in Point Six of his Fourteen Points address, asking for the evacuation of all Russian territory and a settlement of all questions affecting Russia that would assure that nation "an unhampered and unembarrassed opportunity for the independent determination of her own political development and national policy and assure her a sincere welcome to the society of free nations under institutions of her own choosing ... " (*Lansing Papers*). The Bolsheviks were not impressed.

Russian diplomacy, in its defiance of the Allies, moved irresistibly toward an accommodation with Germany. The Bolsheviks signed an armistice with the Kaiser's government on December 15, 1917, with the proviso that both nations move rapidly toward the negotiation of a permanent peace treaty. Before Christmas, the two nations dispatched delegates to Brest-Litovsk. The Russians sought a peace without annexations or indemnities, but the Germans had no intention of withdrawing their forces from Russia's occupied territories before the end of the war, especially from Russian Poland and the Baltic

---

[40] Lansing's report on Russia, December 4, 1917, *Papers of Woodrow Wilson*, 45: 205–07; *War Memoirs of Robert Lansing*, 343–44.
[41] Lansing to the President, January 2, 1918, *Lansing Papers*, 2: 348.

states. Meanwhile, the Bolsheviks pressed the Allies to end their war and join the Russians in a general peace. Unable to move the Allies to the peace table, the Bolsheviks threatened to appeal to the popular masses of Europe to rise up and save Russia from German injustice. The Germans, conscious of Russia's inability to resume the struggle, refused to modify their territorial demands. When the Russian and German negotiators resumed their peace talks at Brest-Litovsk in January 1918, the Germans were in complete control; all Russian efforts to gain support had failed. The Treaty of Brest-Litovsk, completed in March, freed the Ukraine and portions of Poland from Russian control, as well as Finland, Estonia, Latvia, Lithuania, Bessarabia, Crimea, and the Caucasus Mountain region.

Wilson and his advisers believed that an American policy that distinguished between Bolshevism and Russian liberalism could return the Russian revolution to its initial democratic course. On January 10, 1918, Lansing advocated recognition only when the Russian people exercised their sovereign authority. To recognize the Bolsheviks before the Russian people could express their will, he warned, "would encourage them and their followers in other lands."[42] Writing to Wilson on January 10, 1918, American labor leader Samuel Gompers argued for continued opposition to Lenin. "The real, democratic, practical revolutionaries of Russia, men who have made the revolution," he assured the President, "are standing firmly for the democratization of Russia, and for the proper orderly government of the country."[43] Wilson agreed that, given time, Russia would return to the liberal-democratic principles of the Provisional Government. Until then, he would not recognize the existence of Russia's Leninist regime.[44]

When Brest-Litovsk freed forty German divisions for duty on the Western Front, British and French leaders proposed Allied landings at Vladivostok in Siberia, as well as at Murmansk and Archangel in northern Russia. Japan would carry the burden at Vladivostok, while the United States would support the Anglo-French effort in the north. Backed by Russian forces loyal to the Allied cause, these landings would establish an Allied front from Siberia to the Upper Volga and compel Germany to reestablish its Eastern Front. In May, the British dispatched a force to Archangel, and requested an American contingent. Wilson remained reluctant to commit U.S. forces to Russia, but relented in response to growing Allied pressure. Accepting General Foch's argument that American military involvement was more essential in Russia than on the Western Front, Wilson, in June, agreed to join the Western intervention. Rather quickly, the Allied presence in Russia shifted from the establishment of a second front to the defense of that country's anti-Bolshevik elements – a decision that Wilson condemned.

What drew Wilson into his Siberian intervention was the plight of Czecho-Slovak prisoners of war who, with the Russian collapse, hoped to join the Allied

[42] Lansing memorandum, January 10, 1918, *Papers of Woodrow Wilson*, 45: 563–64.
[43] Samuel Gompers to Wilson, January 19, 1918, ibid., 46: 39.
[44] Ibid., 47: 35–36.

forces on the Western Front and thereby strengthen Czech claims to national independence. Unfortunately, German and Austro-Hungarian prisoners of war blocked their westward passage. With access to the Trans-Siberian Railway, they moved eastward to reach the Western Front through Vladivostok. In July 1918, Wilson dispatched a small contingent of U.S. soldiers to join Japanese forces in eastern Siberia to aid the beleaguered Czecho-Slovaks.[45] Soon the U.S. presence in East Asia clashed with possible Japanese territorial ambitions in Siberia and Manchuria, where the Japanese, by November, had stationed over 72,000 troops. For Wilson, that Japanese presence threatened the Open Door in Manchuria and northern China.[46] Britain's Prime Minister, David Lloyd George, summarized accurately Wilson's full response to the Russian challenge of 1918. The President, he noted, was not pro-Bolshevik, but much opposed to the Allied Archangel and Murmansk expeditions. In Siberia, wrote the Prime Minister, Wilson's "principal anxiety was ... the conduct of the Japanese, who were apparently taking the whole of eastern Siberia into their own hands ... and generally behaving as if they owned the country."[47]

V

Wilson's wartime contribution to an Allied victory in Europe was designed to assure his and the nation's leadership in designing the post-war peace. The President appointed General Tasker Bliss to represent him on the Supreme War Council, organized in late 1917 by Britain's Lloyd George to break the power of the military commanders over the conduct of the war, as well as to involve the United States in Allied wartime and post-war planning. Allied commanders requested the immediate assignment of American units to the British and French armies.[48] Under the President's directive, however, U.S. General John J. Pershing, commander of the American Expeditionary Force in Europe, resisted Allied pressure to disperse his forces. By keeping American units intact on the Western Front, he enabled them to play a definable role in the final victory over Germany.[49] The initial American battles

[45] Wilson to Lansing, September 17, 1918, ibid., 51: 25–26.
[46] For a detailed evaluation of the Allied intervention in Russia during 1918, with emphasis on Wilson's determination to defend Russian self-determination and China's Open Door, see Betty Miller Unterberger, *Intervention against Communism: Did the United States Try to Overthrow the Soviet Government, 1918–1920?* (Texas A&M University, University Lecture Series, 1986), 4–19.
[47] Ibid., 17. For a general critique of Wilson's response to Bolshevism and other social revolutions, see Lloyd C. Gardner, *Safe for Democracy: The Anglo-American Response to Revolution, 1913–1923* (New York, 1984).
[48] Seymour, *Papers of House*, 3: 442–45.
[49] On keeping the U.S. forces intact, see David F. Trask, *The Supreme War Council* (Middletown, 1961), 71–99. More specific is Trask, *The AEF and Coalition Warmaking, 1917–1918* (Lawrence, 1993). A general study of American forces in the war is John S. D. Eisenhower and Joanne Thompson Eisenhower, *Yanks: The Epic Story of the American Army in World War I* (New York, 2001).

at Cantigny and Belleau Wood, followed by St. Mihiel in September and the Meuse-Argonne in October, contributed markedly to stopping the mammoth German offensive of March 1918 and assuring the success of the Allied counteroffensive of July and August.[50] By early autumn 1918, the German armies were in rapid, if orderly, withdrawal across northern France toward the German border.[51]

With the approach of peace, Wilson's immediate challenge lay in Europe, where his leadership hinged on an armistice based on his Fourteen Points. The President understood fully that the European Allies did not share his vision of the post-war world, especially after the Russian publication of the Allied secret treaties. To protect his diplomatic independence, Wilson rejected a formal alliance with Britain and France, designating the United States officially as an "associated power" in the Western coalition. Throughout the final months of the war, he refused to compromise his principles by recognizing the secret treaties, or to prejudice any post-war Allied negotiations with wartime concessions to known British and French interests. During 1918, moreover, Wilson acquired a prestige that, he believed, towered over a stricken Europe, assuring him a dominant role in the post-war peace settlement. The swelling voice of mankind, he averred, would crush those who stood in his way. In his noted New York address of September 27, 1918, he admonished those who would challenge his command of the European masses:

> National purposes have fallen more and more into the background and the common purpose of enlightened mankind has taken their place. The counsels of plain men have become on all hands more simple and straight-forward and more unified than the counsels of sophisticated men of affairs, who still retain the impression that they are playing a game of power and playing for high stakes.... Statesmen must follow the clarified common thought or be broken....[52]

Wilson's world leadership hinged as well on his success in designing the emerging League of Nations. Already a plethora of competing proposals were appearing on the horizon. On April 11, league advocates such as Elihu Root, A. Lawrence Lowell, William Howard Taft, and Edward House gathered at lunch to discuss the shape of the future league. They could not agree among themselves, but all questioned the known views of the President, as did Secretary Lansing. Wilson, on the other hand, informed Taft and Lowell that he rejected the views of the League to Enforce Peace.[53] What all proposals

[50] For the German and Allied offensives of 1918, see Martin Gilbert, *The First World War: A Complete History* (New York, 1994), 406–96.

[51] Bliss's full report of the U.S. role as a member of the Supreme War Council, February 19, 1920, in *Lansing Papers*, 2: 199–215.

[52] Wilson's address at the Metropolitan Opera House, New York, September 27, 1918, *Papers of Woodrow Wilson*, 51: 131–32.

[53] For the difference of opinion on the league issue, see Roland Stromberg, "Uncertainties and Obscurities About The League of Nations," *Journal of the History of Ideas*, 33 (January-March 1972), 139.

had in common was their failure to resolve acceptably the taunting issue of ends and means. Viscount Grey advised prospective league members that they must understand that any league, to be effective, would demand limitations on sovereignty, obligating all members to act in defense of collective decisions.[54] Elihu Root averred that any country, including the United States, unwilling to make such a commitment, should not join the league.[55]

Such stark realism was unacceptable to those who viewed the league as an escape from power politics. Ignoring such profound questioning of collective security, Wilson, in his New York address, reminded the country that a league of nations would be the essential element in any peace settlement. The league would terminate alliances that entangled, and "clear the air of the world for common understandings and the maintenance of common rights."[56] The league's formation, he added, required a post-war conference. If constructed earlier, it would be merely an anti-German alliance among the great powers; if formed after the peace settlement, it would be an inconsequential afterthought.[57]

Wilson relied on House to prepare the required league draft. In his search for the means to enforce the peace, House suggested to Britain's Lord Robert Cecil that the nations of the world required a moral standard. Any country that defied that standard should suffer moral condemnation – something that all countries would avoid.[58] In submitting his draft of a league covenant to the President on July 16, House emphasized the need for a higher standard of honor and behavior in international life. He included references to Wilson's notions of collective security, using much of Wilson's phraseology regarding "territorial integrity and political independence." But he recommended no means to achieve these essential objectives.[59] After studying the House draft on August 15, the President made two important changes. He eliminated House's provision for a world court, and added military force to House's list of league sanctions, which were largely economic.[60]

VI

House warned the President that his power to coerce the Allies would recede with the fighting. He wrote to Wilson on September 3: "As the Allies succeed, your influence will diminish.... I believe you should commit the Allies now to as much of your program as is possible." Similarly, General Bliss, troubled by Wilson's absolute refusal to bargain with the Allies while they still required

[54] Viscount Grey of Fallodon, "Viscount Grey on the League of Nations," *The Survey*, 40 (July 8, 1918), 401.
[55] Elihu Root to House, August 16, 1918, Seymour, *Papers of House*, 4: 46.
[56] Wilson's address of September 27, 1918, *Papers of Woodrow Wilson*, 51: 131.
[57] Ibid., 129–30.
[58] House to Lord Robert Cecil, June 25, 1918, Seymour, *Papers of House*, 4: 18–20.
[59] House to Wilson, July 14, 1918, ibid., 24–25; House's draft of the covenant, ibid., 29–36.
[60] Ibid., 48–49; David Hunter Miller, *The Drafting of the Covenant* (New York, 1928), 2: 15.

U.S. support, predicted that Europe, once it had achieved peace, would reject both the President's leadership and his program.[61]

By the end of September, General Ludendorf pressed Prince Maximilian von Baden, head of Germany's civilian government, to seek an armistice to end the fighting. Even more bluntly, Field Marshal von Hindenburg, on October 2, informed the Kaiser's Crown Council that the army could not wait another forty-eight hours.[62] The German government set out to convince the Allies, but especially Wilson, that it had become more democratic. Wilson had warned Prince Maximilian: "If we must deal with the military masters and monarchical authorities ... [the United States] must demand, not peace negotiations, but surrender." On October 12, Prince Maximilian proposed an armistice based on the Fourteen Points. Wilson, in response, demanded the full democratization of the German government. Then, in deference to British and French pressures, he demanded the abdication of the Kaiser as a condition of peace. On October 20, as the Kaiser accepted exile, Prince Maximilian accepted the President's terms and promised sweeping democratic reforms. The new German government now faced the task of preserving order at home and reaching a settlement with the Allies. When Wilson presented the German capitulation to London and Paris, he discovered that both Allies, anticipating an immediate German collapse, had no interest in an armistice based on the Fourteen Points.

Wilson, in response, threatened to repudiate any Allied peace terms that conflicted with his program. House warned London and Paris that unless they agreed to the Fourteen Points, the United States would leave the war. On November 4, the Supreme War Council approved a Pre-Armistice Agreement based on the Fourteen Points, but with important qualifications on the question of freedom of the seas and compensation for damage suffered by civilians in German-occupied territory. Finally, on November 11, German officials signed the Armistice Agreement to bring the long, exhaustive war to an end. During the final negotiations, it seemed that Wilson had reenforced his leadership role. House wrote contentedly from Europe: "I doubt whether any of the heads of government with whom we have been dealing quite recognize how far they are committed to the American peace program."[63] Actually, the President's power to coerce Allied spokesmen had evaporated with the end of war.

Simultaneously with the retreat of his influence abroad, Wilson faced a serious assault on his leadership at home. His wartime speeches had stirred the country's patriotic emotions as well as its sense of importance, but they had failed to consolidate his public appeal or the country's devotion to a league of nations. It was nowhere apparent that he could carry his league commitment through the U.S. Senate. The Senate harbored its own traditions of

[61] House to the President, September 3, 1918, Seymour, *Papers of House*, 4: 64; House and Bliss quoted in Trask, *Supreme War Council*, 143, 155–56.

[62] William L. Shirer, *The Rise and Fall of the Third Reich* (New York, 1962), 57.

[63] House to Wilson, November 5, 1918, *Papers of Woodrow Wilson*, 51: 594.

isolationism and independence, enhanced in 1918 by an upsurge of political partisanship. Republican leaders who supported Wilson's wartime leadership had long criticized him for excluding members of Congress, both Republican and Democratic, from his councils. Now they would reassert their party's normal majority status.

Conscious of his burgeoning domestic opposition, Wilson made his leadership the central issue in the 1918 congressional elections. In October, he appealed to the nation's electorate to strengthen the Democratic control of Congress. "The return of a Republican majority," he warned, "would ... certainly be interpreted on the other side of the water as a repudiation of my leadership."[64] Even Democratic leaders regarded the President's partisan appeal as a major political error. Republicans accused him of reducing the quest for peace to a partisan venture; they resented deeply his gratuitous charges of disloyalty against Republican congressmen who had supported his wartime leadership. The President's earlier liberal support had long disappeared. In November, the Republicans, still by far the country's normal majority party, easily captured control of both houses of Congress. They charged logically that the President had asked the nation for a vote of confidence, and had lost. Some Republicans denied that Wilson still possessed the authority to speak for the nation.[65] Thus the President emerged from the 1918 election faced with diminished public support and a rebellious congressional majority as he prepared to manage the forthcoming peace negotiations in Paris.

Wilson followed his failed intervention in the congressional election with another questionable decision. So completely had he identified the world's concern for a stable peace with his own conception of the American mission that many regarded his presence at the Paris Peace Conference both logical and sound. Still, Democratic friends advised him to remain in Washington. Frank Irving Cobb, Democratic editor of the *New York World*, argued emphatically that the President should avoid the Paris negotiations. Cobb observed early in November:

> The moment Wilson sits at the council table with these Prime Ministers and Foreign Secretaries, he has lost all the power that comes from distance and detachment. Instead of remaining the great arbiter of human freedom, he becomes merely a negotiator dealing with other negotiators.[66]

Upon his return from London in December, Cobb remarked to his wife, "Wilson does not know what he is up against." House cabled the President from Paris: "Americans here whose opinions are of value are practically

---

[64] Wilson's appeal to voters, October 15, 1918, ibid., 51: 343–44; October 17, 1918, ibid., 353–55.

[65] For the impact of the election on Wilson's leadership, see Stewart W. Livermore, *Politics Is Adjourned: Woodrow Wilson and the War Congress, 1916–1918* (Middletown, 1966), 246–47.

[66] Cobb to House, November 4, 1918, Seymour, *Papers of House*, 4: 210. See also Memorandum of Frank Irving Cobb, November 4, 1918, *Papers of Woodrow Wilson*, 51: 590–91.

unanimous in the belief that it would be unwise for you to sit in the Peace Conference. They fear that it would involve a loss of dignity and your commanding position."[67]

Senator Key Pittman, representing thirty Wilson supporters, advised the President not to go to Paris.[68] Even Secretary Lansing observed that the President should remain at home. "I am convinced," he wrote, "that he is making one of the greatest mistakes of his career and imperiling his reputation."[69] Wilson rejected such advice, and on November 18 announced that he would enter the peace negotiations in person.[70] On December 2, in his Annual Message on the State of the Union, he explained his special responsibilities to Congress and the nation. But he confessed to a group of senators that it was his responsibilities to Europe that gave him no choice but to attend the Paris conference. "Her stricken peoples," he said, "are imploring me to do so. They say and perhaps truly that if I refuse they are forsaken, that if I deny them they are wholly abandoned.... I must go and trust to the future for my vindication and I hope for theirs."[71]

If the President required congressional cooperation in treaty-making, his choice of a peace commission did nothing to assure it.

Convinced that the Paris negotiations were purely an executive responsibility, he refused to appoint any prominent Republicans, or even one member of the Senate, to the commission. It would be unfair, Wilson observed, to influence the free judgment of the Senate by appointing one or more of its members to the negotiating team. Eventually he selected four men associated with his administration, and all without major political influence: Robert Lansing, Colonel House, General Bliss, and Henry White, an experienced diplomat and nominal member of the Republican Party. The President added his name to the list of commissioners.[72] Not only had he rejected the advice of his political friends in his appointments to the commission, but he had also refused to discuss peace terms with members of Congress. Despite his political setbacks, growing opposition in Congress, and warnings of trouble in Paris, Wilson sailed for Europe on December 4 aboard the *George Washington*, still convinced that he possessed the power to overwhelm his adversaries both at home and abroad.

[67] House to Wilson, November 14, 1919, Seymour, *Papers of House*, 4: 213.
[68] Key Pittman to Wilson, November 15, 1918, *Papers of Woodrow Wilson*, 53: 94–95.
[69] Memorandum by Robert Lansing, November 18, 1918, ibid., 128.
[70] Telegram to Colonel House, November 18, 1918, ibid., 108–09.
[71] Annual Message, December 2, 1918, *Papers of Woodrow Wilson*, 53: 284–86. Wilson's response to Europe's pleas quoted in Fite and Graebner, *Recent United States History*, 141.
[72] Press release, November 29, 1918, ibid., 243.

3

Versailles

A Study in Arrogance

I

Wilson's reception in Paris was tumultuous. The throngs that lined the streets cheered and wept, hailing him as the savior of France.[1] His reception in London was scarcely less rapturous. The King lauded the American contribution to victory. The President, in response, included no reference to Britain's role in the Allied triumph. Nor in addressing the French House of Representatives later did he recognize the heavy price that France had paid for victory.[2] What mattered to him was the American role. The public adulation the President experienced in Paris and elsewhere reaffirmed his conviction that he alone carried the hopes of the world's masses for a peaceful and progressive world order. The vision was glorious; the realities, less so.

Wilson's conception of a Europe united behind his leadership contrasted with the actual state of European opinion. When the peace conference opened on January 12, 1919, with delegates from thirty-two countries jamming the city, the crowds in Paris were tense and unruly. David Lloyd George later declared before Parliament: "I am doubtful whether any body of men with a difficult task have worked under greater difficulties – stones crackling on the roof and crashing through windows, and sometimes wild men screaming through the keyholes."[3] Correspondents had warned Washington repeatedly that the inflamed state of French opinion made Paris the least desirable of all European cities for the conduct of peace negotiations."[4]

Wilson approached the peace conference with a well-established vision of a triumphant post-war world, leaving a doubtful role for the many renowned

[1] Cary Travers Grayson, *Woodrow Wilson: An Intimate Memoir* (New York, 1960), 62.
[2] David Lloyd George, *Memoirs of the Peace Conference* (2 vols., New Haven, 1939), 1: 110–14.
[3] Quoted in Ray Stannard Baker, *Woodrow Wilson and the World Settlement* (3 vols., Garden City, 1923), 2: 38.
[4] Sally Marks, *International Relations in Europe, 1918–1933* (New York, 1976), 4.

experts on international affairs who had accompanied him to Paris. The President stayed at Murat Palace, guarded by French soldiers; members of the American Peace Commission and other delegates took up residence at the Hotel Crillon. Wilson maintained a liaison only with Colonel House, his longtime counselor. Despite its high level of competence, the American Peace Commission was never permitted to make recognizable contributions to the work of the conference. From the outset, Bliss and Lansing complained that the Commission lacked the unity and direction required to act effectively. "I am disquieted," Bliss wrote to his wife on December 18, "to see how hazy and vague our ideas are."[5] Bliss wondered what would happen when other delegations arrived. He confided to Lansing, "I think that our present course is dangerous, dangerous to the point of threatening the success of the Commission."[6]

Wilson made no effort to encourage or coordinate the work of the U.S. Commission. Stephen Bonsal, a seasoned journalist who served as House's secretary in Paris, described its role: "When, as rarely happened, their signatures were wanted, the President would summon the delegates to House's office and then dismiss them."[7] Bliss complained that he never knew the President's precise views on any subject.[8] The President rarely attended Commission meetings, a practice the Commission found humiliating.[9] So persistently did Wilson ignore the Commission that Lansing contemplated resigning and returning to the United States.

Outside the five-man Peace Commission, the huge American delegation at Paris comprised career State Department and embassy personnel, some War Cabinet bureaucrats, noted American students of European affairs, and military officers. At the core of the delegation was the Inquiry, experts who had advised the President since 1917. Each group in the delegation remained a separate entity, without access to the President. John Foster Dulles complained early that it was "practically impossible for anyone to get to see him or for him to give time to purely American conferences."[10] Countless Europeans looked to Wilson for salvation, from war and the full spectrum of social ills confronting Europe. But at no time did Wilson establish contact with the spokesmen of labor, women's rights, racial minorities, or other groups aroused by his promise of social justice.

[5] Bliss to Mrs. Bliss, December 18, 1918, David F. Trask, "Tasker Howard Bliss and the 'Sessions of the World' 1919," *Transactions of the American Philosophical Society*, vol. 56, part 8, 1966. 11; Bliss to Lansing, December 18, 1918, ibid.
[6] Bliss to Lansing, December 26, 1918, United States Department of State, *Papers Relating to the FRUS: The Paris Peace Conference* (13 vols., Washington, 1942–1947), 2: 297–98. Hereafter cited as *Paris Peace Conference.*
[7] Stephen Bonsal, *Unfinished Business* (Garden City, 1944), 42–43.
[8] Bliss to Baker, January 11, 1919, Trask, *Tasker Howard Bliss*, 13.
[9] Arthur Walworth, *Wilson and the Peacemakers: American Diplomacy at the Paris Peace Conference, 1919* (New York, 1986), 43.
[10] Ibid., 22.

Wilson's design for an ideal world soon ran the gauntlet of big-power interests. In theory, the nations represented at the Paris Peace Conference were to conduct business in plenary sessions, with all delegations in attendance. Because of the generally acknowledged complexity of the issues confronting the conference, the Supreme Council – those who managed the war – would dictate the peace. Within the Supreme Council, Wilson faced Europe's self-assigned spokesmen: David Lloyd George of Britain, Georges Clemenceau of France, and Vittorio Orlando of Italy. These men, as a Council of Four, conferred in private behind well-guarded doors. The press challenged the tight restrictions, but the conference procedure never provided more than official news releases. Newsmen wondered why Wilson, whose success hinged on the continued support of public opinion, would confine his arguments to secret meetings where his colleagues could outvote him.[11] In late January, *The Nation* reported a press rebellion in Paris against the decision to give the public only summary statements, officially prepared.[12]

Wilson had offered his Fourteen Points as the foundation of the post-war international order, but a profound divergence of interests quickly governed the proceedings. Wilson's peace program faced its initial challenge in the secret Treaties of London, dated April 26, 1915, wherein the European Allies – France, Britain, Russia, and Italy – had promised each other territorial gains as compensation for the emerging horrors of war.[13] Wilson's refusal to recognize these treaties in no measure undermined their influence; Lloyd George, Clemenceau, and Orlando were determined from the outset to fulfill their treaty obligations. Wilson's disapprobation, accompanied with claims that the United States stood on a higher moral plain, both puzzled and angered the cynical Clemenceau. After one session, the Frenchman observed bitterly, "Talk with Wilson! How can I talk to a fellow who thinks himself the first man in two thousand years to know anything about peace on earth?" Clemenceau once remarked to Colonel House, "I get on with you. You are practical. I understand you, but talking to Wilson is something like talking to Jesus Christ."[14] Unwilling to assert the national interest of the United States in his devotion to such principles as self-determination, Wilson could not prevent other members of the Big Four from asserting the concrete interests of their countries.

II

Wilson regarded the integration of a league of nations into the peace treaty the primary task of the Paris Peace Conference. On December 21, 1918, addressing

---

[11] For a complaint against the secrecy imposed on the Paris conference by the major powers, see *The Nation*, 107 (December 28, 1918), 732; also Richard V. Gulahan, "Majority Imposes Secrecy," *The New York Times*, January 16, 1919.

[12] *The Nation*, 108 (January 25, 1919), 107.

[13] For the provisions of the treaties, see Rene Albrecht-Carrie, *Italy and the Paris Peace Conference* (New York, 1938), 334–39.

[14] Clemenceau quoted in Fite and Graebner, *Recent United States History*, 143.

a convocation at the University of Paris, he predicted that the League of Nations would "operate as the moral force of men throughout the world, and that whenever or wherever wrong and aggression are planned or contemplated, this searching light of conscience will be turned upon them...."[15] The President presented his resolution for the creation of a league at the second plenary session on January 25, 1919. In his address, he averred that the American delegation would suffer his nation's scorn if it failed to carry out this assigned mandate.[16] What remained was the preparation of the final draft of the League Covenant for presentation to the conference.

Sir Robert Cecil of the British Foreign Office had developed his own plan for a league, based on the traditional responsibility of the great powers for maintaining the peace. A permanent secretariat in Geneva would handle administrative duties. Members would avoid armed conflict by seeking agreement through arbitration, public discussion, and diplomacy.[17] General Jan C. Smuts of South Africa offered a similar plan, based largely on Anglo-American cooperation.[18] Wilson's plan, drafted largely by Colonel House, emphasized the protection, through collective action, of "the territorial integrity and existing political independence" of all league members. Unlike the British proposal, with its emphasis on peaceful procedures, Wilson's league would react directly against aggression, even as the United States reserved the right to determine unilaterally when it would exercise that right. Wilson provided for later alterations of boundaries "if it could be shown that injustice had been done or the conditions had changed." But he offered no specific provision for treaty revision.[19]

Wilson's colleagues on the American Commission generally supported the creation of a league of nations, but many rejected his conception. Robert Lansing, Tasker Bliss, and Henry White preferred Cecil's emphasis on diplomacy to Wilson's positive guarantee of peace through the forceful preservation of the status quo. Lansing warned the President that any positive pledge to oppose aggression would meet vigorous opposition in both Europe and the United States.[20] He thought so little of Wilson's draft that he refused to engage in its formulation.

Wilson faced major opposition in London. Britain's Lloyd George revealed no interest in Wilson's league. He condemned the President for his self-appointed role as missionary "to rescue the poor European heathen from their age-long

[15] Address at the University of Paris, December 21, 1918, Arthur Link, ed., *The Papers of Woodrow Wilson* (69 vols., 1966-1994), 53: 462.
[16] Wilson's address to the Plenary Session, January 25, 1919, ibid., 54: 266.
[17] For Cecil's proposal, see Miller, *The Drafting of the Covenant*, 1: 51–64.
[18] Ibid., 34–39. For commentary on these plans, see Lloyd Ambrosius, *Woodrow Wilson and the American Diplomatic Tradition* (New York, 1987), 55–56.
[19] Ibid., 57; David Hunter Miller, *My Diary: At the Conference of Paris* (New York, 1924), I, 370ff.
[20] For White's views, see Allan Nevins, *Henry White: Thirty Years of American Diplomacy* (New York, 1930), 487; Robert Lansing, *The Peace Negotiations* (Boston, 1921), 135,147; on Bliss, see Frederick Palmer, *Bliss, Peacemaker: The Life and Letters of General Tasker Howard Bliss* (New York, 1934), 166–67.

worship of false and fiery gods." Whatever the British view of collective security, Lloyd George shared Wilson's call for the reduction of armaments, under the presumption that the League offered security against external attack. At the meeting of the Imperial War Cabinet on December 25, 1918, the Prime Minister argued that disarmament was the ultimate measure of the League's validity.[21] Despite the widespread doubts regarding the League's promise, when Wilson addressed the plenary session on January 25, the Paris conference was prepared to accept his formal proposal. The small-power delegates generally approved the creation of a league, but complained of their exclusion from the drafting process. Lansing observed that the great powers were running the conference.[22] House and Cecil assumed responsibility for drafting a final Anglo-American design for the League of Nations.[23] British and American leaders assigned the task of polishing the draft to David Hunter Miller, the American expert on international law, and Sir Cecil J. B. Hurst.[24]

When British leaders accepted the Hurst–Miller draft, that draft, in general, became the Covenant of the League of Nations, with its unaltered Article X as a guarantee against international aggression. Still, Cecil wondered whether anyone really took Wilson's program of collective security seriously. Much of Britain agreed with him. George Dewar expressed a widespread English view of the League when he asserted that "no nation on earth is prepared, or ought to be prepared, to subordinate its own vital interests to some general idea of what is good for the world." He focused his condemnation on Wilson, who, he wrote, "considered himself to know more than all mankind before him or contemporary with him."[25] Whatever the conference's pervading doubts, the plenary session of February 14 accepted the draft.

France, from the outset, challenged the official Anglo-American assertion that collective security would guarantee the peace. Clemenceau understood that Lloyd George and Wilson were determined to avoid any future entanglements on the European continent. The French leader favored a league with coercive power, backed by the United States and Britain, as the only guarantee of French security. Wilson agreed, in response to French demands, that military and economic sanctions might become necessary, but he rejected any precise formula for their employment. Wilson managed to eliminate Clemenceau's demand for a military staff.[26] Jules Cambon, the noted French diplomat, questioned the League's effectiveness. "France," he wrote, "would have time to be

[21] Lloyd George, *Memoirs of the Peace Conference*, 1: 420–21.

[22] Ambrosius, *Woodrow Wilson and the American Diplomatic Tradition*, 67.

[23] For American and British collaboration in drafting the League Covenant, see ibid., 61, 65, 69.

[24] The Hurst–Miller draft, February 2, 1919, in Miller, *The Drafting of the Covenant*, 1: 65–71.

[25] George A. B. Dewar, "Peace – or Truce: After the Signature," *The Nineteenth Century* (July 1919), 29.

[26] For the opposition of France to U.S. and British domination of the league issue, see Ambrosius, *Woodrow Wilson and the American Diplomatic Tradition*, 70–76.

swallowed up before it was even decided whether the league of nations would act...." Future peace, Cambon argued, depended not on leagues but on the quality of diplomacy. Paul Cambon, his brother and an equally renowned diplomat, wrote on February 10: "Wilson ... continues to play a disintegrating role. His society of nations which doesn't even exist seems to him to be equal to everything."[27] Paul Cambon, conscious of the burgeoning opposition that Wilson faced in the United States, proposed that French newspapers ignore the plight of the American prophet. "The less we concern ourselves with President Wilson," he wrote on February 19, "the more the opposition that he arouses at home will avail.... It is of the highest importance to let the position of Wilson break up of itself."[28]

III

When Wilson left Paris on February 15 to return briefly to the United States, his star was at its zenith. By postponing the most divisive issues confronting the conference, the President had managed to command the agenda. Upon his arrival in Boston on February 24, Wilson informed an enthusiastic crowd that Europeans were hopeful because they believed that they were "on the eve of a new world, when peoples will understand one another, when nations will support one another in every just cause, when nations will unite every moral and every physical strength to see that the right shall prevail." Any man who resisted the present tides running in the world, he added, would "find himself thrown upon a shore so high and barren that it will seem as if he had been separated from his human kind forever." Those who sought to diminish the country's commitment to the fulfillment of that promise, he warned, did not know America.[29] Actually, Wilson's needed support at home was already waning.

Republican leaders in Washington had opened their assault on the flawed assumptions of collective security as early as December 1918. If a vote in defense of territorial integrity required unanimity, then, as Felix Morely suggested, any country accused of aggression could negate collective action by voting against it.[30] The rule of unanimity limited league action to moral force alone. In December, Senator Henry Cabot Lodge repeated his earlier assault on Article X. A league, he declared, "must be either a mere assemblage of words, ... or it must be a practical system. If such a league is to be practical and effective, it cannot possibly be either unless it has authority to issue decrees and force to sustain them." He added his own rejoinder: "Are you ready to put your soldiers and your sailors at the disposition of other nations? If you are not, there will be no power of enforcing the decrees of ... whatever may be established."[31] *The Washington Post*, in January, summarized

---

[27] Quoted in Walworth, *Wilson and the Peacemakers*, 122–23.
[28] Ibid., 123.
[29] Wilson's address in Boston, February 24, 1919, *Papers of Woodrow Wilson*, 54: 238–44.
[30] Felix Morley, *The Society of Nations* (Washington, 1932), 89.
[31] *Cong. Record*, 65th Cong., 3rd Session (December 21, 1918), 727, 728.

the Republican charges against collective security. First, an effective league, it asserted, required the employment of armed force, compulsory for all members of the league. If the league's authority rested merely on "moral force," it would be ineffective and "merely a waste of time to make it part of the peace treaty."[32] Second, the Republican critics charged that a league of nations would carry the burden of defending the status quo, an obligation that it could not sustain. Why should the league, asked Senator Borah, uphold the British Empire? On February 21, he commented on the magnitude of such a commitment: "She to-day holds possession of one-fifth of the habitable globe, and we in article 10 guarantee the integrity of her possessions on the three continents of the earth."[33] It was essential, added Senator Irvine Lenroot of Wisconsin, that league involvement in the affairs of nations be on the side of liberty, not the preservation of despotism.[34] Elihu Root gave this assault on Article X classic form when he observed on March 29 that "if perpetual, it would be an attempt to preserve for all time unchanged the distribution of power and territory made in accordance with the views and exigencies of the Allies in this present juncture of affairs." This would be not only wrong, but also futile.[35]

Lodge leveled a direct warning to Wilson in early March when he circulated his so-called "Round Robin" resolution among Senate Republicans. This statement declared pointedly that the League of Nations Covenant, in its present form, was not acceptable to the Senate. Lodge assumed accurately that the chairman would rule him out of order. He then proceeded to read aloud the names of the thirty-seven Republican signers – more than one-third necessary to block Senate approval of Wilson's treaty.[36] Ignoring his inescapable dilemma, the President on March 4 vowed to embody the League in a peace treaty and thereby fulfill the purpose for which America had gone to war.[37]

On the following day, Wilson sailed for France to address the troubling challenges still confronting the Paris conference. When he arrived on March 14, he found that much had changed. He received none of the applause he had experienced on his triumphal arrival three months earlier. The French press was now openly critical of him. During his absence, Colonel House, who believed the President too obstructive in his dealings with Allies in Paris and the Senate at home, had accepted a French demand for a preliminary treaty without the League Covenant. Wilson quickly recaptured his earlier success

[32] Quoted in D. F. Fleming, *The United States and the League of Nations* (New York, 1932), 90–91.
[33] *Cong. Record*, 65th Cong., 3rd Session (February 21, 1919), 3913; William E. Borah, *American Problems*, ed. Horace Green (New York, 1924), 102.
[34] *Cong. Record*, 65th Cong., 3rd Session (February 28, 1919), 4570.
[35] See Elihu Root, *Men and Policies*, eds. Robert Bacon and James Brown Scott (Cambridge, MA, 1924), 265.
[36] William C. Widenor, *Henry Cabot Lodge and the Search for an American Foreign Policy* (Berkeley, 1980), 314–16.
[37] Address at the Metropolitan Opera House, March 4, 1919, *Papers of Woodrow Wilson*, 55: 413–20.

in incorporating the Covenant in the treaty, but he found House's independent dealing with European leaders, generally in search of compromise, unbearable. The relations between the two men approached the breaking point. The President reluctantly accepted several minor changes in the Covenant. Members now gained the right to withdraw from the League. Wilson successfully rejected another French attempt to strengthen the League with an international military organization.

IV

Germany confronted the Allies with their most demanding and divisive decisions. On March 27, Wilson warned his colleagues that an unjust peace would provoke a German desire for revenge. Both Lloyd George and Clemenceau agreed, but Clemenceau observed that persuading the Germans that the Allies were just was another matter.[38] From the outset, Wilson's quest for moderation had no chance against peacemakers who were determined to inflict on Germany the harsh peace that, they believed, it deserved and alone would guarantee the Continent's future peace. For the French, the recovery of Alsace-Lorraine seemed little compensation for the human and physical price that France had paid for victory. France had lost 1,400,000 men, 10 percent of its male population, with an equal number maimed by the German war machine. Clemenceau understood that France lacked the power to counter any resurrection of German might and ambition. His defense strategy at Paris assumed many forms, not the least a guarantee of Germany's western frontier. It was essential, General Ferdinand Foch assured Colonel House, that France have control of the Rhine.[39]

At issue was the future of the Rhineland, a 10,000-square-mile region on the left bank of the Rhine between Alsace-Lorraine and the Netherlands. It included not only the cities of Cologne and Mainz, but also much of Germany's industrial capacity, with numerous fortresses, munitions factories, and strategic railroads required for any German military advance into western Europe. Its population of somewhat over 5 million shared strong economic and political ties with Germany. But Paris was determined to gain a new political regime for the region. As early as December 1918, the Foreign Affairs Committee of the Chamber of Deputies voted overwhelmingly for the permanent demilitarization of the Rhineland.[40] Clemenceau drove to the heart of the security issue by demanding the creation of one or two Rhenish republics along the west bank of the Rhine.

[38] Paul Mantoux, *The Deliberations of the Council of Four* (March 24-June 28, 1919), trans. and ed. Arthur S. Link, with the assistance of Manfred F. Boemeke (2 vols., Princeton, 1992), 31, 33.

[39] Seymour, *Papers of House*, 4: 120–23.

[40] George Bernard Noble, *Policies and Opinions at Paris, 1919* (New York, 1935), 239; Louis Yates, *United States and French Security* (New York, 1957), 23; Arno J. Mayer, *Politics and Diplomacy of Peace-Making* (New York, 1967), 178.

For France, the Saar Valley in the southern Rhineland held a special attraction. The Saar was exceedingly rich in coal deposits, and France was notably deficient in coal resources. Moreover, the Germans, in their retreat, had wantonly destroyed the French coal mines at Lens and Valenciennes. France had lost the Saar at the Congress of Vienna in 1815. For reasons of restitution and reparation, France now sought economic control of the region, to be guaranteed by some measure of political domination. The Chamber of Deputies voted for the annexation of the Saar.[41] Unfortunately, most Saarlanders had long become distinctly German in their sympathies.

For President Wilson, French territorial demands on Germany required conformity with both the Pre-Armistice Agreement and the principle of self-determination. In Point Eight of his Fourteen Points, he declared that "the wrong done by Prussia in the matter of Alsace-Lorraine ... should be righted." Beyond that, the President refused to consider any assaults on the principle of self-determination. When Foch insisted that the German Empire could, under no circumstance, extend beyond the Rhine, Wilson responded that he opposed even a temporary separation of the Rhineland from Germany.[42] Lloyd George, torn between his opposition to a permanent military occupation of the Rhineland and his recognition of the French need for security, turned to the offer of an Anglo-American guarantee to France. On March 14, he suggested the idea to Wilson. The President readily accepted it, convinced either that he could persuade the Senate to agree, or that the issue would ultimately become irrelevant inasmuch as the League of Nations would provide France the necessary guarantees.[43]

Clemenceau understood that neither Wilson nor Lloyd George desired any military involvement in post-war Europe. For good reason, he refused to entrust French security to ephemeral Anglo-American pledges under the League. French Foreign Minister Andre Tardieu observed that Britain and the United States possessed ample physical guarantees of security. "To ask us to give up occupation," he declared, "is like asking England and the United States to sink their fleet of battleships. We refuse."[44] General Foch, on March 31, argued that Germany could, with available power, defeat France before an English army could appear.[45]

By late March, the conflict between Wilson and Clemenceau over French security had reached an impasse. On the key issues of the guarantee treaty and occupation of the Rhineland, Wilson had the support of the American Commission. On April 3, Bliss reported to his wife: "Things here have come to a dangerous pass. The French military party are pushing their government to its downfall. They are making demands for the occupation *in perpetuity* of the Rhine by our Allied Army including 100,000 Americans and other things

[41] Ibid.
[42] Seymour, *Papers of House*, 4: 333, 335–36.
[43] David Lloyd George, *Memoirs*, 253, 265–66.
[44] Andre Tardieu, *The Truth About the Treaty* (Indianapolis, 1921), 175–77, 181.
[45] Foch quoted in Mantoux, *Deliberations of the Council of Four*, 1: 87.

which we cannot yield. And if we don't yield, there is no treaty."[46] House urged the President to offer concessions to the French. On April 7, Wilson called a meeting of the American Commission. Bliss reported the outcome: There should be no more secret conferences of the "Big Four" and all differences should be discussed openly in a plenary conference.[47] That day, the President ordered the *George Washington* prepared for a return voyage to the United States. It was now up to the Council of Four to resolve the issue of French security. In the required compromise, the French yielded on the question of the Rhenish republics, but gained the right to occupy the Rhineland for fifteen years and the permanent demilitarization of the west bank of the Rhine.

Wilson's position on the Saar issue was initially no less uncompromising. He agreed that France should have whatever Saar coal it required, but not at the expense of the Saarlanders's right to self-determination. Wilson and Lloyd George agreed that German sovereignty over the region should remain inviolate. Unfortunately, such an arrangement would create a perpetual state of conflict that all desired to avoid. Clemenceau, on March 28, reacted violently to the Anglo-American defense of German sovereignty over the Saar, demanding that the issue go before the Council of Four. There, Tardieu argued that French annexation of the Saar was essential for the industries of Alsace-Lorraine. Lloyd George consented to give the Saar mines to France as reparation, but proposed that the Saar Valley be made an autonomous state. Wilson remained wedded to his earlier position: France could mine the coal but acquire no territorial sovereignty. The United States, he added, was morally obligated to uphold the Armistice Agreement that granted France only the territory lost in 1871. When the President denounced as hypocrites all who would place national interests above the Armistice Agreement, Clemenceau accused Wilson of being pro-German, and stormed out of the room.[48]

France, isolated on the Saar issue, suggested a League mandate over the Saar for fifteen years, with France overseeing the administration of the region. Wilson objected to even this limited suspension of German sovereignty. Tardieu's argument that French ownership of the mines was incompatible with German political sovereignty compelled Wilson to offer a solution that would infringe on Germany's monopoly of political power. His answer lay in an administration commission under League control. This arrangement satisfied both Lloyd George and Clemenceau, creating a political regime that would give France the coal without the danger of a renewed conflict with Germany. Wilson agreed to the suspension of German sovereignty for fifteen years.[49] The French failed to gain control of the Saar, but acquired a political regime that would enable them to exploit its mines.

[46] Bliss to Mrs. Bliss, April 3, 1919, Trask, *General Tasker Howard Bliss*, 45.
[47] Bliss to Mrs. Bliss, April 7, 1919, ibid., 45.
[48] Thomas A. Bailey, *Woodrow Wilson and the Lost Peace* (Chicago, 1963), 221.
[49] Saar settlement of April 9, 1919, Mantoux, *Deliberations of the Council of Four*, 1: 215–17; Mantoux's Notes of the Council of Four, April 9, 1919, *Papers of Woodrow Wilson*, 57: 161–64.

Clemenceau's quest for guarantees of French security applied to military as well as territorial restraints on Germany. France demanded and received the limitation of the German army to 100,000 men, and the total elimination of German offensive weapons such as the German navy and air force.[50] In addition, Clemenceau extracted from Wilson and Lloyd George the guaranty treaty, whereby the two nations promised to come to France's aid in the event of some future German attack. On the matter of German reparations, accepted in part to enhance French security, Wilson recognized the extensive British and French claims against Germany. He agreed in principle to a large payment, the actual amount to be determined later by a special reparations commission. The many restrictions on German power and influence reestablished Anglo-French dominance of the European continent, or so it seemed.

This Allied treatment of Germany was scarcely logical. Throughout the war, Wilson had deliberately pointed to the Kaiser's government, not the German people, as the source of Europe's tragedy.[51] At the time of the Armistice, he declared that the United States "cannot deal with any but veritable representatives of the German people who have been assured a genuine constitution...." Thereafter, a popular revolution swept away the old regime and paved the way for the new Weimar Republic. But at Paris, representatives of the new Germany were excluded from all deliberations. Carrying the burden of disapprobation supposedly reserved for the Kaiser's regime, the new German government was denied representation at the Paris conference until the victors had completed the treaty. Bliss reminded Wilson that reports from Germany indicated that the new government was attempting to reconstitute the state on a truly democratic foundation. "[I]f the spirit of her government is anything like that which is indicated in these memoranda," Bliss added, "It seems a pity that she cannot in any way be heard while the peace terms are being discussed."[52]

Without reference to Germany's wartime regime, Articles 231 and 232 of the treaty declared, in part, that "the Allied and Associated Governments affirm and Germany accepts the responsibility of Germany and her allies for causing all loss and damage...."[53] Thus the Weimar Republic, by Wilson's definition not even the enemy, ultimately carried the full burden of German war guilt and reparations. Absent from the Paris deliberations, Germany was powerless to defend its historic national boundaries. In drawing Germany's new borders, the victors

---

[50] For the debate on the size of the German army, see Minutes of the Council of Ten, March 7, 10, 1919, *Paris Peace Conference*, 4: 263–65, 296.

[51] In April 1917, Wilson declared that Americans had no feeling toward the German people "but one of sympathy and friendship." Again, in June, he declared that "we are not the enemies of the German people and ... they are not our enemies." Wilson repeated such words as he assured Germany of a just peace. See Address to Joint Session of Congress, April 2, 1917, *Papers of Woodrow Wilson*, 41: 523; May Day Address, June 14, 1917, ibid., 42: 500.

[52] Bliss to Wilson, April 1, 1919, in David F. Trask, *General Tasker Howard Bliss and the "Sessions of the World,"* 1919 (Philadelphia, 1966), 33.

[53] On Wilson's error in compelling the new German government to carry the burden of war guilt, see Louis J. Halle, *Men and Nations* (Princeton, 1962), 54–56, 158–61.

deprived Germany of 27,000 square miles of territory and 6.5 million inhabitants, half of whom spoke the German language. For most Germans, there was little in these impositions and penalties that represented the Fourteen Points.[54]

Wilson agreed readily that Germany should lose its former colonies, but he intended to achieve this massive transfer of territory under the principle of self-determination. He had supported national aspirations only when the populations in question seemed to conform to some form of organic state that could achieve political order and coherence. Other transferals, he believed, should be left to the League of Nations. During the war, Britain, Australia, New Zealand, France, and Belgium occupied the German colonies in Africa and the south Pacific. Japan seized the German islands in the Pacific north of the equator. The occupying states demanded that the peace conference recognize their new acquisitions.

Eventually, Wilson accepted their right of occupation, but held tenaciously to the principle that all newly acquired colonies come under the political mandate of the League of Nations for the protection of the native peoples. These new governments would exercise mandatory, not sovereign, rights. Lansing opposed the system of mandates because it left unresolved the question of sovereignty. Did the mandates belong to the League of Nations or to the mandated countries?[55] For Wilson, the mandates comprised an alternative to colonialism, and thus defended, in some degree, the principle of self-determination. In practice, the mandates were scarcely distinguishable from colonies.

V

Superficially, Wilson gained his greatest victories in the Eastern European settlement. Austria, having rejected his December 1917 offer of special treatment if it left the war, now faced total disintegration under the promise of self-determination. That glowing promise presumed the existence of established political units within the former Austro-Hungarian Empire, with recognizable boundaries, prepared to resolve, through democratic procedures, the territorial and political challenges confronting them. With the military collapse of Germany and Austria in 1918, the peoples of Austro-Hungary proclaimed new states based essentially on historic national groupings. Every nationality had its spokesmen at the Paris conference in search of recognition and ample boundaries. The notion that every nationality could now enjoy a state and government of its own was appealing, but the dispersal of nationalities demanded such a massive redoing of maps and movement of peoples that the quest for self-determination quickly became disillusioning. For Wilson, the triumph of self-determination lay in the very creation of the new states.

54 Hans A. Schmitt, "The Treaty of Versailles: Mirror of Europe's Postwar Agony," *The Treaty of Versailles: The Shaping of the Modern World*, Proceedings of the Virginia Humanities Conference, April 7–8, 1989, Published by the Center for Programs in the Humanities, Virginia Tech, 1989.

55 Robert Lansing, *The Peace Negotiations: A Personal Narrative* (Boston, 1921), 83–84.

Ethnic boundaries defied clear definition because national groupings did not inhabit watertight ethnic compartments. All great cities of the Austro-Hungarian Empire had strong multinational constituencies. The establishment of new states unleashed a plethora of boundary disputes that taxed the knowledge and ingenuity of experts assigned the responsibility of resolving them. Lansing had concluded early that the principle of self-determination would impose impossible demands on the peace conference. He wrote as early as December 30, 1918:

> The phrase is simply loaded with dynamite. It will raise hopes which can never be realized. It will, I fear, cost thousands of lives. In the end it is bound to be discredited, to be called the dream of an idealist who failed to realize the danger until too late to check those who attempt to put the principle into force. What a calamity that the phrase was ever uttered! What misery it will cause! ... A man, who is a leader of public thought, should beware of intemperate or undigested declarations. He is responsible for the consequences.[56]

So general became the demand for self-determination that Colonel House complained in April, "It has become a craze and in many instances ridiculous."

Many boundary decisions reflected the interests and ambitions of those with the power to demand them. Austria, Hungary, Bulgaria, and even Russia lost territory to Poland, Czechoslovakia, and Rumania, the specially favored among the new states. France desired a strong Poland and Czechoslovakia as potential allies against German and Russian expansionism. With French support, the two countries seemed to win their boundary disputes. Poland's ethnic claims, bolstered with historical arguments, created a multiethnic Poland in which the Poles constituted less than 70 percent of the population. Czechoslovakia demanded and received a southern boundary that included 750,000 Hungarians. Rumania emerged as the special defender of East-Central Europe against Bolshevik expansionism. Thus favored, Rumania enlarged its boundaries at the expense of Ukrainians, Hungarians, Bulgarians, and Russians. So devoid of principle were the boundary settlements that Isaiah Bowman of the American delegation hoped that the United States would not sign the peace treaty without reservations. Bliss complained of the impossibility of satisfying the new states. "The 'submerged nations,'" he wrote, "are coming to the surface and as soon as they appear, they fly at somebody's throat. They are like mosquitoes, vicious from the moment of their birth. All their energies are devoted to raising armies and all begging the United States for troops, for money, for arms and what not."[57]

The Paris Conference compounded Europe's future peace by assigning German territory to two Slavic countries. Wilson, in his thirteenth point, promised Poland access to the sea – a promise that he could fulfill only at

---

[56] Robert Lansing's statement of December 30, 1918, ibid., 97–98.

[57] Bliss to Mrs. Bliss, February 26, 1919, in Palmer, *Bliss, Peacemaker*, 375. Bliss found the Polish representatives the most demanding, transforming every issue before the conference into a Polish question. See ibid., 370.

Germany's expense. The only developed harbor in the area was Danzig, a city with 200,000 loyal German inhabitants. How could Danzig become a Polish port without making the city Polish? The answer lay in designating Danzig a free city, separated from Germany, governed by a democratically elected senate and city council. Poland received the Polish Corridor to give it access to the free city of Danzig.[58] The strategic German Sudetenland went to Czechoslovakia, even as Germany accepted the permanent independence of Austria. By assigning primarily German areas to Slavic states, the Paris conference served neither the principle of self-determination nor the cause of peace.

Italy claimed and received, under the 1915 secret Treaty of London, the Austrian Trentino up to the Brenner Pass, as well as Trieste on the Dalmatian coast below the port of Fiume. Orlando presented Italy's case for annexing Fiume on April 19.[59] Wilson, despite British and French support for Italy, rejected the Italian claim to the port – the new state of Yugoslavia's only outlet to the sea. He denied that the Treaty of London justified Italy's defiance of the principle of self-determination.[60] As the debate resumed on the following day, Orlando repeated his demands, and threatened to leave the conference if they were refused. Wilson, on April 23, responded with a dramatic public appeal to the Italian people.[61] That day, the British and French, supporting the American position, asked the Italians to reconsider.[62] Orlando, in defiance, returned to Italy and there received a huge ovation, demonstrating Italy's support for his demands. The issue of Fiume had reached an impasse. Orlando ultimately protected the Italian interest by gaining postponement of the final decision. In 1920, Italy came to terms with Yugoslavia, receiving Fiume as a "separate body," with a strip of coast connecting the city with Italy.[63] Again, as in the clash of territorial claims elsewhere in the former Austro-Hungarian Empire, self-determination lost.

What created fundamental instability in the vast and critical region of the former Austro-Hungarian Empire was the failure of the Paris Conference to create a successor. That empire had exploited its non-German minorities, but it had created an economic unit that had given considerable stability and some prosperity to a large and important region of Europe. For this reason, Britain hesitated to endorse the breakup of the old empire. No one saw more clearly the price of Balkanizing the Austro-Hungarian Empire than Winston Churchill.[64] The conference refused to organize East-Central Europe into a confederation or a free-trade area that might have granted the new states some chance of

[58] Schmitt, "The Treaty of Versailles," 23.
[59] Mantoux, *Deliberations of the Council of Four*, 1: 276–80.
[60] For Wilson's response on April 19, see ibid., 282–84; *Paris Peace Conference*, V: 85–93.
[61] Baker, *Woodrow Wilson and the World Settlement*, 3: 287–90.
[62] Mantoux, *Deliberations of the Council of Four*, 1: 346–50.
[63] Trask, *General Tasker Howard Bliss*, 50.
[64] See Winston S. Churchill, *The Gathering Storm* (Boston, 1948), 10.

economic and political progress. Yet on the stability and resilience of the region hinged much of the future of the Paris settlement.

Elsewhere, Wilson failed to apply the doctrine of self-determination to the victors. The Paris Conference did not touch the empires of Britain, France, Italy, Belgium, Holland, or the United States. The resulting disillusionment among Armenians, Persians, Indians, Indochinese, Koreans, and some Africans, was profound. In Paris, such nationalists as Indochina's Ho Chi Minh took Wilson's promises seriously. They quickly learned that his principle did not extend to yellow, brown, and black peoples living under white rule. In effect, self-determination became a readily available device for punishing the losers. As the veteran Irish nationalist, John Decoy, observed, Wilson's concerns for nationality apply "only to a portion of the world – that controlled by Germany and her allies – and utterly ignore the rest."

Turkey, as a German ally, paid the price of defeat in the loss of its empire, largely to Britain and France. In late October 1914, Turkey attacked Odessa, a Russian port on the Black Sea. That action invited immediate declarations of war by Russia, Britain, and France. Turkey had lost its southeast European empire in the Balkan War of 1912, but its capital, Constantinople, still controlled the vast Ottoman Empire that stretched southward from Asia Minor to the Indian Ocean. Britain and France planned the region's dissection as early as January 3, 1916, when Britain's Mark Sykes and France's Georges Picot negotiated the Sykes–Picot Agreement. That arrangement awarded France Greater Lebanon, with exclusive influence over the rest of Syria and claims extending to Mosul. Britain claimed Barra and Baghdad, the two Mesopotamian provinces. Both countries wanted Palestine, but could reach no agreement on its disposal.

Britain's conquest began with the occupation of Baghdad in March 1917, followed by the taking of Ramadi on the Euphrates and Tikrit on the Tigris before the end of the year. Meanwhile Colonel T. E. Lawrence, with his Arab forces, crossed the Sinai Desert and captured Aqaba in July 1917. This permitted the Royal Navy to transport Arab forces to aid Britain in the conquest of Palestine. General Sir Edmund Allenby occupied Jerusalem on December 11, 1917, prepared now to advance on Damascus and Constantinople with Arab support. On November 12, 1918, a British squadron steamed triumphantly into Constantinople. The disposal of the Ottoman Empire fell to the Council of Four. At the war's end, Britain recognized Arab independence within the Arab peninsula; elsewhere Britain and France displayed little interest in Arab self-determination. Britain had carried the burden of the conquest. The disappearance of the Ottoman Empire brought the British Empire to its zenith. Lloyd George had added almost a million square miles.[65]

---

[65] David Fromkin, *A Peace To End All Peace: The Fall of the Ottoman Empire and the Creation of the Modern Middle East* (New York, 1989), 383, 400–01. Fromkin's volume comprises a complete history of the fall of the Ottoman Empire during the war.

VI

Russia's absence from the Paris Conference was not that country's choice. For reasons of ideology and politics, the conference excluded that former ally. Lloyd George favored a Russian presence, but Clemenceau argued that the peace settlement did not concern Russia.[66] Still, the Bolshevik revolution and the continuing pressures it exerted, not only within Russia, but also on Hungary, Germany, and other European states, never ceased to plague the conference. Throughout the spring of 1919, the Paris Peace Conference contemplated the prospect that Germany might succumb to Bolshevism.[67] This fear of Bolshevik expansion was reinforced when in March the Communist, Bela Kun, gained power in Hungary. Many agreed that Bolshevism, as a danger to civilization, should be destroyed, but no one could propose a policy for achieving that goal.[68] The danger of Communist expansion fell heavily on France. In January 1919, Marshal Foch launched a drive to rescue Russia from the Bolsheviks, suggesting that the Allies negotiate an immediate peace with Germany and embark on a crusade to crush Bolshevism. When Foch, in late March, submitted an even more ambitious plan to eliminate Bolshevism, Wilson expressed his firm opposition.[69]

On February 15, the day before Wilson left Paris for his trip to the United States, Winston Churchill traveled to Paris to gain Wilson's support for a major Allied Russian intervention. Wilson's reply was predictable and clear. An Allied intervention, he warned, would be ineffectual, even detrimental. He advised an immediate withdrawal of all Allied forces from Russia. Churchill asserted that an Allied withdrawal would place the White elements in Russia at the mercy of the Bolsheviks. Upon his return to London, Churchill initiated an Allied effort, allegedly with U.S. support, to aid the White Russians in their struggle against the Bolsheviks. Wilson was outraged. He instructed Colonel House to inform the Allies that the United States is "not at war with Russia and will in no circumstances that we can now foresee, take part in military operations there against the Russians."[70]

Even then, Allied intervention had no future. During 1919, the Red Army, conscripted, trained, and toughened under Leon Trotsky's driving leadership, proved superior to the diverse forces that comprised the White counterrevolutionaries. The appeals to patriotism against foreign intervention, the failure of the Whites to coordinate their actions, and the Bolshevik promise of self-determination to outlying minorities in Armenia, Georgia, and central

---

[66] Lloyd George, *Memoirs of the Peace Conference*, 1: 211–12.
[67] See, for example, the Diary of Colonel House, April 4, 1919, *Papers of Woodrow Wilson*, 56: 585.
[68] Ibid., 219.
[69] Baker, *Wilson and the World Settlement*, 1: 166.
[70] Wilson to Commission, February 19, 1919, *Papers of Woodrow Wilson*, 55: 208; Seymour, *Papers of House*, 4: 348.

Asia – all assured the ultimate Bolshevik triumph. With their victory, they reincorporated the non-Russian minorities in the Caucasus and central Asia into the Soviet state.

Russia was neither an ally nor an enemy vulnerable to dismemberment through the application of self-determination. But Russia contained a variety of ethnic nationality groups, concentrated largely along its European border: Finns, Latvians, Estonians, Lithuanians, Poles, and Ukrainians. As well-established nationality groups, all seemed qualified for the political restructuring of Europe, based on the principle of self-determination. Wilson and Lansing, in their desire to preserve Russia's territorial integrity, challenged the application of self-determination to Russian territory. Poland and Finland were unique. Wilson had singled out Poland for self-determination in his Fourteen Points address; Finland had been less integrated into the Russian Empire than other non-Russian nationalities. The Soviet regime had granted Finland independence. The Inquiry [the post-war panel of experts] judged that the right to self-determination granted to Poland belonged as well to Finland, Estonia, Latvia, Lithuania, and the Ukraine. On April 30, Lansing reported to the Council of Foreign Ministers on the Baltic situation. The staff report recommended the extension of de facto recognition to the provisional governments of the three Baltic states, without provision for prior Russian approval.[71]

Lansing objected to the report, insisting that the recognition of the Baltic States comprised a dissection of Russia that the United States had sought to avoid. Lansing's position faced a challenge when the plenary session of May 6 approved the statement that "Germany recognizes and shall fully respect the national independence of all territories which formed the former Russian Empire."[72] That German precedent did not influence Wilson or Lansing, who remained committed to Russia's territorial integrity. The Baltic region achieved independence while the Bolshevik regime reabsorbed much of the Russian borderlands elsewhere.[73]

VII

Japan's strong delegation in Paris based its case for the retention of Shantung on Tokyo's contribution to the Allied war effort, its wartime treaties with the European allies, and its rights of conquest and occupation. Japan threatened to leave the conference rather than give up Shantung. China's demands at

---

[71] Report of Lord and Morison, cited in Miller, *My Diary*, 16: 175–77, 218.

[72] Ibid., 20: 159.

[73] For an excellent survey of the national sovereignty issue as it applied to Russia at the Paris Peace Conference, see Linda Killen, "Self-Determination vs. Territorial Integrity: Conflict within the American Delegation at Paris over Wilsonian Policy toward the Russian Borderlands," *Nationalities Papers: The Association for the Study of the Nationalities (USSR and East Europe)*, Spring 1982, X, No. 1, 65–78.

the conference were no less clear and uncompromising: to protect the territorial integrity of China.[74] U.S. addiction to the Open Door policy placed the President under extreme pressure to defend Chinese interests. Minister Paul Reinsch warned Washington of the accumulating Chinese doubts regarding the seriousness of U.S. obligations to China.[75] In Paris, Chinese and American delegates sought to formulate a joint policy on the Far Eastern problem. By early 1919, China's Cheng-ting Wang and American experts David Hunter Miller, James T. Shotwell, and Stanley Hornbeck had prepared their case for China.[76] On January 6, 1919, Reinsch submitted a strong appeal to the American peace delegation. "Only the refusal to accept the result of Japanese secret manipulations ... ," he warned, "can avert the onus of making China a dependence of a reckless and [boundlessly] ambitious caste which would destroy the peace of the entire world."[77]

Wilson not only embraced the Chinese cause, but also insisted that V. K. Wellington Koo, Chinese minister to the United States and head of the Chinese delegation in Paris, address the Big Four. Koo reminded the delegates that Japan had extracted its wartime agreements from China through force. China, he concluded, had a right "to the restoration of these territories."[78] For Lansing, Koo had "simply overwhelmed the Japanese with his argument."[79] But Koo failed to dissuade British and French leaders from honoring their wartime pledges to Japan. Isolated on the Shantung question, Wilson accepted Shantung's transfer to Japan, but managed to gain a verbal promise that Japan would eventually restore Shantung to China. The Chinese delegation refused to accept the Shantung decision or to sign the Versailles Treaty.[80]

As the world's most advanced and powerful nation in the Afro-Asian world, Japan hoped to secure U.S. support in Paris for a statement on racial equality in the Covenant of the League of Nations. Despite his apparent devotion to self-determination, Wilson still harbored his racial prejudices and assumed that the Senate would not approve the League Covenant if it included a declaration of racial equality. Unsure of Wilson's support, the Japanese delegation took its proposal for racial equality to the League of Nations Commission. There, Wellington Koo supported the measure.[81] For Japan, the issue of

---

[74] Detailed evaluation of the issues confronting China in Reinsch to Lansing, November 23, 1917, ibid., 2: 491–504.

[75] Reinsch to Lansing, March 10, 1919, *FRUS, 1919* (2 vols., Washington, 1934), 1: 282.

[76] James T. Shotwell, *At the Paris Peace Conference* (New York, 1937), 132–33.

[77] Reinsch to Acting Secretary of State, January 6, 1919, *Paris Peace Conference*, 2: 524.

[78] Wellington Koo's statement, January 28, 1919, ibid., 3: 755–57.

[79] Lansing, *The Peace Negotiations*, 253.

[80] For a full account of the Shantung question in Paris, see Wunz King, *Woodrow Wilson, Wellington Koo and the Chinese Question at the Paris Peace Conference* (Leyden, 1959).

[81] Quoted in Paul G. Lauren, "Human Rights in History: Diplomacy and Racial Equality at the Paris Peace Conference," *Diplomatic History*, 2 (Summer 1978), 265.

racial equality had become a matter of national pride. Viscount Kikujiro Ishii, now Japan's ambassador to the United States, asked, "Why should this question of race prejudice, of race discrimination, of race humiliation be left unremedied?"[82] On March 4, Ishii delivered his government's special plea on racial equality to the President in Paris.[83] Japanese Americans joined the appeal; some sent telegrams to the U.S. delegation in Paris urging support for the principle of racial equality.

On April 11, 1919, in the final session of the League Commission, Baron Makino Shinken of the Japanese delegation introduced an amendment to the League Covenant on the recognition of racial equality. In defense of the amendment, Makino asserted that "the principle of the equality of nations and the just treatment of their nationals should be laid down as a fundamental basis of future relations in the world organization." Moved by Makino's appeal, eleven of the seventeen members of the Commission voted for the Japanese proposal. The American, British, and Australian delegates opposed it. Wilson, who chaired the session, then ruled that majority approval was insufficient for the inclusion of the racial equality measure in the Covenant. It required, he announced, unanimous endorsement. Most of those present were shocked. They knew that on two other occasions, with Wilson himself involved, the Commission had not demanded unanimity. The Japanese condemned Wilson for employing one voting arrangement to support his ethno-racial prejudices and another for everything else.[84]

Having failed to win approval of the Japanese amendment on racial equality at the Commission session on April 11, Makino introduced the original Japanese proposal at the plenary session of the peace conference on April 28, convened to consider the League of Nations Covenant. Makino explained that it was only "to see the League established on a sound and firm basis of good-will, justice, and reason that we have been compelled to make our proposal." Facing the same uncompromising British and American opposition, the Japanese acquiesced in their final defeat on the racial question. The subsequent unanimous vote in favor of the Anglo-American conception of the League Covenant scarcely reflected the true sentiments of the peace conference on either the racial question or the efficacy of the League itself.[85]

---

[82] Speech in New York City, March 14, 1919, quoted in Lauren, "Human Rights in History," 268.

[83] Breckinridge Long to Wilson, March 4, 1919, *Papers of Woodrow Wilson*, 55: 436–37.

[84] For Wilson's disposal of the Japanese proposal, see ibid., 270–73.

[85] The final draft of the League Covenant, April 21, 1919, in Miller, *The Drafting of the Covenant*, 2: 683–93. For a detailed and generally favorable treatment of the Paris Peace Conference, see Margaret MacMillan, *Paris 1919: Six Months that Changed the World* (New York, 2002). Its value lies in its portrayal of the intricacies of decision making on highly complex and divisive issues.

VIII

At Versailles on May 7, Clemenceau, as president of the conference, submitted the treaty's conditions to Count Ulrich von Brockdorff-Rantzau, German foreign minister and leader of the German delegation. He addressed the German delegates:

> This is neither the time nor the place for superfluous words. You have before you the accredited plenipotentiaries of the great and lesser Powers, both Allied and Associated, that for four years have carried on without respite the merciless war which has been imposed upon them. The time has now come for a heavy reckoning of accounts. You have asked for peace. We are prepared to offer you peace.... There will be no verbal discussions, and observations must be submitted in writing.[86]

Brockdorff-Rantzau, in his response, was defiant. "We are under no illusions," he acknowledged, "as to the extent of our defeat and the degree of our powerlessness.... [W]e have heard the victor's passionate demand that as the vanquished we shall be made to pay, and as the guilty we shall be punished." He declared that Germany would seek no escape from its responsibility for the war, but denied that Germany "should be burdened with the sole guilt of that war."[87] He demanded a just peace and Germany's immediate admission to the new League of Nations. In declaring that no nation could endure or implement the treaty's harsh terms, the German delegation hoped to spare Germany the full consequences of military defeat.

Brockdorff-Rantzau submitted the German proposals for revision on May 29, including mandates, under League jurisdiction, for the former German colonies. The German defense emphasized the ostensible contradiction between the treaty and Wilson's Fourteen Points.[88] British leaders throughout the political spectrum urged Lloyd George to seek an accommodation. General Smuts favored a "drastic revision" of the treaty, especially its military, territorial, and reparation clauses. "I strongly urge settling up with the Germans now," he wrote. "Now is the time, and it may be the only time, to reap the fruits of victory." On June 2, Lloyd George informed Wilson and Clemenceau of the British consensus in favor of revision.[89] Bliss agreed that the conference leaders should listen to the Germans if they hoped to avoid another war.[90] The President, opposing all compromise, denied that the treaty

---

[86] Clemenceau's address, Plenary Session, May 7, 1919, *Paris Peace Conference*, 3: 415–16.

[87] Ibid.,17–20.

[88] Observations of the German Delegation on the Conditions of Peace, May 29, 1919, ibid., 6: 795–901.

[89] Council of Four, meeting held at Lloyd George's flat, June 2, 1919, ibid., 6: 139–46; Lloyd George, *Memoirs of the Peace Conference*, 1: 461–81. Lloyd George observed that Clemenceau "was annoyed and Wilson righteously indignant."

[90] Bliss to Mrs. Bliss, June 6, 1919, Trask, *General Tasker Howard Bliss*, 60.

deviated substantially from his Fourteen Points. Members of the U.S. delegation generally shared Wilson's reluctance to revise the treaty. In the end, Wilson acknowledged that the terms were harsh, but he regarded them justified. "I think," he concluded, "it is profitable that a nation should learn once and for all what an unjust war means in itself."[91]

On June 12, the conference agreed to reject the German demands for revision, except for minor changes, as well as immediate membership in the League. Clemenceau presented the conference's reply to the German counter-proposal on June 16, shattering the German expectations. Brockdorff-Rantzau and German Chancellor Philip Scheidemann resigned to avoid the necessity of signing the treaty. President Friedrich Ebert ended the crisis by appointing Gustav Bauer as Chancellor. Bauer formed a new cabinet that recognized Germany's need to accept the treaty. The new foreign minister, Hermann Miller, and another cabinet member, Johannes Bell, traveled to Paris to sign the treaty. At a plenary session held at Versailles's Hall of Mirrors on June 28, the fifth anniversary of the Sarajevo assassination, delegates from the Allied and Associated powers, as well as Germany, signed the Versailles Treaty, with its League of Nations Covenant.[92] Also at Versailles, the United States and France signed a security treaty to go before the U.S. Senate with the Versailles Treaty.[93] At Wilson's immediate departure for Brest, Colonel House, who had carried the burden of reconciling Wilson's views with those of Lloyd George and Clemenceau, stepped forward. The President looked at him and said coldly, "Goodby, House."

Doubts and warnings regarding the wisdom and longevity of the treaty permeated the entire conference. Britain's John Maynard Keynes wrote to Foreign Secretary Sir Austen Chamberlain on May 26: "We have presented a Draft treaty to the Germans which contains in it much that is unjust and much more that is inexpedient.... The settlement ... for Europe disrupts it economically.... The New States we are setting up cannot survive in such surroundings."[94] Britain's Harold Nicolson condemned the terms on June 8 in a letter to his father: "Now that we see them as a whole we realise that they are much too stiff. They are not stern merely but actually *punitive*.... [T]he real crime is the reparation and indemnity chapter, which is immoral and senseless."[95] General Smuts agreed. For him, the treaty's only hope

---

[91] Report of Meeting Between the President, the Commissioners, and the Technical Advisers of the American Commission, June 3, 1919, *Paris Peace Conference*, 11: 218–22.

[92] Plenary Session of June 28, 1919, ibid., 3: 421–23. The Peace Conference with Austria (Saint Germain), June 2, 1919, ibid., 3: 426.

[93] Mantoux, *Deliberations of the Council of Four*, 2: 590–92.

[94] Roy Forbes Harrod, *The Life of John Maynard Keynes* (New York, 1969), 251.

[95] Harold Nicolson, *Peacemaking 1919* (London, 1933), 359. There is a certain irony here, and proof of the extremity of the indemnity clauses. Technically speaking, the final act of World War I did not take place until October 3, 2010, when the German government paid the last installment of the 33 billion dollar indemnity levied on Germany at Versailles. See *Time*, October 11, 2010, "What They're Ending in Germany," 15. *Time* conjectured this meant that World War I had finally ended.

lay in its future revision.[96] Even Clemenceau acknowledged to Herbert Hoover: "[T]here will be another world war in your time and you will be needed back in Europe."[97] Much of the American delegation had become equally disconsolate. In mid-May, five young members of the American Commission staff, including the noted Harvard historian, Samuel Eliot Morison, resigned in protest against the treaty provisions. On May 17, William C. Bullitt joined them.[98] Not even House harbored much respect for the treaty.[99]

Those who impose treaties on the world carry the responsibility for their defense; the victims have no intention of doing so. Three states that regarded themselves victimized in Paris were Germany, the Soviet Union, and Japan – three of the five most powerful in the world. Britain and France were in no condition to defend the treaty.[100] For Wilson, that mattered little. He had arranged for the world to confront unwanted threats with a system of collective security, a system whose limited viability had been universally exposed. But for Wilson and his supporters, the demonstrated necessity of lasting peace had long overwhelmed the problem of means. Colonel House assured the President as early as July 1918 that the world, weary of war, now relied on his peace program.[101] Wilson once quieted the doubts of his adversaries, who questioned the effectiveness of the League, by assuring them that "if it won't work, it must be made to work."[102] Failure was too disastrous to contemplate. This propensity of laudable purposes to cloud the importance of means led the economist Alfred Marshall in another context to compare utopian programs – those that lacked the means for their achievement – to the "bold facility of the weak player who will speedily solve the most difficult chess problem by taking on himself to move the black men as well as the white."[103]

At Wilson's urging, the Paris Conference had accepted his solution for war. But what would limit aggression in the future as in the past was diplomatic accommodation or the threat of counterforce, not appeals to international law and the superior morality of the status quo. Defense of the post-Versailles order rested on the United States, in alliance with Britain, France, and perhaps others, to maintain the preponderance of power that had defeated Germany,

[96] Smuts to Lloyd George, May 22, 1919, quoted in Trask, *General Tasker Howard Bliss*, 59.

[97] Herbert Hoover, *The Memoirs of Herbert Hoover* (2 vols., New York, 1951–1952), 1: 468, 482.

[98] Bullitt to Wilson, May 17, 1917, ibid., 58.

[99] Seymour, *Papers of House*, 4: 474.

[100] For the price that Britain and France paid for their apparent military and diplomatic triumphs, see A. N. Wilson, *After the Victorians* (New York, 2005); Robert A. Doughty, *Pyrrhic Victory: French Strategy and Operations in the Great War* (Cambridge, MA, 2005).

[101] House to the President, July 11, 1918, Seymour, *Papers of House*, 4: 22.

[102] Wilson quoted in Carr, *The Twenty Years' Crisis*, 8.

[103] Alfred Marshall, "The Social Possibilities of Economic Chivalry," *Economic Journal*, 17 (March 1907), 16n.

with the clearly conveyed willingness to use it.[104] At the war's end, American diplomatist Lewis Einstein reminded the nation:

> At no time even unknown to us, were European politics a matter of indif-
> ference to our vital interests, but if hitherto we were impotent to alter their
> march, a fortunate destiny preserved the existing balance independently of
> us.... [W]e have today a distinct and legitimate duty in the family of great
> nations in contributing to preserve those elements which compose the bal-
> ance of power, and to which we can only be blind at our later cost.[105]

IX

Upon his arrival in New York on July 8, President Wilson met the burgeoning Republican challenge head-on. He assured a reporter that the Senate would ratify the treaty.[106] On July 10, he laid his treaty before the Senate, informing that body that he expected no less than prompt and unqualified approval. "The only question," he declared, "is whether we can refuse the moral leader-ship that is offered us, whether we shall accept or reject the confidence of the world."[107] After tracing the events that led to the construction of the treaty, he concluded: "The stage is set, the destiny disclosed. It has come about by no plan of our concerning, but by the hand of God who led us into this way. We cannot turn back."[108]

Lodge had prepared the Republican opposition for the coming debate on the League issue. His "Round Robin" resolution had demonstrated his power to kill Wilson's League in the Senate, but he required a countering proposal that would satisfy all elements of his party – irreconcilable iso-lationists, such as Senator Borah, who opposed any commitment to the League of Nations, as well as Republicans who favored a League in some form. Lodge proposed to Borah a maneuver whereby the Republican major-ity would load the League Covenant with reservations that would protect U.S. sovereignty. If isolationists supported these reservations and thereby

---

[104] Margaret MacMillan, in *Paris 1919*, argued, to the approval of others, that the work at Paris was in no way responsible for what occurred later. To blame the treaty, she writes, is "to ignore the actions of everyone – political leaders, diplomats, soldiers, ordinary voters – for 20 years between 1919 and 1939." But it was the creators of the Versailles Treaty, led by Woodrow Wilson, who saddled the world with the attractive post-war notions regarding international life, as embodied in the promise of collective security. Those suppositions, flowing from the deliberations at Paris, determined the behavior of nations between 1919 and 1939. That behavior, marked by the refusal of all the victors at Versailles to assume responsibility for the defense of the treaty, ended with the catastrophe of another world war. For a defense of MacMillan's judgment, see Hew Strachan, "To End All Wars? Lessons of World War I Revisited," *Foreign Affairs*, 82 (January/February 2003),148–49; "Versailles Revised," *U.S. News & World Report*, December 2, 2002, 44–45.

[105] Lewis Einstein, *A Prophecy of War* (New York, 1918), 45–46.

[106] Press conference, July 10, 1919, *Papers of Woodrow Wilson*, 61: 424.

[107] Ray Stannard Baker and William E. Dodd, eds., *The Public Papers of Woodrow Wilson* (6 vols., New York, 1925–1927), 5: 551.

[108] *Papers of Woodrow Wilson*, 61: 436.

eliminated Wilson's League, they could still, if they desired, vote against the final approval. If the Senate rejected the treaty with reservations, the isolationists would emerge triumphant; a League of Nations adopted with reservations would be preferable to Wilson's Covenant. Borah's acceptance of this strategy assured Lodge a united party until the final vote. During June 1919, Lodge prevailed upon Elihu Root to draft the necessary reservations, designed essentially to assure congressional approval of any American resort to force. These reservations, Lodge insisted, were designed only to limit U.S. obligations to the League's security system. Lodge, meanwhile, packed the Foreign Relations Committee with Republicans known to oppose Wilson's version of the League.[109]

Lodge had repeatedly posed the collective security dilemma facing Wilson before the debate began. For him, the League was either a useless assemblage of phrases or a practical and effective organization based on force. Any reliable League, Lodge warned, would require infringements on national sovereignty that no one, not even the President, would favor. "What will your league amount to," asked Borah, "if it does not contain powers that no one dreams of giving it?" This question required an answer, but no one could resolve the conflict between the obligation to act and the sovereign right to avoid it.

Wilson, on August 19, met the challenge by inviting the Senate Foreign Relations Committee to the White House.[110] There, for three hours, he attempted to explain the country's obligation under Article X and to assure the Committee that the treaty would not undermine the constitutional powers of Congress in external affairs. Every member state, he told the senators, was free to reject decisions of the League Council. Still, he added, the United States, under Article X, would accept a moral obligation to act. "But it is a moral, not a legal, obligation," he emphasized, "and leaves our Congress absolutely free to put its own interpretation upon it in all cases that call for action." Moral obligation, Wilson declared, was superior to legal obligation, but moral obligation left a country the right to exercise judgment regarding the circumstances for action.[111] Wilson argued that moral force, representing the convictions of humanity, would be sufficient to maintain the peace without obligation. This presumed a common interest in peace that would reject aggression, and thus sustain the status quo. All countries preferred peace to war, but not all, as Root had warned, accepted the existing treaty structure.[112]

Convinced that American opinion would ultimately desert the administration, Lodge resorted to the tactics of delay by reading the huge text of the Versailles Treaty. Tormented by the fear that time was running against him,

[109] Widenor, *Henry Cabot Lodge and the Search for an American Foreign Policy*, 341–44.
[110] For a verbatim report of the White House conference of August 19, see Henry Cabot Lodge, *The Senate and the League of Nations* (New York, 1925), 297–379.
[111] On Wilson's critical distinction between moral and legal obligation, see Fleming, *The United States and the League of Nations, 1918–1920*, 312–14.
[112] *Cong. Record*, 65th Cong., 1st Session (August 20, 1919), 4025.

Wilson decided to take his case to the country. The President's personal physician, Admiral Gary Travers Grayson, warned him that he could not withstand the rigors of a long and exhausting speaking tour. In rejecting that warning, the President demonstrated his almost fanatical conviction that the treaty required ratification in its original form.[113] On September 3, the President left Washington on his final crusade to convince the American people that the Lodge reservations resulted from intense partisanship or bad judgment. In either case, they threatened U.S. interests in peace and international stability.

Wilson opened his campaign at Columbus, Ohio, on September 4, before a small and unenthusiastic audience. The treaty was harsh, he acknowledged, but not unjust. With its acceptance by the Senate, he promised, the men in khaki would never need to cross the seas again. The League of Nations would eliminate that necessity.[114] On the same day, Wilson spoke to a more enthusiastic audience at the Indianapolis Coliseum. Again, to the cheers of the crowd, the President proclaimed that the League would eliminate the possibility of future wars. "The heart of the Covenant of the League," he declared, "is that the nations solemnly covenant not to go to war for nine months after a controversy becomes acute." Had there been nine days of discussion, he added, Germany would not have gone to war.[115] Many in his audience seemed unconvinced.

In St. Louis on September 5, the crowds were more receptive. Speaking at the St. Louis Coliseum, the President again defended the treaty, declaring that it presented the country the choice of joining the League of Nations and thereby redeeming its pledge to extend liberty and justice in the world.[116] On September 6, he admonished his Kansas City audience to accept the Versailles Treaty without change. "To reject that treaty, to alter that treaty," he averred, "is to impair one of the first charters of mankind."[117] In Des Moines, later that day, he assured his listeners that Germany, in accepting the treaty, had surrendered to the world.[118] Two days later, Wilson defended the treaty in Omaha, declaring it a work of majesty – the achievement of a world without war.[119] After addressing generally enthusiastic audiences in Sioux Falls, St. Paul, and Minneapolis, the President traveled westward to Bismarck, Billings, Helena, Coeur d'Alene, Spokane, and Tacoma.

In his address in the Seattle Arena on September 13, Wilson dwelled at length on the Covenant of the League of Nations and the unprecedented obligations assumed by its members.[120] As he proceeded down the Pacific coast

---

[113] Quoted in Joseph P. Tumulty, *Woodrow Wilson As I Knew Him* (Garden City, 1921), 435.
[114] Address at the Columbus Chamber of Commerce, September 4, 1919, *Papers of Woodrow Wilson*, 63: 7, 17.
[115] Address at the Indianapolis Coliseum, September 4, 1919, *Papers of Woodrow Wilson*, 63: 20–21.
[116] Address at the St. Louis Coliseum, September 5, 1919, ibid., 51.
[117] Address at Convention Hall, Kansas City, September 6, 1919, ibid., 72.
[118] Address at the Des Moines Coliseum, September 6, 1919, ibid., 87.
[119] Address at the Auditorium in Omaha, September 8, 1919, ibid., 101.
[120] Address at the Seattle Arena, September 13, 1919, ibid., 255–64.

from Washington to California, the President experienced the large, almost fanatical throngs that promised success to his venture. In San Francisco's Civic Auditorium on September 17, he again defended the League Covenant as a guarantor of peace.[121] In the San Diego Stadium on September 19, the President proclaimed the treaty's triumph of self-determination:

> We went into this war not only to see that power of that sort never threatened the world again, but we went into it for even larger purposes than that.... [T]he heart and center of this treaty is that it sets at liberty people all over Europe and Asia who have hitherto been enslaved by powers that were not their rightful sovereigns and masters. Only by removing such wrongs, he continued, could or should there be peace.[122]

At Los Angeles on September 20, he proclaimed the elimination of force in international affairs. Every great fighting nation in the world, he declared, solemnly agrees that it will never resort to war without first submitting any matter in dispute to arbitration, discussion, and the judgment of mankind.[123]

From Los Angeles, the President traveled eastward to Ogden, Salt Lake City, Cheyenne, and Denver, and on September 25, reached Pueblo. There, in the City Auditorium, he implored his listeners to support the League so that Americans would never again die on foreign battlefields. In the peroration of his speech, Wilson asked why mothers of soldiers lost in France would weep and call down "the blessings of God upon me.... They believe, and rightly believe," he concluded, "that their sons saved the liberty of the world."[124] That speech ended the tour. Exhausted by the strain of more than thirty major addresses, the President, at the urging of his physician, cancelled his remaining engagements and returned to Washington.[125] Several days later he suffered a stroke. For the remaining eighteen months of his presidency, the nation conducted its affairs with little White House direction.

X

Secretary Lansing sought to fill Washington's political void on the issue of treaty ratification. During October, his congressional liaison informed him that the Senate would not approve a treaty without the Lodge reservations. The burden of creating the necessary two-thirds majority for approval rested on Lansing's success in gaining wide Democratic support for the reservations. His office became the center of activity between the senatorial supporters of the treaty and the Executive Office. Britain's Viscount Edward Grey landed in

---

[121] Addresses in San Francisco, September 17–18, ibid., 323–36, 349.
[122] Address in the San Diego Stadium, September 19, 1919, ibid., 371–72.
[123] Address in Los Angeles, September 20, 1919, ibid., 404, 409.
[124] Address in the Pueblo City Auditorium, September 25, 1919, ibid., 503, 511.
[125] For Wilson's declining health during the trip, see Tumulty, *Woodrow Wilson As I Know Him*, 439–40.

New York on September 27, as the special ambassador to the United States, to urge U.S. ratification of the treaty.[126] Grey plunged headlong in the treaty fight. Unable to see the President, he turned to Lansing with his case for the reservations, even as he convinced London that Europe would have the treaty with reservations, or not at all.[127]

Much of the pressure for compromise centered on Senator Gilbert M. Hitchcock of Nebraska, Democratic leader in the Senate. To maintain unity within the Democratic Party, Hitchcock on November 15 insisted that he needed to know the President's stand on the reservations. The President's response was clear: "I trust that all true friends of the treaty will refuse to support the Lodge resolutions." Hitchcock, blocked in his search for compromise, assured Colonel House that most Democrats favored ratification in almost any form. House addressed the President: "A great many people, Democrats, Progressives, and Republicans, have talked with me about ratification of the Treaty and they are all pretty much of one mind regarding the necessity for its passage with or without reservations."[128] Again there was no response.

During November 1919, the struggle over ratification reached its first crisis. Informed that the voting would commence on the Lodge reservations, Wilson pleaded with the Senate Democrats to oppose any modification in the treaty. The Republican majority, voting as a unit, passed the reservations, one by one. If the Democrats still possessed the power to defeat the treaty with reservations, Lodge made it equally clear that the Republicans would kill it without the reservations. This placed the burden of passage on the President. Wilson, on November 18, instructed Democrats to reject the treaty with reservations, arguing that the reservations nullified the treaty. The Senate rejected the amended treaty by the overwhelming vote of 39 to 55, Republican irreconcilables joining the Democrats. The Democrats moved the approval of the unaltered treaty. Again the treaty fell, 38 to 53.

During succeeding weeks, many Democrats broke ranks, convinced with Allied leaders that U.S. membership in the League with reservations was preferable to no membership at all. Joining those now beseeching a settlement, Mrs. Wilson urged her husband to accept the reservations rather than see the Paris Peace Pact go down in defeat. Mrs. Wilson recorded his reply:

> Little girl, don't you desert me; that I cannot stand. Can't you see that I have no moral right to accept any change in a paper I have signed without giving every other signatory, even the Germans, the right to do the same thing? ... [T]he Nation's honor that is at stake.[129]

---

[126] Ibid., September 27, 1919.
[127] For Viscount Grey's efforts to break the political deadlock between Wilson and his opponents, see Leon E. Boothe, "A Fettered Envoy: Lord Grey's Special Mission to the United States, 1919–1920," *The Review of Politics*, 33 (January 1971), 78–94. See also Boothe, "Lord Grey, the United States, and the Political Effort for a League of Nations," *Maryland Historical Magazine*, 65 (Spring 1970), 50–51.
[128] House to the President, November 24, 1919, Seymour, *Papers of House*, 4: 509–10.
[129] Edith Bolling Wilson, *My Memoir* (Indianapolis, 1938), 297.

On December 6, Grey divulged his plans to leave for Britain in January. He wrote to the Foreign Minister secretly: "President continues to be too ill to see any of his own Ministers.... There is no one with whom I can discuss anything effectively in Washington." Lansing surmised correctly that Grey would not return. The President discovered that Lansing had been conducting cabinet meetings in his absence. On February 11, upon rejecting the Secretary's defense that he acted from necessity, he accused Lansing of repeatedly rejecting his judgment, and advised him to resign his position immediately.[130] Lansing noted briefly upon submitting his resignation, "Thank God an intolerable situation is ended."[131] In the final vote, of March 1920, on the treaty with the Lodge reservations, Democrats joined Republican reservationists to produce a majority of 49 to 35, still seven votes short of the necessary two-thirds. Convinced to the end that reservations were synonymous with nullification, the President accepted defeat with the expectation of total vindication later.[132]

XI

Wilson emerged from the League fight in the Senate, determined to carry the issue into the coming presidential election. Shortly after the treaty vote, he confided bitterly to his physician and friend: "I am a sick man lying in bed, but I am going to debate this issue with these gentlemen in their respective states whenever they come up for reelection.... And I will get their political scalps when the truth is known to the people."[133] Republicans accepted the challenge, convinced that neither Wilson nor the League question could arouse widespread enthusiasm for the Democratic cause. During the Senate debates, Lodge predicted that the President, if he went before the nation on the League issue, "would be the worst beaten man that ever lived." Boies Penrose, the Republican boss of Pennsylvania, observed confidently, "Any good Republican can be nominated for President and can defeat any Democrat." The collapse of wartime emotions and the increasing disillusionment over the war, that Wilson seemed powerless to counter, presaged an easy Republican victory.

Lodge required a Republican stand on the League issue that would hold the leading elements within the party together and guide the party and the nation through the coming decade. As temporary chairman of the Republican convention, he suggested a platform based on the reservations. But Borah demanded that he reject the League completely. Lodge met the challenge by requesting Root to examine the phraseology of the League platform adopted by the Indiana Republicans. The Indiana plank condemned the League, but

---

[130] Wilson to Lansing, February 11, 1920, *Papers of Woodrow Wilson*, 64: 404.
[131] For Lansing's resignation, see Lansing to Wilson, February 12, 1920, ibid., 408–10.
[132] For a superb analysis of the League fight, see John Milton Cooper Jr., *Breaking the Heart of the World: Woodrow Wilson and the Fight for the League of Nations* (New York, 2001).
[133] Cary T. Grayson, *Woodrow Wilson: An Intimate Memoir* (New York, 1960), 102–07.

favored an "association of nations" that would recognize the country's sovereignty. Root accepted the formula and constructed a League plank that satisfied all except the Republican minority that took the League seriously. That plank, eventually adopted without debate, committed the Republican Party to world peace through "an international association ... based upon international justice." Lodge thought the statement somewhat vague. William Allen White, the noted Republican editor, observed that the platform had "successfully met the requirement of saying nothing definite in several thousand well chosen words." Senator Warren G. Harding of Ohio appeared the ideal candidate to carry out the platform.

That choice offered the Democrats some chance of recovery. Eventually, after thirty-eight ballots, the party agreed on James M. Cox, the former governor of Ohio. For the vice presidency, the convention selected the handsome and engaging Assistant Secretary of the Navy, Franklin Delano Roosevelt. On the League question, the party adopted the Lodge reservations that the Republican Party had deserted. Harding's ineptness in thought and phraseology on questions of foreign policy tested the patience of sophisticated Republicans and members of the press, but the public cared little about details. Cox took up the League issue with little conviction. Astute observers had difficulty in distinguishing the views of Cox from those of Harding. James Bryce, the astute British observer of American politics, wrote to an American friend: "I understand the perplexity for your friends between two such candidates as Cox and Harding. I am glad not to have to make the choice."[134] On election eve, *The New Republic* passed final judgment on what it described as "one of the most joyless, futile and irritating campaigns in our history.... On the great issues of foreign policy there has been no contribution from the candidates."[135]

From the campaign, the Republican Party again emerged as the country's normal majority party. So overwhelming was the reaction to Wilson and the war that Harding received 16 million votes, 61 percent of the total, to 9 million for Cox. Eugene V. Debs, running as a Socialist candidate from behind prison bars in Atlanta, received over 900,000 votes. Clearly the country had repudiated the League of Nations. "We have torn up Wilsonism by the roots," concluded Lodge. There were other issues in the campaign, but the overwhelming Republican victory demonstrated that the vast majority of the American people were not prepared to analyze and define the nation's interests, or the means for their defense, in the emerging post-war world.

---

[134] The noted Republican editor, William Allen White, commented on the campaign's lack of intellectual seriousness in *The Autobiography of William Allen White* (New York, 1946), 596–97.

[135] For the victorious Republican Party's failure to present a positive foreign policy, see *The New Republic*, 24 (November 10, 1920), 254.

4

The Retreat to Utopia

America's involvement in the Great War demonstrated graphically the role of U.S. economic and military power in the affairs of the world at war. Diplomatic tradition properly understood and applied, presented the only program available to sustain the hard-won peace. But Woodrow Wilson's vision of a new world order, based primarily on democratic and judicial procedures, was designed specifically to eliminate both force and an accommodating diplomacy as the essential, historical ingredients in international peace and stability. Wilson defied history and experience in his assumption that he had actually created a new world order through the negotiations at Versailles and the resulting treaty. Certainly the British and French negotiators did not really agree with Wilson's perception of what had been accomplished there, but tragically they all behaved as if the new world order had actually been achieved and universally accepted thereafter, and assumed that this world order needed only the reliance of moral force to ensure its compliance. Realists in the British, French, and U.S. governments, and Maxim Litvinov in the Soviet government, warned that the treaty either needed revision or the implementation of collective security agreements to enforce it, or both, but to no avail. These people understood that what provided the president his fleeting moment of leadership in world affairs was not his appealing design for a peaceful future, but the fact that he led a country with a remarkable capacity to wage total war – indeed, the nation that had made the defeat of Germany possible.

If the country's supreme venture into European policies revealed its limited capacity to exorcise traditional modes of behavior from international affairs, it predicted as well that the American people would not escape any future war on the European continent that endangered their interests in the Atlantic. The United States, in the future as in the past, would exercise its influence in a world of power politics, facing challenges that it could neither escape nor control. Thus, sound national policy would of necessity avoid the extreme goals of shunning world responsibilities and of rescuing, with appeals to self-determination and peaceful change, oppressed and endangered humanity everywhere. It would be directed rather toward the recognition and pursuit of a variety of specific national interests in competition with nations that could discover in the international system no effective substitute for the established rules of power politics.

That the American people drew exactly the wrong conclusions from their wartime experience was a tribute to Wilson's influence over their thoughts and emotions. Indeed, so profound, yet so divisive, was his impact on the Republic that it drove American behavior toward the extremes against which the recent diplomatic past had warned. Wilson had promised the transformation of world politics in accordance with his principles. Much of the American populace chose to measure his success by the goals he had set for himself and the nation; by those standards, he had failed. If few Americans asked themselves what influence a German victory might have had on United States security, it was because the President and members of his administration consistently refused to formulate national purposes in terms of preserving the traditional balance of power – the only real emolument of victory available to the American people. Indeed, Wilson succeeded in eliminating the concept of international equilibrium from the main currents of the nation's thought altogether. In veiling the nation's considerable contribution to the defense of the old order, he managed to convert a successful national effort into a lost crusade.

In proclaiming goals whose achievement always eluded him, Wilson laid the foundation for a pervading isolationism. For countless Americans, nothing in the country's experience dictated the necessity of a permanent or continuous American involvement in European politics. The widespread disillusionment with the war merely reinforced that conviction. Not without reason they concluded that the United States had gained little more from its trans-Atlantic experience than Prohibition and the Spanish flu or, as Henry L. Mencken suggested, American Legion parades and the new Russian colossus. The disillusionment quickly focused on the country's wartime associates, Britain and France, whose leaders had warred so effectively on American neutrality and now refused to pay their countries' wartime debts to the United States. The powerful newspaper publisher, William Randolph Hearst, reminded his readers that Britain had often been the target of American patriotism.[1] Unable to discern any demonstrable gain from their European venture, millions of Americans entered the 1920s determined to prevent its repetition. "We ask only to live our own life in our own way," declared California's Hiram W. Johnson in March, 1922, "In friendship and sympathy with all, in alliance with none."[2] For Indiana's Albert J. Beveridge, the country's "divinely ordained mission [was] to develop and exercise, by friendship to all a partnership with none, a moral influence circling the globe."[3]

[1] On William Randolph Hearst, see Selig Adler, *The Isolationist Impulse: Its Twentieth Century Reaction* (New York, 1957), 79.

[2] Johnson quoted in Alexander DeConde, ed., *Isolation and Security* (Durham, 1957), 10–11.

[3] Albert J. Beveridge, "George Washington and Present American Problems," *American Monthly*, 13 (April 1921), 46.

Isolationists recognized no danger to the nation's interests in political and military detachment from European affairs. Europe's peace, they charged, was not the responsibility of the United States. Isolationism would not prevent another European war, but it would enable the United States to avoid it. Indeed, argued Beveridge, the European powers would carefully avoid any action that might involve the United States in their future conflicts. "After the incredible blunder of the German High Command in attacking us and forcing us into the war," he asked, "does anybody imagine that any other nation hereafter at war with another nation will repeat that tragic folly?"[4] Isolationists admitted that the United States was not isolated from Europe commercially or intellectually; they insisted simply that the country could avoid the quarrels, intrigues, politics, ambitions, and animosities that had for centuries driven other countries to war.

Isolationists centered their attack on the League of Nations, a program for peace at once too ambitious and too threatening to national sovereignty. If the United States entered the League, declared Hiram Johnson, "I must abandon the lessons of my youth, which until this moment have been the creed of my manhood, of American ideals, American principles, and American patriotism." Idaho Senator William Borah's distrust of the League was equally profound. To submit a vital issue to the decision of foreign powers, he complained, was nothing less than moral treason. As the Senate's leading proponent of isolationism, Borah insisted that he did not oppose cooperation with other nations. "What I have opposed from the beginning," he declared, "is any commitment of this nation to a given line of procedure in a future exigency, the facts as to which could not be known before the event." Congressman Ogden L. Mills of New York agreed that effective cooperation did not require prior commitment. "We believe," he said, "that the United States can better serve by maintaining her independence of action than by pooling her influence in advance."[5]

Such isolationists never explained how the country could prepare for an emergency unless it had ordered its affairs with such exigencies in mind. Borah denied that cooperation and independence were incompatible. By setting a good example and limiting cooperation to voluntary behavior, the United States could exert that leadership only if it stayed out of European affairs. "I do not think we can have here a great, independent, self-governing republic," he said, "and do anything else. I do not think it is possible for us to continue to be the leading intellectual and moral power in the world and do anything else."[6]

Anti-League sentiments informed President Warren G. Harding's policies toward Europe. At a celebration of his election in Marion, Ohio, in November 1920, he offered his obituary to the League. "You didn't want a surrender of the U.S.A.," he reminded his fellow townsmen, "you wanted America to go

---

4 Albert J. Beveridge, *The State of the Nation* (Indianapolis, 1924), 8–9.
5 Johnson quoted in Adler, *The Isolationist Impulse*, 104. For Borah's views, see Charles W. Toth, "Isolationism and the Emergence of Borah: An Appeal to American Tradition," *Western Political Quarterly* 14 (June 1961), 555–56. Mills quoted in *The New York Times*, October 29, 1924, 6.
6 Borah quoted in Karl Schriftgiesser, *This Was Normalcy* (Boston, 1948), 132.

on under American ideals. That's why you didn't care for the League which is *now deceased*."[7] In his inaugural, Harding declared that the United States was "ready to associate with the nations of the world, great and small, for conferences and counsel ... [and] to participate in suggesting plans for mediation, conciliation, and arbitration."[8] For Borah, Harding's commitment to associate was unnecessarily dangerous to the country's freedom of action. Such doubts conformed to the nation's mood; thereafter, the Republican administration exercised greater care. Until 1923 it refused to answer League correspondence. Shortly before his death that year, Harding remarked: "I have no unseemly comment to offer on the League. If it is serving the world helpfully, more power to it. But it is not for us. The Senate has so declared, the people have so declared. Nothing could be more decisively stamped with finality."[9] Apparently the anti-League forces had triumphed.

II

For other Americans – often intellectuals and academicians – Wilson's vision of a new world order, free of all reliance on force, was too essential for the world's future to be discarded in deference to isolationism. If post-war Wilsonians ignored the persistent role of power in affairs among nations, it was because they regarded the end of lasting and universal peace sufficiently overwhelming to negate the problem of means.[10]

Thus, Wilsonian internationalism denied, as did isolationism, that the United States need be concerned with any specific configurations of political or military power in Europe or Asia. Both were equally antagonistic to the conservative tradition of American diplomacy. Whereas isolationism insisted that the nation had no external interests that merited the use of force (although it never recognized the necessity for curtailing the country's commitments in the Far East), internationalism declared that American interests existed wherever governments challenged the peace or human rights. Isolationism preached that events outside the hemisphere were inconsequential; internationalism insisted not only that they mattered, but also that the universal acceptance of democratically inspired principles of peaceful change would control them. Every program fostered by American internationalists during the 1920s – membership in the League of Nations or the World Court, the employment of arbitration conventions, the resort to consultation in crises, collective security, naval disarmament, and the outlawry of war – denied the need of any precise definition of ends and means

---

[7] Harding quoted in ibid., 131 (emphasis in the original).

[8] Harding's inaugural address, *Cong. Record*, 67th Cong., special sess., March 4, 1921, 5; Toth, "Isolationism and the Emergence of Borah," *Western Political Science Quarterly*, 14 (June 1961).

[9] Schriftgiesser, *This Was Normalcy*, 133.

[10] The almost total neglect of means as an essential element in international relations characterized the nation's thought during the 1920s. It informed the followers of Wilson everywhere – in the successive presidential administration, the Congress, the press, and the country's leading universities.

in American foreign policy. Every program anchored the effectiveness of policy to the power of world opinion to bring aggressors before the bar of justice.

Internationalists in the 1920s consisted largely of the pro-League forces that insisted the United States redeem its pledges to the past and the future. League proponents, unlike isolationists, argued that the United States could not avoid a future European war. The country, therefore, would fulfill its obligations to its own and the world's peace by preventing, not merely by trying to escape, a breakdown of the peace. For many internationalists, the League of Nations wielded that necessary authority to prevent war. The central issue before the American people, pro-League editors argued, was whether or not they would play their part in eliminating dangerous competition from international life by joining the League.[11] John Eugene Harley, professor of political science at the University of Southern California, explained that the League would maintain international order by making international law the rule of conduct. To achieve this purpose, the League might require sanctions, but not war. "The desire for order as expressed by public opinion of the world," he wrote, "is the true and ultimate force which will sustain the League in the effort to maintain order through international law."[12] Raymond B. Fosdick, briefly Under-Secretary General of the League and thereafter a New York lawyer, noted that the League would prevent war by making compulsory all the forces for peace that were absent in 1914 – delay, discourse, arbitration, and law.[13] He, no less than others, assumed that all countries would follow League rules, that governments, having argued the issues, would ultimately prefer any settlement to war. Should a crisis demand League intervention to prevent aggression, the Council, as a last resort, would recommend military force. But membership would not require any country to enter military or naval action.[14]

If League membership carried no military obligations, then its power to prevent aggression was moral or nonexistent. Indeed it was the League's reliance on moral force that made American adherence so essential. Specifically, internationalists agreed, United States membership would guarantee the League its needed effectiveness by increasing its prestige and its command of world opinion, the only genuine foundations of peace. "The League lives by and through public opinion," noted author G. Lowes Dickinson reminded readers of The *New Republic* in October, 1923. "It has practically no other power. To refuse to mobilize this opinion, to damp it down, to pretend that it does not exist, is in effect to destroy it."[15] Yale economist Irving Fisher argued

[11] Hamilton Holt, "The Successful League of Nations," *Independent* 104 (October 23, 1920), 124.

[12] John Eugene Harley, *The League of Nations and the New International Order* (New York, 1921), 7.

[13] Raymond B. Fosdick, "Will the League Stop Wars?" *The New York Times Book Review and Magazine*, October 17, 1920, 1.

[14] Irving Fisher, *America's Interest in World Peace* (New York, 1924), 61.

[15] G. Lowes Dickinson, "Can These Bones Live?" *The New Republic* 36 (October 24, 1923), 229–30.

that United States adherence to the League would give the organization the moral influence it required to sustain international order. This country, he explained, was the world's "greatest reserve of moral power, with ideals ... more unselfish than those of other countries and therefore [able to] exert a special moral influence against the ill-conceived and little restrained European scramble for spoils."[16]

Internationalists attributed the apparent successes of the League in the early 1920s to the growing force of world opinion. Fosdick noted in *The Atlantic* of August 1922 that the League had settled the boundary dispute between Yugoslavia and Albania. "The method was effective," he wrote, "not because it represented force, but because it had behind it the moral judgment of civilization." Again, Fosdick attributed Italy's retreat from Corfu in 1923 to the opinion of mankind, given cohesion and force by the League of Nations. Fisher arrived at the same conclusion. The small states, he wrote, "made their protests vociferously in the Assembly of the League, and public opinion throughout the world was quickly mobilized against Italy."[17] Internationalists pondered the additional triumphs that the moral leadership of the United States might have brought to the League. Franklin D. Roosevelt observed as early as August, 1920, that, except for the American rejection of League membership, Poland would not be fighting the Russians with its back to the wall. Had the United States entered the League, Fisher argued in 1924, "war would be outlawed, universal disarmament would be no longer a dream, and reparation and debts and balanced budgets and currency stabilization and gigantic standing armies would be problems solved or on their way to solution."[18]

Still, Republican leaders, following Harding's death, remained adamantly opposed to membership. On October 23, 1923, President Calvin Coolidge explained his party's foreign policy. "We have," he averred, "a well defined foreign policy, known to all men who will give it candid consideration. It has as its foundation peace with independence. We have abstained from joining the League of Nations mainly for the purpose of avoiding political entanglements and committing ourselves to the assumption of obligations of others, which have been created without our authority and in which we have no direct interest."[19] By 1924, the Coolidge administration had inaugurated a policy of cooperation with the League's humanitarian ventures. Under Republican leadership, observed Secretary of State Charles Evans Hughes, the United States had achieved much for peace and humanity without entangling or injurious commitments.

[16] Irving Fisher, *League or War?* (New York, 1923), 159.

[17] Raymond B. Fosdick, "The League of Nations After Two Years," *Atlantic Monthly*, 130 (August 1922), 262. In the Yugoslav–Albanian conflict, financial pressure and the threat of a blockade contributed to the settlement. On the Corfu question, see Fosdick, "Mussolini and the League of Nations," *Review of Reviews*, 67 (November 1923), 482; Fisher, *America's Interest*, 57. Actually, the Council of Ambassadors in Paris arranged the return of Corfu to Greece in exchange for a payment of damages to Italy.

[18] Roosevelt in *The New York Times*, August 13, 1920, 3; Fisher, *America's Interest*, 27.

[19] *The New York Times*, October 24, 1924, 4.

At its 1924 convention, the Republican Party reaffirmed Coolidge's decision to avoid League membership. "The Government," its platform declared, "has definitely refused membership in the League of Nations, and to assume any obligations under the Covenant of the League. On this we stand." The United States, continued the platform, would maintain both its independence and its concern for other nations "through cooperation without entangling alliances."[20]

So thoroughly did Coolidge's victory reflect public approval of Republican foreign policy that the Democratic Party dropped the League issue completely. The Republican conquest of the nation's mind on matters of external affairs was complete.

III

Consigned by adverse opinion to failure on the League issue, internationalists seized upon World Court membership as an alternative approach to effective international cooperation. Eventually the Court battle constituted the most determined internationalist counterattack of the decade. When, in May 1922, the Court officially opened for business, the noted American international law expert, John Bassett Moore, was among its eleven judges. Many anti-League Republicans such as Elihu Root shared the confidence of pro-League leaders in the World Court. Secretary of State Hughes pressed Harding to submit the question of Court membership in the Senate. To satisfy congressional isolationists, he suggested four reservations that would absolve the United States of all commitments to the League but would demand for the United States all powers on the Court enjoyed by League members. Harding proposed membership to the Congress on these terms as early as February, 1923, but Borah, as chairman of the Senate Foreign Relations Committee, opposed the plan as overcommitment of American power and prestige to the League cause.[21] Both major parties endorsed Court membership in their 1924 platforms.

Still, anti-League isolationists in the Senate continued to stall, convinced that adherence to the World Court, a creation of the League, would gradually entrap the United States in the League itself. Coolidge argued for Court membership in his March 1925 inaugural. "The weight of our enormous influence," he declared, "must be cast upon the side of a reign not of force, but of law and trial, not by battle, but by reason."[22] Finally, in December 1925, when the issue of Court membership had won the support of peace societies, women's clubs, pro-League forces, countless mass meetings, and much of the press, the Senate agreed to act. Early in 1926, it approved membership by a vote of 76 to 17. To forestall an assault of the question of advisory opinions, Senator Claude A. Swanson of Virginia introduced a fifth reservation, which denied

[20] George D. Ellis, ed., *Platforms of the Two Great Political Parties* (Washington, 1932).
[21] Denna F. Fleming, *The United States and the World Court* (Garden City, 1945).
[22] Ibid., 48; Adler, *The Isolationist Influence*, 204–05.

the Court the right to render an advisory opinion on any question touching the interests of the United States.[23] In response, the Court demanded the right to impose reservations of its own. Coolidge acknowledged the impasse, and in November 1926 announced that United States membership in the World Court had become a dead issue.

Unfortunately, the World Court, without compulsory jurisdiction or means of enforcement, was scarcely the agency to settle issues on which hinged the future of peace and war. Thus the great debate over Court membership that raged across the nation during the mid-1920s had little relationship to the realities of world politics and the limited role reserved for the Court on questions of importance. Court proponents viewed membership simply as a matter of moral obligation – the obligation of the country to support any movement or institution that contributed to peace. During the final Senate debates over membership, Senator Swanson argued characteristically: "I am strongly persuaded from every moral consideration ... that we should adhere to this World Court."[24] United States membership, argued Irving Fisher, would strengthen the Court's influence. "The Court has no sheriff except public opinion," he declared, "America's adhesion would double its authority in the minds of men."[25]

What made United States membership so appealing was the Court's alleged capacity, magnified by American support, to assert the primacy of law over force. The Federal Council of Churches of Christ in America appealed to its congregations, "Pray and speak for the extension of the sway of law over force and for wholehearted readiness on the part of our nation to play its part in bringing this about." By joining the World Court, Harding assured a St. Louis audience in July 1923 that the United States would promote the substitution of, "reason for prejudice, law for obduracy, and justice for passion...."[26] Fisher reminded Americans that courts had replaced conflict in every field where they had been instituted. "It only remains," he added, "to apply this great principle between nations ... to abolish war as an institution wholly and forever." Students of international law took the lead in urging the American people to accept their responsibility for promoting international justice through Court membership. Manley O. Hudson of Harvard University asked the nation to throw "the full weight of [its] moral influence [behind] a movement for the substitution of law for force in international affairs." Not even the absence of enforcement machinery seemed detrimental to the Court's effectiveness. "It is not unreasonable to believe," asserted the University of Southern California's Harley, "that civilized nations will honor the awards of a tribunal which they

[23] Fleming, *The United States and the World Court*, 56.
[24] On the World Court's limited jurisdiction, see Edward Hallett Carr, *The Twenty Years' Crisis, 1919–1939* (London, 1956), 193, 206. Swanson, quoted in *Congressional Digest*, February 1926, 71.
[25] Fisher, *America's Interest*, 117.
[26] "A Prayer for the World Court," *Literary Digest*, June 23, 1923, 34; James W. Murphy, ed., *Speeches and Addresses of Warren G. Harding, President of the United States*, Washington, 1923, 37–38.

have solemnly created to make such awards."[27] World opinion would enforce the Court's decrees.

Court membership, finally, would solidify the world's peace structure without any specific American obligation to a system of force. Herbert Hoover, Secretary of Commerce, reminded a Des Moines audience in April 1923 that in joining the Court, the United States would "enter into no obligations to use arms or take no commitment that limits our freedom of action."[28] Indeed, the United States, through Court membership, would undertake only two commitments: to participate in the selection of judges and to pay its share of the Court's expenses, estimated at $40,000 per year. But whatever the annual cost of maintaining the Court, Congress would reserve the right to determine what the nation's share would be. During the final Senate debate, spokesmen for the Court insisted repeatedly that membership carried no national obligation except to the Court itself. As Senator Thomas A. Walsh of Montana declared, "We enter into no covenant to do or refrain from doing anything."[29] The battle over Court membership, like that over the League, revealed the nature of American internationalism in the 1920s. The United States would support world peace, not through specific commitments to the defense of the Versailles settlement, but through the encouragement of any organization or procedure that promised to limit change in international life to peaceful processes.

Internationalists agreed that neither the League nor the World Court had confronted any major political issues; nor had they demonstrated any capacity to restrain a major power. "The League," noted the *Independent* "in April 1923, "is discreetly keeping its hands off crucial matters, and the 'balance of power,' which has been held as a devilish thing still goes on."[30] The cooperative effort was new, Raymond Fosdick reminded the skeptics. In time, he predicted, the League would become a "central rallying-point around which the forces of law and peace may gather and slowly develop new approaches to common dangers and new methods of common action." Similarly, journalist and historian Francis Hackett observed in July 1924 that the League, given time, would grow into an effective organization. "The more complex the creature," he wrote, "the more helpless its youth. When the League's members recognize the full value of their creation, it will become incredibly strong."[31]

Realists, that tiny minority who challenged the decade's euphoria, saw no future in either the League or the World Court as guarantors of the peace. Their reasoning was clear. Such international agencies, whatever their devotion to peaceful change, would always serve the status quo; they would therefore

[27] Fisher, *America's Interest*, 36; Manley O. Hudson, "The Permanent Court of International Justice – An Indisputable First Step," *Annals of the American Academy*, 108 (July 1923), 188–90; John Eugene Harley, "The World Court of Justice," *Journal of Applied Sociology* 7 (May-June 1923), 245.

[28] *Congressional Digest*, May 1923, 239.

[29] *Cong. Record*, 69th Cong., 1st session, December 18, 1925, 1085.

[30] "The League on Its Merits," *Independent*, 109 (April 14, 1923), 242.

[31] Francis Hackett, "The League at Half Stage," *Survey*, 52 (July 1, 1924), 388.

never find a standard equally acceptable to all countries. No state dissatisfied with the distribution of power, resources, or territory would entrust its future to an international agency. The fallacy in the concept of peaceful change lay in the fact that international disputes were overwhelmingly political, not judicial, in nature; their resolution would reflect interests and power, not the judgments of deliberative bodies. For that reason, the satisfied powers would protect their world, not with law and peaceful procedures, but with superior force. "The League conception," warned H. H. Powers, an economist and student of European affairs, in 1924, "is that world order, as regards the nations, is static. The nations are finalities. They are to stay at home, avoid trespass, and maintain neighborly relations.... Mussolini and his like regard the world order as still dynamic. The nations are not finalities. The forces of aggression and absorption are perilously active, and the nation that assumes a passive attitude is doomed."[32] The impulse toward self-assertion and change would keep the world dynamic and sorely troubled.

Those who dominated the public's education during the 1920s did not prepare the country to recognize this central admonition. Little in their teaching challenged the notion that the United States could fulfill its obligations to international stability without power, commitments, and alliances. Seldom did the teaching of the decade propose any strategic concept capable of guaranteeing the country's minimal security requirements. Neither isolationists nor internationalists assigned the country any historically recognizable role in world affairs.

Neither on matters of tariff policy nor on attitudes toward Allied war debts did the United States accept its role as the world's leading creditor nation. So protective of American industry was the Fordney–McCumber Tariff of 1922 that it prevented many debtor nations from reducing their financial obligations to the United States. The Republican administrations after 1921, moreover, refused to recognize Allied debts as an American contribution to the war effort. Washington insisted rather that they were legal obligations to be paid in full. Nor would the United States government accept the argument that Allied payments be anchored to German reparations. Still, the Coolidge administration in 1924 endorsed the Dawes Plan, named after banker Charles G. Dawes, whereby United States banks agreed to extend loans to Germany to ease that nation's reparations payments. Later, in 1929, the United States participated in the formulation of the Young Plan, named after another American banker, Owen D. Young. This reduced German reparations from $33 billion to $9 billion with the expectation that Germany would now fulfill its financial obligations to the European Allies. At the same time, the United States continued to press the Allies for payment on their war debts, but with scant success. Unable to acquire dollars in payment for goods, partly because of the high tariff barriers of the United States, the European nations could, in practice,

---

[32] H. H. Powers, "After Five Years," *Atlantic Monthly*, 133 (May 1924), 694–95. Powers expected little of the League, but believed that the United States should enter it. See p. 696.

acquire extensive dollar holdings only in the form of German reparations, financed largely by American loans to that country.

If United States tariff and debt policies remained narrowly nationalistic, Washington encouraged the outflow of capital to support much of the world's economy. Secretary of Commerce Herbert Hoover expanded the overseas operations of his department after 1921 by dispatching commercial agents abroad to discover new outlets for trade and investment. Through pamphlets, speeches, articles, and press releases, the Department of Commerce advertised opportunities for American economic expansion to serve the nation as well as the individual requirements of the American people. "Foreign trade," declared Hoover in a speech before the Export Managers' Club of New York in 1926, "has become a vital part of the whole modern economic system. ... In peace time our exports and imports are the margins upon which our well-being depends. The export of our surplus enables us to use in full our resources and energy...." With almost $4 billion of United States capital moving into Europe, Asia, and Latin America during the 1920s, and $3 billion of foreign trade entering the markets of the world annually, the United States was scarcely isolated from the pressures of international life. "These vested interests," Curtis Wilbur, Secretary of the Navy, warned the Connecticut Chamber of Commerce in May 1925, "must be considered when we talk of defending the flag.... To defend America we must be prepared to defend its interests and our flag in every corner of the globe."[33]

That the United States had interests abroad, some of which it would defend by force if necessary, was clear enough. But they were not as widespread, or as universal, as Wilbur's rhetoric would suggest. Neither the Republican leadership nor any elements in American society cared to blanket the globe with an American military presence, or commit the nation to adventurous policies. At times during the 1920s, the United States played the role of a dominant power, but always without accepting any responsibility for the international system.

IV

American power had contributed substantially to the shape of the Versailles settlement. If that treaty defined the interests of the United States in its distribution of power and territory, then, of necessity, any major threat to the post-war treaty structure would be a matter of American concern. Any forthright national response might contribute either to the defense of the Versailles decisions or to their modification as interests might dictate. Except for Washington's preparedness to make such decisions, the United States possessed no foreign policy at all.

France above all other European countries understood the necessity of an American role in maintaining the stability of Europe. From the moment of its establishment in 1870–71, the German Empire had outdistanced France

---

[33] Fite and Graebner, *Recent United States History*, 336.

militarily. For that reason, French supremacy on the Continent required nothing less than the dismemberment of Germany. Having failed to achieve this objective at Paris, French negotiators extracted from Wilson a Guaranty Treaty whereby the United States would assure France protection against future German aggression. Britain offered the French government similar guarantees contingent upon the ratification of the Franco-American treaty. At Paris in 1919, these pacts were the means whereby Wilson and British Prime Minister David Lloyd George encouraged France to give up its extreme demands on Germany. The subsequent failure of the United States Senate to accept either the Guaranty Treaty or the Versailles Treaty threw France on its own resources and contributed to that country's post-war bitterness and insecurity.[34]

Thereafter, France pursued a vindictive course in world affairs. Its unrealistic demands for German reparations, followed by its occupation of the Ruhr in 1923, contributed to a vengeful and aggressive nationalism in Germany. The Socialist Leon Blum criticized French President Raymond Poincaré in the Chamber of Deputies for the French action. "You have upset world opinion," he charged, "you have weakened German democracy." France approved the Geneva Protocol of 1924, which defined aggression and bound all members of the League of Nations to submit their disputes to compulsory arbitration. However, Sir Austen Chamberlain, Foreign Minister of the new Conservative government in London, rejected the Protocol as an overextension of British power. U.S. and British officials condemned France's refusal to disarm as well as its restrictive policies toward the rehabilitation of the German economy.[35] They questioned France's search for allies in Eastern Europe, in defiance of the spirit of the Versailles Treaty. Whether France was motivated by insecurity or by the determination to achieve an unchallengeable first-rank position in European affairs remained unclear. But French policies designed to limit an aggressive Germany that did not exist, and that could hardly have been predicted, succeeded merely in alienating much of the Western world.

U.S. policy revealed no greater concern for the future of Eastern Europe than it did for France, although French primacy on the Continent and the independence of the Slavic states made up the heart of the Versailles settlement. Western interests among the new Slavic nations would not long survive the lapse of French military dominance on the Continent. By the early 1920s, both Russia and Germany had made clear their ultimate intentions toward the regions of Eastern Europe.

Washington's dismissal of the Soviet and German challenges to the Versailles settlement began with its determined isolation of Russia from the main currents of European diplomacy. In the aftermath of the war,

---

[34] For the French problem, see Stephanie Lauzanne, "France and the Treaty," *North American Review*, 210 (November 1919), 604–12; Robert H. Ferrell, *Peace in Their Time: The Origins of the Kellogg–Briand Pact* (New Haven, 1952), 52–62; Hajo Holborn, *The Political Collapse of Europe* (New York, 1951), 125–27.

[35] Oswald Garrison Villard, "Britain's Failure," *The Nation*, CXIII (December 7, 1921), 641–42.

Russia, economically prostrate and underdeveloped, sought to escape its diplomatic isolation in pursuit of American trade. But Washington, anticipating the rapid demise of Soviet communism, ruled out recognition and commercial relations that might sustain the hated Communist regime. After Harding's election, the Soviets assumed that the spokesman of big business would favor any expansion of U.S. trade and diplomacy, but Secretary of State Hughes, acting through the French embassy, informed Soviet Deputy Foreign Commissar Maxim Litvinov that under present conditions, recognition and commerce were impossible. Already the burgeoning Russian challenge to the post-war Versailles order suggested that non-recognition was an unaffordable luxury.

Russia began its assault on the Eastern European settlement as early as 1920 when the new Bolshevik regime, recoiling from the unsuccessful invasion of White armies into Soviet territory during the previous year, dispatched the Red Army into Poland. Immediately, J. Pierrepont Moffat, a member of the American embassy staff in Warsaw, warned Washington that a Russian triumph over Poland would ignite revolutions in Germany, Austria, and perhaps even Italy. Hugh Wilson, another distinguished American diplomat, responded to the Russian siege of Warsaw by observing that "we have to go back to the defense of Vienna against the Turks and other crucial battles in the world's history to find one of equal significance."[36] France sent token aid to the Polish government; the United States and England sent none. Newly appointed American Secretary of State Bainbridge Colby placed his reliance on another Russian revolution. Poland held on by a narrow margin, and the crisis passed. But the lessons were clear for all to observe. Having only recently created at Versailles the political structure of Eastern Europe as a great democratic achievement, the Western democracies revealed no intention to fight for its preservation.

German resentment and ambition after Versailles also focused on Eastern Europe. The treaty's Eastern provisions, especially those regarding Austria, Czechoslovakia, Danzig, and the Polish Corridor, had the effect of directing German attention toward Eastern Europe, where the obviously minimal interests of the Western powers, added to the internal confusion of the new states, created opportunities for unlimited political and military encroachments. Perhaps no one stated with greater precision Germany's long-term interest in destroying the Versailles arrangement in Eastern Europe than did Adolf Hitler in his book *Mein Kampf* (1925). In his ideal world, Britain would exist as a great nation, but would abandon its balance of power politics on the Continent and maintain only its traditional maritime and imperial interests. France would retain its national integrity and colonial empire, but would return to the status of a secondary power in European affairs.

[36] Nancy Harvison Hooker, ed., *The Moffat Papers: Selections from the Diplomatic Journals of Jay Pierrepont Moffat, 1919–1943* (Cambridge, MA, 1956), 20–21; Hugh R. Wilson, *Diplomat between Wars* (New York, 1941), 18.

These changes, coming with time, would permit Germany the freedom to pursue its real interests – the occupation and colonization of Eastern Europe.[37] Beyond Eastern Europe loomed Russia, but Germany had already come to terms with the Soviet colossus. Russian delegates attended the Genoa Economic Conference of April 1922. The failure of that conference led to the Treaty of Rapallo between the two outcast powers, Russia and Germany. The treaty provided for economic cooperation and established close political – and ultimately military – ties. Despite the indignation of Europe's other powers, the Rapollo Treaty held fast, supplemented by a commercial treaty in October 1925, and periodically renewed.

Germany's Foreign Minister, Gustav Stresemann, reestablished a legitimate German role in European affairs by calling the Locarno Conference of October 1925, marked by a festive mood and countless expressions of goodwill. Germany agreed to arbitration treaties with Poland and Czechoslovakia, while France signed alliances with these two nations on Germany's eastern frontier. Britain refused to enter any Eastern security arrangements and limited its commitments to guaranteeing the Franco-German and Belgo-German boundaries of Western Europe. As Foreign Minister Sir Austen Chamberlain phrased it, England's obligations were "narrowly circumscribed to the conditions under which we have an actual vital interest." While Britain refused to enter any agreement to defend the Versailles arrangements for Eastern Europe, it permitted the French to enter such a commitment, limiting Britain's future action. In the event of any aggression, Britain would either persuade the French government to ignore its obligations, or follow France into a war to preserve the status of Eastern Europe. Such undesirable choices were lost in the "spirit of Locarno" and the general sense of European security that it created. In September 1926, changes in the Versailles settlement appeared consonant with their interests and security. Such inescapable questions regarding Europe's future were far too precise and potentially troublesome for the vagaries of American thought. For British leaders, they were equally unwelcome. In February 1925, Sir James Headlam-Morley, historical adviser of the British Foreign Office, warned his government that the Vistula, not the Rhine, was the real danger point in Europe and thus of vital concern to the Western powers. In a remarkably prophetic memorandum to Foreign Minister Sir Austen Chamberlain, he posed a critical question:

> Has anyone attempted to realize what would happen if there were to be a new partition of Poland, or if the Czechoslovak state were to be so curtailed and dismembered that it in fact disappeared from the map of Europe? The whole of Europe would at once be in chaos. There would no longer be any principle, meaning, or sense in the territorial arrangements of the continent. Imagine, for instance, that under some improbable condition, Austria rejoined Germany; that Germany using the discontented minority in Bohemia, demanded a new frontier far over the mountains, including

---

[37] Adolf Hitler, *Mein Kampf* (New York, 1940), 894–932, 944–49, 967–63.

Carlsbad and Pilsen, and that the same time in alliance with Germany, the Hungarians recovered the southern slope of the Carpathians. This would be catastrophic, and, even if we neglected to interfere in time to prevent it, we should afterwards be driven to interfere, probably too late.[38]

V

The American reliance on paper – stocks and bonds at home and treaty arrangements abroad – culminated in the late 1920s in the Kellogg–Briand Peace Pact. Aristide Briand, the French Foreign Minister, created an unprecedented stir in American peace circles when in April 1927 he proposed a pact between the United States and France for the bilateral renunciation of force in any future conflict in which the two nations might become involved. By the mid-1920s, the concept of outlawry, as the ultimate means of applying rationality to international affairs, had caught the national mood. Senator Borah quickly emerged as a leading champion of the idea, arguing that as all human evils were vulnerable to an outraged public sentiment, supported by law, so war could be banished from the earth by educating the people of the world that it was immoral.[39]

Secretary of State Frank B. Kellogg resisted the pressure for Washington to accept the opportunity to eliminate war as a legitimate exercise of national power. To him, as he explained to a number of Senators, the Briand proposal was nothing less than a bilateral alliance. But during the spring of 1928, the idea of a general outlawry pact, to include all nations, began to push all opposition aside, for a multilateral treaty would eliminate the danger of war everywhere and, at the same time, universalize the American commitment to peace so completely that it would destroy all sense of specific national obligation to any country or region threatened by aggression. So popular was this new approach to outlawry that Kellogg eventually claimed it as his own.[40] Some Washington realists, however, found the trend disheartening. William R. Castle, a State Department official, visited his office on Sunday in late May 1928 and discovered the Secretary in an adjoining office involved in a discussion of multilateral treaties. Castle confided his dismay to his diary:

> They think that they are remaking the world and actually it is nothing but a beautiful gesture while the Jugoslavs tear down Italian consular flags and the Chinese fight and the Japanese stand at attention. The gesture is worthwhile if is made just right and with force.... [But otherwise it] may seriously tie our hands, as the originators of the plan, if the time comes when as honorable people we must step in with force ... words can never take the place of actions ... the only way to achieve peace is by quietly and steadily standing for the right and fair thing. We could change the whole attitude of Latin

---

[38] Sir James Hedlam-Morley, *Studies in Diplomatic History* (London, 1930), 182, 184.
[39] William E. Borah, "Public Opinion Outlaws War," *Independent*, 113 (September 13, 1927), 147–49.
[40] See Ferrell, *Peace in Their Time*, 140–41.

America toward the United States by getting other nations to cooperate with us in our police measures. We have stood for moderation in China and we can be careful not to suspect and offend the Japanese. We can learn courtesy in our dealings without losing any of our firmness. We cannot remake humanity in a day. We cannot abolish war with a pen but we can take the lead in making war unnecessary.[41]

Eventually the proponents of outlawry achieved their triumph in the Kellogg–Briand Peace Pact, signed with appropriate pomp in Paris on August 27, 1928. President Calvin Coolidge's observations on the pact carried the utopian spirit of the decade to a new high. "Had an agreement of this kind been in existence in 1914," he informed a Wausau, Wisconsin, throng, "there is every reason to suppose that it would have saved the situation and delivered the world from all the misery which was inflicted by the Great War.... It holds a greater hope for peaceful relations than was ever before given to the world.... It is a fitting consummation of the first decade of peace."[42]

Officially, the signers had consigned war to oblivion. Within the United States, the Kellogg Pact excited anew the enthusiasm of the peace advocates. Nicholas Murray Butler, president of Columbia University, lauded the treaty with an appealing display of optimism: "It represents a magnificent victory of public opinion over prejudice, indifference and legalism.... To attempt to outlaw war by an act of free will ... is wholly practical and about to be accomplished." Upon his return to the United States following the ceremonies in Paris, Kellogg proclaimed the treaty a national achievement, not to be exploited by the Republican Party either in the presidential campaign or in the Senate. The Republican Convention in 1928 had already endorsed the Kellogg proposal. The Democratic Party accepted Kellogg's victory with only slightly reduced enthusiasm. For Kellogg, the entire country appeared to favor the treaty. With varying degrees of enthusiasm, the Senate ratified the treaty in January 1929, by a vote of 85 to 1.[43]

What made the Kellogg–Briand Pact attractive to American isolationists and internationalists alike was the absence of enforcement machinery and the Secretary of State Kellogg's firm denial that the United States assumed any obligations under the pact. Many lauded the treaty's reliance on international morality, and such reliance seemed to assure success with a minimum of risk. Still, Roland S. Morris, professor of international law at the University of Pennsylvania, wondered how a pact based on moral force alone could protect the peace. Speaking before the American Society of International Law at the University of Pennsylvania in April 1929, Morris questioned the pact's importance. "I am not unmindful of the moral obligations which are implied in such a strong statement of intention to avoid all war and to seek pacific means. But

[41] Castle quoted in ibid., 185n.
[42] Coolidge's Wausau speech quoted in ibid., 208.
[43] The quotes and results can be found in, Norman A. Graebner, *Ideas and Diplomacy: Readings in the Intellectual Tradition of American Foreign Policy* (New York 1964). 493 ff.

let us never forget that the legal import of a national or international document is no measure whatsoever of its social or political potentialities."[44]

For more resolute internationalists, however, the pact opened new possibilities for binding the United States more closely to the European security system through active consultation with the League of Nations. David Hunter Miller, a drafter of the League Covenant, declared that the anti-war treaty "links the United States to the League of Nations as a guardian of peace; it makes the aim of that institution and the aims of our foreign policy in the largest sense identical. It is not too much to say that the Treaty in fact, though not in form, is a Treaty between the United States and the League."[45]

For other internationalists, the Kellogg–Briand Pact's essential contribution to peace lay in its challenge to neutrality. Columbia University's Joseph P. Chamberlain reminded the American Society of International Law in 1929 that the pact gave nations both the opportunity and the right to stall aggression by pledging not to aid any treaty-breaking power. Similarly, Quincy Wright, professor of international law at the University of Chicago, argued that aggression against any state was aggression against all, including the United States. If the pact imposed no obligation to act, it did not deny any country the right to help the victims of aggression. [B]y ratifying the Kellogg Pact," he concluded, "the United States gave up the rights of neutral trade with violators of the Pact and was relieved of duties of neutrality for the benefit of such states...."[46]

Clyde Eagleton, professor of government at New York University, insisted again that the United States would strengthen the Kellogg Pact most effectively by rejecting the rights of neutrality and threatening sanctions against would-be aggressors. "The world," he wrote, "stands waiting for us to translate our frequent words in behalf of peace into some form of actual support for peace.... If we want peace, as we have said in the Pact of Paris, we must support peace when the Pact is broken. We must consult and cooperate with other states to that end."[47] Eventually, those who favored peace enforcement advocated consultation, non-recognition and neutrality revision. These responses to aggression did not imply any commitment to the direct use of force; nor did they receive the support of the American public or congressional isolationists.[48]

[44] Roland S. Morris in *Proceedings of the American Society of International Law* (1930), 90.

[45] James T. Shotwell, "The Pact of Paris: With Historical Commentary," *International Conciliation*, 243 (October 1928), 453, 458; David Hunter Miller, *The Pact of Paris: A Study of the Briand–Kellogg Treaty* (New York, 1928), 132.

[46] Joseph F. Chamberlain in *Proceedings of the American Society of International Law* (1929), 93; Wright in ibid., 1930, 84.

[47] Eagleton, ibid., 90, 94, 113.

[48] For a more extensive analysis of the Kellogg–Briand Pact in American internationalist thought, see Harold Josephson, "Outlawing War: Internationalism and the Pact of Paris," *Diplomatic History*, 3 (Fall 1979), 377–90. See also Richard N. Current, "The United States and 'Collective Security': Notes on the History of an Idea," DeConde, *Isolation and Security*, 39–44.

Such expressions of victory for the cause of peace had little effect on the minority of writers and analysts who knew better. What disturbed the realists was the absence of enforcement machinery. No nation or group of nations assumed any responsibility under the treaty for the prevention or punishment of aggression. By condoning wars of self-defense, the Kellogg–Briand Pact seemed tolerant enough to recognize the legitimacy of any European war fought during the preceding century. Professor Edwin M. Borchard of Yale University observed in *The Nation* that the treaty, "far from constituting an outlawry of war.... [constituted] the most solid sanction of specific wars that has ever been given to the world." Columnist Walter Lippmann warned that an agreement to renounce war as immoral would not abolish it. The Kellogg–Briand Pact, no less than the League or the World Court, he wrote, comprised an effort of the favored nations to sustain the Versailles structure without change or war. It was clear to Lippmann that peace rested less on a moral declaration in behalf of the status quo than a system that accepted change in the international order.[49]

Some regarded the Kellogg Pact merely as worthless; others viewed it as a positive danger to peace. Like all utopian proposals, it eliminated the need of either diplomatic precision or military commitment. As Salvador de Madariaga observed with remarkable perception, the outlawry of war scheme enabled the United States to "bridge over the gap between its two favorite tendencies: the tendency to isolation (from Europe at any rate), and the tendency to see itself as a leading nation in moral as well as in material progress."[50] Frank H. Simonds, the noted American journalist, feared that the American involvement in the pact would mistakenly encourage Europeans to believe that the United States had deserted isolationism.

Many U.S. senators wondered whether any agreement could guarantee peace without imposing some obligation on the major powers. Kellogg himself reassured the Senate Foreign Relations Committee that the pact contained no commitment except the commitment not to go to war. His correspondence with other nations, he said, made it clear that the United States would never sign a treaty whereby it accepted any obligation to come to the rescue of another nation. Some Senators simply dismissed the question of means as irrelevant; for others, the absence of provisions for enforcement of the peace rendered the pact meaningless.

During the debates over ratification, one critic likened the treaty to "throwing peace paper wads at the dogs of war expecting that they will injure the dogs or destroy their appetite for a more palatable diet." Senator Reed of Missouri added sarcastically, "What the proclamation of Sinai did not accomplish in four thousand years, what Christ's teachings have not achieved in twenty centuries of time, is to be produced by the magic stroke of Mr. Kellogg's

[49] Cited in Fite and Graebner, *Recent United States History*, 355.
[50] Salvador de Madariaga, "Disarmament – American Plan," *Atlantic Monthly*, 143 (April 1929), 537–38.

pen.... The armies of earth have marched across the realms of time over high-ways carpeted by treaties of amity." Carter Glass of Virginia summarized the views of many when he announced that he would vote for the treaty but did not want anyone to think that he considered it worth a postage stamp.[51] Another disillusioned senator had the last word in the debate with lines from François Villon:

> To Messur Noel, named the neat
> By those who love him, I bequeath
> A helmless ship, a houseless street
> A wordless book, a swordless sheath
> An hourglass clock, a leafless wreath
> A bed sans sheet, a board sans meat,
> A bell sans tongue, a saw sans teeth,
> To make his nothingness complete.[52]

So pervading was the illusion that the United States, through moral leadership alone, could sustain global security that senators dared not, by their votes, disapprove of Kellogg's widely heralded achievement in behalf of peace and the status quo.

VI

Herbert Hoover, who became President in March 1929, approached the new worldwide peace structure with profound seriousness. For him, the United States naval establishment was quite adequate, and since the Kellogg–Briand treaty had indeed eliminated war, except for defense, the continued drain of naval expenditures away from more useful and humane projects had lost its rationality. Armaments not only comprised an unconscionable burden for mankind but also generated ill will and rivalries among nations. During his first month in office, Hoover initiated discussions with British officials on the question of further naval reduction. In his Armistice Day Address of November 11, 1929, he recounted the progress in disarmament achieved since the war. He assured the American people that the key to world peace lay not in prepared-ness or diplomacy but in the existence of a spirit of goodwill among nations.[53]

Hoover's actual negotiation with British Prime Minister J. Ramsey MacDonald in August and September 1929 illustrated fully the extent to which American naval power was divorced from policy. For the Prime Minister, England possessed an empire that required nothing less than a global defense effort. For Britain, moreover, the United States fleet was a source of security,

[51] *The New York Times*, January 16, 1929.

[52] *Time*, January 28, 1929.

[53] Hoover's Armistice Day address, Washington, November 11, 1929, in William Starr-Myers, ed., *The State Papers and Other Public Writings of Herbert Hoover* (Garden City, 1934) I, 125–32.

not a threat of war. Thus MacDonald had little interest in either British or American further naval reduction.[54]

Eventually, at Hoover's prodding, the London government called the London Naval Conference of 1930. Its five delegations represented the United States, Britain, France, Italy, and Japan. From the outset, the conference ran into insurmountable difficulties. All the nations present, except the United States, pointed to specific interests and potential rivals that necessitated either adequate naval power or other security guarantees. The Japanese, for example, made it painfully clear that they had interests and ambitions in the Pacific that demanded naval expansion. The United States, too, had its distant and vulnerable commitments; it simply refused to recognize any relationship between those outposts and the power to defend them. The United States alone among the great nations refused to be burdened by the obligations of empire.

At length, the United States, Great Britain, and Japan signed a new naval agreement on lesser naval craft. It failed to limit anything larger. Indeed, the United States required a major naval building program if it was to reach its allowable quota. France held the key to genuine naval reduction, but French officials established early one immutable condition to any naval agreement: a security pact with the United States. The American delegation, headed by Secretary of State Henry L. Stimson, hoped to coerce France by arousing public sentiment against the French demands. They discovered, as did Woodrow Wilson eleven years earlier, that the French government, whatever its views on naval reduction, had the full support of French public opinion. Eventually, Stimson had to choose between the collapse of the conference and a consultative pact for France. He chose the latter course, only to be repudiated in Washington.

At the end of the conference, France and Italy refused to sign any treaty at all. Frank H. Simonds, writing in *The Review of Reviews* of May 1930, summarized the security dilemma at London: "The British and Americans were always seeking formulas which would give the French the semblance of security without the reality, the French were always demanding the reality and rejecting the semblance...."

From Versailles to the London Conference, the predominant foreign policy mood of the United States had gradually conformed to the pattern of utopian internationalism that found its ultimate expression in the Kellogg–Briand Peace Pact. Lewis Einstein, writing in *The North American Review* of September 1931, predicted that the outbreak of another war in Europe would find the United States as unprepared physically and emotionally as it had been in 1914. For him, in that Depression year, American foreign policy was nonexistent. "Beyond certain platitudes of peace and goodwill, beyond a predilection for forms of legal remedy which we are only ready to accept for questions

---

[54] MacDonald to Charles G. Dawes, August 9 and September 24, 1929, *FRUS*, 1929 (Washington, 1943), I, 1886–88, 254–56.

of secondary interest, beyond pushing our dwindling exports on impoverished Europe," he wrote, "what more has been our recent foreign policy."[55]

Even the internationalists who believed that the United States should play a leading role in world affairs seldom acknowledged the obligation that the country act responsibly – that it measure events carefully to judge how and where its interests were involved, that it be prepared to engage in the immediate defense of positions of vital concern and to negotiate on matters of secondary importance.

At times, the attention that American officials gave to international bodies and conferences created a semblance of genuine world leadership, whereas the utopian methods employed permitted the country to escape its responsibilities totally. The perennial avoidance of hard political settlements turned the concepts of conciliation, cooperation, consultation, and peaceful adjustment into ends in themselves. American leadership had led the nation to expect perfection in diplomacy at little expense to itself. It was easier and cheaper to allow potentially costly issues to drift. The peace of the 1920s was no demonstration of either a general acceptance of the Versailles settlement (symbolic of the status quo) or even the universal rejection of force.

What sustained the assumption that all wars had been fought and all issues resolved was the predominance of Western power, which permitted the spokesmen of the democracies to manage the game of international politics so effortlessly that they were quite unconscious of the role that power had played in their success. Thus, peace rested primarily on the weakness of those countries – especially Russia, Germany, and Japan – whose governments had already made clear their dissatisfaction with the Versailles settlement (symbolic of the status quo) or even the universal rejection of force. Any collapse of the Western monopoly of power would witness the almost immediate return of force to international life.

But Americans, experiencing the prospect of perennial peace without demonstrable risks or heavy costs, assumed that the world of the 1920s had responded to American principles of peaceful change rather than the West's near-monopoly of power, based largely on the potential might of the United States. No one saw the error in such assumptions more clearly than did Edwin L. James of *The New York Times*. James argued that America's world position resulted not from moral leadership but from the country's wealth and material resources. Were the United States a poor and weak nation, the world would care no more about what it thought than did it before the Great War. James continued:

> Now those that still believe that "the moral sense" of America is a real factor in international affairs will surely cite the Kellogg pact as an example of how we do good and do it altruistically. But no one who has lived in Europe in recent years can believe in the dominant moral effect of the Kellogg pact as

[55] Lewis Einstein, "Our Still Dubious Foreign Policy," *North American Review*, 232 (September 1931), 210–18.

an active factor in world affairs. Almost the only attraction Europe ever saw in it was the line the United States signed on. No European nation promised anything in the anti-war pact that it had not already agreed to in the covenant of the League of Nations. But there was the signature of the United States, which seemed to promise the co-operation of our great material power in curbing the aggressor in another war. And that made a powerful appeal.... Does any one believe seriously that the deference and respect Britain has shown for us in the past decade represent a belief in our moral superiority, a realization of a superior civilization on this side of the Atlantic or a better system of government and social order? Not at all. Britain is extremely practical in foreign affairs. There is no new approval of America and Americans, but there is a realization of our material power as something to reckoned with seriously, and Britain does just that.[56]

---

[56] Edwin L. James, "Our World Power and Moral Influence," *International Digest*, I (October 1930), 21–24.

5

Manchuria and the Triumph of Non-Recognition

I

As an Allied power, Japan emerged triumphant from the Paris Peace Conference. It had acquired Shantung as well as Germany's Pacific islands north of the equator. Yet ultimately Japan found the post-war settlement no more satisfactory than did Germany or Russia. Not only were Japan's wartime designs on China, as embodied in the Fifteen Demands of 1915, generally unfulfilled, but also, as the self-appointed leader of Asian independence, Japan had failed to replace the Western imperial structures in the Orient with a body of independent Asian states in a Japanese-led East Asian hegemony. Post-war Japan possessed two powerful weapons: its own expansive energy, backed by an efficient economy and an impressive navy, as well as the force of anti-colonialism, aggravated by the failure of self-determination at Paris. For Asian leaders generally, the Versailles settlement was intolerable. Confronted by the dual forces of Japanese expansionism and Asian nationalism, the Western powers could anticipate pressures for change in the Orient that presaged the retreat of Western power and influence. Predictably, Japan would lead the assault.

Japan, burdened with an excess of population and a shortage of resources, could expand nowhere on the Asian mainland or across the Pacific without inviting condemnation, if not retaliation, from the Western imperial nations. Japanese ambitions had long made clear that Britain, France, The Netherlands, and the United States – the primary guardians of the Far Eastern status quo – would either accept a more equitable distribution of territory, authority, and resources in Asia, or they would maintain their hegemony at increasingly high cost.

In response to Japan's aggressiveness during the war, President Woodrow Wilson committed the United States to an extensive naval building program, designed especially to contain Japanese power in the Pacific. That program had the support of naval officers, as well as members of Congress and the press, who regarded an expanded navy a more promising defense of U.S. interests than the League of Nations.[1] What drove the more determined opposition to an expanded naval program was the challenge of costs amid a burgeoning isolationist mood. For the *Newark News*, naval costs were exceeding reasonable limits. The *San Francisco Chronicle* declared that "the best use of all navies is to make junk of them." *The Saturday Evening Post* termed the naval program "a punishment inflicted by stupidity."[2] The *Washington Herald* observed that no danger required the United States to have the largest navy in the world. Naval competition merely aggravated international tension. A cartoon in the *Chicago Daily News* revealed a warlord walking behind a taxpayer weighted down with arms and stating, "I always capture this one."

In April 1920, *The Nation* posed a response to the looming naval arms race: invite Japan and England to stop ship building. "France, England, Japan, and America," ran the proposal, "can disarm on the seas by mutual agreement ... and the glory of leading the way should belong to the United States."[3] It was left for Senator William Borah of Idaho to capture the country's headlines in December 1920 with a resolution requesting the President to invite British and Japanese representatives to a conference on naval reduction. Editors and public officials responded with enthusiasm. Vice President Calvin Coolidge doubted that naval reduction would guarantee the peace, but it would bring relief from taxation. Journalist Frank I. Cobb reminded the country in the *Atlantic Monthly* that rich nations contained their own necessary elements of defense, that the drain of resources in military preparedness weakened rather than strengthened national security. Even many who opposed unilateral disarmament agreed that naval reduction, achieved through negotiation, might serve the cause of tax reduction without undermining national security. Facing no opposition in the Executive, Borah carried his resolution with ease through both houses of Congress during May 1921.

Responding to the prospect of an international conference on naval limitation, Secretary of State Charles Evans Hughes determined to use the occasion to strengthen the East Asian defenses against Japanese expansionism through international agreement, with limitations on Japanese naval power in the Western Pacific and additional guarantees of the Open Door principle in China.[4] U.S. officials also sought the annulment of the Anglo-Japanese Treaty of 1902. That treaty had neutralized British opposition to Japanese expansion during the recent war at China's expense, and thus appeared to Washington as an encouraging element in Japan's continuing encroachment on Chinese territorial integrity. British officials differed among themselves as to the value of the alliance. Some had no interest in the Open Door principle and believed

[1] See, for example, *Literary Digest*, January 11, 1919, 13; *Philadelphia Bulletin*, February 3, 1919; *Detroit Free Press*, February 2, 1919.
[2] *Newark News* in *Literary Digest*, June 14, 1919; *San Francisco Chronicle*, February 1, 1919; *Saturday Evening Post*, March 26, 1921.
[3] *The Nation*, April 10, 1920, 453.
[4] See William E. Borah, "Disarmament," *Nation's Business*, IX (September 1921), 7–8.

that Japan had the right to pursue its destiny as a Far Eastern power, even at the expense of China. The British understood, moreover, that for many Japanese leaders, the Anglo-Japanese Treaty was an essential element in their country's prestige and security. Secretary Hughes, however, transformed the issue of the alliance into a simple one of moral and political choice. Britain, he declared, must support either the United States or Japan; it could not do both. Such pressure brought the British government, along with Australia and Canada, into line.[5]

Hughes, in August 1921, sent invitations not only to Britain and Japan, but to France and Italy as well. Only Japan, knowing that the conference would be designed to curtail its influence in East Asia, balked, demanding that Hughes publish the conference agenda. Eventually, Japan sent a powerful delegation to the conference despite Hughes's refusal to offer an agenda. To include all nations with major interests in East Asia, Washington invited four lesser powers to the conference, including China itself. The Washington Conference opened on November 11, 1921. In his opening address, Secretary Hughes offered his formula for naval reduction. He quickly disposed of much of U.S. naval tonnage, then quickly sank four new British battleships and nineteen older ones, scrapped seven partly built Japanese ships and ten older ones, striking out for a 5-5-3 ratio in naval strength for the United States, Britain, and Japan. Eventually Japan accepted its naval inferiority as it gained strategic advantages elsewhere.

Several treaties were negotiated at the conference. In the Five Power Naval Limitation Treaty, signed by the United States, Britain, Japan, France, and Italy, Japan accepted its permanently inferior naval position, compared with Britain and the United States. At the same time, the Five Power Treaty denied the Western powers the right to fortify those islands in the Western Pacific from which they might launch an effective campaign against the Japanese homeland.[6] In the Four Power Treaty, the secretary managed to replace the older Anglo-Japanese alliance with a vague agreement among the United States, Britain, France, and Japan to consult in case any question of aggression should arise in the Orient.[7] In the Nine Power Treaty, Hughes secured another formal Japanese acceptance of the Open Door principle of the commercial and territorial integrity of China.

---

5 For an analysis of Hughes's pressure on the British government, see J. Chal Vinson, "The Imperial Conference of 1921 and the Anglo-Japanese Alliance," *Pacific Historical Review*, XXXI (August 1962), 258. Prime Minister Jan Smuts of South Africa responded to Hughes's request with the remark that "the only path of safety for the British Empire is the path which can be trodden with America." Ibid., 261.

6 Diplomatic exchanges on Hughes's naval limitation proposal can be found in *FRUS, 1922* (Washington, 1938), I, 252–53; non-fortification agreement, ibid., 252–53.

7 For the diplomatic exchanges on the Four Power Pact, see ibid, 2–50. The State Department assured Senator Medill McCormick of Illinois on March 13, 1922, that the United States undertook no obligations except to communicate in case of aggression. Ibid., 51.

As a parchment arrangement, the Washington treaties were magnificent, assuring East Asia's lasting peace. Senator Oscar Underwood expressed the general mood: "I do not see how anyone can conceive ... that any differences of opinion or conflict of interests between the signatory powers thereto can arise." The *Kansas City Star* proclaimed the conference "Probably the greatest practical endeavor against war in all history."[8] For the *Philadelphia Public Ledger*, the Washington treaties comprised "the world's greatest achievement for peace in all its long and crowded history."[9] The *Times* (London) praised President Harding for saving the world from both war and bankruptcy.[10]

Naval and press observers noted even before the pacts were signed that there was little relationship between the actual treaty provisions and Far Eastern realities. The Five Power Naval Treaty granted Japan unlimited freedom to increase the number of its naval vessels in categories other than battleships, as well as to extend the range and firepower of its existing warships. The agreement on the non-fortification of the Central and Western Pacific denied to the United States the right to maintain naval bases on Guam or the Philippines. For Washington, this was no sacrifice because Congress had no interest in such distant fortifications, and Guam was too small to serve as an adequate naval base.[11] For some naval analysts, the Five Power Treaty comprised an unprecedented victory for Japan.[12] Elmer Davis, the noted journalist and critic, observed in *The New York Times* of February 6, 1922: "As the score stands at present, it seems hardly too much to say that this conference has been the greatest success in Japanese diplomatic history.... Japan retains her strategic supremacy, military and political, on the continent of Asia.... Japan has Asia to herself."

The Senate refused to approve the Four Power Pact before it had attached an amendment that declared that it was understood to contain "no commitment to armed force, no alliance, no obligation to join in any defense." Even then it passed by a margin of only four votes. The United States gained nothing from the dissolution of the Anglo-Japanese alliance. Years later, Winston Churchill was to write: "The annulment caused a profound impression in Japan, and was viewed as the spurning of an Asiatic Power by the Western World. Many links were sundered which might afterwards have proved of decisive value to peace."[13] The Japanese at Washington gave up their claims to Shantung as they had agreed in advance. What remained after 1922 to guarantee the status quo in the Western Pacific was the Nine Power Treaty whereby Japan again agreed to uphold the Open Door. The fulfillment of this ultimate U.S. objective rested on Japan's continued acceptance of the limitations imposed by the East Asian treaty.

---

[8] *Kansas City Star* in *Literary Digest*, LXXI (November 26, 1921), 9.

[9] *Philadelphia Public Ledger* in ibid., LXXI (December 31, 1921), 9.

[10] *Times* (London) in ibid., LXXI (November 26, 1921), 10.

[11] The *Washington Post*, December 17, 1922.

[12] For one example of this view, see William Howard Gardiner, "A Naval View of the Conference," *Atlantic Monthly*, 129 (April 1922), 522–39.

[13] Winston Churchill, *The Gathering Storm* (Boston, 1948), 14.

II

Amid the decade's continuing peace and stability, East Asia approached the end of the 1920s with the assurance that the Washington treaties still ruled. It seemed to matter little that China had suffered a bitter civil war, accompanied by an intense anti-foreignism, that left China with a growing Communist movement and the rise of a nationalist government under the leadership of Chiang Kai-shek, China's new strongman. Also during the late 1920s, Manchuria experienced intense economic development under Japanese investment and industrial leadership, rendered possible by Chinese economic concessions. So successful were Japanese investments and industrial leadership in Manchuria that by 1930, almost 30 million people, mostly Chinese, resided in Manchuria's three eastern Japanese-occupied provinces. That massive migration ignited an anti-foreign movement that threatened to eliminate the non-Chinese residents – who began to leave.

Japan's stake in Manchuria was too pervasive to permit a Japanese withdrawal. For Japan, the occupation of Manchuria had become a vital necessity. The Japanese islands had limited arable land, no mineral resources, and a population increasing at the rate of a million each year. Occupied Korea and Formosa had failed to satisfy Japan's requirements for land and resources. But Manchuria, with its abundant natural riches, supplied the food and raw materials necessary for Japan's economic expansion. Japanese interests dictated the continued conversion of Manchuria into a Japanese dependency.

Japanese expansionism was in the air. The Tanaka Memorial of 1927 revealed that expansionist mood. This Memorial, sent to the Japanese Emperor by Premier Tanaka Giichi, was a blueprint for the Japanese conquest of East Asia. The document was secret; its public exposure created embarrassment and denials in Tokyo that it had any significance. But it reminded the world that Japan harbored an imperialist element, especially within its military elite. By 1931, a confrontation between Japanese and Chinese forces in Manchuria was inevitable.

With the armed clash outside Mukden, Manchuria, on September 18, 1931, Japanese officials in Manchuria were determined to exploit the destruction of track along the South Manchurian Railway to alter the region's political status. Japan's special privileges in Manchuria included the right to station troops along the vital South Manchurian Railway. That right Japanese officials would not compromise. The struggle for control of Manchuria had begun.

III

For Herbert Hoover, President since March 1929, the issues raised by the Manchurian crisis were clear and disturbing. Again Japanese military forces had struck a neighboring region, with force and without warning, to alter the political status of East Asia. If, on former occasions, Washington had ignored the display of Japanese power, it could hardly do so in 1931. For Japan threatened not only the U.S. commitment to China's political and commercial integrity, but also the credibility of the entire international treaty structure. The United States had rejected membership in the League of Nations, but it had taken the lead in negotiating the Nine Power Pact of 1922 and the Kellogg–Briand Peace Pact of 1928. For Washington, these two treaties comprised the world's greatest hope for global peace and stability. Japan, in signing them, had agreed to share the world's responsibility for maintaining them. At stake in Manchuria, therefore, was less that region's future than the entire post-Versailles international order.[14]

Chinese editors moved quickly to universalize the significance of events in Manchuria. To Shanghai's *China Press*, Japan threatened not only Manchuria, but also the peace and security of all nations. "Unless immediate international pressure is exerted," it concluded, "The Kellogg Pact, the League of Nations Covenant, and other similar world declarations will be thrown into the dust bin." Soon, such themes appeared in the American press. Japan's war against China was serious enough, agreed the Washington *News*, but it was "insignificant compared with the larger issue of rescuing the world's peace machinery." If the U.S. government, charged the *News*, "cannot make these peace treaties operate – by diplomatic demands, or by economic boycott, if necessary – how does it expect the American people or the world to retain any faith in peace treaties and disarmament?" U.S. Minister to China Nelson T. Johnson acknowledged his indifference to Manchuria's future. He advised the State Department in late November 1931: "The fate of Manchuria is of secondary importance compared to the fate of the League." Similarly, Stanley K. Hornbeck, chief of the Division of Far Eastern Affairs, urged the administration to base any protests to Tokyo on the issue of international peace, not on the principles of the Open Door.

Secretary of State Henry L. Stimson, like Johnson and Hornbeck, was troubled less with Chinese integrity than with the structure of world peace. At a cabinet meeting on October 9, Stimson warned President Herbert Hoover against involving the United States in any humiliating position should Japan refuse to honor its signatures on the Nine Power and the Kellogg–Briand pacts. But the secretary recorded in his diary why there could be no negotiated alterations in the Far Eastern treaty structure:

> The question of the "scraps of paper" is a pretty crucial one. We have nothing but "scraps of paper." This fight has come on in the worst part of the world for peace treaties. The peace treaties of modern Europe made out by the Western nations of the world no more fit the three great races of Russia, Japan, and China, who are meeting in Manchuria, than, as I put it to the Cabinet, a stovepipe hat would fit an African savage. Nevertheless they are parties to these treaties and the whole world looks on to see whether the treaties are good for anything or not, and if we lie down and treat them like

---

[14] *The Memoirs of Herbert Hoover, II: The Cabinet and the Presidency, 1920–1933* (New York, 1952), 364–65.

scraps of paper nothing will happen, and in the future the peace movement
will receive a blow that it will not recover from for a long time.[15]

An unopposed Japan, Stimson feared, would undermine the credibility of the
whole system of collective security, based essentially on the force of world
opinion. For that reason, he could offer Japan, as a signatory of the Nine
Power and Kellogg pacts, no choice but to sacrifice its interests and ambitions
to the higher goal of world peace, that, as it happened, underwrote the worldwide interests of the United States.

Even before the end of September, Stimson outlined a program to bring Japan
to terms. Writing to Hugh Wilson, the U.S. minister in Geneva, Switzerland, he
stated his preference for direct Sino-Japanese negotiations. If they required outside leadership, Japan and China should submit their dispute to the League. If
that approach failed, the United States would consider sanctions.[16] When, in early
October, it became clear that Japan and China would not resolve their conflict
peacefully, Stimson placed the available responses before the President: collective economic sanctions against Japan, diplomatic pressure based on the power
of public opinion, or, if necessary, a vigorous moral judgment against Japan to
recover as much respect as possible for the peace treaties.[17]

Hoover rejected economic sanctions outright, arguing in his *Memoirs*: "Ever
since Versailles I had held that 'economic sanctions' meant war when applied
to any large nation.... [N]o nation of spirit would submit to having her whole
economy totally demoralized.... Sanctions or the threat of them also meant rising emotions, the development of incurable hatreds, and an insensate opposition to any remedial action."[18] The President defined his countering policy at
a cabinet meeting in mid-October. He acknowledged that the Nine Power and
Kellogg pacts were only moral instruments based on the hope that peace could
be enforced solely by the moral reprobation of the world. The United States,
therefore, would confine its role in the Sino-Japanese conflict to friendly counsel,
especially since the United States possessed no interests in China that would recommend a war over Manchuria. Still, the President concluded, the United States
had an obligation to use every influence short of war to "uphold the moral foundations of international life."[19] The reliance on moral suasion was sufficient to
assure a Japanese retreat. Hoover and Stimson agreed that ultimately the power
of world opinion would compel all signatories to honor their agreements.

IV

On October 8, news reached Washington that the Japanese were bombing
Chinchow in southern Manchuria, distant from Mukden. "I am afraid,"

[15] Henry L. Stimson and McGeorge Bundy, *On Active Service in Peace and War* (New York, 1948), 233.

[16] Stimson to Hugh Wilson, September 23, 1931, *FRUS, 1931* (Washington, 1946), III, 49.

[17] Hoover, *Memoirs*, II, 366–67.

[18] Ibid., 366.

[19] Ibid., 365.

Stimson recorded in his diary, "we have got to take a firm ground and aggressive stand toward Japan."[20] Unwilling to act unilaterally, Washington turned to the League. Stimson instructed the American consul in Geneva, Prentiss Bailey Gilbert, to sit with the League Council at its meeting on October 13. Stimson limited Gilbert to League action taken under the Kellogg Pact.[21] On October 17, the Council, in secret session, agreed to urge all signatories of the Kellogg–Briand Pact to remind China and Japan of their obligations to sustain the peace of the Far East. For Hoover and Stimson that was enough, for they wanted no U.S. responsibility for a Manchurian settlement. Indeed, on October 19 the Secretary ordered Gilbert to avoid all League deliberations that involved the employment of League machinery rather than appeals under the Kellogg Pact. London and Paris argued that Gilbert's withdrawal from the Council would discredit the organization in a time of crisis and lend encouragement to Tokyo.

During subsequent days, the boundaries of U.S. involvement in League actions became clear. Stimson permitted Gilbert to "go on sitting at the damned table," as he complained in his diary. "He is, however," continued the Secretary, "to keep his mouth shut and let it be shown in that way that he is nothing but an observer."[22] Thereafter, Washington followed the League at a distance. Stimson even held up his note to China and Japan under the Kellogg Pact for three days after Britain and France had sent theirs. On October 24, the League Council passed a resolution that called upon Japan to evacuate Chinese territory by November 16. This decision Stimson refused to endorse, for it might commit the United States to some future forceful intervention. Hoover agreed. William Castle, Under Secretary of State, recorded in his diary on November 4 that the President had remarked at lunch that "he wants to get completely out of the League connection and thinks it might have been wise politically, to make Stimson keep out."[23]

Japan's open contempt for the November 16 deadline measured the League's ineffectiveness. Yet some editors viewed the League action of October as evidence that reason was indeed overcoming force in international affairs. The Buffalo *Courier Express* termed the League's "interference" as a "notable victory for the organized opinion of the world against war as an instrument of national policy." The Baltimore *Sun* proclaimed, with equal satisfaction: "The gain for peace is at once a vindication of the League and the Kellogg Pact.... The League has not, to be sure, imposed its demands on Japan in their entirety. But it has so mobilized the forces of world opinion and world diplomacy as to check Japan in her career of Manchurian aggression." Not all were convinced. The Philadelphia *Record* termed the League action

[20] Stimson quoted in Richard N. Current, "The Stimson Doctrine and the Hoover Doctrine," *The American Historical Review*, LIX, No. 3 (April 1954), 516–17.
[21] For the constraints on Gilbert, see *Literary Digest*, CXI, (October 31, 1931), 3–4.
[22] Current, "The Stimson Doctrine," 518.
[23] Castle quoted in ibid., 519.

both unwise and ineffective, leading not to the triumph but the destruction of the League. The New York *Daily News* wondered why the administration was so insistent on preserving the status quo in Asia when the United States was protecting no tangible interests in opposing Japan. "The answer as we see it," ran its judgment, "is that Japanese expansion is not going to stop. We believe that by sitting on the safety-valve, the United States is only piling up trouble for itself."

When the League Council reconvened at Paris in mid-November, Hoover sent Ambassador Charles G. Dawes from London to represent the United States as observer and consultant.[24] Stimson informed Dawes that the United States would not join any League embargo against Japan. He hoped thereby to avoid driving the Japanese moderates from power amid the worldwide depression, which struck Japan in 1931. At issue at the Council session in Paris was the establishment of a neutral commission, under the Earl of Lytton, to investigate the entire Sino-Japanese controversy. During the deliberations, Dawes refused to sit with the Council, maintaining contact from his suite at the Ritz. Tokyo's open support permitted the Council, with the necessary unanimous vote, to establish the Lytton Commission on December 10.[25]

V

Having wedded American interests to the perpetuation of the international treaty structure, Hoover and Stimson required some means to close the gap between their determination to stop Japan and their desire to avoid trouble. Increasingly, they found the answer in some recourse to moral sanctions. During November 1931, Stimson concluded that it might be wise to "outlaw Japan and let her sizzle [under a Chinese boycott] and all the moral pressure of the world."

Woodrow Wilson had created a ready and appealing response to foreign governments whose nature or behavior failed to conform to his moral or constitutional standards. In March 1913, he rejected the traditional policy of de facto recognition in refusing to recognize the revolutionary Victoriano Huerta regime of Mexico. In 1915, he warned the Japanese government that the United States would not recognize any territorial or political Japanese impositions on China. He eliminated the need to deal with the Bolshevik government of Russia by denying it recognition. If non-recognition failed to eliminate any unwanted conditions that mattered, it eliminated the need to deal with them. Non-recognition applied to events in Manchuria might have no bearing on Japanese policy, but it would relieve Washington of any responsibility for confronting it realistically.

[24] Hoover, *Memoirs*, II, 372.
[25] J. B. Donnelly, "An Empty Chair in Paris: Dawes, Sweetser, and the Manchurian Crisis," *Topic: A Journal of the Liberal Arts*, No. 19, Washington and Jefferson College, Spring 1970, 37–49.

Early in December, Hoover proposed to the cabinet that the League instruct its members not to recognize any changes in Manchuria that resulted from violations of the Kellogg Pact.[26] If the United States could not prevent further Japanese aggression, it could, through non-recognition, express feelings of deep moral disapprobation toward events in Manchuria, thereby satisfying public demands that it take its stand against Japanese aggression, and do so without involving the country in war. Columnist Walter Lippmann, that month, favored the non-recognition of treaties, "negotiated at the point of a bayonet," as a promising vindication of the world's peace efforts. Such non-recognition would compel the Japanese to contemplate the price of undermining their country's legal position as well as its credit and prestige throughout the world.

Before the end of December, the Hoover administration settled on the doctrine of non-recognition as the means best designed to reenforce the Versailles treaty system. Stimson rationalized the administration's move toward non-recognition in his memoirs. "If the fruits of aggression should be recognized," he wrote, "the whole theory of the Kellogg Pact would be repudiated, and the world would be at once returned to the point of recognizing war as a legitimate instrument of national policy. Nonrecognition might not prevent aggression, but recognition would give it outright approval."[27]

With the January 2, 1932, Japanese invasion of Chinchow, Stimson was ready to act. On the next day, he prepared identical letters to the governments of China and Japan, based on the non-recognition notes of 1915. After conferring with foreign policy specialists, Stimson revised the draft and secured the President's approval. On January 7, the secretary sent identical notes to Japan and China which declared that this nation could not "admit the legality of any situation *de facto* nor does it intend to recognize any treaty or agreement entered into between those Governments" that might impair either the treaty rights of the United States or the territorial and administrative integrity of the Republic of China.[28] It was a unilateral demarche by the United States. Britain and France refused to endorse the U.S. statement, declaring that they had no interests in Manchuria that merited even a legal sanction against Japan.[29] But the President argued that the Kellogg Pact was the world's primary moral force against aggression and that the note of January 7 had effectively mobilized world opinion against Japanese behavior. Indeed, Hoover predicted that the note would stand as one of the country's great state papers.[30] With that judgment much of the American press agreed. The Providence *Journal* thought the note one of "clear and far-reaching importance in the history of

[26] Hoover, *Memoirs*, II, 373.
[27] Stimson and Bundy, *On Active Service*, 235.
[28] Stimson's note of January 7, 1932, *FRUS*, 1932 (Washington, 1948), III, 8; Stimson and Bundy, *On Active Service*, 235–36.
[29] Hoover, *Memoirs*, II, 373.
[30] Stimson and Bundy, *On Active Service*, 244.

twentieth-century diplomacy." But some members of the press warned that non-recognition would not serve the peace. U.S. Ambassador in Tokyo, W. Cameron Forbes, found Stimson's toughness a meaningless verbal exercise that would, under no circumstances, serve the interests of the United States. Far better, explained Forbes, to recognize the actual conditions that governed the Sino-Japanese relationship.[31] Upon departing from Tokyo in March 1932, Forbes announced that his staff was unanimous in its opposition to the moral pressures emanating from Washington, convinced that they would ultimately lead the United States into war.

As some critics predicted, the verbal strictures against Japan had no apparent effect on Japanese behavior. On January 28, 1932, Japanese forces attacked Shanghai, largely in retaliation against a Chinese boycott. Hoover ordered U.S. naval vessels to that city to protect American civilians.[32] Stimson warned Tokyo that if the Japanese failed to protect the International Settlement in Shanghai, the result could be catastrophic.[33] More than events in Manchuria, those in Shanghai raised the specter of global war, and thereby dictated caution. Even members of the press who condemned Japan for its brutality demanded that Washington move with extreme delicacy.

For Stimson, it appeared essential that the United States continue to express official recognition of its pro-Chinese sympathies, even as it adhered to its principle of peaceful change. On February 16, the League Council supported the non-recognition doctrine and called upon Japan to fulfill its obligations under the Nine Power Pact. "As I reflected on it," Stimson recalled, "it seemed to me that in future years I should not like to face a verdict of history to the effect that a government to which I belonged had failed to express itself adequately upon such a situation."[34] Indeed, Stimson hoped, as he confided to his diary, that Japan would not withdraw from Shanghai before the United States could pass moral judgment on its latest aggression.[35]

What Stimson had in mind after February 8 was a restatement of the non-recognition doctrine. He hoped to secure British cooperation, but London preferred to act with the League. The secretary, determined to express himself again on the morality of the situation in Manchuria without making a speech, turned to the idea of writing an open letter to someone, eventually deciding on Senator William E. Borah. The letter, dated February 23, 1932, was designed to strengthen public sentiment for the Open Door and define for the League the limits of U.S. policy.[36]

---

[31] For Forbes's realist critique, see Gary Ross, "W. Cameron Forbes: The Diplomacy of a Darwinist," in Richard Dean Burns and Edward M. Bennett, eds., *Diplomats in Crisis* (Santa Barbara, 1974), 55–60.

[32] Hoover, *Memoirs*, II, 374.

[33] *FRUS: Japan, 1931–1941*, I, 178–79.

[34] Henry L. Stimson, *Far Eastern Crisis: Recollections and Observations* (New York, 1939), 157.

[35] Stimson in Current, "The Stimson Doctrine and the Hoover Doctrine," 529.

[36] For the Borah letter, see Stimson and Bundy, *On Active Service*, 249–54.

Basing his new appeal on the Nine Power Treaty rather than on the Kellogg Pact, Stimson argued that nothing had occurred to challenge the validity of the two treaties. Together, he wrote, they "represent independent but harmonious steps taken for the purpose of aligning the conscience and public opinion of the world in favor of a system of orderly development by the law of nations...." Stimson's letter included a warning to Japan that the American decision for non-recognition, if taken by other governments of the world, "will effectively bar the legality hereafter of any title or right sought to be obtained by pressure or treaty violation, and which ... will eventually lead to the restoration to China of rights and titles of which she may have been deprived."[37] Never before had Stimson made such claims for the coercive power of non-recognition.[38]

Addressing the American Conference on International Justice in Washington on May 4, during Stimson's absence, Acting Secretary Castle carried even further the administration's faith in the burgeoning Hoover–Stimson doctrine. "The President," said Castle, "... realized that in the mechanism of international relations a stern deterrent of the use of force would be to make valueless the results of war.... I believe that this 'Hoover Doctrine,' accepted by most nations of the world, through the League vote, is welcomed because it accomplished as nearly as may humanly be possible the purpose of peaceful prevention of war."[39]

Again the reliance on non-recognition received the public approval that Stimson had anticipated. For the *Christian Science Monitor,* Stimson's letter ranked with the most important state papers in the country's history. The *Wall Street Journal* termed it "a lucid, forceful statement of the correct American attitude toward the dangerous outbreak of extreme nationalism in the Orient." The *Washington Post* heralded non-recognition as "the most important contribution to the machinery of international justice since the Kellogg Pact was signed." Some were not convinced. Again a minority defined non-recognition less as an American response to Japanese aggression than as a device to avoid the necessity of creating a response. Neither Stimson's strong historical defense of the Nine Power Treaty, nor even his veiled threat of a naval race in the Pacific under the Washington treaties, stopped Japan or brought any country to China's defense. London made clear its refusal to follow the U.S. policy of non-recognition. But soon the British championed non-recognition before the League, and, on March 11, the League Assembly adopted a resolution incorporating the principle.[40]

VI

During March 1932, the Japanese smuggled former Emperor of China, Henry Pu Yi, into Manchuria and installed him as head of the new puppet state of

---

[37] Stimson and Bundy, *On Active Service,* 246–49.

[38] Stimson's letter, he recalled, was intended "to encourage China, enlighten the American public, exhort the League, stir up the British, and warn Japan." Ibid., 249.

[39] For Castle's statements, see *Literary Digest,* CXIII (May 21, 1932), 9.

[40] Stimson and Bundy, *On Active Service,* 257.

Manchukuo.[41] While Japan proceeded with the creation of its puppet state, Washington's reaction became increasingly tense and ambivalent. Stimson anticipated an armed clash with Japan. At a cabinet meeting in early April, the secretary dwelled on the Japanese challenge to Western civilization and the need for war preparation. The Secretaries of War and Navy approved. Stimson questioned the country's top military leaders on the state of national preparedness. The President was not impressed; his continuing search for a Manchurian peace was not based on military power or its use.

President Hoover's continuing disclaimers of any intention to use force troubled League officials in Geneva. Norman Davis returned to Washington on March 29 to report on the unfortunate reactions to Hoover's statements opposing any resort to force. With the President's approval, Stimson agreed to visit Geneva, departing on April 5. Hoover announced that the secretary would discuss disarmament and the Far Eastern crisis. But Stimson, in his memoirs, assigned himself the task at Geneva of obtaining "a world judgment against Japan" so that "it would lay a firm foundation of principle upon which the Western nations and China could stand in a later reckoning."[42]

While Stimson was pursuing his line of policy in Geneva, Hoover and Castle were proclaiming quite another at home. During Stimson's absence in April, Castle made two speeches in which he assured his audiences that U.S. policy excluded sanctions of economic pressure or military force.[43] For good reason, the President dreaded Stimson's return. Indeed, the secretary was incensed by Castle's speeches. He now argued that the fleet, after completing its war games, should remain in Hawaii, and advocated another official statement in behalf of non-recognition. Meanwhile, the situation in East Asia remained quiet. On May 5, Japan and China signed a peace treaty; before the end of the month, the Japanese had withdrawn all troops from the Shanghai area. Ambassador Joseph C. Grew reported from Tokyo on June 13 that the Japanese public continued to regard Manchuria as essential for their well-being, but did not regard non-recognition or the League as barriers to Japan's firm control of the region. The Japanese people, Grew concluded, stood firmly behind their government.[44]

Stimson soon turned to the preparation of a speech in defense of non-recognition in accordance with his own interpretation, based on the fulcrum of the Kellogg Pact. "The speech," he recorded, "is intended to rally the European countries around the Pact, so that when the issue with Japan comes up, they will support us intelligently on this central point." When he submitted his draft to the President, he ran into opposition. He received instructions to cancel part and revise some of the rest. Even his censored address, delivered through arrangements with Walter Lippmann before the Council on Foreign Relations in New York on August 8, 1932, was a powerful assault on world sentiment.

[41] *FRUS, 1932,* IV, 76–77.
[42] Stimson and Bundy, *On Active Service,* 258.
[43] Castle in Current, "The Stimson Doctrine and the Hoover Doctrine," 534.
[44] Grew to Stimson, June 13, 1932, *FRUS, 1932,* IV, 76–77.

Stimson proclaimed the Kellogg Pact as the bulwark of peace. By declaring war illegal, he declared, the Pact compelled the world to condemn aggressors as law breakers. The necessary exercise of this broad obligation to denounce aggressive war, he declared, was in itself a powerful force for peace. "The Kellogg-Briand Pact ...," he continued,

> rests upon the sanction of public opinion which can be made one of the most potent sanctions in the world.... Public opinion is the sanction which lies behind all international intercourse in time of peace. Its efficacy depends upon the will of the people of the world to make it effective. If they desire to make it effective, it will be irresistible.[45]

"Moral disapproval," Stimson added, "when it becomes the disapproval of the whole world, takes on a significance hitherto unknown in international law. For never before has international opinion been so organized and mobilized."[46]

Stimson received his customary adulation. The New York *World Telegram* praised the Hoover–Stimson doctrine as "the most important international step taken by the United States since the World War." The *Washington Post* added: "It is little wonder that Japan is acutely concerned over the purport of the American exposition of the Kellogg Pact and the consequences which are now sure to flow from a willful rupture of the mutual pledge of all nations to remain at peace." *The Nation* observed that public sanction "on which rests the Kellogg Pact can be one of the most potent sanctions in the world." Robert Shaw concluded in the November 1932 *Review of Reviews* that the doctrine of non-recognition supplied teeth to the Kellogg Pact even while it permitted the world to avoid any commitment to the use of force.[47] The Japanese press, recognizing no Japanese aggression in Manchuria, termed the speech highly improper, imprudent, and vile.[48]

So popular and pervading was the Hoover–Stimson doctrine, as it evolved between 1931 and 1933, that both the President and Stimson claimed sole authorship. Yet the two men never agreed on what it was. For Hoover, non-recognition remained a final and sufficient response to aggression, without recourse to economic pressure or military force, a formula that anticipated conciliation and peace, relying for its success on public opinion. That was the Hoover Doctrine. For Stimson, non-recognition was not an alternative but a prelude to economic and military sanctions, as a means of drawing a sharp and persistent conflict of purpose between the United States (with the League) and Japan, defining the ideological grounds for war that he expected would eventually come. That was the Stimson Doctrine, the response to Japan that ultimately prevailed.[49]

---

[45] Stimson and Bundy, *On Active Service*, 259.
[46] Stimson's speech, entitled "The Pact of Paris: Three Years of Development," was published as a special supplement to *Foreign Affairs*, XI (October 1932).
[47] For a wide reaction to Stimson's speech, see *Literary Digest*, CXIV (August 20, 1932), 6.
[48] Grew to Stimson, August 10, 1932, *FRUS*, 1932, IV, 198–99.
[49] Current, "The Stimson Doctrine and the Hoover Doctrine," 541–42.

On September 15, 1932, while the Lytton Commission was completing its report to the League, the Japanese government announced its recognition of the state of Manchukuo. That decision added another challenge to both the U.S. policy of non-recognition and the forthcoming Lytton Report. From Tokyo, Ambassador Grew warned Stimson that Japan regarded the United States as its most persistent antagonist. It expected little and received little from the Lytton Commission. If Stimson accepted the necessity of confronting Japanese behavior, he wanted the moral position of the United States to be absolutely clear. For that reason, he welcomed the Lytton Report; the report condemned Japan and refused to recognize the new state of Manchukuo.[50] But Castle regarded the report "judicial in temper and fair to both countries." The President and his cabinet, to Stimson's disgust, revealed little interest in the Lytton Report. Stanley Hornbeck complained that Washington after August 1932 had offered no support to the League as it sought to complete the Lytton Report.[51] Walter Lippmann noted that the report and non-recognition were not compatible. Whereas the Lytton Report recommended a new government for Manchukuo, non-recognition demanded the restoration of the status quo.[52] On February 24, 1933, the League Assembly adopted the Lytton Report with the recommendations that Stimson desired. If it did not provide for the return of the status quo, it did exclude recognition of the existing regime of Manchuria.

VII

Japan's conquest of Manchuria in 1932 comprised the first serious threat to the world's post-Versailles international peace structure. The challenge was inescapable. The victors of 1919 who dictated the peace treaty would either accept serious modifications in its provisions, both in Europe and Asia, or use superior force to sustain their decisions. Few contemplated that such unwelcome choices would ever arise, for the League of Nations, with the Nine Power Treaty of 1922 and the Kellogg-Briand Peace Pact of 1928, had ostensibly eliminated any recurrence of aggression that might demand a military response. These mechanisms presumed that all nations would abjure objectives attainable only through a resort to armed force. But Japan had demonstrated graphically that the presumed triumph of universal peace remained elusive.

Japan's deep concern for Manchuria reflected not only its own heavy investment and vital interests in the region, but also the problem of China itself. Japan was not the only country that threatened China's territorial, economic, and administrative integrity. All the world's major powers, including the United States, had marked China for spoilation, acquiring special privileges

---

[50] For an analysis of the Lytton Report, see *Literary Digest*, CXIV (October 15, 1932), 15–16.

[51] Hornbeck memorandum, January 9, 1933, *FRUS, 1933*, III, 28–29.

[52] For Lippmann's comments, see Current, "The Stimson Doctrine and the Hoover Doctrine," 537.

and otherwise undermining China's sovereignty. Long before 1900, they had reduced China to a colonial status. Even after Versailles, the imposed unequal treaties remained in full force. Japan had no assurance that other powers would not reveal ambitions in Manchuria. The Washington Conference of 1922 could have resolved the issue of China's territorial integrity, but the Nine Power defense of China had avoided the challenge. The burden of protecting the Open Door in Manchuria fell to Japan alone.

With its full commitment to the status quo in world affairs, no less than to the Open Door in China, Washington assumed major responsibility for the protection of Chinese interests in Manchuria. What rendered that commitment troublesome was the total absence of U.S. interests in the region. Compared with Japan's, those of the United States were infinitesimal. U.S. trade with Manchuria was almost nonexistent. American residents in Manchuria were scarcely numerous enough to fill a small hotel. With no tangible interests at stake, the United States, with its long commitment to China's Open Door, assumed the chief burden for the defense of Manchuria, again deliberately challenging Japan, a militant, determined power that it had been confronting for decades. Tokyo's commitment to Manchuria had the full support of the Japanese people. As Columbia University's noted Asian expert, Nathaniel Peffer, observed in February 1933: "The Japanese people will support their government on Manchuria. Against the United States they will support it on anything."[53]

Historically, nations faced external dangers with offers of accommodation or threats of counterforce. For the victors at Versailles, such responses were no longer regarded as proper or necessary. Through the League, the Nine Nation Treaty, and the Kellogg–Briand Pact, the world had eliminated the necessity of accommodation with states challenging the treaty structure with force. When Japan absorbed Manchuria, Washington eliminated the issue of accommodation with the simple process of refusing to recognize unwanted change. Non-recognition granted the status quo a special morality that negated the interests and rights of others to pursue change. Secretary Stimson proclaimed that non-recognition, if adopted by other powers, would assure a peaceful, stable future. "If a similar decision should be reached... by other governments of the world," he predicted, "a caveat will be placed upon such action which, we believe, will effectively bar the legality hereafter of any title or right sought to be obtained by pressure or treaty violation."[54]

Non-recognition, whose broad appeal lay in its avoidance of action, was unprecedented in the demands it imposed on the international community. For it offered its adherents the unprecedented authority to command the behavior of nations everywhere by judging the acceptability of their demands on the international treaty structure. As a universal defense of the status quo,

---

[53] Nathaniel Peffer, "Manchuria: A Warning to America," *Harper's Magazine*, CLXVI (February 1933), 303–04.

[54] Stimson and Bundy, *On Active Service*, 254.

non-recognition was either meaningless or a massive, unprecedented commitment of the Versailles powers to sustain the world of their creation, and to do
so with little reference to power or diplomacy. For Nathaniel Peffer, the U.S.
commitment to Manchuria's future independence was demanding enough. As
he warned:

> The pronouncements of the American government with reference to
> Manchuria, ... will constitute, unless revoked, a pledge and policy no less
> binding than the Monroe Doctrine but infinitely harder to effectuate. They
> will ... make us the protagonist of the *status quo* in a region where the *status
> quo* is inherently unstable.... And of this fact the American people remain
> singularly unaware and wholly uncritical.[55]

What, Peffer wondered, prompted the United States to assume such vast commitments, with objectives achievable only through war. For him, events in
Manchuria scarcely touched any American interests. Nor did such broad commitments, he noted, flow from public demand, but from the decisions of a
tiny clique in Washington, creating a point of honor that supported the government. If the American public favored such a pervading confrontation with
Japan over Manchuria, it would pay the price. Few asked whether those in
office committed the United States to Manchuria's future with wisdom and
the consent of the governed.

During its final weeks in office, the Hoover–Stimson administration
received ample reassurance of non-recognition's longevity. One welcome
assertion of the principle followed Stimson's trip to Hyde Park on January 9,
1933, for a conversation with President-elect Franklin D. Roosevelt on U.S.–
East Asian relations. In a press release of January 17, Roosevelt declared that
"American foreign policies must uphold the sanctity of international treaties.
That is the cornerstone on which all relations between nations must rest."[56]
On February 25, Stimson noted that the League Assembly had affirmed the
principle of non-recognition, placing the United States and the League on
common ground. For Stimson, that "clear expression of world opinion"
would encourage nations to settle their disputes only by peaceful means.[57]

Hoover never softened his demand that sanctions be limited to peaceful
procedures, but he argued, as late as February 24 that, under the principle of
non-recognition, public opinion "would be continuous and [would] ultimately
be triumphant."[58]

Non-recognition became the ultimate international response to any threatened assault on the Versailles peace structure, under the doubtful assumption
that it would release moral disapproval in such abundance that no country

---

[55] For a long, realist judgment of non-recognition, see Peffer, "Manchuria: A Warning to
America," 301–08.
[56] Stimson to Grew, January 18, 1933, *FRUS: Japan 1931–1941*, I, 109.
[57] Stimson to Hugh Wilson, February 25, 1933, *Peace and War: U.S. Foreign Policy, 1931–1941*
(Washington, 1943), 176–77.
[58] Hoover to Stimson, February 24, 1933, *FRUS, 1933*, III, 209.

could long defy it. This reduced diplomacy to a simple demand for capitulation. Even Stimson acknowledged that the Nine Nation Treaty no longer
reflected the military and political realities of East Asia, but to him it was law,
and the law still governed. Furthermore, the law governed universally, appli-
cable wherever the peace structure appeared threatened, sustaining international stability by rejecting any treaty revision. Unfortunately, the Versailles
Treaty was replete with territorial arrangements whose perpetuation remained
unacceptable to their victims. The moment had dawned for the victors at Paris
to frame responses to demands for treaty revision that were sure to come.
Responses to such challenges scarcely mattered. Non-recognition still offered
the perennial guarantee that the Versailles structure could withstand all
pressures for change unscathed.

6

The Rise of Hitler

I

It is easy to judge the Versailles Treaty a failure. Within a decade, many of its key provisions faced inescapable assault. States carrying the responsibility for formulating a treaty become the automatic defenders of its provisions; certainly the victims of either diplomatic or military defeat would not defend it. Historian Arthur Link, in his defense of Woodrow Wilson, argued that World War II was primarily the result of the Depression. But the Depression, whatever its magnitude, could not set the world on the road to war unless the conditions for conflict were already well established. Three of the world's major powers – Germany, Japan, and the USSR – believed themselves sufficiently victimized by the Versailles Treaty to tear it to shreds at the first opportunity. Only the Soviet Union deviated from this perspective for a time in its drive for collective security in the 1930s.

In a similar vein, historians who accept Fritz Fischer's verdict of 1961 that Germany was as responsible for the disaster of 1914 as that of 1939, see the two episodes as revealing German ambitions to expand eastward, rendering German aggression as the defining feature of both wars. This converted the two wars into a single entity. The notion of continuity makes little distinction between the Kaiser's Germany of 1914 and that of Adolf Hitler. The Kaiser had abundant company in creating the crisis of 1914; Hitler had none that mattered in 1939. The Holocaust and other Nazi crimes were not shared by the Kaiser's Germany. In addition, the democratic powers at Versailles had the opportunity in 1919 to set an aggrieved Germany, one that scarcely resembled Hitler's, on a different course. Against ample warnings, they failed to do so.[1] Without an Adolf Hitler, would there have been another war? From the outset, Hitler desired and planned on war. His memoir, *Mein Kampf*, declared clearly his aim of eliminating the Jews, conquering the Poles and Slavs, to make room

[1] Charles Hawley, "Hot Topic in Germany: Aggression in World War I," *The Christian Science Monitor*, August 2004, 6–7.

for the expansion of the "Aryan" race.[2] He would continue his warfare until Germany achieved predominance, eliminating France as Europe's traditional primary power. Meanwhile, he would exploit the realities and possibilities he faced.

Given the differences between the Germany of 1914 and Hitler's Germany, how does one describe the conditions that created this change? It is not possible to understand the rise of Hitler without, at the same time, analyzing the source of his power and the means he used to attain it. Admittedly he was mesmeric in his speaking technique and could sway a crowd, but that alone was an insufficient basis for his power. What themes did he discover as the means of gaining power over the populace in Germany? Certainly the economic disaster of world depression gave him an inroad to the masses who suffered from joblessness and the necessity of taking a wheelbarrow load of reichsmarks to buy a loaf of bread during Germany's economic collapse of the early 1920s. The promise of food, employment, and the restoration of national pride constituted a powerful appeal.

Who received the blame for the economic disaster that befell Germany after 1920? Hitler attributed the disaster to the Treaty of Versailles. For him, the politicians, not the generals, lost the war in 1918; they then accepted the humiliating peace thrust upon the nation in Paris. These political leaders came to be known as the "November Criminals." Correspondent William L. Shirer observed that the German generals, "shrewdly and cowardly, had maneuvered the republican government into signing the armistice which the military leaders had insisted upon, and that thereafter had advised the government to accept the Treaty of Versailles."

Shirer noted that the old regime had forced the new government into a position in which the onus could be shifted to it "even though it was not responsible for the German collapse. The blame for that rested on the old order, which had held power. But millions of Germans refused to believe this. They had to find scapegoats for the defeat and ... their humiliation and misery." This left a ready-made rationale for Hitler to follow.[3]

When did Hitler's intentions become visible to the world? He proclaimed them in *Mein Kampf*, published in Germany in 1925, and in England in 1933, but most people who read the book discounted it as the ravings of a disgruntled loser. Many, however, took it seriously. Soviet Commissar for Foreign Affairs Maxim Litvinov concluded that it was not necessary to examine anything else to understand what Hitler intended to do as leader of Germany.[4] Franklin Roosevelt listened to Hitler's first speech as Chancellor of Germany,

[2] Ian Kershaw, *Hitler: 1889–1936, Hubris* (New York, 1999). Kershaw points out that Hitler stated his intent in *Mein Kampf*, but also in other writings and early speeches. See pp. 149–153.
[3] William L. Shirer, *The Rise and Fall of the Third Reich* (New York, 1960), 32.
[4] *The New York Times*, March 18, 1936.

turned to Eleanor Roosevelt, and declared the man a menace. He never changed his mind.[5]

An examination of Hitler's speeches reveals even more graphically what he planned for Germany and the world as his role for Germany materialized in the 1930s. He gave evidence at the trial of Reichswehr officers in September 1930 where he charged that Germany was unfairly restricted by Versailles: "The National Socialists do not regard these treaties as law, but as something imposed upon Germany by constraint.... If we protest against them with every means in our power then we find ourselves on the path of revolution." The president of the court asked if this meant using illegal means, to which Hitler responded: "I presuppose for the moment that we have won the day: then we shall fight against the treaties with every means, even from the point of view of the world, with illegal means."

In an interview of September 1930, with Rothay Reynolds of the London *Daily Mail*, Hitler made his case more specifically. Already the Nazis had won 107 seats in the Reichstag. "If Europe decides to make Germany serve a life sentence," he warned, "then she must face the danger of having an embittered nation, desperate to the verge of crime, in her midst." That September, Hitler published an article in the London *Sunday Express* in which he declared: "Germany may still be saved by reopening the Versailles Treaty and the Young Plan. When delirium sets in it will be too late...." Then, in October, he granted an interview to a correspondent of the *Times* who asked if a Nazi foreign minister would insist on a complete repudiation of the Treaty. Hitler answered: "That is a question which cannot be answered with a simple negative or affirmative." However, sooner or later the treaty's open repudiation would come.[6]

Hitler's necessary support in his rise to power came largely from German industrialists, the press, aristocrats, and disgruntled army officers, all of whom thought they could control him. Without their financing and backing, Adolf Hitler, with his strutting and posturing, would have been a comic relief in the German and European political scene. With their support, he was a force not to be discounted. His adherents were largely extreme nationalists who wanted to emasculate the Versailles Treaty and "rearm Germany, break out from the encirclement of Britain, France and their allies, expand into Eastern Europe, where they would have access to grain and oil and eventually dominate Europe."[7]

The Nazi elite's economic power was immense. The group included "Emil Kirdorf, the union-hating coal baron who presided over a political slush fund

[5] Edward M. Bennett and Margery Harder Bennett, interview with Eleanor Roosevelt, Hyde Park, New York, Summer 1959.
[6] Norman Baynes (ed.), *The Speeches of Adolf Hitler* (New York, 1969), II, 992–96.
[7] James Pool, *Hitler and his Secret Partners: Contributions, Loot and Rewards, 1933–1945* (New York, 1997), xi–xii.

known as the 'Ruhr Treasury' which was raised by the West German min-
ing interests, [and who] had been seduced by Hitler at the party congress
in 1929." Also "Fritz Thyssen, the head of the steel trust, ... was an even
earlier contributor.... Joining Thyssen was Albert Voegler, also a power in
the United Steel Works." This list included newspaper publishers, coal mine
operators, and numerous large banking establishments. After initially opposing Hitler's rise to power and warning Hindenberg against making him chancellor, Gustav Krupp von Bohlen und Halbach cast his lot with Hitler and
became vehemently pro-Nazi. Hitler's major supporters included numerous
ultra-nationalist generals.[8]

English historian A. J. P. Taylor explained Hitler's political triumph on the
fiftieth anniversary of his seizure of power. It began with frightening Germans
by the burning of the Reichstag – which Hitler attributed to Communist ter-
rorists threatening the nation.[9] Taylor argued that in less than five years, Hitler
transformed Germany, changing it from a society respectful of laws and civil
responsibility into "a state ruled by violence and barbarism," a process so
gradual as to not appear startling. Conservatives thought they had a puppet
they could manipulate; they became the puppets.[10]

To understand Adolf Hitler's appeal to Germans requires delving into both
his and ordinary German's psychological proclivities. Ralph Manheim, the
translator of *Mein Kampf*, observed that Hitler was self-educated, a poor
writer of German because of his minimal education and south Austrian background. Manheim also stressed that if people had read Hitler's diatribes and
took them seriously, they would have been horrified. That the outside world
gave little credence or attention to Hitler's nationalistic appeals became more
apparent when not even his own party members considered them important.
As Manheim noted, "The average party member did not read the book, and
among the leaders it was a common saying that Hitler was an extraordinary
speaker, a great leader, a political genius, but it's too bad he had to write that
silly book."[11]

Hitler attributed Germany's collapse in 1918 to politicians, Jews, economic
exploiters – those people who blamed the German army for the national disaster that led to defeat and the Versailles Treaty. It was the creators of that
treaty in Paris who were Germany's enemies; it was they who denigrated the
"bastion of ... national freedom against the power of the stock exchange."[12]

---

[8] Shirer, *The Rise and Fall of the Third Reich*, 142–45.
[9] Herman Goering bragged to his interpreter at the Nuremberg trials that he personally set the
    fire that burned the Reichstag. Richard W. Sonnenfeldt, *Witness to Nuremberg* (New York,
    2006), 40–41.
[10] A. J. P. Taylor, "January 30, 1933," *The New York Times*, Sunday, January 30, 1983.
[11] Quote from Ralph Manheim in Hitler, *Mein Kampf*, trans. Ralph Manheim, xviii.
[12] Ibid. 278. The sections in the book on the economy and the army run rampant with accusa-
    tions about the "real" traitors of the German state, who were international bankers; Jews;
    Communists, who were also led by Jews; and the intelligentsia, who looked down on peo-
    ple like Hitler. The anti-Semitic overtones run literally through the whole book and foretell

He attacked the war-guilt clause of the treaty, comparing the Treaty of Versailles with the Treaty of Brest-Litovsk, which he said was fair and just compared with the Versailles settlement. He said that his enemies assailed the Brest-Litovsk Treaty as "one of the most shameful acts of rape in the world." This, in turn, accounted for millions of Germans believing that "the peace Treaty of Versailles [was] nothing more than just retribution for the crime committed by us at Brest-Litovsk,"[13] thus viewing any condemnation of Versailles as an injustice. This became the reason "why the shameless and monstrous word *'reparations'* was able to make itself at home in Germany." Hitler asserted that his lectures on "'The True Causes of the World War' and on 'The Peace Treaties of Brest-Litovsk and Versailles,' [were] the most important of all" until his followers understood his ultimate objective: the revision of the Versailles Treaty.[14]

II

In his essay "Hitler: Obsession Without End," Hans Schmitt contended that libraries contain more books about Hitler than any reader could deal with in a lifetime, and that only the Bolshevik Revolution takes more space on the library shelves. It was the Bolshevik Revolution that taught Hitler that opponents are not overcome by debate but by exile or extermination. "Yet," Schmitt concluded, "it took years before [Hitler] generated the same revulsion as his Russian models, years before most Europeans, not just Germans, persisted in viewing him as the lesser evil." He asserted that "Anti-communism became the sacred shield behind whose cover other forms of fraud and tyranny advanced upon a stubbornly unaware humanity."[15] It is debatable whether Neville Chamberlain, even when forced to face an aggressive Hitler, was convinced the Nazi dictator was a worse menace than Stalin's Russia. When all sorts of evidence presented itself to Chamberlain that Britain and the Soviet Union faced a common threat, he could not bring himself to make the requisite deal with the Soviets.[16] It was this fear of Bolshevik solutions and menaces that Hitler exploited both at home and abroad.

the fate of German Jews if Hitler ever gained power. But the most prophetic sentence lies in the section entitled "Development of Jewry," where Hitler wrote, "For once this book has become the common property of a people, the Jewish menace may be considered as broken," 308.

[13] The Treaty of Brest-Litovsk cost Russia 1.3 million square miles of territory and 62 million inhabitants, plus Bessarabia, which was annexed by Rumania in December 1917. For details, see Michael T. Florinsky, *Russia: A History and an Interpretation* (New York, 1958), II, 1473.

[14] Hitler, *Mein Kampf*, 468 ff.

[15] Hans A. Schmitt, "Hitler: Obsession Without End," *The Sewanee Review*, XCVI, No. 1 (January–March 1988), 158–59.

[16] Edward M. Bennett, *Separated by a Common Language: Franklin Delano Roosevelt and Anglo-American Relations, 1933–1939: The Roosevelt-Chamberlain Rivalry* (Lincoln, 2002), 216–17.

Hitler focused his attention, when he achieved power, primarily on two areas: foreign policy and preparation for war. Those who ignored this focus, in Germany or elsewhere, did so at their peril. This was the salient fact noted by Alan Bullock, in *Hitler: A Study in Tyranny*, when listing Hitler's objectives as Führer. He quoted Goering's testimony at Nuremberg when he told the court, "Foreign policy above all was the Führer's very own realm. By that I mean to say that foreign policy on the one hand, and the leadership of the armed forces on the other, enlisted the Führer's greatest interest and were his main activity."[17] Bullock went on to write that Hitler's focus on the military and foreign policy was essential because his total concentration was on consolidating and exercising power with the intent of expanding the German role in Europe.

From his school days in Linz, Hitler was first and foremost an extreme nationalist. He considered Germany's defeat (in 1918) as equivalent to personally losing the war. From the beginning of his political career, he identified his own ambition with the reestablishment and extension of German power. Hitler had but one objective: overturning the Versailles Peace, followed by "the Pan-German dream of a German-dominated Europe." This provided the "core of his political programme." At Düsseldorf in 1932 he expanded on this theme. He argued that it was not the treaty itself on which German misfortunes rested; it was on German weakness in accepting it. First, the "weak" republic had to be replaced. Then the new and strong German state could reverse the disasters imposed on the nation at Versailles and take action to recreate a dominant Germany.[18] In his interview with Rothay Reynolds, Hitler argued that the alternative to the Nazis and revision of Versailles could be understood even by a child – it was "Bolshevism."[19]

Some people have argued that the real failure of the Versailles Treaty rested on an indisputable fact that it was created in one mood and failed of enforcement in another. Examining this thesis becomes necessary if the slow death of Versailles is to gain some measure of clarity. The French mood at Versailles was to saddle Germany with such a large burden of economic responsibility, with reparations, that it would be unlikely the Germans could again pose a threat, especially if the concept of *securité* was amplified in French and Allied policy thereafter. In part, the viability of this approach depended on the Americans and the British abiding by the implications of the policy set forth in the treaty, especially those provisions that kept Germany from rearming and that limited German territory. The first failure of this approach came when the United States withdrew from the Versailles settlement. Some leaders in France blamed the Americans for all the failures of the next fourteen years, including the Great Depression itself. Also, when the French sought British support for French *securité* policy, they discovered that Great Britain had a different view of the requisite foreign policy relating to Germany.

[17] Alan Bullock, *Hitler: A Study in Tyranny* (New York, 1962), 313.
[18] Ibid., 314.
[19] Baynes, *Speeches of Hitler*, II, 993.

Howard Payne defined the French problem most succinctly when he observed that the French discovered that their national security against future German resurgence was inextricably woven into a triangular policy dilemma. The dilemma was inherent in France's separate and often tense relations with Great Britain and the United States.[20] The problem began with the French perception at Versailles that only a punitive peace could keep the Germans from rising against France again. The French position rested on a promise by the Americans and the British to help France apply the policy of "artificial inferiority" to Germany by a treaty that would provide automatic Anglo-American military aid if Germany attacked France. When this Guarantee Treaty reached the United States Senate, it was repudiated, releasing the British from the necessity of guaranteeing French security. This left France entering "the twenties with a nagging, triangular policy problem."[21] Paris tried various approaches to obtain American support to no avail.[22]

Hitler understood the intention of the French and made it clear that whatever it required to eliminate the Versailles restrictions he would undertake. He wrote to Chancellor Brüning on October 14, 1931: "The Peace Treaty of Versailles is no Peace Treaty. On the contrary it belongs to the category of those *Tribut-Diktats* which bear in themselves the seeds of later wars." He rejected the clauses that made Germans second-class citizens.[23]

At the outset in 1933, many of Hitler's potential critics refused to take his objectives seriously. George S. Messersmith, chargé at the American embassy in Berlin and ultimately one of the severest and most accurate critics of the Nazi movement, did not see what was happening in Hitler's Germany during the early days of Hitler's assumption of power. Messersmith reported to the State Department that "extremists" in the Nazi party attempted to eliminate Jewish participation when in April 1933 the party decreed that government contracts would go only to "Aryan" companies free of Jewish, Communist, and foreign influence. Foreign companies that did not dismiss all Jews from their operations would be excluded. Such actions were not official. Economic minister Alfred Hugenberg, reacting to such orders, urged businessmen to resist unauthorized interference. Herman Goering publicly threatened to dissolve the Combat League, which was organizing the picketing of non-Aryan businesses and demanding bribes and kickbacks. Hitler's deputy, Rudolph Hess, ordered the removal of department store pickets. Viewing these actions,

[20] Howard C. Payne, Raymond Callahan, and Edward M. Bennett, *As the Storm Clouds Gathered: European Perceptions of American Foreign Policy in the 1930s* (Durham, 1979). Republished by Regina Books, Claremont, n.d., 3

[21] Ibid., 5.

[22] Aristide Briand proposed the Pact of Paris specifically to attract the United States back onto the international stage. Secretary of State Frank B. Kellogg understood what Briand was trying to do and proposed that it be a multilateral agreement to thwart Briand's intent. See ibid., 9, 13, 16.

[23] Baynes, *Speeches of Hitler*, II, 998.

Messersmith believed that the regime had overcome the party extremists, led
by Joseph Goebbels.[24]

Like Ambassador Cudahy in Poland,[25] Messersmith characterized the clear
signs of rising militarism as "relatively harmless diversions for the unem-
ployed that, like the April anti-Jewish boycott, aimed to steal the thunder of
the party radicals." Even in the realm of foreign policy, Hitler's announced
objectives did not ring bells of alarm. In his biography of Messersmith, Jesse
Hiller noted: "Hardly a Westerner outside of France in 1933 disputed [Hitler's]
contention that modifications in Versailles were long overdue. Certainly there
was room for talk among reasonable people, and Messersmith, as late as the
early summer, was inclined to see the current German leadership as such." He
contended that Germany would be a "trouble spot" for a long time, "but for
now ... Germany's leaders could be dealt with."[26]

This perception changed radically in late 1933 and early 1934. Messersmith
saw the resurgent attacks on Jews and foreigners, especially Americans, as
well as the renewal of restrictions on foreign businesses that did not surrender
to German demands on their practices, as causes for concern. He observed
that the life of the Jews had "become absolutely impossible." By late 1933, the
German intent to rid the country of Jews became clear, as did Hitler's objective of annexing Austria."[27] The renewal of trade restrictions on American
companies, which contradicted Secretary of State Cordell Hull's free-trade
orientation, infuriated Hull. He began to speak more forcefully to the German
representatives in Washington – who always responded with reassuring
answers.[28]

What equally angered Hull was the treatment of Jews and Americans
in Germany. The German chargé in Washington, Rudolf Leitner, called on
August 11, 1933, to protest a boycott of German commerce because of the
German treatment of Jews. Hull told him the best remedy was for Germany to
stop harassing Jews. On September 5, 1933, he called Leitner back to protest
another attack on Americans who had failed to give a Nazi salute, and told
him that because the attacks occurred in front of police who did nothing, he
was considering a formal, vigorous, and open protest to the German government. A lame excuse by Leitner brought forth a warning from Hull that "if
such attacks continued the U. S. government would ... warn all Americans to
stay out of Germany."[29]

---

[24] Jesse H. Stiller, *George S. Messersmith: Diplomat of Democracy* (Chapel Hill, 1987),
    38–39.
[25] Cudahy wrote to FDR telling him there was nothing to worry about in what was happening
    in Germany, comparing the SA and SS to the Moose and the Elks in the United States, and
    contending that the Germans liked to put on uniforms and march around to martial music
    to let off steam. Cudahy to FDR, January 8, 1934, PPF 1193, John Cudahy Folder, Franklin
    Delano Roosevelt Library, Hyde Park. Cited hereafter as *FDRL*.
[26] Stiller, *Messersmith*, 39.
[27] Ibid., 44.
[28] Cordell Hull, *The Memoirs of Cordell Hull* (New York, 1948), I, 238.
[29] Ibid., 240–41.

III

July 13, 1933, marked the arrival of the new ambassador to Germany, William E. Dodd, whom George Messersmith judged to be an effective appointment. Dodd had received his Ph.D. from the University of Leipzig in 1900, was fluent in the German language, and had numerous contacts among the intellectuals in the German universities. Unfortunately these Germans were the antithesis of the country's new leadership. Dodd liked Messersmith because he tended to business, as Dodd visualized the "real" business of the embassy. During the first month of Dodd's tenure, Messersmith wrote to the State Department that Dodd's appointment was "one of the wisest that could have been made."[30]

This judgment changed, but not immediately. Dodd understood the German character, and did not find it revealed in the Nazis, who expected him to say something positive about their rule. Instead, he reminded "Germans of the futility of extremism." Messersmith soon observed that Dodd was an ivory-tower academic who possessed "little knowledge of economics or business" and had "very little contact with some of the realities of life."[31] Nor were these Dodd's only limitations. He greatly admired Thomas Jefferson and disdained career diplomats who thought going to social events and observing diplomatic traditions were important. He especially disliked people who had money and Eastern educations.[32]

One can admire Dodd's perception of the Nazis as repugnant and dangerous, but the degree to which he revealed his sentiments as ambassador made him less than useful. U.S. ambassador to the USSR William Bullitt wrote to FDR after a visit to Berlin, relating a conversation he had had with the German Foreign Minister Konstantin von Neurath, who brought up the subject of the American ambassador and the German desire to have him removed. Von Neurath bluntly told Bullitt that neither he nor his government would have any further dealings with Dodd, and if Dodd stayed, the United States would in essence have no ambassador in Berlin. What really surprised and alarmed Bullitt was the same message coming from André Francois-Poncet. The French Ambassador told Bullitt, "For Heaven's sake, get Dodd moved out of Berlin. He used to be bad as an Ambassador but now he is impossible. He scolds me because I invite members of the German Government to my Embassy." He continued, "And he embarrasses all of us ambassadors by taking the line that we should not be ambassadors to the Government to which we are accredited but should carry on a sort of holy crusade against National Socialism." He suggested that if Dodd wanted to be a crusader against Nazism, he should

[30] Stiller, *George S. Messersmith*, 41. Michael Polley wrote a very good assessment of Dodd's ambassadorship, pointing not only to his deficiencies but also to the fact that Dodd's diaries are an invaluable resource for perceiving the Germany of the 1930s and the record of Nazi oppression. Michael J. Polley, "William E. Dodd," in Cathal J. Nolan, ed., *Notable U.S. Ambassadors since 1775* (Westport, 1997), 83 ff.
[31] Ibid.
[32] Ibid.

cease to be an ambassador. Poncet concluded that the United States would never exercise influence on Germany with Dodd as its ambassador.[33]

Dodd failed to maintain contacts with those who could tell him what really went on in the German hierarchy. In fact, he tried to provide some guidance in an interview with Hitler on March 7, 1934, when he attempted to illustrate to Hitler how much was to be gained by reestablishing the better commercial and academic relations that had meant so much to both countries. Hitler ignored this initiative and complained about the Jews in Germany. Dodd said perhaps the answer might lie in establishing quotas on political and academic positions. Hitler responded that what was really wrong in Germany and in German-American relations was the influence of Jews in both countries. Dodd never attempted to achieve an accommodation with the Nazis again.[34]

IV

By 1933, Europe and the Atlantic world faced two inescapable challenges: the deepening worldwide depression and Germany's burgeoning threat to the Versailles Treaty's design for Europe. To address the international economic crisis, the League of Nations, in 1932, called the London Economic Conference. This multi-power conference received President Hoover's full approval. League experts had prepared the conference agenda before Roosevelt entered the White House. The new president assured the forthcoming London conference his full cooperation, but accepted Hoover's request that the conference keep the troublesome issues of reparations and war debts off the agenda.

The London conference was planned essentially to negotiate a general reduction of tariffs and a series of international monetary agreements that might stimulate trade and pull the world out of the Depression. In April 1933, Britain's Ramsay MacDonald assured reporters in Washington that the London conference, about to open, might possibly save democracy from the world's economic challenges. Dealing with unemployment, overproduction, and international economic blight, it could achieve a settlement of equally important and related concerns, including arms limitation – a serious economic challenge. The accumulation of larger and larger armaments, MacDonald observed, were leading less to peace than to overexpanded national budgets.[35]

Such objectives conformed to the liberal free-trade doctrines of the Secretary of State, Cordell Hull. Without the restoration of international commerce and finance, Hull believed, there would be little business recovery. Roosevelt appeared to agree, adding that the London conference "must establish order in place of the present chaos by the stabilization of currencies, freeing the flow of world trade, and by international action to raise price levels." Roosevelt's

[33] Orville H. Bullitt, ed., *Correspondence Between Franklin D. Roosevelt and William C. Bullitt: For the President, Personal and Secret* (Boston, 1972), 235.
[34] Polley, "William E. Dodd," 83.
[35] Address of Ramsay MacDonald, National Press Club, April 22, 1933, OF 48, Box 4, *FDRL*.

selection of an American delegation was not promising. It included such a mishmash of personalities and viewpoints, even bitter animosities, that it was destined for failure.[36] So obvious were the portents of disaster that some prominent national leaders rejected appointments to the delegation.

When the London conference opened in June 1933, the central issue was currency stabilization. France, speaking for Europe's gold-bloc countries, favored an agreement based on gold. To that end, France submitted a detailed plan whereby the United States would join Europe in maintaining the gold standard as the basis of international monetary stabilization. This determination of the gold-bloc countries to give precedence to monetary stabilization irritated Washington. Soon, Roosevelt, under the influence of Raymond Moley, an economic nationalist, lost interest in the conference; his own domestic program, the New Deal, had made some impressive advances against the American Depression.[37] By July, the President had deserted the movement for world currency stabilization. Explaining his decision to rely on a planned national currency, Roosevelt argued that the "sound internal economic system of a nation is a greater factor in its well-being than the price of its currency in changing terms of the currencies of other nations."

Not even the search for a tariff formula in London conformed any longer to American purpose, for the U.S. National Recovery Act of 1933 had authorized higher duties to insulate American wage and price policy from world pressures.[38] Roosevelt's economic nationalism assured the breakup of the conference. Still, the causes of failure were general, not specific. That Britain or other gold-standard countries would have agreed to any specific currency and tariff program remained doubtful to the end. Nor was it clear that any decisions made in London could have relieved the worldwide Depression.[39] It remained for Congress to establish the foundations of freer trade when it passed Hull's Reciprocal Tariff program in 1934, authorizing the Executive to negotiate trade agreements with foreign countries that might increase or lower existing rates by as much as 30 percent. Not even that program brought any substantial results.[40]

V

To confront Germany's burgeoning rejection of the military clauses of the Versailles Treaty, the League of Nations in February 1932 called the World Disarmament Conference, to meet in Geneva. Before the conference opened, the United States, in December, engineered the "No Force Declaration," under which Germany, France, Great Britain, and Italy promised "not in any

[36] Michael A. Butler, *Cautious Visionary: Cordell Hull and Trade Reform* (Kent, 1998), 48–49. This volume contains a full account of the London Conference, 46–81.

[37] For Moley's important role, see ibid., 57–60, 69–71.

[38] Ibid., 63.

[39] Fite and Graebner, *Recent United States History*, 369–70.

[40] Ibid., 370.

circumstances to attempt to resolve any present or future differences between them by resort to force." To limit future controversy, the four powers suggested that Germany and others, largely disarmed by the Versailles Treaty, should be granted equality of armaments under a system that would provide security for all.[41]

In imposing extensive restrictions on German rearmament, the victorious allies in 1919 had added the corresponding promise that other powers would limit their armaments, and thereby eliminate any future arms race. The Versailles powers did not totally disarm, but their reduced land forces scarcely exceeded those of Germany. No former Allied power favored large expenditures for arms. Indeed, all were determined to avoid them. Germany proposed that all nations either reduce their defenses to Germany's level or permit Germany to alter the Versailles formula. In an economically depressed world, that proposal received wide approval.

Against such attractive and promising formulas for the defense of the status quo, Hitler, who became German Chancellor on January 30, 1933, had to move cautiously. As historian Gerhard Weinberg expressed it, the Germans required a route that would avoid retaliation against them and would not become apparent until it was too late. "Determined to rearm," he wrote, "the Germans used the negotiations to secure whatever advantages they could without committing themselves to agreements they would have to break conspicuously and quickly. Care was exercised, however, that Germany not give the appearance of sabotage of the conference."[42] Some Germans feared that other countries might intervene to stop German rearmament, but they became increasingly confident that this would not occur. Everyone knew that Germany was violating the military provisions of the Versailles settlement. They feared the consequences, but did not know how to respond.

As German ambitions became more apparent, the victors of the recent war seemed paralyzed by the realities they faced. With no interest in either retreating from its world position or in rearming, Britain took the lead in framing a response to the burgeoning German challenge. This required an arrangement that would accommodate some form of appeasement, one that recognized the changing international circumstances. It demanded that both sides acknowledge in some degree the previous errors that needed correction. Those who shared this view regarded Hitler's attacks on the Versailles Treaty as logical and warranted. They sought, in their search for accommodation, to limit Germany's demands to what satisfied its security requirements.

At the disarmament conference in Geneva, Ramsay MacDonald presented the British plan on March 16, 1933. It recommended the size of the armies allowed to the various powers, and restrictions on the number of military units, all designed to conform to the pressures created by Germany and the

---

[41] Gerhard L. Weinberg, *The Foreign Policy of Hitler's Germany: Diplomatic Revolution in Europe, 1933–1936* (Chicago, 1970), 40.

[42] Ibid., 46.

Depression. To ease the price of security, MacDonald's plan would reduce Europe's armies by almost half a million men. Germany and France would be granted equality. The plan presented no formula on defense requirements, or any defense against the demands of each power for alterations that would fit its special interests. This played directly into Hitler's hands. Yet in its aim to satisfy all nations represented at Geneva, the MacDonald Plan became the most acceptable solution to the German-led arms competition. It demanded no commitments to the Versailles order and provided for no common action against anyone. The plan's popularity rested on its promise of peace and defense of the status quo at little cost or danger. At most, it provided for some negotiated settlement in opposition to those who believed that peace rested on firmness and the refusal to compromise.

In June 1933, the conference adjourned to meet again in October. In the interval, the desperate attempts to reach a weapons agreement, based on the MacDonald Plan, continued. In Britain, the plan received the full support of Neville Chamberlain, his powerful political faction in Parliament, and the multitude who favored accommodation and the avoidance of war. What motivated the willingness of much of the British populace to tolerate almost anything that Hitler did was the widespread fear of Bolshevism. The Russian revolution of 1917 sent shock waves across Europe that rolled up on the shores of England, creating fear, especially among the upper classes. The Duke of Northumberland termed it "a Jewish-Bolshevik conspiracy." The only adequate response seemed to be the creation of a force equal to that led by Mussolini and, subsequently, by Hitler.[43] The more extreme members of this group feared the German Jews, whom they considered part of the emerging Russian conspiracy.[44]

Chamberlain's most powerful and determined antagonist was cabinet member Sir Robert Vansittart, concerned with military affairs, who perceived that the route Britain was following would lead to disaster. Versailles, as he saw it, was being abandoned without any real attempt to find an alternative course to deal with the crisis. He complained that the British at Geneva were abandoning too many of the Versailles restrictions and limitations. He placed no faith in the French request for a League of Nations investigation, under Article 213 of the Versailles Treaty, that Germany was infringing on the treaty's military, naval, and air clauses.

Vansittart was equally troubled by the French military and France's Foreign Minister, Edouard Daladier. He complained that the French army was led by "a collection of mediocre generals visibly afraid of the Germans. One, to my horror, told them so." Vansittart found the Paris government equally hopeless. He thought Edouard Daladier less than effective as Foreign Minister. But he was no more pleased with leaders in the British Foreign Office. He

---

[43] Ian Kershaw, *Making Friends with Hitler: Lord Londonderry and Britain's Road to War* (London, 2004), 4–12.

[44] Ibid., 5.

charged that British foreign policy was being influenced in London by powerful men totally inexperienced in foreign affairs, who talked of France as an honorary first-class power, without understanding that Britain was headed in the same direction. For Vansittart, the West was nearly finished, and Britain would be fortunate if it could "prop it up enough to tide over the next onset."[45] Vansittart's condemnation of British policy focused on Chamberlain. To him, Chamberlain totally misunderstood the Germans and could not conceive of people who were abnormal in abnormal times. For Vansittart, Chamberlain was a disaster.[46]

French leaders found the British equally unresponsive to their efforts at cooperation in facing the German military challenge. Later, when France, in search of support, asked the British for consultation about what should be done, the War Office strongly opposed a response. The government informed the French that Britain did not believe the time opportune to take any action. Yet when the disarmament conference threatened to break down in 1934, British Foreign Secretary Simon warned the London government that Britain required close cooperation with the French. An armed Germany, he warned, meant that the League of Nations, as an international influence, would be reduced to the vanishing point, rendering rearmament mandatory. Simon concluded that Britain needed either to bring about a disarmament agreement or seriously consider a rearmament program.

British policy gave France the same choice. Facing British rejection of cooperation, the French could look to the United States or grudgingly accept the British wait-and-see posture, leading to the appeasement of Germany. In 1934, both the French public and the U.S. Congress denied every country the freedom to act. The French Ambassador in Washington, Andre de Labouleye, warned Europe that domestic pressures would turn the United States away from any cooperative program. In the end, none of the Western victors of 1918 could discover sufficient interest in the Versailles Treaty's military and territorial decisions to justify their military defense. This reality was clear admission that they had overreached in Paris.

VI

President Roosevelt in Washington, distant across the Atlantic, sought to fathom what alternatives confronted the United States in Geneva. Clearly, the former allies desperately desired an American presence in Europe to lead in arms limitation or, failing that, a reassertion of influence in European affairs. Unfortunately for Europe, isolationists formed a brick wall around any attempt of Roosevelt's to confront what he foresaw as a threat to American security and other national interests. Isolationists cared little for the outcome at Geneva as long as the United States remained outside the competition.

---

[45] Sir Robert Vansittart, *The Mist Procession* (London, 1958), 410.
[46] Ibid., 430.

Washington passed responsibility to the British as they were closer to the threat than was the United States.[47]

Roosevelt appointed Norman Davis as his delegate to the Geneva conference, assuring Davis that he had not given up hope for its success. He believed it important that the conference succeed. Upon Davis's departure, the President exclaimed, "Bon voyage and all the good luck in the world. If you pull off disarmament they will bury you in Arlington." He instructed Davis to support the MacDonald Plan, because Anglo-American cooperation was crucial. Arms limitation, he asserted, would improve the world's outlook and promote immediate and permanent economic welfare. Roosevelt remained hopeful that if MacDonald, Daladier, Mussolini, and Hitler gathered at the conference table, they might reach a satisfactory agreement. He authorized Davis to promote such a meeting.

In April 1933, Davis reported that European disarmament representatives were considering a plan that would come into effect if a state violated the Kellogg–Briand Peace Pact. The European powers would consult, but not interfere with any collective action organized to confront an aggressor. Britain would not be considered in this plan, limited as the plan was to the European continent. Thus, U.S. adherence would never compel the United States to take action against Britain. Davis informed Washington that under the plan, there would be no problem of entanglement with Europe in anything resembling a treaty because it would involve only economic sanctions against an aggressor.

When the wrangling at Geneva appeared to stall any genuine progress toward an agreement, Roosevelt moved to stimulate action, as well as to forestall a speech that Hitler was scheduled to deliver in the Reichstag on May 17. On May 16, the President presented his address entitled "An Appeal to the Nations of the World for Peace by Disarmament and for the End of Economic Chaos." He expressed hope for success at both the London Economic Conference and the Disarmament Conference at Geneva. He offered concrete proposals for a general non-aggression pact and agreements to respect national frontiers.

Roosevelt's speech was followed by a Davis speech that emphasized U.S. willingness to consult with other states when the peace was threatened. This consultation would seek collective measures agreed to by the powers represented at the disarmament conference "to refrain from any action tending to defeat the collective effort which these states may thus make to restore peace." This policy of parallel action would align the United States with the Western powers to pursue peace by restraining aggression. The lead would need to be taken in Europe. The Europeans would be responsible for the necessary collective action, but once they agreed on a policy, the United States would not interfere. By implication, this meant a possible "commitment to a sanctions policy, subject to U.S. domestic constitutional and political inhibitions."

---

[47] Roosevelt to Davis, August 30, 1933, Roosevelt to MacDonald, August 30, 1933, *FRUS, General, 1933* (Washington, 1950), 208–210.

Facing the suspicions in the Senate regarding an outreach program to Europe, this offer was as bold as any the President could afford.

Davis's plan made clear that the United States would enter no contractual agreement for any European action. Secretary Hull was emphatic in approving this decision. Hull argued that a contractual arrangement was not possible in part for political reasons. American isolationism demanded that the United States reserve to itself the right to interpret the plan's meaning and to emphasize American independence of judgment on the matter.[48] The British Foreign Office failed to understand that U.S. cooperation with Britain and Europe rested on the success of the MacDonald Plan at Geneva. When later MacDonald visited the United States, Roosevelt reminded him that he could not, for political reasons, sign a multilateral treaty, because it would need to go before the Senate for ratification. He would, however, support Davis's proposal. It is probable that Roosevelt believed that he had the authority ro impose sanctions of a non-military nature against any aggressor. This would be merely an economic move and would not involve any commitment to collaborate in any other way with the League powers.

VII

By early 1934, it became clear to Britain's Sir John Simon that the Geneva conference was disintegrating. Germany had long departed. In March, Simon sent a memorandum to the Cabinet titled "Consequences of a Breakdown of the Disarmament Conference." This recalled the reception given to a British memorandum of January 29 by France and Germany. It was clear that a breakdown of the conference was impending because the suggestions in the British memorandum did not go far enough for Germany. Hitler insisted that Germany be granted a larger air force immediately, a request that the French would not accept.[49]

Spring 1934 was disheartening for France. In the face of Germany's blatant disregard of the provisions of the Versailles Treaty and Hitler's clear obstructionism in the Disarmament Conference, France offered a proposal that went much further than the British one. If a violator should be charged, the Permanent Disarmament Commission would request the offending state to comply, its obligations fixed by the commission. Unless the violation had ceased by the established expiration date, the offending state would no longer be allowed to benefit from the guarantees of the normal rights of member states. If the violation were deemed sufficiently serious, the accused would no longer be protected by the Pact of Paris. A committee of inspection would ensure that the violations ceased. If they continued, there would be joint action

---

[48] D. K. Adams, *FDR, The New Deal and Europe, An Inaugural Lecture*, Given at the University of Keele, October 23, 1973 (published by the University of Keele), 7.

[49] Cabinet document, "Consequences of a Breakdown of the Disarmament Conference," March 1934, C.P. 68 (34), Churchill College, Cambridge.

by the remainder states to coerce the offending state economically, with financial assistance to the offended nation and an economic boycott of the violating state.[50] Led by Louis Barthou, France sought to realign France and Russia inside an encircling alliance system, but the effort failed when Barthou could obtain no British cooperation or reliable support from any other countries. No nation was willing to resort to force in defense of the Versailles structure.

In London, Foreign Minister Simon laid out a scenario that would follow the submission of the French proposal. If the French plan were adopted, and it came to the point of facing Germany and demanding acquiescence, he surmised that Britain would certainly not accept the French plan. It would overcommit Britain in facing Germany. The British rejection left the Versailles Treaty's provisions controlling German rearmament in shambles. Indeed, those provisions had long succumbed to changing conditions. Hitler announced as early as October 1933 that since no one wished to allow Germany adequate defenses in response to other countries' unwillingness to disarm, it had no choice but rearm. Hitler made his move as early as October 14, 1933, with the announcement that Germany was leaving both the Geneva Disarmament Conference and the League of Nations. It would now continue to rearm without regard to the opposition of other nations.

---

[50] French Proposals (Given to Mr. Henderson) on Principles to Govern Guarantees of Execution, C.P. 68 (34), 2–3.

7

Challenge of the Dictators

I

Adolf Hitler's decision to leave the Geneva Disarmament Conference and the League of Nations revealed his intentions to scrap the Versailles Treaty and launch an aggressive campaign against its provisions. This entailed enlisting Mussolini to his cause. First, however, he needed to be in a position to overwhelm foreign foes who would try to hold Germany to the inferior position it had occupied during the first post-war decade. He began this process by addressing the Reichstag in May 1933, informing its members that Germany would not demand equality of armaments for four years, but would sign no agreement that perpetuated the military inequality. Inside Germany, he began to implement his program, set forth in *Mein Kampf*, with speeches that emphasized German nationalism and militarism. His anti-Semitic Nuremberg Laws sent a stream of talented Jews out of the country.

Hitler's open campaign against Versailles began in July 1934 with his dramatic move to annex Austria. The effort failed. The attempted coup resulted in the assassination of Austrian Chancellor Engelbert Dollfuss. It produced no annexation, but it exposed Hitler's expansionist program. Ironically, this move frightened future ally Benito Mussolini, because German possession of the Brenner Pass would give Hitler an open route to northern Italy.[1] Mussolini need not have worried. Hitler's emphasis on *Lebensraum* strengthened his drive for an Italian alliance, while Mussolini's designs in the Mediterranean placed him at odds with France. This gave Germany and Italy a common potential enemy. Hitler, moreover, was an early admirer of Mussolini and his Fascist program. The more Mussolini was attacked by "liberal" elements in Germany and elsewhere, the more Hitler desired to cement an alliance.[2] Hitler's later support of Mussolini's adventure in Abyssinia helped to bring the two dictators together.

[1] Fite and Graebner, *Recent United States History*, 378.
[2] Weinberg, *The Foreign Policy of Hitler's Germany*, 16.

Diplomacy under the threat of force was to become the hallmark of Hitler's assault on the Versailles restrictions. In author John Toland's discussion of the November 2, 1934, Nuremberg Rally and Hitler's actions regarding disarmament that followed, he noted that Germany's expansionist foreign policy depended on power, and Hitler was rearming "at every level." Heartened by public reaction to Germany's impressive military display at the 1934 Nuremberg rally, Hitler issued a secret order three weeks later significantly enlarging the army. That day, Germany enrolled 70,000 recruits, while the defense budget rose to 654 million marks. In London, this unleashed alarming rumors of infringements on the Versailles Treaty. These reactions moved Hitler to consciously woo important Britons. He would require British acquiescence in his eastward expansion. His moves to reassure important British citizens paid huge dividends for years to come.

On December 19, 1934, Hitler hosted a dinner party attended by four English guests among the twenty-five present. Included among the four Englishmen were "a well-known member of the Anglo-German Fellowship, Lord Rothermere, his son, and Ward Price, editor of the *Daily Mail*, the most influential Rothermere newspaper." Ironically, Rothermere had been introduced to Hitler by the half-Jewish Princess Stephanie von Hohenlohe. What attracted Rothermere to Hitler was their common hatred of Bolshevism[3].

In late January 1935, Hitler received two more English guests of importance, Lord Allen of Hurtwood and Lord Lothian. Hurtwood brought a message of goodwill from Prime Minister Ramsay MacDonald, while Lord Lothian was so persuaded of Hitler's "sincerity" that he convinced Foreign Secretary Sir John Simon of its reality. This was the backdrop of Simon's visits to Germany, postponed the first time by Hitler's anger over the publication of a British White Paper criticizing German rearmament and patent violations of the Versailles restrictions. Despite this, Sir John informed Parliament that he intended to continue calling on the German Chancellor.

Hitler's plans for rearmament and territorial expansion moved forward dramatically in 1935. Ironically, one of Hitler's early territorial triumphs flowed from a provision of the Versailles Treaty. On January 13, the League of Nations conducted a plebiscite in the Saar Basin that offered three options: continued League supervision, union with France, or reunion with Germany. Ninety percent of the vote favored reunion. This reaccession of German territory inaugurated Hitler's territorial recovery program. Sir Geoffrey Knox, who headed the governing body of the Saar from 1932 to 1935, found this action unfortunate, although clearly within the provisions of the Versailles Treaty. He did not trust the Germans and did not believe the Saar to be simply a Nazi problem. When Knox was asked if he thought Germany's expansive mood went back to the Treaty of Versailles, he said he thought not: "No, the battle of Leipzig (1631), ... [The Germans] have always conquered by isolating their enemies [the Great War was their only failure]...." Knox contended

[3] John Toland, *Adolf Hitler* (New York, 1976), 500–01.

that Germany never really disarmed, and unless directly confronted, war was imminent. Knox was aghast at the reporting he read in *The Times*, and could not understand "how any paper in this country could believe Hitler's protestations about his peaceful intentions when the whole efforts of the man and his regime in Germany were devoted to making the nation obedient and efficient instruments of war."[4]

Germany's persistent refusal to negotiate on issues that troubled other nations was equally disturbing. Historian Gerhard Weinberg made a shrewd assessment of the misperceptions that dominated the aftermath of the Hitler–Simon and Ribbentrop–Eden meetings in Berlin during early 1935. That no agreements on anything emerged was evidence of Germany's uncompromising mood. The British sought Hitler's agreement to a pact ensuring Austrian independence, a return to the League, and the signing of an Eastern Locarno agreement, only to be met by absolute refusal. Eden concluded that none of these quests would be realized in the future, while Simon continued to anticipate some German accommodation.

When Britain and France confronted Germany with nothing but angry words, Berlin proclaimed a vast expansion of the German military machine. On March 10, 1935, Goering announced that Germany was building an air force in defiance of the Versailles military restrictions. Then, on March 16, Hitler denounced the provisions of the Versailles Treaty that restricted German arms. He reinstated conscription, declaring that the German army would be expanded to 36 divisions, amounting to 550,000 men. He cited the provisions of the Versailles Treaty that other states should reduce their arms. Their failure to do so was the rationale for German action.[5] On Sunday March 17, German officials celebrated their Memorial Day with special ceremonies at the State Opera House. "Ostensibly," wrote correspondent William L. Shirer, "this was a ceremony to honor Germany's war dead. It turned out to be a jubilant celebration of the death of Versailles and the rebirth of the conscript German army."[6]

Hitler's bold elimination of the Versailles clauses limiting Germany's military land forces produced a vocal condemnation – nothing more. French Ambassador Francois-Poncet accused Germany of violating the Versailles Treaty. Hitler responded that German rearmament was aimed at Communism and the Soviet Union. When the British delegation at Geneva condemned the German arms program as a treaty violation, Hitler countered that he could hardly violate a treaty that Germany had not signed.[7] Britain rejected sanctions, while the League issued a communiqué calling for peace "within the framework of the League of Nations."[8]

---

[4] W. T. Crozier, *Off the Record: Political Interviews, 1933–1943* (London, 1973), 36–37.
[5] Robert H. Ferrell, ed., *The Twentieth Century: An Almanac* (New York, 1984), 182–83.
[6] Fite and Graebner, *Recent United States History*, 378.
[7] Toland, *Adolf Hitler*, 501–03.
[8] Fite and Graebner, *Recent United States History*, 378.

In a Reichstag speech of May 21, Hitler attacked the validity of a dictated peace. He warned the Versailles victors that their efforts to defend such a treaty were doomed. Germany would no longer be bound by terms that the state had no hand in writing. He condemned conferences, treaties, or agreements that touched German interests without Berlin's participation. He spoke of peace in the terms of war when he added that the German government would help safeguard the peace only if others agreed "to recognize the law of perpetual evolution by keeping open the way to treaty revision." Any attempt to depart from this principle, he warned, would provide a "preparation for future explosion."[9] Hitler's early warning gave the Versailles victors the ultimate choice between accepting serious treaty modifications, or war.

Even as Hitler was successfully reestablishing the foundations of German military dominance on the European continent, he also was challenging the near-monopoly of British naval power on the seas. The Versailles Treaty had denied Germany any naval authority. But amid the military discussions of 1935, Britain agreed to a naval treaty with Germany, signed on June 18. The treaty recognized Germany's right to naval rearmament to 35 percent of Britain's tonnage. But Admiral Raeder, commander of the German navy, was already planning German naval construction equal to that of Britain, exceeding Britain in submarines. British naval intelligence knew of it and warned of it, but without effect.[10]

London had negotiated this treaty without informing or consulting the French, unleashing protests and alarm across France. The French press expressed outrage. Paris officials complained that Britain had agreed to exchange naval information with Berlin that it had denied Paris, making it appear that London was making a deal with the enemy while snubbing an ally. British spokesmen assured the French that such British naval information was available to them, but that they had never requested it. Additionally, the French accused Britain of further abandoning the Versailles settlement. If Germany could, at no cost, secure London's acquiescence on matters of naval construction, the military clauses of the Versailles Treaty had indeed become obsolete.

II

As Hitler's rearmament plans became apparent, the British and French sought ways to confront Germany's rising power and provide further guarantees of the Versailles peace structure. To that end, the French organized the Stresa Conference with Britain and Italy, which met on April 11, 1935. The conference intended to create a strategic response to Germany's announced program to rearm. Italy supported the conference because of its fears of a rearmed Germany, positioned on the Italian border. That nothing came of

[9] Baynes, ed., *The Speeches of Adolf Hitler*, II, 1241.
[10] Weinberg, *The Foreign Policy of Hitler's Germany*, 208–09.

the conference may be attributed to Mussolini's rising territorial ambitions in Northern Africa.

Having failed to obtain the desired response to possible German aggression at Stresa, the French turned to the Soviet Union, where the Russians shared their concern over German arms and territorial ambitions, as outlined in Hitler's memoirs. The designs on Soviet territory openly expressed by German delegates at the London Economic Conference also troubled the French. Thus the French quest for a Little Entente in Eastern Europe touched mutual concerns that resulted in the May 2, 1935, signing of a Franco-Soviet defense agreement. The Soviets, in search of additional support, signed a defense pact with Czechoslovakia on May 16. The long-sought Franco-Soviet pact was a complete failure from the outset.[11]

For Hitler, the existence of an opposing alliance was undesirable. His response was immediate. In his Reichstag speech of May 21, he offered bilateral non-aggression pacts to all his neighbors, except for Lithuania, which had incurred his wrath. He promised to adhere to the Locarno pact, including the demilitarization of the Rhineland and guarantees of Austrian independence.[12] Columnist Dorothy Thompson questioned Hitler's dissimulation. In a *Foreign Affairs* article of July 1935, she asserted that National Socialism was not a peaceful movement. Having established a wartime economy, she warned, Hitler required a war to sustain his power. She contended that the German political system was built on the presumption of an enemy, concluding that Germany planned aggression.[13]

Like Thompson, much of the international community received Hitler's assurances with skepticism.[14] Hitler took no notice of the stiffening British posture, perhaps misled by the repeated display of Simon's preference for accommodation. As Sir John failed to recognize that Hitler wanted war, based on his own timing, Hitler failed to understand that the genuine British desire for peace did not mean that England would not fight under any circumstances. Thus mutually deceived, both countries continued to stumble toward the inevitable confrontation.[15]

III

The first test of any form of collective security came not from Berlin, but from the Italian threat in the summer of 1935 to North Africa's Abyssinia. British editor G. Ward Price noted how completely the move was Mussolini's alone. The Fascist dictator had little public support, and even his military leaders

[11] William Evans Scott, *Alliance against Hitler* (Durham, 1962), 196.
[12] Baynes, *Speeches of Adolf Hitler*, II, 1241.
[13] Dorothy Thompson, "National Socialism: Theory and Politics," *Foreign Affairs*, XIII (July 1935), 573.
[14] Weinberg, *The Foreign Policy of Hitler's Germany*, 208–09.
[15] Ibid., 206.

thought a war would be a long and costly process. Price visited Italy in April, five months before the war commenced, and found "many Italians full of anxiety about the risks and cost of the approaching campaign."[16] American journalist Anne O'Hare McCormick visited Italy in early 1935 and also found little support for the impending assault. Even Mussolini's close friends thought the idea total madness, doomed to failure.

Mussolini's supporters were mostly young men indoctrinated in the Fascist principle that the individual counted for nought when weighed against the affairs of state. Although much of the older generation opposed war, they understood that opposition in a Fascist state could be suicidal. Still, dislike for the war appeared in anti-war inscriptions. "In the narrow lanes of Venice and Genoa and in the slums of Naples," Italian writer Caetano Salvemini reported, "the walls are covered with anti-war inscriptions."[17]

In October 1935, Mussolini, undeterred, plunged ahead with his planned attack, assured that he would face no reprisal from Britain and France. In part, this conviction lay in the British failure to reveal any concern for Abyssinia. When Simon and Chamberlain conferred with the Italians at Stresa, they did not address the subject. This silence, added to the known English opposition to war, convinced Mussolini that London would not confront his African venture with force. Initially, Britain responded to the Italian invasion of Abyssinia with an appeal for League action. There, London received no support from France, for the Paris government had apparently won Italian support in a common resistance to German aggressiveness. The failure of Anglo-French cooperation in resisting Italian aggression assured Mussolini that he could safely pursue his conquest of Abyssinia. What underscored the guarantee of Anglo-French inaction was the replacement of Ramsay MacDonald with Stanley Baldwin as British Prime Minister in June 1935. Baldwin appointed Sir Samuel Hoare as Foreign Minister.

Hoare soon emerged as Britain's leading advocate of appeasement, determined to end the African war by satisfying Mussolini's territorial ambitions. With France's Pierre Laval, he framed a Franco-British peace agreement that offered Mussolini two-thirds of Abyssinia in exchange for peace. This proposal, made in December 1935, Mussolini readily accepted; his army had encountered unexpectedly stiff resistance from the Abyssinians. In explaining the offer, Hoare argued simply that Abyssinia was not worth saving, especially at the cost of European peace. His decision, he explained, rested on the fact that "a frontier incident in an African desert seemed likely to involve Europe and the world in a very serious crisis." This led him to the question: "Could we ... prevent a remote and unknown corner of Africa from becoming the starting point of a general conflagration?"

Chamberlain agreed with that judgment, arguing that Abyssinia was not worth saving. He defined the African state as "an islet of the Dark Ages in a

---

[16] Quoted in Gaetano Salvemini, *Prelude to World War II* (London, 1953), 471.
[17] Ibid.

modern ocean." He quoted Winston Churchill, no stranger to imperial reasoning, who asserted that Abyssinia was not a worthy or equal member of a league of civilized nations. In defending the Hoare–Laval agreement, Chamberlain concluded that "if in the end the league were demonstrated to be incapable of effective intervention to stop this war, it would be practically impossible to maintain the fiction that its [Abyssinia's] existence was justified at all."[18] For Britain, a friendly Italy in the Mediterranean assured an open supply line to its colonies. For France, it eliminated the need to maintain troops on the Italian frontier. In London, the British Parliament refused to agree. On December 18, 1935, it rejected the Hoare–Laval Agreement to end the war by ceding Abyssinian territory to Mussolini. Both men were forced to resign in disgrace. Four days later, Anthony Eden became British Foreign Minister.

As the African war continued, the British government, under intense pressure to act, asked the League for oil sanctions to curtail the Italian air and ground onslaught. In its quest of oil sanctions, the League invited non-League nations to participate. This search for broader involvement was aimed largely at the United States. Roosevelt and Hull, determined to prevent any American involvement, warned Americans not to deal with either belligerents. Any trade would favor the Italians; without ships, the Abyssinians had no access to U.S. markets. The President met the crisis by establishing a "moral embargo," asking Americans not to trade with Italy in strategic goods, especially oil.[19] Mussolini acknowledged later the impact of the oil embargo on the Italian war effort. Italy, he said, could not have sustained the Abyssinian campaign one more week if Eden's proposed oil embargo had been accepted by all the powers.[20]

Throughout the spring of 1936, Mussolini's superior military technology began to determine the course of the war. Unopposed by the League or the Western powers, Mussolini's legions, armed with bombers, tanks, and mustard gas, proceeded to complete the conquest of Abyssinia. It was left for correspondent William L. Shirer to record the ending on May 2, 1936:

> The Italians entered Addis Ababa today. The Negus has fled. Mussolini has triumphed – largely with mustard gas. That's how he's beaten the Ethiopians. He's also triumphed over the League, by bluff. That's how he kept off oil sanctions which might have stopped him. We picked up a broadcast of him shouting from the balcony of the Palazzo Venezia in Rome. Much baloney about 30 centuries of history, Roman civilization, and triumph over barbarism. Whose barbarism?[21]

Haile Selassie, Abyssinia's exiled king, passed final judgment on the Italian conquest. Addressing the League of Nations in Geneva in June 1936, he

---

[18] Keith Feiling, *The Life of Neville Chamberlain* (New York, 1946, 1970), 264–65.
[19] Hull, *The Memoirs*, I, 428ff.
[20] Robert A. Friedlander, "New Light on the Anglo-American Reaction to the Ethiopian War, 1935–1936, *Mid-America*, XLV (April 1963), 115–25.
[21] William L. Shirer, *Berlin Diary: The Journal of a Foreign Correspondent,1939–1941* (London, 1941), 61.

recalled that fifty nations, eight months earlier, had "asserted that aggression had been committed in violation of international treaties." He charged that never before had a state been subjected to systematic extermination by the barbarous resort to mustard gas against civilian targets. But the issue, he continued, transcended what occurred in Abyssinia; it had raised the broader question of collective security – the proclaimed foundation of international peace – and found it wanting. "Should it happen," he concluded, "that a strong Government finds it may with impunity destroy a weak people, then the hour strikes for that weak people to appeal to the League of Nations to give judgment in all freedom. God and history will remember your judgment."[22]

IV

Nothing in the troubling international scene after 1933 challenged American isolationism, established in the early 1920s by the supposition that American involvement in the Great War was unnecessary, and gained nothing that mattered for international security. Initially, Hitler's belligerent rhetoric created some sense of national insecurity, but few public or congressional demands for confrontational diplomacy and military retrenchment. Washington, moreover, sustained a reassuring response that quickly banished the sense of insecurity and sustained the national mood of confidence, unilateralism, and isolationism.

That isolationist mood permitted the United States only a minor role in Europe's international affairs, eliminating any U.S. support for collective security. Providing aid to victims of aggression in the form of arms or ammunition was illegal. There could be no financial aid. The Johnson Act of 1934 prohibited the U.S. government or private agencies from lending money to any country in default on its war debts. President Roosevelt attempted to eliminate the continuing issue of war debts, but without success.

Events in Europe and Asia troubled some officials in Washington, but aroused determination in Congress and much of the press to ensure the United States a certain escape from foreign crises. Helmuth C. Engelbrecht's and Frank C. Hanighen's book, *Merchants of Death*, published in 1934, traced U.S. entry into the World War to a conspiracy of munitions makers. This theme dominated the hearings of the congressional committee, headed by Senator Gerald P. Nye of North Dakota, designed to ensure an American escape from another war. The Nye hearings received full press coverage, gaining overwhelming public support for isolationist legislation and the principle of neutrality. The committee, through long and careful interrogation, unveiled the effective lobbying and sordid business practices, as well as the wartime profiteering, of American industries. But Nye could not prove that Wall Street bankers and munitions makers had single-handedly carried the nation into war, or had influenced Woodrow Wilson more than did the German submarine. In

[22] Haile Selassie, "Appeal to the League of Nations" (June 1936).

the atmosphere of 1935, such details were lost on the isolationist millions. The committee's report stressed the incompatibility between neutrality and uncontrolled wartime shipping and investment. Nye's conclusions of June 1936 charged that loans and shipments to belligerents favored those who controlled the seas, converting the United States into an auxiliary arsenal. Thus the success of American neutrality lay in the control of credit and trade with those at war.[23]

Congress had already acted. Early in April 1935, Nye introduced a set of resolutions into the Senate that comprised an impartial arms embargo in another European war, with restrictions on loans to belligerents. Congress passed the Neutrality Act, embracing these principles, in August 1935. It granted the President authority in time of war to ban the export of arms to belligerents. It warned Americans traveling on the vessels of warring nations that they did so at their own risk. Opponents of the law argued that in time of war, the United States would be powerless to defend the weak or affect the war's outcome.[24] The President signed the law because, he said, it expressed the will of the American people. Isolationism had become a national phenomenon, embraced forcefully in a series of addresses by Roosevelt in 1935 and 1936.

Isolationism embraced a peculiar Anglophobia. War in Europe would again pit England and France against Germany. The United States would fight on the side of England, or not at all. Britain, therefore, constituted a perennial threat to American neutrality. But if American isolationism combined a distrust of England with an intense determination to avoid another European war, it did not share the pro-Axis sympathies of the nation's almost infinitesimal pro-German minority. This distinction was not lost on the German ambassador, Hans Heinrich Dieckhoff, who reported to Berlin in December 1937: "From the German standpoint, the position and the activity of the supporters of isolationism are to be welcomed.... But we must be clear about one thing: the pacifists – with the exception of a few groups, particularly of German-Americans – have their position in no way determined by friendship or sympathy for Germany."[25]

Frank Simonds, a major analyst of the day, delivered the Albert Shaw lectures at Johns Hopkins University in 1935. In devastating style, he addressed the central dilemma that the Versailles Treaty imposed on the international order. Simonds observed that nations responsible for the treaty would not revise what was advantageous to their own interests. Nor would they use their armies to enforce League policies that did not directly concern them. He contended that there existed no universally understood standard that would lead to easy identification of a just or unjust demand.[26] As long as there were

[23] Fite and Graebner, *Recent United States History*, 375–76.
[24] Robert Divine, *The Illusion of Neutrality* (Chicago, 1962), 115.
[25] Fite and Graebner, *Recent United States History*, 377.
[26] Frank H. Simonds, *American Foreign Policy in the Post War Years: The Albert Shaw Lectures on Diplomatic History* (Baltimore, 1979), 16.

nations that believed themselves victims of unjust, imposed treaties, with no means to change them peacefully, there would be wars to redress grievances. Nations that refused to accept changes peacefully, he charged, wanted something for nothing. They wanted a peace profitable to themselves without cost or responsibility. The Versailles victors, including the United States, he charged, lived in an unreal world, behaving like the gambler who, after winning all his playing partners' money in a poker game, "invokes the law to prohibit future gambling."[27] This was the impulse of the Versailles victors, including an isolationist United States, in their pursuit of an unchanging world.

V

This perennial effort of the Allied powers to defend their world, not with power but with appeals to the sanctity of the Versailles Treaty, convinced Hitler that he faced nothing but words. This assured him that he could assault the treaty's territorial arrangements, with bluff or violence, picking off the victims one by one. Isolationism ensured U.S. inaction; changes in the British government were equally encouraging. On January 20, 1936, King George V died and was succeeded by Edward VIII, who was fully in favor of a rapprochement with Germany. This objective was not pleasing to Eden. But the king announced that he was prepared to talk to Hitler, either in London or in Germany. This prospect offered consolation to Hitler, who was convinced that if Britain could not muster enough support at home or elsewhere to stop Mussolini in Abyssinia, what would it do if he chose to remilitarize the Rhineland? He believed he knew the answer.

Hitler required a rationale for invading the Rhineland. He began to lay the groundwork in 1935. Noting the impending Franco-Soviet Treaty, he warned the Polish ambassador that if his country concluded a treaty with France, he would denounce the Locarno Pacts.[28] This moved the French to ask London for support if Hitler terminated the Locarno guarantees; the response was ambiguous. It seemed clear that neither Britain nor France was prepared to defend the Rhine frontier.[29]

Even as Hitler gave the order for the German invasion of the Rhineland, he asked the Wehrmacht adjutant, Colonel Friedrich Hossbach, whether his marching orders could still be withdrawn. He received an assurance that it was possible. Still fearing that the invasion might fail, he permitted the invasion order to stand. The British and French did nothing.[30] This was an occasion when Hitler's plans for conquest might have suffered from a severe response. His generals believed the move premature, his popular support uncertain.

---

[27] Ibid., 58–66.
[28] Salvemini, *Prelude to World War II*, 432.
[29] Ibid.
[30] Toland, *Adolf Hitler*, 23–24.

The immediate Anglo-French response threatened reprisal. The French termed the German invasion "a return of the mailed fist in diplomacy [providing] a menace and provocation." The French asserted that "rather than submit to this last crashing piece of Teutonism, France will fight."[31] In London, Prime Minister Stanley Baldwin declared as early as 1934 that thanks to aerial warfare, the White Cliffs of Dover were no longer the first defense of Britain. Instead, he warned, "you think of the Rhine. That is today where our frontier lies." British reaction was strongest among that minority who believed the German invasion to be a crucial test of the Versailles guarantees, to be met with force.

Among those who favored action was Winston Churchill. When France took its case to the League of Nations, Churchill judged this a key case for the League. "Strangely enough," he confessed, "there never was a moment or occasion when the League of Nations could command such overwhelming force."[32] On March 13, 1936, Churchill proposed that Britain uphold its commitment to the Locarno Treaty.[33] Anthony Eden thought otherwise. He informed the cabinet that the French wanted to invoke their authority over the Rhineland, but there was no public support for such a move, either in England or in France. Ultimately, the British escaped responsibility by suggesting that the Rhineland was a League issue.[34]

Washington officials, with Americans generally, followed the Rhineland crisis with concern, but with no inclination to support a national response. Roosevelt instructed Ambassador Dodd in Berlin to inform him immediately if the United States could make any gesture toward peace. But the peace, he added, "must be a peace with justice but the kind of peace which will end without threat for more than a week or two."[35] FDR's ambassadors in Europe recognized the Rhineland crisis as a major one. Breckinridge Long in Italy judged the situation "more dangerous than any since 1918."[36] U.S. Ambassador John Cudahy in Poland offered Roosevelt a full and accurate assessment of the Rhineland crisis. He noted that the French were driven by panic, and stood firm, but Britain would offer no help, miffed by the French refusal to support London in the Abyssinian crisis. Cudahy was convinced that collective security "has crashed in European international affairs and the League of Nations and collective action are illusory." He concluded: "Only a miracle can prevent a war in Europe.... The catastrophe may be averted for a time but if the Hitler Government is not overthrown a war in Europe is as certain as the rising sun."[37]

---

[31] Guido Enders, "Versailles Curb Broken," *The New York Times*, March 11, 1936, 1ff.

[32] Sir Winston Churchill, *Step by Step: 1936–1939* (London, 1939), 14–15.

[33] Ibid., 15.

[34] Toland, *Adolf Hitler*, 524.

[35] Robert Dallek, *Franklin D. Roosevelt and American Foreign Policy, 1932–1945* (New York, 1979), 124.

[36] Long to Roosevelt, March 13, 1936, Edgar B. Nixon, ed., *Roosevelt and Foreign Affairs* (Cambridge, MA, 1969), III, 254.

[37] Cudahy to Roosevelt, March 20, 1936, ibid., 267–68.

Cudahy knew that the President was aware of the danger, that he recognized and accepted the certainty of war. The United States had to act accordingly, but Cudahy found it amazing, given the challenges facing the United States and Europe, to be faced with petitions from peace societies protesting the President's national defense appropriations in the Congress. He lamented the decision of Congress to deny the President discretionary authority under the Neutrality Act. "Arguments opposed to this," he said, "have not changed my viewpoint that it would give us a powerful weapon in a warring world."[38]

Ambassador Dodd warned from Berlin that the situation the world confronted, following the invasion of the Rhineland, was extremely serious. Germany's dictatorship, he added, was "stronger than ever. If she keeps the pace three more years she can beat the whole of Europe in a war." The blunders of fifteen years, he concluded, were coming home to roost, creating a dangerous world, with "Germany dominating Europe, Japan dominating the Far East...."[39] Actually, the German occupation of the Rhineland marked the end of the Versailles Treaty's devices for protecting international security. As British historian A. J. P. Taylor concluded, "The League of Nations was a shadow; Germany would rearm, free from all treaty restrictions; the guarantees of Locarno were no more. Both Wilsonian idealism and French realism had failed." Europe had returned to the conditions that existed before 1914.[40] The President agreed. He wrote to Ambassador Bullitt, referring to the Rhineland crisis, "The fat is in the fire again. What a thoroughly disgusting spectacle so-called civilized man in Europe can make [of] himself."[41] Security again rested on strength, alliances, and diplomacy.

VI

With Germany rearmed and Italy alienated by the combination of French and British indecision in the Abyssinian crisis, the balance of forces in Europe faced a new challenge in the Fascist rebellion against the Republican Government of Spain. This rebellion, led by Spanish General Francisco Franco, began on July 17, 1936. Franco's rebel forces seized control of Spanish Morocco. From that African base they launched an invasion against the elected Spanish government in Madrid. The issues in the Spanish conflict had been gathering for years. The Spanish army and church had long condemned the Madrid regime's control of education and its seizure of church properties. In October 1934, the Catholic Popular Action Party gained a number of seats in the cabinet of Prime Minister Alejandro Lerroux.[42] The struggle for power had begun.

[38] Ibid.
[39] Dodd to Roosevelt, April 1, 1936, ibid., 278.
[40] A. J. P. Taylor, *Origins of the Second World War* (New York, 1962), 102–03.
[41] Roosevelt to Bullitt, March 16, 1936, Nixon, *Roosevelt and Foreign Affairs*, III, 258.
[42] For these developments see Lester Brune, *Chronological History of United States Foreign Relations 1776 to January 20, 1981* (New York, 1985), II, 723.

Meanwhile, Communist parties entered elections in France and Spain, winning support for the radical Popular Front, sworn enemies of Fascism and Nazism. German and Italian leaders viewed these political forces, presumably directed from Moscow, as dangerous. In July 1936, days after the rebellion began, Fascist Italy and Nazi Germany entered the fray by supplying Franco's forces. In supporting the rebellion, Hitler had two objectives: first, to prevent a Bolshevik state from securing a land bridge between France and Africa; second, to create in Spain a faithful ally, not aligned with Britain or France. Spain, moreover, would be a source of raw materials in any future struggle.[43]

Spanish officials turned to France for arms and munitions. After initially supporting Spain's ruling government, France backed away when Eden warned Leon Blum, the French Premier, that if France entered a war against Germany over the Spanish issue, Britain would offer no support.[44] Although Eden issued the warning, it reflected the views of Chamberlain, then Chancellor of the Exchequer, who contended that Britain was not prepared militarily or financially to enter the Spanish conflict.

Under the 1935 Franco-Soviet Pact, Moscow owed some support to France, and, with it, a commitment to the Spanish government – to which its sympathies naturally flowed. The French retreat left the USSR the sole defender of the Spanish regime. Moscow's full commitment to the Spanish cause came on August 3, 1936, with a public demonstration in Moscow's Red Square. As Germany and Italy poured men, weapons, and aircraft into the fight, the USSR now met the challenge head-on with shipments of soldiers and equipment. The Spanish government relied on the Soviets for its survival, as the war became more violent, with German aircraft raining death and destruction on Spanish targets.

What troubled an observant world was the magnitude of the external, largely ideological involvement in the Spanish conflict. There were both political and ideological elements in the Spanish Civil War, but the larger issue that troubled Europe was the possible emergence of a continental power revolution. Surely, with their involvement, the German and Italian governments presumed that they were in the first stages of a contest for dominant influence in Europe. The troubled Soviet government agreed with that assessment. Here was the dress rehearsal for the large-scale international drama unfolding in Europe. Herman Goering acknowledged this when he urged Hitler to respond quickly to the Spanish challenge, thereby testing the German army and its equipment in combat, steeling them for the next phase of German expansion.[45] The U.S. ambassador in Spain was the historian-turned-diplomat, Claude Bowers. He was not far off target when he judged: "World War II started in Spain in 1936."[46]

[43] Burnett Bolloten, *The Spanish Civil War: Revolution and Counter Revolution* (Chapel Hill, 1991) 97–98.
[44] Brune, *Chronological History of American Foreign Relations*, 723.
[45] Bolloten, *The Spanish Civil War*, 97–98.
[46] Claude Bowers, *My Mission to Spain: Watching the Rehearsal for World War II* (New York, 1954), vi.

What troubled Britain was less the prospect of a Nazi–Fascist victory in Spain than the countering presence of Soviet power. Chamberlain opposed any dealing with the Russians in Spain. His fear of a Soviet victory governed the views of most of his supporters in the Foreign Office, the Conservative Party, and the military. Baldwin advised Secretary Eden that "on no account … must [we be brought] to fight on the side of the Russians." Sir Samuel Hoare agreed. In a minute to the Cabinet on August 5, 1936, he wrote that Britain must do nothing "to bolster up Communism in Spain, particularly when it is remembered that Communism in Portugal … would be a grave danger to the British Empire." In the same vein, Sir Maurice Hankey, who presided over the operations of the Cabinet and Imperial Defense, issued a warning on July 20. "In the present state in Europe with France and Spain menaced by Bolshevism," he wrote, "it is not inconceivable that before long it might pay us to throw in our lot with Germany and Italy, and the greater our detachment [from aid to the loyalists] the better."[47] Many in high positions in the British government and ruling circles viewed Hitler as Europe's ultimate bulwark against the Russian Bolsheviks.

Fears of a Russian menace guided official French reactions to the Spanish Civil War as well. As in Britain, French fears did not invoke any military involvement. A general war, French Foreign Minister Georges Bonnet explained to the German ambassador, Count von Welczeck, would merely render the conflict more destructive and unleash Communism across the globe. Minister of Justice Paul Reynaud repeated that warning. Premier Daladier reminded the German count that, given the modern equipment that would be used in a general war, there would be an "utter destruction of European civilization." Cossack and Mongol hordes would pour forth into the breach. "This," he concluded, "must be prevented even if it entailed great sacrifices." Later, Daladier repeated the warning, predicting that in the event of war, the Soviets would bring forth world revolution.[48] German officials sustained this illusion. The German military attaché in Paris warned General Gamelin, chief of the French general staff, predicting how a European war would end: "[W]hen Germany and France are exhausted Russia, which will have bided her time, will intervene and that will mean world revolution."[49]

Both Britain and France overwhelmingly favored a policy of neutrality toward the Spanish conflict, and thus sustained a remarkable consensus on matters of policy. But not all shared the conservative fears of the Soviet Union. For them, it mattered little who triumphed. In supporting the policies of Britain and France, Churchill advocated the strictest neutrality, with the hope that others would do the same.[50] Spain could pay the price of its own failures. This policy of inaction the French willingly followed. The Spanish

---

[47] These quotations are from Bolloten, *The Spanish Civil War*, 175.
[48] Ibid., 171–72.
[49] Ibid., 172.
[50] Churchill, *Step by Step, 1936–1939*, XVIII, 50–53.

war became another of those episodes along the road to a wider European war where Anglo-French action, supported by the USSR, might have cut a swath through the totalitarian war machine.

Neither Britain nor France considered this course of action. For some, the more appealing solution lay in forming an alliance with the Soviets and turning the power of Germany eastward. Nothing less than such an alliance would keep Germany "in a wholesome state of apprehension."[51] But British and French leaders in command thought otherwise. They refused to confront Germany in Spain and thereby defend their country's interests in the Mediterranean, including France's southern borders. Elsewhere in Western Europe, they would seek peace by appeasing Germany in the East, using Berlin as a countervailing force against the Soviet Union.[52] Such ambitions, requiring German and Soviet compliance, expected too much from their limited power and influence. Meanwhile, the end in Spain was the triumph of the Fascist forces.

VII

Franco's bid for control of Spain divided the American people by challenging both their ideals and their isolationist sentiments. Many liberals sympathized with the Madrid government; several thousand fought for the Loyalists as members of the Abraham Lincoln Brigade. But within the United States were Catholics and conservatives who judged the Spanish Civil War in religious rather than political terms. For them, Franco represented not totalitarianism, but property, stability, and the Church. In the American press, both sides received support. The most vehemently pro-Franco news came from the Hearst newspapers, which branded the Madrid government as "Red" and recounted real and imagined atrocities, while failing to mention such actions on the other side.

Most newspapers supported the Loyalists because they represented democracy and a duly elected government, while magazines tended to support Franco, reflecting the editorial opinions of their owners. Most Catholics supported the government forces, and therefore stood in opposition to the Catholic hierarchy, which supported the rebels. Most Americans surveyed by public policy pollsters did not care who won. A Gallup poll of January 11, 1937, placed 66 percent in that category.[53] Ironically, some who advanced and supported neutrality most vehemently advocated intervention, whereas others who had opposed neutrality favored its strict implementation. William E. Borah and Gerald P. Nye requested suspension of the neutrality rules, while Cordell Hull asked for their vigorous enforcement.[54] The President resisted

---

[51] Bolloten, *The Spanish Civil War*, 94.
[52] Ibid., 184.
[53] Hadley Cantril, ed., *Public Opinion* (Princeton, 1951), passim.
[54] Bolloten, *The Spanish Civil War*, 178.

the pressures from Borah and Nye on grounds that the very Neutrality Acts they favored required the United States to maintain a policy of abstention from the Spanish Civil War.

Roosevelt recognized the belligerent status of the contending forces and invoked a moral embargo on military shipments to both sides in the Civil War. When the Spanish ambassador in Washington complained of German interference, Secretary Hull reminded him that the United States had pursued an independent course with respect to the Spanish Civil War, and would continue to do so. The nation, he said, "is interested in keeping out of war and incidental to this is interested in peace everywhere; that in accordance with this attitude I have made it a practice up to this hour of preaching peace generally in every part of the world...." When American exporters demanded the right to ship arms to the Loyalists, Congress underwrote official U.S. neutrality by extending the Neutrality Act to include the Spanish Civil War.

Pressures for U.S. involvement in the Spanish Civil War prompted Congress to perfect its neutrality program. Previous measures had avoided the issue of non-contraband trade in time of war – a highly profitable trade that U.S. shippers hoped to maintain – despite its obvious defiance of American neutrality. Roosevelt favored a more flexible embargo program that would permit him to distinguish between aggressors and their victims. The Neutrality Act of May 1937, partially mandatory and partially discriminatory, gave the President greater freedom in determining the outflow of American goods to belligerents. The established prohibitions on the export of arms, ammunition, or implements of war to any belligerent, as well as the purchase, sale, or exchange of bonds and other securities of any nation named in a presidential proclamation of neutrality, still held. But the prohibitions against the solicitation of funds in the United States did not apply to medical aid, food, or clothing to relieve human suffering when the soliciting agent was not itself a belligerent. The 1937 law renewed the ban on American trade in belligerent passenger and merchant vessels. The President could, at his discretion, remove belligerent submarines and armed merchant vessels from the ports or territorial waters of the United States. Finally, the new act embodied the right of discretion toward belligerents by permitting the sale of non-military goods, including vital raw materials, to nations at war (ostensibly the Western democracies) on a cash-and-carry arrangement. Congress had apparently discovered a formula that would guarantee both commercial profits and the avoidance of war. At the same time, Congress refused to waive any of the rights and privileges of the United States. The nation would have peace, and solely on its own terms.[55]

Congress had warned Britain and France that, whatever the circumstances of any crisis, they could anticipate little military aid from the United States. At the same time, the neutrality policy rendered the nation's interests in the status quo increasingly vulnerable to the aggressiveness of the totalitarian powers. But in Spain, official neutrality permitted the United States to escape

---

[55] Fite and Graebner, *Recent United States History*, 382–83.

responsibility for what occurred. There, German and Italian air, land, and naval forces continued to support Franco with ever-greater effectiveness. Finally, in March 1939, Franco entered Madrid in triumph to end the long and destructive Spanish Civil War.

VIII

U.S. neutrality policy in the Spanish Civil War defied the broad tradition of permitting aid to a country under attack. For good reason, however, Roosevelt accepted the limits that isolationism placed on national behavior. Avoiding the minority pressures that favored American involvement in the Spanish war, Roosevelt recognized the overwhelming opposition among the multitudes that supported his administration. He understood also that U.S. arms shipments would mean little in the face of the active participation of German and Italian forces, aided by the military equipment that flowed through the leaky quarantine along the French border. Russian aid was less helpful and harder to place with necessary effectiveness on the Spanish battle front. Russia alone could not defeat the Nazi–Fascist coalition.

Hitler's objectives in the Spanish conflict were best described by American foreign correspondent William L. Shirer, who noted graphically what Hitler's plans entailed. The German Chancellor wished, from the outset, to draw Mussolini into an alliance. In the end, the Spanish war cemented the German-Italian relationship. On November 7, 1937, Hitler told his generals and members of his foreign office: "A hundred per cent victory for Franco is not desirable from the German point of view. Rather we are interested in a continuance of the war and in keeping up the tension in the Mediterranean."[56] Hitler's plan succeeded. Not only was Mussolini separated from any deal with the British and French, but instead was pulled into the Rome–Berlin Axis. He signed the Anti-Comintern Pact with Germany and Japan on November 26, 1937. Thereafter, Mussolini was committed to his new allies for the long haul.

It had long been clear that Germany was determined to contest the Versailles territorial provisions for Austria, Czechoslovakia, Poland, and even the Soviet Union. These German territorial ambitions, now amply supported by Europe's predominant military structure, permitted the Versailles victors two choices – either to challenge Germany's military expansion or come to terms with Berlin on territorial issues. If the German demands on the Versailles structure were diplomatically, even morally, unacceptable, they were, nevertheless, real and inescapable.

---

[56] Quoted in Shirer, *The Rise and Fall of the Third Reich*, 297.

8

The Elusive Response

I

By 1937, Adolf Hitler's challenge to Europe had become overt and threatening. Through two years of unrestrained defiance of the Versailles Treaty's military provisions, German rearmament had become the dominant factor in European politics. Why Germany's military effort had emerged as a special danger to Europe's security, American diplomat Hugh R. Wilson explained from Switzerland. "The ability of a dictator to devote practically the entire resources of his country to armament," he wrote, "cannot be matched by democratic countries in time of peace." From Berlin, Ambassador William E. Dodd warned Washington that "the development of the [German] army and the recent throwing off of restraints of these past 17 years have brought matters back to a place where Germany is even more dangerous to the world than in 1914."[1] In his diary notation of April 20, 1937, foreign correspondent William L. Shirer recorded Europe's declining confidence:

> Hitler's birthday. He gets more and more like a Caesar. Today a public holiday ... and a great military parade. The Reichswehr revealed a little of what it has: heavy artillery, tanks, and magnificently trained men. Hitler stood on the reviewing stand in front of the Technishe Hochschule, as happy as a child with tin soldiers, standing there more than two hours and saluting every tank and gun. The military attachés of France, Britain, and Russia, I hear, were impressed. So were ours.

On May 1937, French Premier Leon Blum acknowledged to U.S. Ambassador William C. Bullitt that "Hitler had the political initiative on the continent of Europe...."[2]

On January 30, 1937, Hitler reminded the Reichstag that he had assumed responsibility for restoring German honor and prestige by bringing the

[1] Wilson to Hull, January 27, 1936, Dodd to Hull, February 6, 1936, *FRUS, 1936,* I (Washington, 1953), 186, 195.
[2] Shirer, *Berlin Diary*, 63. Bullitt to Hull, May 20, 1937, *FRUS 1937,* I (Washington, 1954), 94.

Versailles humiliation to a close. "Above all," he continued, "I solely with-drew the German signature from that declaration which was extracted under duress from a weak government, acting against its better judgment, namely the declaration that Germany was responsible for the war." He asserted that the boldest task he ever faced, and the most difficult, was "the restoration of universal military service, the creation of a new air force, the reconstruc-tion of the German navy, and the reoccupation of the Rhineland...." This he did without negotiation with the former victors, because national honor, he asserted could not be bartered away. "It can only be taken away. And if it cannot be bartered away it cannot be restored through barter; it must simply be taken back." He had not consulted Germany's former enemies or informed them of his actions, he concluded, because it would be easier for them to accept a fait accompli, which they would need to accept in any case.[3]

Hitler's ambitions were no secret. German officials acknowledged freely the intention of the Reich not only to dominate Central and Eastern Europe, but also to secure the return of Germany's pre-war colonies (or their equivalent). No longer, they added, would Germany condone the vindictive clauses of the Versailles Treaty. Nazi aggressiveness had a quality of its own. Internally, Hitler, divorced from the German past, operated in a moral void, accepting no limits on his determination to dismantle the German state machine and substitute organized chaos, with himself in absolute command. Still, Hitler's external challenge was not unlike those posed by ambitious rulers of neigh-boring states in previous generations. Essentially, he gave Europe the choice of accepting massive changes in its treaty structure, or face the probability of war. For the United States, as well as for Europe, the threatened destruction of the Versailles order carried a heavy penalty, presaging the decline of Britain and France as great powers, with the consequences damaging to Western security. Beyond the decline of Western supremacy lay the predictable conflict between Germany and Russia – the ultimate issue in Europe's faltering stabil-ity. How the European balance of power could survive that clash was nowhere apparent. Nor was it clear how the creators of Versailles intended to protect their world from such a disaster.

II

This impending collapse of the Versailles order troubled Washington without creating the foundation of an adequate American response. What separated Americans and Europeans alike in their reaction to the Nazi challenge was not their desire to avoid war, but their varying perceptions of the price and proce-dures to achieve such avoidance. Many American isolationists, in their deter-mination to sustain the peace, presumed that its continuance would exact its demands in diminished trade and some revision of the Versailles order. For them, the Paris Peace Conference had imposed unfair restriction on Germany;

[3] Baynes, *The Speeches of Adolf Hitler, II*, 1335–36.

the democracies, therefore, could serve their interests more effectively through treaty revision than through sanctions against Germany, which would save neither the treaty nor the peace.

For such leading isolationists as William E. Borah, revisionism was a necessary and responsible policy to confront the burgeoning dangers of German expansionism. Isolationist Senator Gerald P. Nye insisted that the American people would not "consciously endorse a war which had no other object than to maintain the particular status quo which was established at Versailles." Similarly, the *Alexandria* (Virginia) *Gazette* argued that the Fascist nations making trouble in Europe would not remain at peace unless they had better access to new territory and raw materials.[4] Although convinced that the United States was safe from European attack, isolationists after 1935 voted overwhelmingly for military appropriations in their desire to strengthen the country's hemispheric defenses. Such preparedness would keep order in the Western Hemisphere. There, the republic could flourish regardless of what happened in the outside world – while it paid some diplomatic and economic price for peace.

Internationalists, who dominated the Roosevelt administration, along with many isolationists, did not regard every territorial arrangement embodied in the Versailles Treaty as sacred, or even just. In practice, however, they rejected treaty revision as an acceptable guide for national policy. The admittedly arbitrary boundaries defined the international legal structure; any effort to alter them by force would produce legitimate resistance and thereby endanger the peace. Sharing the Wilsonian presumption that the breakdown of the peace anywhere threatened the peace everywhere, internationalists contended that U.S. peace and security required the rejection of every diplomatic or armed assault on the Versailles treaty structure. They discovered the means to uphold the status quo in international law and the principles of peaceful change and self-determination – the moral bulwarks of the established order. As operating forces in international life, these constraints eliminated the legitimacy, even the necessity, of any diplomatic accommodation of aggression.

Roosevelt and his Secretary of State, Cordell Hull, required a formula that would convey the administration's deep concern for international stability, even while it permitted the United States to escape all responsibility for its preservation. The occasion for its formulation came suddenly on July 7, 1937, when Japanese troops on maneuvers near the Marco Polo Bridge outside Peking, exchanged shots with Chinese forces stationed in the vicinity.

Ambassador Joseph C. Grew reported from Tokyo that "no one seemed to know who started the trouble," but Japanese officials seized on the clash to unleash a full-scale invasion of China. The absence of U.S. interests in China

---

[4] Wayne S. Cole, *Senator Gerald P. Nye and American Foreign Relations* (Minneapolis, 1962), 164, 168–69; Manfred Jonas, *Isolationism in America, 1935–1941* (Ithaca, 1966), 107–08; *Alexandria* (Virginia) *Gazette*, October 14, 1937, 4. The neutrality legislation after 1935 assumed that the United States, to avoid war, would pay a heavy price in lost commerce.

whose defense merited war compelled Washington either to dismiss the issue or try to save China without direct assistance or costly sanctions. Its formal response consisted of a reassertion of U.S. principles on non-recognition and peaceful change, fully promulgated in the Manchurian crisis of 1931–1932.

On July 16, 1937, Secretary Hull released a statement to the press that reaffirmed the sanctity of the international treaty structure and the country's uncompromising devotion to it. Asserting that serious hostilities anywhere affected the rights, obligations, and concerns of the United States, Hull continued:

> This country constantly and consistently advocated maintenance of peace. We advocate national and international self-restraint. We advocate abstinence by all nations from the use of force in pursuit of policy and from interference in the internal affairs of other nations. We advocate adjustment of problems in international relations, by processes of peaceful negotiation and agreements. Upholding the principle of the sanctity of treaties, we believe in modification of provisions of treaties, when need therefore arises, by orderly processes carried out in a spirit of mutual helpfulness and accommodation.[5]

These principles reduced the area of legitimate change in the international treaty structure almost to the vanishing point. The statement addressed the burgeoning crisis in China, but its application was global. The State Department's political adviser on Far Eastern affairs, Stanley K. Hornbeck, commented that Hull's program embodied "a comprehensible statement of the fundamental principles" of U.S. foreign policy.[6] On August 23, the State Department formally acknowledged that the July 16 statement was directed primarily at the immediate events in China.[7]

Much of the world that favored the status quo lauded Hull's principles. Predictably, the Chinese replied that they had "always sought to settle international controversies by any of the pacific means known in international law and treaties." Still, they were not impressed; they wanted more. Dr. C. T. Wang, the Chinese ambassador acknowledged on August 20 the validity of the principles, but what China required, he argued, was action. Three days later, Chinese President Chiang Kai-shek criticized the Roosevelt administration for its refusal to take a firm stand in the Far East. "I do not want the United States to be dragged into the war," he admitted, "but I do look to her to maintain her position in the Pacific and to maintain the peace there."[8] Hull responded with a reassertion of established U.S. policy: "From the beginning of the present controversy in the Far East we have been urging on both the

---

[5] Hull, *Memoirs*, I, 535–36; Cordell Hull, *Principles of International Policy* (Washington, 1937), contains a full statement of his principles and the international responses to them.
[6] Stanley K. Hornbeck, *The United States and the Far East* (Boston, 1942), 36.
[7] *FRUS: Japan, 1931–1941* (Washington, 1943), 356.
[8] Ambassador Nelson T. Johnson to Hull, August 23, 1937, *FRUS: The Far East, 1937* (Washington, 1954), III, 460–61.

Chinese and the Japanese governments the importance of refraining from hostilities and of maintaining the peace."[9]

Japanese comments on Hull's statement of U.S. principles were generally approving, but with the added notation that the principles could succeed only "by full recognition and practical consideration of the actual particular circumstances of that region." Hull complained that Japan was prepared to acknowledge U.S. principles only after it possessed all it wanted in the Orient.[10] On September 2, Hull instructed Ambassador Grew in Tokyo to impress upon Japanese officials the importance that the United States government attached to his July 16 and August 23 statements. Grew regarded Hull's July 16 statement as wise in that it did not brand Japan as an aggressor, which he doubted would have any effect.[11]

Portugal's response to Hull's principles reflected the view of the skeptics. It asserted that effective policy demanded some direct confrontation with the current troubles in China, requiring the passage "from the field of intention into that of action, or, more concretely what is to be done so that events ... will not contradict the good intentions." Moral pressure alone, the Portuguese warned, would "produce rather limited practical action."[12] Still, Hull never compromised his reliance on peaceful change, repeating that principle in his advice to Norman Davis, who headed the U.S. delegation to the Brussels Far Eastern Conference of October 1937, called by the League of Nations. "The essential first step in building for peace," wrote Hull, " is development of an understanding and awareness ... of the vital importance of the principles indispensable to normal international relationships." That month, Hull assured the Soviet ambassador in Washington that effective resistance to aggression required not military force or economic coercion but "a combination of all possible moral and other influences to outlaw war."[13]

How appeals to international law and the precepts of the Kellogg Peace Pact, which avoided both commitments and risk, could be effective in curtailing aggression was not clear. In the past, non-recognition and the enunciation of principles had served only as devices to escape responsibility for what occurred. Roosevelt's occasional references in private to sanctions, blockades, international cooperation, and the need for relaxation of the neutrality laws suggested that he doubted the power of principles to command world affairs. Publicly, however, the President never acknowledged the essential roles of power and diplomacy in dealing with the unstable and resistant international order. His refusal to confront the dictators with choices that defined U.S. interests reflected in part his acceptance of the internationalist creed, in part, his conviction that he would lose an open political battle with the isolationists.

[9] Fite and Graebner, *Recent United States History*, 387.
[10] Hull, *Fundamental Principles*, 34; Hull, *Memoirs*, I, 536.
[11] Joseph C. Grew, *Ten Years in Japan* (New York, 1944), 212.
[12] Hull, *Fundamental Principles*, 46.
[13] Hull, *Memoirs*, I, 659–60.

Skilled politician that he was, Roosevelt would balance what was desirable with what was practicable.

III

Great Britain was scarcely better prepared, physically or emotionally, to respond decisively to Hitler's challenge. Britain, no less than France, had long ceased to be a first-class military power. Pacifist sentiment, fed by memories of the Great War and the assumption that peace was secure, had undermined Britain's capacity for war. So weak had Britain and France become that not even the military clauses of the Versailles Treaty possessed any value as a bargaining counter.[14] Germany's reoccupation of the Rhineland destroyed what remained of the Allied strategic gains from the recent war. Nevertheless, Hitler faced in Britain a highly vocal opposition determined to limit, if not eliminate, any further German assaults on the Versailles settlement. Among Hitler's leading critics in the British government were Robert Vansittart, Permanent Under Secretary of the Foreign Office, Duncan Sandys, former member of the Foreign Service, Cabinet member Duff Cooper, and Foreign Secretary Anthony Eden. But the anti-German leadership in London fell to Winston Churchill, a Member of Parliament, but outside the Cabinet. For this group, the German defiance of the military clauses of the Versailles Treaty represented more than a potentially dangerous shift in the European balance of power; it exhibited a totally unacceptable triumph for unilateralism and a philosophy of force. Such behavior suggested that Germany had moved beyond international control, that any concessions would merely fuel additional demands. Backed by assumptions of power and prestige commensurate with Britain's imperial tradition, Churchill and others had no doubt about Britain's capacity to preserve its primacy in European and world affairs, as well as its self-assigned role as arbiter of the international order.

What troubled British officials in 1937 was the knowledge that Hitler's ambitions now included the Versailles Treaty's territorial arrangements for Central Europe, including Austria, Czechoslovakia's Sudetenland, Danzig, and Memel. Throughout the summer and autumn of 1937, British diplomats reminded London of the possibility of immediate German aggression against Austria and Czechoslovakia.[15] Eden thought Britain might be able to come to terms with Germany on the issues of Central Europe, but only under the condition that German expansionism be limited to peaceful procedures. Vansittart

[14] On British weakness, see Vansittart, *The Mist Procession*, 40; Viscount Templewood, *Nine Troubled Years* (London, 1954), 144; Lord Halifax, *Fullness of Days* (New York, 1957), 182–83.

[15] Examples of the British recognition of the German threat to Central and Southeast Europe: report of the Cabinet's Committee on Germany, February 1936, II 2/2, Vansittart Papers, Roskill Library, Churchill College, Cambridge; Eden's memorandum on Spain, January 8, 1937, *DBFP, Second Series*, XVIII (London, 1980), 38; Cadogan to Henderson, July 8, 1937, ibid., XIX (London, 1982), 47; Selby to Eden, July 13, 1937, ibid., 57.

explained why Britain dared not negotiate any agreement with Germany at the expense of others. "You may not be able," he noted, "to prevent the destruction of liberties or independence (Abyssinia). That is different from conniving in their destruction. If we try anything of that kind we will soon be made to appreciate the difference."[16] Changes emanating from force would challenge British security no less than British principles because, as Churchill warned his constituents in Chingford, a Germany unrestricted by peaceful methods would eventually overrun all Eastern and Southeastern Europe. Were Britain to tell Germany it could have what it wanted in the East, Harold Nicolson argued, that country, within a single year, "would become dominant from Hamburg to the Black Sea, and we should be faced by a confederacy such as had never been seen since Napoleon."[17]

Britain's capacity to sustain the Versailles settlement for Central Europe required far more power than the country possessed. For Churchill, Hitler's successful violation of the Rhineland was evidence enough of British weakness. "Five years ago," he declared, "all felt safe; five years ago we were all looking forward to peace, to a period in which mankind would rejoice in the treasures which science can spread to all classes if conditions of peace and justice prevail.... Look at the difference in our position now! We find ourselves compelled once again to face the hateful problems and ordeals which those of us who worked and toiled in the last struggle hoped were gone forever."[18]

For Churchill, Britain had never been so vulnerable. The country's very survival as a great power depended on its willingness to embark on a major rearmament program. After 1934, Churchill had responded to Germany's military expansion with a preparedness crusade of his own. Despite his perennial appeals to British greatness and tradition, his impact on British rearmament remained elusive. Britain lacked not only the industrial capacity and financial resources, but also the political will, to match Germany's military program.[19] For Churchill, an anti-German coalition could still terminate the drift

[16] Vansittart's marginal comment on Minute by O'Malley on Anglo-Italian Relations, June 2, 1937, *DBFP*, Second Series, XVIII, 838.

[17] Churchill's speech at Chingford, October 19, 1936, Martin Gilbert, ed., *Winston S. Churchill, V, Companion to the Coming of the War, 1936–1939* (Boston, 1983), 373n; Nicolson diary July 16, 1936, ibid., 243.

[18] Quoted in William Manchester, *The Last Lion: Winston Spencer Churchill, Alone 1932–1940* (Boston, 1988), 189. Many shared Churchill's conclusion that the world had entered a new age of force. For a long, excellent analysis of the change resulting from the breakdown of Versailles, see Eric Phipps, ambassador to Berlin, to the Foreign Office, November 6, 1935, 7/6, Phipps Papers, Roskill Library, Churchill College, Cambridge. United States Minister to Ireland John Cudahy observed: "When Hitler invaded the Rhineland it was clear to all that the treaty system had been replaced by force and show of force in diplomacy...." Cudahy to Roosevelt, March 1, 1938, PSF: Ireland, TS, *FDRL*.

[19] Churchill's crusade for a stronger British defense dominated his speeches in Parliament and his newspaper columns throughout the years from 1934 to 1937. See his volume of speeches, *While England Slept: A Survey of World Affairs, 1932–1938* (New York, 1938), and his collection of newspaper articles, *Step by Step, 1936–1939* (London, 1975). See also Churchill, *The Gathering Storm* (Boston, 1948), 147–64.

toward war. "But there must be," he advised, "Concert and Design guided by far-sighted unselfishness and sustained by inexorable resolve. This is no task for France; no task for Britain; no task for the Locarno Powers or any group of powers; no task for small Powers nor for the great; it is a task for all." For Sir Norman Angell, an effective deterrent required no less than a firm Anglo-French alliance, backed by the Soviet Union.[20] An effective system of collective security necessitated, above all, a general consensus regarding the nature and immediacy of the danger. That consensus did not exist in Great Britain.

IV

Most British citizens and members of Parliament did not share the conviction that Britain faced external dangers requiring heavy military expenditures and a posture of toughness. "They believe, as they always do," Duff Cooper complained, "that war is a fearful catastrophe that must be avoided at all cost."[21] Countless Englishmen detected the real threat to peace not in German militarism but in the unfairness of the Versailles Treaty. Sir Norman Angell warned as early as 1933 that it was "now almost everywhere admitted that there can be no peace until [the treaty] is revised." In November 1934, Earl Winterton informed the House of Commons that "what is standing between Europe and peace are the conditions which are laid out [at Versailles]." Lord Lothian reminded his readers in the *Manchester Guardian* that National Socialism triumphed in Germany because Germany's neighbors failed to negotiate revisions in the post-war treaties.[22] For some British observers, the Rhineland clauses were the ultimate monument to blind statecraft. Lord Allen of Hurtwood phrased such convictions thus: "If we are ever to be in a position to protect the peace of the world, we must first of all be just to Germany." Sir Nevile Henderson confided to Lord Lothian in May 1937 that, to his mind, "the British empire is something infinitely too valuable to be risked for principles, which are not yet based on real justice. Amend first the injustices ... in the Versailles Treaty."[23]

Churchill explained why British revisionism would have no place in Anglo-German relations. Earlier he had urged revision of the Versailles Treaty, but only "in a calm atmosphere and while the victor nations still have ample supremacy...."[24] For him, treaty revision was acceptable only so long as Britain

[20] Churchill, *Step by Step*, 18–19; Churchill, *While England Slept*, 255; Churchill to Viscount Cecil of Chelwood, April 9, 1936, Martin Gilbert, ed., *Winston S. Churchill*, V, 94; Angell to Churchill, March 15, 1937, ibid., 620; Anthony Eden, *Facing the Dictators* (Boston, 1962), 211, 377.
[21] Duff Cooper, *Old Men Forget* (New York, 1954), 204.
[22] Angell quoted in Herman Lutz, *German-French Unity: Basis for European Peace* (Chicago, 1957), 81; Winterton and Lothian quoted in Martin Gilbert, ed., *Britain and Germany between the Wars* (London, 1964), 16–17.
[23] Lord Allen of Hurtwood quoted in Christopher Thorne, *The Approach of War, 1938–1939* (London, 1968), 12; Gilbert, *Britain and Germany*, 17.
[24] Manchester, *The Last Lion*, 62.

could govern the results. Benito Mussolini's subsequent aggression against Abyssinia in October 1935 troubled Churchill, not because it touched any vital British interests but because Mussolini used force. "We don't need to worry about the Italians," he assured American journalist Vincent Sheean. "It isn't the thing. It's the kind of thing." Churchill acknowledged that Britain had often profited from the use of force in building its empire. But, he assured Sheean, "that belongs to the unregenerated past.... The world progresses. We have endeavoured, by means of the League of Nations and the whole fabric of international law, to make it impossible for nations to infringe upon each other's rights."[25]

If Hitler and Mussolini were permitted to attack the whole established treaty structure, Churchill warned, the results would be incalculable. "All the nations of Europe," he wrote, "will just be driven helter-skelter across the diplomatic chessboard until the limits of retreat are exhausted, and then out of desperation ... the explosion of war will take place."[26] The time for revision had vanished because England could no longer assure the settlement of grievances through peaceful means alone.

From Berlin, British diplomats warned the London government that its attitudes were rapidly placing Britain and Germany on a collision course. German officials complained that there were no German aspirations, however legitimate, that Britain did not oppose. "Cannot Messrs. Baldwin, Eden, Neville Chamberlain, and Churchill," Ambassador Sir Eric Phipps asked in March 1937, "see that Germany is just keen to maintain her bloc in Central Europe as England her far-flung territories? ... [I]f England cannot, or will not, see this, an Anglo-German understanding is difficult and indeed impossible to attain."[27] British policy, wrote Phipps,

> bars the way to Germany in every direction. Germany's colonial demands are passed over... ; in the South-East the Anschluss with Austria has been consistently opposed, whilst in the East, where no British interest is involved, Great Britain declines to give Germany a free hand or even to join the anticommunist crusade. The same dog-in-the-manger policy is adopted in the case of Memel and Danzig. Wherever Germany attempts to recover what is hers or to extend her influence she is met with suspicion and covert or open opposition.[28]

If Britain, warned Phipps, continued to interfere in German affairs as "a kind of self-constituted League of Nations, or super-nation ... [or] go on butting

---

[25] Martin Gilbert, *Winston S. Churchill* (London, 1976), V, 666.
[26] Churchill, *While England Slept*, 313.
[27] Phipps to Eden, March 16, 1937, *DBFP*, Second Series, XVIII, 443. Malcolm Grahame Christie, a British confidante of Vansittart's residing in Germany, discovered the same pattern in German thought in a long interview with Herman Goering on February 3, 1937, 1/5 Christie Papers, Roskill Library, Churchill College, Cambridge.
[28] Phipps to Eden, April 13, 1937, *DBFP*, Second Series, XVIII, 619; Phipps to Eden, April 13, 1937, 1/18, Phipps Papers.

in as we did in Memel, Danzig and elsewhere, ... it will lead inevitably to a revulsion of German public opinion...."[29]

Lord Lothian shared such views. After a stormy session with German air force commander Herman Goering on May 4, 1937, he concluded that Berlin now regarded Britain as the enemy. Then, on May 10, Sir Nevile Henderson, Britain's newly appointed ambassador to Berlin, recorded his opposition to London's uncompromising posture toward Germany. Did that country, he asked, have no right to an Eastern policy? There would be a clash, he predicted, "if Europe as constituted under the Treaty of Versailles is regarded as sacrosanct.... Much of the Treaty has already been swept away but many seeds for future wars remain unless it is modified by peaceful negotiation...."[30]

Henderson observed that the Versailles settlement, unless revised, would not "exist a day longer than Germany can afford to wait.... [S]he will not only tear up any part which offends her but secure similar benefits to the smaller ex-enemy Powers who suffer under it, thus securing their goodwill and gratitude at our expense."[31]

Britain's policy of toughness, based on the anticipation of mounting trouble, appeared self-fulfilling. For that reason, Goering's repeated accusations that everywhere Britain stood in Germany's path disturbed the British government. Eden instructed Henderson to press Goering for an enumeration of Germany's grievances toward Britain. "[W]hat the Germans take for obstruction," Henderson reported, "is our insistence on peace and peaceful evolution."[32]

For Vansittart, the German government had no right to speak of grievances before it had defined its objectives everywhere and explained precisely by what methods the allegedly hostile country was preventing the attainment of any particular objective. The Foreign Office, still troubled by Goering's charges, informed the German government that Britain, as a member of the League of Nations, could not ignore any forceful disturbance of the status quo. For that reason, it would not condone any change in the status of Austria if achieved by force against the will of its inhabitants. Britain favored a Sudeten settlement that was consistent with Czech sovereignty.[33] Certainly Goering could not regard such solutions as unreasonable. Goering responded simply that

---

[29] Phipps to Sir Orme Sargent, February 24, 1937, *DBFP*, Second Series, XVIII, 300.

[30] Lothian's meeting with Goering on May 4, reported in Henderson to Vansittart, May 10, 1937, ibid., 727–28; Christie's report on Lothian's meeting with Goering, 1/21A Christie Papers; Lothian to Halifax, May 11, 1937, A4.40.3.1, Halifax Papers, Roskill Library, Churchill College, Cambridge; Henderson's memorandum on British policy toward Germany, May 10, 1937, A4.410. 3.3, Halifax Papers. William C. Bullitt, United States Ambassador to France, agreed with Phipps, Lothian, and Henderson that the Versailles Treaty was at the root of Europe's troubles. Bullitt to Roosevelt, January 10, 1937, PSF: France: Bullitt: TS, *FDRL*.

[31] Henderson's memorandum on British policy toward Germany, May 10, 1937, *DBFP*, Second Series, XIX, 104.

[32] Henderson to Eden, June 8, 1937, ibid., XVIII, 870.

[33] Vansittart's comment on Henderson's dispatch of June 8, 1937, ibid., 870; Eden to Henderson, July 15, 1937, ibid., XIX, 68–69.

Britain, in preaching peaceful evolution, really sought to control the future of Central and Eastern Europe, regions vital to Germany's well-being but of little direct interest to Britain.[34] The British debate over revisionism, often incredibly perceptive, failed to underwrite a British-led search for a negotiated redesign of the Versailles Treaty.

V

Nothing in the post-Versailles American experience had prepared Roosevelt or the country to accept the need for either the negotiation of settlements or the preparation for war. Yet, as President, Roosevelt could not ignore Europe's drift toward disaster. As advisors pressed him to act, Roosevelt concluded from time to time that he might display world leadership, without accepting any unwanted commitments, by calling an international conference. Such a conference, conforming to Secretary Hull's emphasis on orderly and peaceful procedures, would search for the principles whereby nations might resolve their differences through mutual agreement. Unfortunately, this reliance on rules of conduct, with its concomitant burden of eliminating Hitler's demands totally without the necessity of war, rendered United States diplomacy irrelevant. Ambassador to Poland John Cudahy advised Roosevelt that a conference would settle nothing. His note to the President, dated January 7, 1937, acknowledged the difficulty of dealing with Hitler when no one could anticipate his actions. He advised Roosevelt that any intervention "without some specific remedy for the difficulties over here would not only be unavailing but would be a mistake from the viewpoint of American prestige.... I do not like to clutter your very much over-cluttered desk with letters," he added, "but I do want to impress upon you the futility of attempting any gesture toward Europe at this time unless this be based upon realistic remedies for the relief of existing troubles."[35] Cudahy concluded that only if Roosevelt were prepared to face Germany's demands directly would the effort achieve anything.

Whatever his limited expectations for European cooperation, Roosevelt refused to discard the conference idea. In January 1937, he suggested to Dodd in Berlin that "if five or six heads of important governments could meet together for a week with complete inaccessibility to press or cables or radio, a definite, useful agreement might result...."[36] Limited to the contemplation of conference proposals, Roosevelt reacted impatiently to assertions that he alone could terminate Europe's difficulties. When Secretary of the Treasury Henry Morgenthau suggested in March that Europe looked to him, Roosevelt retorted, "I feel like throwing either a cup and saucer at you or the coffee pot.

---

[34] Henderson to Eden, July 20, 1937, ibid., 94–95.

[35] Cudahy to Roosevelt, January 7, 1937, Nixon, ed., *Franklin D. Roosevelt and Foreign Affairs*, III, 572–73. See also Cudahy to Roosevelt, December 26, 1936, *FRUS, 1937*, I, 24.

[36] Roosevelt to Dodd, January 9, 1937, Elliott Roosevelt, ed., *FDR: His Personal Letters, 1928–1945* (New York, 1950), III, 649.

Well," he continued, "I had Hull [and] Norman Davis to lunch and Davis said the only person who can save this situation is Roosevelt and then I said to Davis how, and Davis said by sending an envoy to Europe."[37]

Morgenthau, deeply concerned over Europe's drift toward financial bankruptcy, recommended a disarmament conference. Roosevelt advised a meeting of a half dozen countries. "He would tell their delegates," Morgenthau recorded, "that the problem was theirs, and send them to some other building to work out a solution and come back with it." Those who defied the agreements would be faced with an economic boycott. On March 16, Neville Chamberlain, Britain's Chancellor of the Exchequer, argued against such a conference.

Armaments, he reminded Washington, were Europe's only deterrent to German aggression. "No other country," he wrote, "not Italy, since she had her hands full with the task of consolidating her Abyssinian conquest, not Russia with all her military preparations, certainly not France, England, or any of the smaller Powers, is for a moment credited with any aggressive designs." Germany would resist any military arrangements that deflected its aggressive purposes. "The only consideration which would influence her to a contrary decision," Chamberlain concluded, "would be the conviction that the efforts to secure superior force were doomed to failure by reason of the superior force which would meet her if she attempted aggression."[38] But no Versailles power was inclined to build such a force.

European leaders joined the quest for a Rooseveltian peace initiative. The President's dismissive reply came in July 1937 when he told newsmen that people were looking "for somebody outside Europe to come forward with a hat and a rabbit in it. Well," he added, "I haven't got a hat and I haven't got a rabbit in it."[39] What Europeans wanted of Roosevelt was not a call for a world conference, but some positive display of America's intention to support the forces opposed to Hitler. For British and French leaders, living under the immediate threat of German expansionism, the economic and military power of the United States was indeed relevant to Europe's peace and stability. Chamberlain had reminded Morgenthau in May that "the greatest single contribution that the United States could make at the present moment would be the amendment of the existing neutrality legislation.... The legislation in its present form constitutes an indirect but potent encouragement to aggression, and it is earnestly hoped that some way may be found of leaving sufficient discretion with the Executive to deal with each case on its merits."[40]

---

[37] John Morton Blum, *From the Morgenthau Diaries: Years of Crisis, 1928–1938* (Boston, 1959), I, 458.

[38] Ibid., 459, 463–64.

[39] Quoted in Dallek, *Franklin D. Roosevelt and American Foreign Policy, 1932–1945,* 144.

[40] Chamberlain memorandum, May, 1937, *FRUS, 1937,* I, 99. Denying the importance of power, the State Department replied that the United States government "firmly believes that the opportunity exists today for directing national policies into a channel of political and economic cooperation, based upon a common-sense harmonization of national interests and upon a spirit of mutual friendliness and fair-dealing." Ibid., 105–06.

For the moment, Roosevelt avoided that challenge, but in September he toyed with a proposal designed to establish a system of economic sanctions. That month, he informed Secretary of the Interior Harold Ickes of his plan to write to all nations of the world (except possibly Germany, Italy and Japan) suggesting that the peace-loving states isolate any country that threatened the liberties of another by denying it trade and raw materials. This program, the President noted hopefully, "would be a warning to the nations that are today running amuck."[41] Roosevelt was not alone in this private advocacy of economic pressure. Assistant Secretary of State George W. Messersmith, deeply distrustful of the Reich, reminded Hull in October that the United States would either continue the temporizing of the past, which predictably would lead to war, or accept a course that offered some chance of maintaining international order.[42] What this concern for power, whether economic or military, had in common with the administration's fundamental reliance on principle was the assumption that the United States could preserve the status quo without coming to terms with the aggressors. Unfortunately, actions that emphasized power rather than principle would be effective only in direct proportion to their defiance of official American neutrality.

Roosevelt's famed Quarantine Speech, delivered in Chicago on October 5, 1937, inaugurated his halting effort to increase the weight of American influence in world affairs. He warned his listeners that terror and lawlessness were endangering the foundations of their civilization. From such international anarchy and instability, he said, there was "no escape through mere isolation and neutrality." It was essential that the United States lead the world to a "triumph of law and moral principles in order that peace, justice, and confidence may prevail in the world." To achieve this internationalist goal, he proposed a quarantine of the aggressors. "When an epidemic of physical disease starts to spread," he declared, "the community approves and joins in a quarantine of the patients in order to protect the health of the community against the spread of the disease." In his moral defense of the status quo, Roosevelt spoke not of interests to be defended or compromised according to circumstances, but of those principles that, if triumphant, would eliminate all unwanted change from the world. In subsequent conversations with the members of the press, Roosevelt admitted only that he sought some new concept of preserving peace; he did not contemplate, he told Cardinal Mundelein of Chicago, the use of military or naval force against aggressor nations. Foreign newspapers, one correspondent informed Roosevelt, described his speech as "an attitude without a program." The President replied: "It is an attitude and it does not outline a program; it says we are looking for a program."[43]

[41] Harold L. Ickes, *The Secret Diary of Harold L. Ickes: The Inside Struggle, 1936–1939* (London, 1955), II, 213.

[42] Messersmith to Hull, October 11, 1937, *FRUS, 1937*, I, 140–41.

[43] For Roosevelt's efforts to explain the meaning of his Quarantine Speech, see Dorothy Borg, *The United States and the Far Eastern Crisis of 1933–1938* (Cambridge, MA, 1964), 381–86.

On October 6, Under Secretary of State Sumner Welles, convinced that the solution of Europe's problems required the worldwide adoption of a framework of diplomatic principles, suggested that the President call a spectacular White House meeting of all the diplomatic representatives in Washington on Armistice Day, November 11. There he would invite the nations of the world to gather at the conference table and arrive at agreements on principles of international conduct, disarmament, and trade. The President accepted the idea, but Hull, arguing against the proposal as a drastic assault on American isolationist opinion, reminded the President that Germany, Italy, and Japan had already taken the offensive and would disregard any treaties or agreements that an international conference might produce. Moreover, to announce a conference without prior consultation with Britain and France would be unfair and unwise. Early in January 1938, Hull withdrew his opposition to a White House meeting and subsequent conference, but insisted that Roosevelt first consult Neville Chamberlain, Prime Minister of Great Britain since June 1937. Only after securing Chamberlain's approval should Roosevelt turn to France, Germany and Italy.

Roosevelt now agreed to send a revised version of Welles's original proposal to Chamberlain. At the contemplated White House meeting, the President would suggest that all governments strive to reach a unanimous agreement on the essential principles that would govern future international relations. Because inequities existed in the post-war settlements, Roosevelt acknowledged that lasting peace required international adjustments of various kinds aimed at the removal of those injustices. But under no circumstances, the President added, would he compromise traditional American freedom from European politics.[44] Should the governments support his plan, the President would not summon a world conference, but would invite Sweden, the Netherlands, Belgium, Switzerland, Hungary, Yugoslavia, Turkey, and three Latin American states to send representatives to Washington and there work out general principles on the questions listed in the draft. Those principles would give Hitler the choice of accepting the limitations imposed on Germany by the treaty system, or defying that system through force and accepting the risks of that decision. Welles delivered the message to British Ambassador Sir Ronald Lindsay on January 11, 1938. He reminded the ambassador that American opinion would not permit a stronger United States commitment to Europe's peace. The President would proceed if by January 17 he received the assurance that the British government supported the proposal. British opposition, Lindsay warned the London government, would annul all progress made in Anglo-American cooperation during the two previous years.[45]

---

[44] Cabinet Notes, January, 1938, CAB 27/626/5887, Public Record Office, London. For Hull's reaction to the Welles proposal, see Hull, *Memoirs*, I, 546–48.

[45] Ambassador Lindsay went even further in warning the British government not to turn down the proposal because he had direct proof from FDR that his purpose was twofold – try to calm the waters with a meeting, but if, as he suspected that Hitler would oppose the meeting

IV

For Chamberlain, Roosevelt's proposal was less than helpful. Unlike the United States, Britain could not escape the immediate threat of German power and ambition. Britain's commitments were global, and vastly exceeded the country's capabilities. In the Pacific, especially, the British position rested on tradition and bluff. London no more than Washington desired to involve itself in the specific problems of East-Central Europe. The British lived under no illusion that they could escape a European war, and a continental struggle against Germany would endanger a rich and vulnerable empire. Unable to renounce its worldwide obligations, London could protect its interests in Europe and elsewhere either by organizing a permanent balance against the Axis or by calming the ambitions of the aggressors through diplomacy. British attempts to reach an understanding with Germany were virtually inevitable. Unless the London government made such an effort, and demonstrably failed, few in Britain, either inside or outside the government, would accept the probability of war that resistance to Germany entailed.

Behind Britain's refusal to meet the German military challenge with a broad and vigorous rearmament program of its own were the terrifying memories of the Great War and the subsequent longing for peace. Predictably, another war, reflecting the gains in aircraft technology, would rain destruction from the skies. After 1935, British leaders acknowledged the speed of German rearmament, but they assumed perhaps correctly, that the British public preferred to discount the German threat. Britain's economy and public finances remained weak; British rearmament, therefore, never exceeded what the British treasury would sanction. Heavy arms expenditures would drain Britain's limited resources, needed for recovery, into wasteful production, and eliminate the possibility for financial solvency. When he was Chancellor of the Exchequer in 1936, Chamberlain had sought above all to protect Britain's needed export trade. "If we were now to ... sacrifice our commerce to the manufacture of arms," he warned late that year, "we should inflict a certain injury on our trade from which it would take generations to recover, ... and we should cripple our revenue." The British defense program focused on the expansion of the air force and the rebuilding of the battle fleet. As Prime Minister, Chamberlain restricted British rearmament to what seemed essential for home defense and the protection of British commitments outside Europe.[46]

Whatever the limitations of British preparedness, the future of collective security seemed promising enough. Every country of Europe, including Italy, opposed German expansion. In 1935, France had negotiated anti-German alliances with Russia and Czechoslovakia. With the exception of France and

or its results, show that it would prove beyond doubt his aggressive intent and solidify the support of peace-loving nations in opposition to him. See Bennett, *Separated By a Common Language*, 163–64.

[46] Feiling discusses the problems and nature of British rearmament in *The Life of Neville Chamberlain*, 312–19.

Czechoslovakia, however, every country in Europe balked at including Russia in a system of collective security. Chamberlain distrusted Russian purpose and discounted Russian power. British cooperation or alliance with Russia, or even with France, moreover, seemed likely to make understandings with Germany more difficult to attain. United States support, on the other hand, would be welcome. It would strengthen British diplomacy without restricting British freedom. Unfortunately, experience suggested to British officials that the United States, despite its great potential power, remained unpredictable and unreliable. "The U.S.A.," Chamberlain wrote, "has drawn close to us, but the isolationists there are so strong and so vocal that she cannot be depended on for help if we get into trouble." Upon reading Roosevelt's Quarantine Speech, Chamberlain concluded again that it was "always best and safest to count on nothing from the Americans but words."[47]

This unpredictability of the United States reinforced Chamberlain's sense of British weakness and provided further argument for a conciliatory policy. For him, the fact that the Germans and Italians were difficult did not eliminate the possibility of dealing with them effectively. Indeed, Chamberlain believed Britain to be uniquely situated to lead Europe through a period of crisis without permitting the impending disruption of the post-war order to end in war. As he assured a Birmingham audience: "There must be something common between us if only we can find it, and perhaps by our very aloofness from the rest of Europe we may have some special part to play as conciliator and mediator."[48] The Prime Minister regarded himself as sufficiently unprejudiced against Hitler and Mussolini to offer Europe disinterested leadership. Above all, Chamberlain recognized the importance of avoiding a direct confrontation with Germany over Central Europe. By establishing a framework for negotiation, the Prime Minister hoped to limit Hitler's assaults on the Eastern European settlement sufficiently to preserve the peace.

Negotiation comprised the necessary means for determining the extent of German ambition. Direct pressure on Hitler, argued Sir Alexander Cadogan, Deputy Under Secretary of State, would compel him to announce a reasonable program or put himself in the wrong. "If everyone in Germany is mad, and if all are bent on our destruction," he wrote in April, 1937, "disaster must come.... Therefore we must try and talk with some of them and encourage some of them. It's no use shutting our eyes and hiding our heads in the sand and doing nothing. If our rearmament is backward, we must have time. We must do something."[49] Chamberlain shared that conviction. "If only I could get on terms with the Germans," he wrote, "I would not care a rap for Musso."

Italy's aggressiveness in the Mediterranean constituted the immediate threat to the peace. Chamberlain, moreover, had defined a reasonable formula

[47] Neville Chamberlain, Diary, February 19, 1938, NC 2/24A, Neville Chamberlain Papers, University of Birmingham; Chamberlain to Hilda Chamberlain, October 9, 1937, NC 18/1/1023, Chamberlain Papers.
[48] Quoted in Feiling, *The Life of Neville Chamberlain*, 321, 324.
[49] David Dilks, ed., *The Diaries of Sir Alexander Cadogan, 1938–1945* (London, 1971), 14.

for settling British differences with Italy. If Mussolini would renounce any territorial designs toward Spain and French North Africa, and withdraw some Italian "volunteers" from Spain, Britain would recognize the Italian conquest of Abyssinia. "We can't go on for ever refusing recognition in the Abyssinian affair," he wrote to his sister Hilda on August 29, "and it seems to me that we had better give it while we can get something in return for it."[50] Through direct, bilateral diplomacy, Chamberlain hoped to satisfy Hitler's demands, but only in accordance with Britain's principle of peaceful change. "I don't see why," he wrote to his sister, Ida, on November 26, "we shouldn't say to Germany, give us satisfactory assurances that you will not use force to deal with the Austrians and the Czechoslovakians and we will give similar assurances that we won't use force to prevent the changes you want if you can get them by peaceful means.'"[51] Chamberlain's proviso separated him only in style from the hardliners in the British government. Vansittart, on November 3, assured German officials in London that Britain would accept the union of Germany and Austria provided that union was not "attempted by means of a Putsch."

Chamberlain inaugurated his personal search for a settlement with Germany in November 1937 when he urged Lord Halifax, Lord President of the Council, to accept the invitation to attend an international sporting exhibition in Berlin and to visit Hitler at Berchtesgaden. The Prime Minister sought no specific German terms, but hoped to reassure Hitler of British sincerity and to determine, in general, what Hitler hoped to gain in Europe and elsewhere. He sought to avoid a territorial settlement with Germany except as part of a general settlement. Such a settlement, in all probability, would require a series of bilateral treaties. British Ambassador in Berlin, Nevile Henderson, warned the London government that Hitler had no interest in bargains, and in particular would not exchange a colonial settlement for one in Europe. The burgeoning Austrian question, Henderson added, was no longer open to discussion.[52]

Clearly the challenges facing Europe could find no solution in Roosevelt's January conference proposal; Chamberlain rejected it. "The plan," he wrote in his diary, "appears to me fantastic and likely to excite the derision of Germany and Italy. They might even use it to postpone conversations with us & if we were associated with it they would see in it another attempt on the part of the democratic bloc to put the dictators in the wrong."[53] Negotiations with Germany and Italy, ran the theme of his reply, required some concrete bases of agreement. Britain would therefore recognize the de jure Italian conquest of Abyssinia and, in time, would propose similar measures to satisfy

[50] Chamberlain to Hilda Chamberlain, August 29, 1937, NC 18/1/108, Chamberlain Papers.
[51] Chamberlain to Ida Chamberlain, November 26, 1937, NC 18/1/1018.
[52] Henderson to Eden, December 15, 1937, annex to Cabinet Notes, January 1938, CAB 27/626/5887, PRO.
[53] Chamberlain's Diary, February 19, 1938, NC 2/24A Chamberlain Papers. This comment was disingenuous on Chamberlain's part as he surely knew from Lindsay's despatches that this was precisely one of Roosevelt's objectives in calling the conference.

German aspirations. Sir Alexander Cadogan, Permanent Under Secretary since early January, like Chamberlain, accused Roosevelt of harboring "wild ideas about formulating a world settlement." The President's proposal, he agreed, presented difficulties. Still, he advised the Cabinet to avoid a break with Roosevelt. "Whatever else may be decided," Cadogan warned, "we must not turn him down."[54]

Chamberlain compromised on his response by suggesting that Roosevelt delay his conference call while the London government tackled some of the specific questions in European politics, especially those involved in territorial aggression.

Roosevelt's second message, withdrawing his project, clarified the depth of his tactical disagreement with Chamberlain and demonstrated his concern for American opinion. The President had an interest in dealing with the aggressors. He reminded the Prime Minister that the de jure recognition of Italy's claim to Abyssinia would undermine the efforts of other countries to defend their territories against aggression. Specifically, noted Roosevelt, it might have a harmful effect "upon the nature of the peace terms which Japan might demand from China." He warned, moreover, that a surrender of the principle of non-recognition would seriously damage public opinion in the United States. The American people would support measures of international cooperation only if they were "destined to re-establish and maintain the principles of international law and morality."[55] In Washington, Hull reminded Ambassador Lindsay that United States policy rested primarily on moral precepts and "the sanctity of agreements and the preservation of international law, both of which rest on this moral foundation...."[56] The desperado nations, he warned, would herald British recognition of the Italian conquest as a virtual ratification of their treaty-breaking policies. The secretary admitted that the policy of non-recognition, as one of indefinite duration, presented difficulties; he insisted, however, that a policy so central to the maintenance of international order could be modified only by general agreement among the nations of the world.

Washington's obvious dissatisfaction with British–Italian relations placed the London government in a dilemma. The Cabinet's Foreign Policy Committee wanted to strengthen British relations with the United States; still, Chamberlain and the Committee found Roosevelt's principles unimaginative and unrealistic. The purpose of British policy was to rid Europe of its immediate perils, whereas the American initiative would both antagonize the dictators and place responsibility for a settlement on small states unsuited for a major international role. By the time Roosevelt's second message reached London, Foreign Minister Anthony Eden had returned from a vacation in the south of

---

[54] Chamberlain to Roosevelt, January 14, 1938, *FRUS, 1938*, I (Washington, 1955), 118–19; Cabinet Notes, January 24, 1938, CAB 23/92/6455, PRO; Dilks, *Diaries of Sir Alexander Cadogan*, 39.

[55] Roosevelt to Chamberlain, January 17, 1938, *FRUS, 1938*, I, 120–22.

[56] Memorandum of Hull's conversation with Lindsay, January 17, 1938, ibid., 133–34.

France. Eden fully accepted Lindsay's advice that Britain should encourage the President's interest in European affairs even at the cost of inconvenience to British diplomacy. Chamberlain's next communication to Roosevelt, which reflected Eden's wishes, informed him that the Prime Minister did not now feel justified in asking the President to postpone his White House meeting, and assured him that the British government would do all in its power to guarantee the success of the effort. Britain, Chamberlain insisted, would seek de jure recognition of Italy's African acquisitions, but only as part of a general Mediterranean settlement. Privately, Chamberlain explained to Lindsay why the British government could not offer more enthusiastic support for Roosevelt's conference proposals. "In case they received a bad reception after they had been launched," he wrote, "we were anxious neither, on the one hand, to share the responsibility with the President for them, nor, on the other, for the President to be able to say that we had given him no warning but unqualified encouragement."[57]

Despite Chamberlain's assurances that he would support the conference call, Roosevelt never renewed his proposal. Chamberlain's opponents argued that the Prime Minister's attitude had angered the President. Perhaps Roosevelt had merely come to share the Prime Minister's skepticism. Ambassador Bullitt offered the President little encouragement. "I remember talking over with you the idea that you might call a world conference, ..." he wrote from Paris. "I feel now that, while such an appeal would be acceptable to American public opinion, it would seem an escape from reality to the rest of the world. It would be as if in the palmiest days of Al Capone you had summoned a national conference of psychologists to Washington to discuss the psychological causes of crime."[58] Still, as late as March 8, Welles informed Lindsay that the United States opposed any direct approach to the German and Italian governments. Editorials as well as personal letters, he informed the ambassador, accused the British government of denying the principle of peaceful change and lending support to the dictators. "It is not," Lindsay replied, "that we like dictators nor that we want to associate ourselves with them, but since we are confronted with a world in which there are dictators, we have reached the conclusion that the only thing to do in order to prevent war is to try to find a basis for peaceful understanding with them."[59] The position that Chamberlain and those who agreed with him took was that Britain, confronted with the

---

[57] Cabinet Notes, January 24, 1938, CAB 23/92/6455, PRO. Eden's reaction to Roosevelt's proposal can be found in detail in Anthony Eden, *Memoirs: Facing the Dictators*, 545–68. To the very end, Eden believed that a comparable opportunity to avoid catastrophe never reoccurred.

[58] Bullitt to Roosevelt, January 20, 1938, Orville Bullitt, ed., *For the President: Personal and Secret*, 252.

[59] Welles's memorandum of conversation with Lindsay, March 8, 1938, *FRUS, 1938*, I, 127. Given the advice Lindsay gave his government about FDR's intent in confronting the dictators and his apparent agreement with this attempt, it is likely that this was Lindsay's 'official' position, in tune with Chamberlain's views and not his own.

rapid deterioration of European stability, had no choice but to pursue direct negotiations.

To Eden and much of the Foreign Office, Chamberlain's handling of Roosevelt had been unsubtle and potentially disastrous. Eden had urged the Prime Minister to do everything possible to abate the isolationist mood in America. War, believed Eden, was inevitable, and without the United States' support, England could not defeat the Germans, Italians, and/or the Japanese.[60] Eden's official secretary, Oliver Harvey, reminded Eden, "The only fatal risk for us is to antagonize Roosevelt and America; without his backing we might be overwhelmed in a war.... We may try to persuade Roosevelt to delay or modify [his] scheme, but if he persists we should heartily concur and co-operate for all we are worth. We should not be forgiven if we turned it down."[61] Eden concluded that Britain should drop the idea of Abyssinia's de jure recognition. Certainly, he argued, Roosevelt's initiative was more important to Britain than an agreement with Mussolini. Ambassador Dino Grandi's assurances that Rome wanted a settlement with Britain merely aggravated Eden's suspicions; the fact that Mussolini wanted conversations was sufficient reason to avoid them.

Even when Grandi informed Eden and Chamberlain in February 1938 that Mussolini accepted the British formula for a Mediterranean settlement, Eden refused to budge. For Chamberlain, his break with Eden was now complete. Late in February, he accepted Eden's resignation and replaced him with Halifax. His quarrel with Eden, Chamberlain wrote, "was not whether we should have conversations now but whether we should have them at all. I have gradually arrived at the conclusion that at bottom Anthony did not want to talk either with Hitler or Mussolini and, as I did, he was right to go on." Cadogan had supported Eden on the matter of Roosevelt's conference proposal, but he agreed with the Prime Minister on the need of pushing the Italian negotiations.[62]

VII

In their conversation at Berchtesgaden on November 19, 1937, Hitler and Halifax made clear why peaceful change was a delusion, a reassuring notion, shared by status quo powers, to avoid the hard, unpleasant realities of international life. Hitler suggested that Britain shed its "Versailles mentality and recognize that the world could never remain in status quo." Halifax replied "that nobody wished to treat Germany as anything but a great Power, and that nobody in their senses supposed the world could stay as it was for ever."

[60] Eden, *Facing the Dictators*, 596.
[61] John Harvey, ed., *The Diplomatic Diaries of Oliver Harvey, 1937–1940* (London, 1970), 69–70.
[62] Chamberlain to Hilda Chamberlain, February 27, 1938, NC 18/1/1040, Chamberlain Papers; Dilks, *Diaries of Alexander Cadogan*, 54.

He added, "The whole point was how changes were to be brought about."[63] Certainly on matters of Danzig, Austria, and Czechoslovakia, Britain did not stand on the status quo. Yet Britain was "very much concerned to secure the avoidance of such treatment of them as would be likely to cause trouble." Britain would not block reasonable settlements reached with the free consent of those directly concerned. Hitler retorted that Britain had special difficulty in facing current realities, that it was living "in a world of it own making, a fairyland of strange, if respectable illusions. It clung to shibboleths – 'collective security,' 'general settlement,' 'disarmament,' 'non-aggression pacts,' – which offered no practical prospect of a solution of Europe's difficulties."[64]

In Geneva, the League of Nations existed for the precise purpose of preventing the dilemma that Europe now faced. Article 19 of the League Covenant accepted the notion that the world's leading powers could not maintain a state of affairs indefinitely against changing conditions. In practice, however, nations did not give up peacefully what they held legally under the sanction of a treaty. "It is true," wrote British author John Strachey, "that governments always tell us that they will never yield to force. All history tells us, however, that they will never yield to anything else."[65] Article 19 of the Covenant remained a monument to the fallacy that countries would voluntarily remedy international grievances at the request of others, except under the limitations of peaceful change. Hitler understood the relationship of force to change, writing in *Mein Kampf*: "The winning back of lost territories is not achieved through solemn invocations of the Lord God or through pious hopes in a League of Nations. But through armed force." Hitler explained to Lord Halifax why the League of Nations could offer nothing to the peaceful settlement of international disputes. "The League system, . . ." he declared, "means the perpetuation of the status quo. It is useless to evade the issue by saying that Article 19 of the Covenant provides for peaceful revision. Such an argument is only another symptom of self-deception, for it is impossible to imagine peaceful revision by general consent, since every member of the League will always require the contribution to be made by others."[66]

VIII

Hitler's assault on the Versailles Treaty's territorial arrangements for Eastern Europe began at a secret strategy conference on November 5, 1937. For him, the choice now lay between accepting the superior morality of the status quo or defying it with force. He explained to his military chiefs that "there had never . . . been spaces without a master, and there were none today; the attacker always comes up against a possessor. The question for Germany was: where

[63] Halifax, *Fullness of Time*, 187. For a full record of Halifax's trip to Germany, November 17–21, 1937, see A4.410.33, Halifax Papers.
[64] John Strachey, *The Menace of Fascism* (London, 1933), 228.
[65] Ibid.
[66] Halifax, *Fullness of Time*, 191.

could she receive the greatest gain at the lowest cost."[67] Hitler noted that German rearmament had progressed sufficiently to permit Germany to pursue actively not only the remaining strictures of Versailles, but also his objective of bringing all German-speaking peoples of Eastern Europe into the German Reich. Britain and France failed to match German rearmament; how long that advantage would last was uncertain. The time to strike had arrived. Ready to gamble Germany's future for high stakes, Hitler stripped his ministry and officer corps of their cautious elements, and by January 1938 was prepared to test the commitments of the Western democracies to the Versailles settlement. The German ambassador assured Washington early in February that the changes in personnel would not effect German policy.[68]

It soon became apparent that the German assault on the Versailles settlement would focus on Austria. British officials had ruled out the appeasement of any German designs on Austria, except with the will of Austria's inhabitants.[69] Anglo-French conversations in London late in 1937 reaffirmed that policy; the Western powers, they agreed, should oppose any German adventures in Central Europe.[70] Early in February 1938, however, Germany began to exert relentless pressure on the Austrian government. The browbeating of Austrian Chancellor Kurt von Schuschnigg at Berchtesgaden on February 12 was scarcely peaceful. Hitler announced his mission to bring the 80 million Germans into one nation, and demanded that Schuschnigg appoint an Austrian Nazi to a key cabinet position. Schuschnigg agreed momentarily, but on March 9 proclaimed an immediate Austrian plebiscite on the question of Austrian independence.

On March 11, with Austria deeply convulsed in a vigorous political debate over the country's future independence, William Shirer, the noted radio correspondent, arrived in Vienna from Prague. To him, as he observed the campaigning, the plebiscite promised to end peacefully, with a victory for Schuschnigg. But late that day, the Austrian resistance to Nazi pressure collapsed with the indefinite postponement of the plebiscite. Unknown to the multitude, Hitler had issued an ultimatum to stop the campaigning. That was the signal for those who favored Austrian independence to disappear, while Nazis by the

[67] Minutes of the conference in the Reich Chancellery, Berlin, November 5, 1937, published in Francis L. Lowenheim, ed., *Peace or Appeasement? Hitler, Chamberlain, and the Munich Crisis* (Boston, 1965), xv, 3. See also Alan Bullock, *Hitler: A Study in Tyranny*, 368. Herman Goering warned Bullitt in November 1937 that Germany would annex the German populations of Austria and Czechoslovakia. Bullitt's report, *FRUS, 1937*, I, 171–72.

[68] George F. Kennan, *Russia and the West under Lenin and Stalin* (Boston, 1961), 317–18.

[69] William Strang of the Foreign Office expressed the official British view when he wrote in November 1937 that Britain "could not condone any change in the international status of Austria achieved by force against the will of the inhabitants." Strang to Halifax, November 6, 1937, *DBFP*, Second Series, XIX, 517–18; also Eden to Henderson, November 6, 1937, ibid., 471–72.

[70] Ibid., 598–605. Chamberlain expressed his satisfaction over Anglo-French agreement on policy toward Central Europe. See Chamberlain to Hilda Chamberlain, December 5, 1937, NC 18/1/1030a, Chamberlain Papers.

thousands seized command of the city. The pro-Nazi masses, now in control, were delirious with excitement and joy, sprouting Nazi uniforms and swastika armbands, yelling "Heil Hitler." In his farewell address, Schuschnigg asked Austrians not to resist the in-marching German troops. The Anschluss was complete; Vienna had become another Berlin.[71]

Hull responded to the Anschluss with a characteristic appeal to the principle of peaceful change. "On March 19 I publicly expressed the concern of our Government over the disappearance of Austria." He lamented the German action as a threat to the peace:

> The extent to which the Austrian incident, or any similar incident, is calculated to endanger the maintenance of peace and the preservation of the principles in which this Government believes is, of course, a matter of serious concern to the Government of the United States.[72]

This moral condemnation failed to impress anyone. What ensured Washington's absence of leadership in the Austrian crisis was an uncompromising isolationist Congress. During January 1938, Representative Louis Ludlow of Indiana introduced into Congress his peace amendment to the Constitution, which declared: "Except in the event of an invasion of the United States or its territorial possessions …, the authority of Congress to declare war shall not become effective until confirmed by a majority of all votes cast thereon in a nation-wide referendum." Public opinion polls revealed that a full 75 per cent of all respondents favored the amendment; the administration, backed by much of the press, bitterly opposed it. Roosevelt warned House speaker William B. Bankhead that the proposal "would cripple any President in his conduct of our foreign relations, and it would encourage other nations to believe that they could violate American rights with impunity."[73] Isolationists distrusted the war-making authority of the President. Inherent in the American system, complained Senator Robert La Follette of Wisconsin, was the "almost unrestricted power of any executive to create a war situation which Congress must accept." Hopefully, 130 million might prevent war when Congress could not. For its supporters, the Ludlow amendment, in short, constituted an epochal advance for democratic government. Eventually, White House pressure overrode such arguments. On January 10, 1938, the House failed by a vote of 188 to 209 to adopt the amendment.

Chamberlain, powerless to act, accepted the Anschluss as gracefully as he could. For him, the consolidation of the two German populations was not unreasonable. He objected only to Hitler's methods, which, he said, "were extremely distasteful to his Majesty's Government...." Having failed to prevent the Anschluss, British officials moved quickly to disavow any British

---

[71] William L. Shirer, *This is Berlin* (Woodstock, 1999), 11–14.
[72] Hull, *Memoirs*, I, 575.
[73] Bennett, *Separated by a Common Language*, 141 (fn 7).

complicity in Hitler's decision to annex Austria. Chamberlain offered his disclaimer to the House of Commons on March 14. He rebuked those who charged that the British government had given consent, if not encouragement, to German aggression. "It is quite untrue," he declared, "to suggest that we have ever given Germany our assent or our encouragement to the effective absorption of Austria into the German Reich."[74] Whereas the London government had never denied Germany's special interest in Austria, it had emphasized its strong disapproval of any solution by violence. The Prime Minister informed the House that Britain had no commitment to come to Austria's defense, and could not have done so except through the use of force. Still, Britain, he argued, had the right to interest itself in Austria's independence because the stability of Central Europe was essential for the greater security and confidence of Europe.[75]

This failure of Chamberlain's appeasement policy in Berlin merely spurred the Prime Minister to reach a settlement with Rome. In the Anglo-Italian agreement of April 16, 1938, Italy pledged to evacuate volunteers from Spain and to seek no permanent advantages in that country. London agreed in exchange to bring the issue of de jure recognition of Abyssinia before the League of Nations, but added that the treaty would take effect only when Italy complied with the Spanish provisions. Surprisingly, Roosevelt viewed the Anglo-Italian pact sympathetically. The United States, he said, advocated the maintenance of international law and order; therefore, it favored the promotion of peace through friendly settlements of controversies between states. Washington, he made clear, would not recognize the Italian conquest. Understandably, Assistant Secretary of State J. Pierrepont Moffat complained of Roosevelt's inconsistency. "In one breath," he wrote, "we praise the British for getting together with the Italians; in the next breath we imply that the Italians are law breakers and unworthy to be dealt with on a footing of equality."[76]

Hitler, in reference to the Anschluss, observed that Germany would tolerate no interference by third parties in the settlement of its relations with countries

---

[74] Chamberlain's statement in the House of Commons, March 14, 1938, *DBFP*, Third Series, I, 47.

[75] Ibid., 47–48; Chamberlain, *In Search of Peace: Speeches, 1937–1938* (London, 1938), 74–75. Also on March 14, Under Secretary of State Sumner Welles had a conversation with German ambassador Hans Heinrich Dieckhoff. The exchange was identical to those of Henderson with Hitler and Ribbentrop earlier in March. Dieckhoff complained that the Versailles Treaty was unjust, yet no country would permit Germany to reverse it, even opposing the Anschluss of Austria. Welles responded that the Germans had not given the Austrians a free choice, but had used force. Welles assured the ambassador that he "had fully appreciated the fact that in their dealings with Germany during the past twenty years injustices had been committed by other powers which [he] had always hoped would some day be righted through reasonable negotiations such as those which Stressemann had endeavored to undertake." PSF: State: Welles: *FDRL*.

[76] Halifax to State Department, March 11, 1938, *FRUS, 1938*, I, 132; Roosevelt's press statement on the Anglo-Italian Treaty, April 19, 1938, ibid., 147–48. For Moffat's observation, see Dallek, *Franklin D. Roosevelt and American Foreign Policy*, 158.

having German elements in their population.[77] He denied that Britain and France had any cause for complaint; the Anschluss had touched the interests of neither country. Germany, he added, had never interfered in the affairs of the British Empire, but was always "obliged to accept a negative reaction by England when Germany tried to solve her own difficulties." Clearly Britain hoped to prevent any change in the status of Central Europe.[78] Germany could take Austria or leave it, but no one in Britain suggested a peaceful procedure other than a German acceptance of the status quo. Goering condemned Britain for its lack of fair-mindedness.

---

[77] Memorandum of conversation, March 3, 1938, *DGFP*, Series D, 1 (Washington, 1949), 241, 243–45. For a British account of the March 3 conversations, see Memorandum from the British Ambassador, March 9, 1938, PSF: State: Welles, *FDRL*.

[78] Ribbentrop to Hitler, March 10, 1938, *DGFP*, Series D, I, 262.

9

Munich

The Continuing Escape from Reality

I

Germany's annexation of Austria did not fulfill Hitler's territorial ambitions. In February 1938, the German leader advised Europe that he would protect the peoples of German origin "who were not in a position through their own efforts to obtain ... for themselves the rights to ... political and ideological freedom." Following the Anschluss, Hitler's irredentism marked Czechoslovakia's Sudetenland, with its large, discontented German majority, as his next objective. The Paris Conference had established the Czech nation on the foundation of the old kingdom of Bohemia, but had added a motley collection of nationalities to round out its frontiers – Poles, Hungarians, Slovaks, Ruthenians, as well as Czechs and Germans. The Sudeten Germans dominated the narrow northern and western border between Czechoslovakia and Germany, as well as the Czech border with Austria in the south. For Czechoslovakia, this mountain frontier, with its strong fortifications, held a strategic importance that far transcended its size and population. The Sudetenland contained the bulk of Czechoslovakia's natural resources and heavy industry, including the famed Skoda munitions works. Equally troubling, the Anschluss demonstrated the diminution of Anglo-French power to sustain what remained of the Versailles settlement.[1]

European and American diplomats, who had scarcely reacted to the Anschluss, recognized the danger in the mounting Czech crisis. Czechoslovakia was allied to both France and the Soviet Union – its major sources of defense. Germany's threat to annex the Sudetenland gave Hitler's opposition the choice of standing together in defense of the Versailles decisions or witnessing their further disintegration. Chamberlain understood why Britain would reject the first alternative. It was evident, he wrote, that "collective security" could not prevent Germany's resort to force until that collective commanded

---

[1] Cudahy to Roosevelt, April 6, 1938, PSF: Ireland: TS, *FDRL*; Bullitt to Roosevelt, May 20, 1938, Bullitt, ed., *For the President, Personal and Secret*, 261.

overwhelming strength and the will to use it.[2] Later, in May, Chamberlain wrote that the Germans were "conscious of their strength and our weakness and until we are as strong as they we shall always be kept in this state of chronic anxiety."[3] In the continued absence of such strength, the Prime Minister regarded resistance to Germany through collective action as a desperate course. In March 1938, he confided to his sister, Ida:

> It is a very attractive idea ... until you come to examine its practicality....
> You have only to look at the map to see that nothing that France or we could
> do could possibly save Czechoslovakia from being overrun by the Germans if
> they wanted to do it ....It would simply be the pretext for going to war with
> Germany. That we could not think of unless we had a reasonable prospect of
> being able to beat her ... and of that I see no sign.[4]

To avoid direct confrontation with Hitler, some in the British Foreign Office favored the "guessing game" that Anthony Eden had outlined in a Leamington speech of November 1936. The theory was simple: as long as Germany was never sure that Britain would not fight, and France was never sure that it would, both countries would seek to avoid trouble. On March 24, before the House of Commons, Chamberlain repeated this formula. He listed the specific British obligations that might demand the resort of force: the defense of Britain, the British Commonwealth, Western Europe, and the Middle East. In rejecting any defense of Czechoslovakia, he warned Berlin that a war over Czechoslovakia would not necessarily be confined to those who had legal obligations for its defense. "It would be quite impossible," he concluded, "to say where it would end and what governments might become involved. The inexorable pressure of facts might well prove more powerful than formal pronouncements."[5] But the status quo for which Britain and France would fight had already proved to be defenseless.[6]

British leaders had long accepted the principle of autonomy for the Sudetenland, a program seemingly acceptable to Germany as well. The key to a peaceful settlement lay in Prague's willingness to offer an acceptable agreement to the Sudeten Germans, and to do so within a reasonable period of time. On April 24, Konrad Henlein, leader of the Sudeten Germans, announced his Karlsbad Program, which set forth the minimum Sudeten demands. These included equality of status, autonomy, removal of all injustices, reparations for past indignities, and full freedom for Germans to proclaim their adherence to German culture and ideology. London and Paris responded favorably

---

[2] Chamberlain to Hilda Chamberlain, March 13, 1938, NC 18/1/1041, Chamberlain Papers, University of Birmingham Library.
[3] Chamberlain to Hilda Chamberlain, May 22, 1938, NC 18/1/1053, ibid.
[4] Chamberlain to Ida Chamberlain, March 20, 1938, NC 18/1/1042, ibid.
[5] Joseph F. Kennedy to Hull, March 23, 1938, *FRUS, 1938*, I, 40; Monica Curtis, ed., *Documents on International Affairs, 1938* (London, 1943), II: 121–23.
[6] Halifax to Phipps, March 15, 23. *DBFP*, 1938, Third Series, 1949, 51, 87–89; Gainer to Henderson, March 24, 1938, ibid., 120.

to the Sudeten proclamation. Its enforcement rested on France and the French alliance system.

Unfortunately, without explicit British support, the French alliance was powerless to act. U.S. Ambassador William C. Bullitt, in Paris, witnessed the alliance's predictable demise. Late in April, French Premier Edouard Daladier and French Minister Georges Bonnet traveled to London to secure the required British commitment to the defense of Czechoslovakia. Chamberlain refused to compromise on his statement of March 24 – Britain's frontier was on the Rhine. Isolated diplomatically in the West and unable to penetrate Germany's western defenses, France sought effective support in the East. Poland, despite its alliance with France, denied that it had any obligation to Czechoslovakia. Moreover, it warned that it would meet with force any Soviet attempt to aid Czechoslovakia by crossing Polish territory. Troubled by Europe's heavy stake in Czechoslovakia, Robert Coulondre, French ambassador in Moscow, urged his government to perfect the Franco-Russian alliance by negotiating a military agreement with Moscow. Paris rejected the advice.[7] It mattered little. Maxim Litvinov, Soviet Commissar for Foreign Affairs, reminded the French government that his country, under all circumstances, would await French action in a war over Czechoslovakia. Moscow, moreover, could not aid Czechoslovakia without defying Poland. The French alliance was dead.

II

Hitler's threat to Czechoslovakia did not touch any historic U.S. interests directly, except that Washington, like London, desired that any changes in the Versailles peace structure be achieved through peaceful processes. President Roosevelt and his advisers favored some response to the burgeoning Czech crisis, but one that did not entail any commitment to specific clauses in the Versailles Treaty. Embracing American escapism in customary fashion, Bullitt advised Roosevelt: "Henceforth, your chief job is going to be to maintain national honor while avoiding involvement in war."[8] If a devastated Europe was not in the interest of the United States, Bullitt reasoned, the United States "should attempt to find some way which will let the French out of their moral commitment."[9]

Meanwhile, U.S. observers in Europe reported a mounting Czech crisis. A trip to Prague convinced American minister to Ireland, John Cudahy, that the Sudeten issue had become explosive. Bullitt, he added, held views more apprehensive than his own.[10] The Czech government, Cudahy feared,

[7] London meeting recorded in *FRUS, 1938*, I, 47–50. Franklin L. Ford and Carl E. Schorske discuss Coulondre in "The Voice in the Wilderness," Gordon A. Craig and Felix Gilbert, eds., *The Diplomats, 1919–1939* (New York, 1963), II, 61, 574. On Poland and the Soviet Union, see Bullitt to Hull, May 16, 1938, *FRUS, 1938*, I, 502.
[8] Reported in Hull to Roosevelt, January 10, 1938, *For the President*, 250.
[9] Bullitt to Roosevelt, May 20, 1938, PSF: France: Bullitt, TS, *FDRL*.
[10] Cudahy to Roosevelt, June 13, 1938, PSF: Ireland: TS, *FDRL*.

would concede no territorial sovereignty to a national minority, nor would the Sudeten Germans or Berlin accept Czechoslovakia's limited concessions.[11] Bullitt predicted that Sudeten demands, underwritten by Berlin, would always outpace any Czech retreat. A clash involving Czech reprisals, Bullitt warned, would invite a German invasion.[12]

For U.S. diplomats in Europe, the Sudeten crisis touched no American interests that demanded a national response. Bullitt argued that the country would serve Europe best by avoiding a war. "I believe that if war starts," he averred, "the destruction of the continent will be so great that, unless we are able to remain strong and relatively untouched, there will be no nation on earth to pick up the pieces."[13] In Warsaw, Ambassador Anthony J. Drexel Biddle Jr. warned the Polish government against making assumptions regarding the U.S. response to any European conflict.[14] U.S. Ambassador to Germany, Hugh Wilson, warned Czech officials in Prague that they should not anticipate American support in the event of war; Bullitt repeated that admonition in Paris.[15] When Halifax, in London, asked Ambassador Joseph P. Kennedy why Britain, rather than the United States, should defend the Versailles order, Kennedy replied that Britain, not the United States, had made the Sudeten issue its own.[16]

Assistant Secretary of State Adolf Berle offered the ultimate rationalization for American abstention from any Sudenten crisis. In a memorandum to the President, Berle argued that Hitler, whatever his methods, was putting a logical end to the mistakes made at Paris in 1919, especially the decision to break up the Austro-Hungarian Empire. The combination of German and Austro-Hungarian power across Central Europe, he recalled, had existed for centuries without endangering Western Europe. The United States, Berle concluded, should not enter a war "to maintain a situation which was untenable from the time it was created by the treaties of Versailles and Saint Germain."[17] State Department officials in Washington, joined by U.S. diplomats in Europe, wondered how the United States could sustain the treaty structure of Europe without undertaking commitments that both isolationists and internationalists opposed.

Bullitt addressed this absence of choice by advising the President to call the ambassadors of England, France, Germany, and Italy to the White House

[11] Cudahy to Hull, June 13, 1938, PSF: State: TS, *FDRL*.

[12] Bullitt to Roosevelt, June 13, 1938, PSF: France, Bullitt: TS, *FDRL*: Bullitt to Moore, July 19, 1938, Bullitt, *For the President*, 277.

[13] Bullitt to Roosevelt, June 13, 1938, PSF: France: Bullitt: TS, *FDRL*.

[14] Memorandum by Anthony J. Drexel Biddle Jr., July 28, 1938, PSF: Poland: TS, *FDRL*.

[15] For Wilson's admonition, see Frederick W. Marks III, *Wind over Sand: The Diplomacy of Franklin Roosevelt* (Athens, 1988), 142–43; Phipps to Halifax, September 2, 1938, Phipps Papers 1/20, Roskill Library, Churchill College, Cambridge.

[16] Kennedy to Hull, September 10, 1938, *FRUS, 1938*, I, 586. Similarly, when French Foreign Minister Georges Bonnet suggested to Bullitt that the United States warn Berlin against the use of force, Bullitt observed that the United States government would not involve itself in the Sudeten question. See Bullitt to Hull, September 12, 1938, ibid., 589.

[17] Berle to Roosevelt, September 1, 1938, PSF: State: Berle: TS, *FDRL*.

and ask them to have their governments send representatives to The Hague to work out a peaceful settlement between Germany and Czechoslovakia. The President, Bullitt suggested, might reinforce his appeal through personal consultations with each ambassador, "stressing to the German Ambassador the fact that France will fight and England will fight, and war in Europe today can end only in the establishment of Bolshevism from one end of the Continent to the other."[18] The warning would remind Hitler of the price that Germany would pay for a European war. Bullitt believed that Roosevelt should delay any meeting with the ambassadors until the proper moment; to do so earlier would encourage the British and French to relax their efforts to find a solution of the Sudeten issue. Again, on August 17, Bullitt suggested that Roosevelt remind the German ambassador that American opinion, being anti-German, could drive the United States into a war against Germany, as it did after 1914. The President would ask the ambassador to transmit that warning to Hitler – and then dismiss him. "You would have done nothing," Bullitt concluded, "except to call his attention to certain facts which are public property and you would have committed yourself to nothing. I think the effect of such a conversation on Germany would be immense."[19]

Roosevelt and Secretary of State Cordell Hull pursued their own formula to bridge the chasm between the administration's desire to exert a telling U.S. influence in European affairs and its determination to avoid any commitment to that continent's future. In mid-August, Berle advised Roosevelt, in planning his forthcoming speech at Queens University, Kingston, Ontario, to create uncertainty regarding U.S. intentions toward the troublesome Czech question.[20] On August 16, Hull addressed the nation in a radio address that conformed to the official standard of ambiguity. "Our own situation," he said, "is profoundly affected by what happens elsewhere in the world." At the same time, he asserted, American policy must develop "within the range of our traditional policies of nonentanglement."[21] Roosevelt's carefully worded speech at Kingston on August 18 assured Canadians that "the people of the United States will not stand idly by if domination of Canadian soil is threatened by any other Empire." Ordinary men and women of the Western Hemisphere could not ignore Europe's troubling issues. "No country where thought is free," Roosevelt warned, "can prevent every fireside and home within its borders from considering the evidence for itself and rendering its own verdict."[22] The President's commitment to the defense of North America was sufficiently traditional to excite no responses. Roosevelt admitted that any president could have proclaimed it fifty years earlier.

---

[18] Bullitt to Roosevelt, May 20, 1938, PSF: France: Bullitt: TS, *FDRL*.
[19] Bullitt to Roosevelt, August 17, 1938, ibid.
[20] Berle to Roosevelt, August 15, 1938, PSF: State: Berle, TS, *FDRL*.
[21] Cordell Hull, *The Memoirs of Cordell Hull* (New York, 1948), I, 584.
[22] Speech by Roosevelt, Queen's University, Kingston, Ontario, Canada, August 18, 1938, Speech File: TS, *FDRL*.

Later that month, Secretary of the Treasury Henry Morgenthau and Roosevelt formulated a plan to impede German expansion with economic sanctions. To secure Hull's approval, the President phoned the secretary: "I have hatched a chicken. Do you want to come over and look at it?"[23] Roosevelt explained to Hull that the plan would enable the government to purchase earmarked British and French gold in the United States for one year at $35 per ounce. Next, the President declared his intention to inform the German ambassador in Washington that the United States would apply countervailing duties against his country if it entered Czechoslovakia. Hull believed the scheme unsound and unnecessarily threatening to American isolationism. His objection reaffirmed the President's own doubts and terminated the project.

Roosevelt and Hull hoped that their August speeches would caution Hitler against any drastic action against Czechoslovakia; their formulations became the basis of subsequent official responses to questions regarding United States policy toward Europe. In answer to a request for guidance from U.S. Ambassador Joseph P. Kennedy in London, Secretary Hull replied characteristically: "[R]ecent public speeches and statements of the President and myself, which were prepared with great care, accurately reflect the attitude of this Government toward the European and world situation, and ... it would not be practicable to be more specific as to our reaction in hypothetical circumstances."[24] Even as Roosevelt and Hull hoped that Europe would take their veiled threats seriously, they avoided any commitments to the territorial arrangements of the Versailles Treaty.

Washington's dilemma became clear when Bullitt agreed to speak at the unveiling of a monument at Port De Grave, Bordeaux, to commemorate the first landing of American troops in the Great War. State Department official R. Walton Moore read the Bordeaux speech and recommended no changes.[25] French Foreign Minister Georges Bonnet hoped that Bullitt would inform the world that the United States would support France in a war against Germany. On September 4, Bonnet heard these reassuring words: "The people of the United States, like the people of France, ardently desire peace.... [But] if war breaks out in Europe, no one can say or predict whether the United States would be drawn into such a war."[26] When those phrases reached American newsstands, isolationists condemned the administration for its interventionism. Bullitt, in Paris, received instructions to insist that his words were misinterpreted. Bonnet declared bitterly that total silence in Washington would have done less damage than Roosevelt's occasional suggestions that he intended to act.[27]

---

[23] John Morton Blum, ed., *From the Morgenthau Diaries, I: Years of Crisis, 1928–1938* (Boston, 1959), 516–17.

[24] Hull to Kennedy, September 1, 1938, *FRUS, 1938*, I: 568. See also Hull to Caffery, September 15, 1938, ibid, 599.

[25] Moore to Bullitt, August 31, 1938, Bullitt, *For the President*, 286.

[26] Ibid., 285.

[27] Marks, *Wind over Sand*, 143.

Roosevelt's subsequent press conferences revealed the confusion produced by the absence of policy. Meeting the press on September 6, the President refused to discuss the Czech crisis, insisting that the information in the press, or received by the State Department, was too contradictory for comment. Three days later, at another press conference, Roosevelt faced the question of America's shifting policy toward Europe, with its implied moral, and possible military, alignment with France and Britain. The President acknowledged that such impressions did indeed appear in the columns of editorial writers. "If they would read the English language about what the Secretary of State has said and what I have said," Roosevelt complained, "they would find their interpretations are about 100 percent wrong." When asked for a definition of United States policy, he replied: "Read what the Secretary of State has said and what I have said. That is the policy. And do not put words into people's mouths that they have not said." At the end, the President admitted that the administration did not mind having its statements construed "a bit strongly for whatever moral effect it might have."[28]

III

Meanwhile, British and French pressure on Prague to avert trouble was unrelenting. Halifax announced as early as March 23 that Britain expected the Czech government to "take all possible measures to do justice to their German minority." On May 2, with no Czech response forthcoming, Halifax admonished the Czech minister in London that the government in Prague needed to reach a settlement of the Sudeten question.[29] In mid-May, Halifax warned Prague that further delay would give the impression that the Czechs were not serious. On May 23, French Foreign Minster George Bonnet agreed to exert any pressure on the Czech government that London believed necessary. "I pointed out," Phipps reported, "that it behooved the Czechs to be more reasonable, for the alternative for them would be total annihilation."[30] As late as July 7, Halifax advised the French government to warn Prague that continued failure to make its full contribution to the cause of peace was about to involve France in a war for which it was not prepared.[31]

Unfortunately, the Czech government, facing a more and more determined, organized, and obstreperous Sudeten opposition, faced only unpromising

[28] Press Conferences, Hyde Park, September 6, 9, 1938, President's Press Conferences: TS, *FDRL*.
[29] Halifax to Phipps, March, 23, 1938, *DBFP*, Third Series, I, 87; Halifax to Newton, May 2, 1938, ibid., 236. The growing British impatience resulted from the announcement on April 24 of the Karlsbad eight-point program, which demanded full autonomy and freedom for the Sudeten Germans.
[30] Halifax to Henderson, May 4, 1938, ibid., 245–46; Halifax to Henderson, May 11, 1938, ibid., 282; Halifax to Newton, May 16, 1938, ibid., 300; Phipps to Halifax, May 23, 1938, ibid., 357.
[31] Halifax to Bonnet, July 7, 1938, ibid., 545.

alternatives. If it employed force to maintain order in the Sudetenland, it invited German retaliation; if it permitted the Sudeten defiance to continue, it invited charges of ineptness. There was evidence that the Sudeten Germans would respond to any Czech proposal with new demands, leading ultimately to complete Czech capitulation or war.[32] Henderson, recognizing Prague's declining capacity to control Czechoslovakia's future, suggested that Czechoslovakia, Britain, and France, in the interest of peace, accept Czechoslovakia's possible dismemberment. "Even if it means cutting down Czechoslovakia," he wrote, "I cannot but believe that it would be to her ultimate peace and advantage to be a homogenous Slav state rather than to maintain ... within her frontiers unwilling blocks of Germans or even Poles and Hungarians."[33]

By mid-summer, Sudeten nationalism had transformed Czechoslovakia into a state of permanent crisis. Gone was the dream that the country could assimilate the Sudeten Germans into the Czech mold. The tidal wave of Sudeten resistance to Czech rule had become irresistible. German threats and propaganda found no resolution in the British and French response, which seemed bewildered in its lack of serious commitment to the Czech cause.[34] Britain's failure to gain a Czech-Sudeten agreement on the future of the Sudetenland compelled Chamberlain to intensify his efforts. In early August, he responded to the Sudeten challenge by dispatching the Runciman Mission to Prague, acting as an independent mediator between the Czech government and the Sudeten German party.

Viscount Runciman's mission to Prague was Britain's final attempt to seek a negotiated solution of the Czech problem. On July 28, Runciman informed Roosevelt that his special mission, independent of all governments, would pursue a settlement through investigation and mediation. "My conferring with both sides may take two or three months," Runciman acknowledged. "But with free hands and the trust and confidence which I enjoy *just now* it *may* be possible to succeed ... and to relieve Europe from its extreme peril."[35] What mattered to London was Hitler's willingness to continue negotiations. To that end, Runciman sought to induce Czech leaders to reach an early agreement with Germany. Hitler did not regard President Edouard Beneš's proposals adequate; the Sudeten question, he said, could be resolved only on the basis of Henlein's Karlsbad demands – which went far beyond Beneš's counteroffers. Late in August, Beneš sent Runciman a new set of proposals that emphasized general principles rather than concrete offers. Runciman noted that the principles left little room for agreement. What gave force to Germany's growing dissatisfaction with Czech delays was the reports of extensive German military preparations and the rocky course of Czech-Sudeten negotiations, with Henlein rejecting each new Czech proposal.[36] Time was running out.

[32] Newton to Halifax, May 8, 20, 1938, ibid., 263, 320.
[33] Henderson to Halifax, April 13, 1938, ibid., I, 625.
[34] Newton to Halifax, August 2, 1938, ibid., II, 33–34.
[35] Runciman to Roosevelt, July 28, 1938, PSF: Great Britain: AS, *FDRL*.
[36] British aide-memoire, September 3, 1939, PSF: Czechoslovakia: CT, *FDRL*.

As Europe entered the critical month of September, Sir Ronald Lindsay, the British ambassador in Washington, assured Hull that the British government was doing everything in its power to obtain a Czech-German settlement. Runciman's failure to achieve the necessary Czech concessions was a measure of the inefficacy of London's endless ambivalence on the question of future action.[37] For Chamberlain, any threat more specific would be a bluff; he had no intention of leading Britain into a war over Czechoslovakia. The Prime Minister assured Kennedy that if France wanted British support, it would enter a war only with British approval.[38] Bullitt reported that the British ambassador in Berlin had warned the German government that if France chose war to counter a German invasion of Czechoslovakia, Britain would follow. Berle informed Roosevelt that the British were either engaging in deception or attempting to bluff the Germans.[39]

IV

With good reason, the troubled world anxiously awaited Hitler's Nuremberg address of September 12. Predictably, the Chancellor harangued his fanatically devoted audience with demands for Sudeten self-determination. He denounced Beneš as a liar, and declared that the deprivation of the rights of 3.5 million Germans in Czechoslovakia must be stopped. If the Sudetens required help from Germany, they would receive it. Hitler's speech was highly offensive, but both European and American observers noted that it did not close the door to further negotiations. The German Chancellor did not demand a plebiscite, but he offered Prague no defense against the probability that he might retaliate against any Czech repression by demanding annexation.[40]

Upon reading the speech, Chamberlain concluded that Runciman could offer no plan that would resolve the crisis. Without asking the Cabinet's permission, he made his long-contemplated move. On September 13, he addressed a note to Hitler, offering to travel to Germany to seek a solution to the Sudeten problem. On the following morning, the Prime Minister received the Cabinet's unanimous approval. Chamberlain had no intention of offering Hitler more than Sudeten autonomy and thereby encouraging further German encroachments on the Versailles Treaty.[41] The Prime Minister had not informed Paris of his plan, but he assured Kennedy that the French, less and less prepared to fight, would applaud his effort to confer with Hitler directly.

---

[37] *DBFP*, Third Series, II (London, 1949), 172–74; Lindsay to Hull, September 3, 1938, *FRUS, 1938*, I, 575–76.

[38] Bullitt to Hull, August 31, 1938, PSF: France: Bullitt, M, *FDRL*; Bullitt to Hull, September 2, 1938, *FRUS, 1938*, I, 570; Berle to Roosevelt, August 31, 1938, PSF: State: Berle: TS, *FDRL*.

[39] Bullitt to Hull, August 31, 1938, PSF: France: Bullitt, M., *FDRL*; Bullitt to Hull, September 2, 1938, *FRUS, 1938*, I, 570; Berle to Roosevelt, August 31, 1938, PSF: State, Berle, TS, *FDRL*.

[40] Kennedy to Hull, September 12, 1938, *FRUS, 1938*, I, 591; Wilbur J. Carr to Hull, September 13, 1938, ibid., 593.

[41] Kennedy to Hull, September 14, 1938, PSF: Great Britain: M, *FDRL*.

Chamberlain surmised correctly. Bullitt noted that the French resolve to fight for France's traditional interests in Central and Eastern Europe had diminished steadily during the previous year. Any French effort to protect Czechoslovakia, Bonnet complained to Bullitt, "would mean the defeat and dismemberment of France."[42] Daladier observed bitterly, in conversation with Bullitt, that France was on the verge "of reaping one of the wars the seeds of which had been sown in the [Versailles] treaty." Daladier and Bonnet had wrecked their careers temporarily by fighting the Versailles settlement. "Both are convinced," Bullitt informed Hull, "that the treaty must be revised and at bottom regard an alteration in the Czechoslovak State as a necessary revision – the necessity for which they pointed out nearly 20 years ago."[43]

Paris advised Prague that it expected the Czech government to carry the Sudeten negotiations to a successful conclusion. French leaders insisted that the French commitment to Czechoslovakia's defense assigned to Paris the right to guide the Prague government in its pursuit of a settlement. Bullitt observed, on September 14, that the French public demanded that France not destroy its youth and the whole European continent "in order to maintain the domination of 7,000,000 Czechs over 3,200,000 Germans." Bonnet informed Bullitt that if Czechoslovakia did not grant autonomy to the Sudeten Germans, France would desert its obligations to that country.[44]

Much of the American press reacted to Chamberlain's trip to Berchtesgaden with astonishment. *The New York Times* commented: "In the history of the British Empire, where protocol is almost as important as the conviction of supreme power, no Prime Minister has ever made a gesture so unconventional, so bold and in a way so humble."[45] *The New York Times*, with other newspapers, feared that Chamberlain's trip was a spectacular admission of desperation, not conducive to a successful negotiation. Roosevelt approved Chamberlain's decision to see Hitler, hoping that it would postpone what appeared to be an inevitable conflict.[46]

At Berchtesgaden, Chamberlain faced the prospect of Germany's absorption of the Sudetenland when Hitler demanded not autonomy, but self-determination, for the Sudeten Germans. That Chamberlain refused to accept, but he agreed to consult his cabinet as well as the French government. Hitler accepted that procedure, promising that he would take no immediate action against Czechoslovakia. It was essential only that Britain lose no time in securing French and Czech approval. At its meeting on September 17, the British Cabinet was reluctant to accept the principle of self-determination at the price of a Czech capitulation. Still, Chamberlain's options had reached the vanishing point. Britain was not prepared for war. It was equally clear that the

[42] Bullitt to Hull, May 16, September 15, 1938, *FRUS, 1938*, I, 501, 601.
[43] Bullitt to Hull, September 8, 15, 1938, ibid., 581, 601.
[44] Bullitt to Hull, September 14, 1938, ibid., 595–96.
[45] *The New York Times*, September 15, 1938, 24.
[46] Roosevelt to Phillips, September 15, 1938, PSF: Italy: Phillips: CT, *FDRL*.

French did not want to fight; indeed, they could not. Chamberlain acknowledged that Czechoslovakia would want British guarantees before it accepted Hitler's demands, but he hesitated to offer them.

On September 18, Chamberlain, with several members of the British cabinet, traveled to Paris for a meeting with Daladier and Bonnet. The discussions continued through the night. The French had few options, but they hesitated to terminate their treaty obligations to Prague. They opposed a Sudeten plebiscite, but insisted that they could obtain Beneš's agreement to a transfer of Sudeten territory by offering a guarantee to defend the Czech state. Chamberlain opposed the guarantee, but needed an agreement with the Czechs before he could return to Hitler. With no time to call the cabinet, the British officials in Paris accepted the guarantee. Ultimately, the British and French leaders agreed, Czechoslovakia's future required the transfer of the Sudeten region to the Reich, whether by plebiscite or by simple cession. Their note warned the Czech government that it alone would carry responsibility for any breakdown of the peace. Bonnet was confident that Prague would accept the Anglo-French proposal that it retreat on the Czech issue. "We will not," he informed Bullitt, "let Benes... drive 40 million French people to their deaths and he knows it."[47]

Roosevelt's State Department advisers urged him to ignore these dramatic and troubling events publicly. Any official statement that emphasized the importance of peace would appear to endorse the Anglo-French effort to satisfy Hitler. Any statement that stressed the importance of a just settlement and encouraged Czech resistance would burden the United States with moral responsibility for any war that ensued. At issue in America's leadership crisis was Roosevelt's determination to escape the mounting pressures of revisionism.

On September 20, Roosevelt called Ambassador Lindsay to the White House for a secret meeting. The President began by calling the Anglo-French pressure on the Czech government "the most terrible remorseless sacrifice that had ever been demanded of a State." Although such demands on Prague would provoke an unfavorable reaction in the United States, he did not blame the British or French governments; he understood the limited choices before them. In the mounting crisis, Roosevelt considered a world conference "for the purpose of reorganizing all unsatisfactory frontiers on rational lines." He would attend such a meeting, provided it was not held in Europe.[48] At the end of the meeting, the President did not even request an answer to that suggestion. In no subsequent communication with London or Berlin did Roosevelt hint at treaty revision. Others could carry the responsibility for the collapse

---

[47] Kennedy to Hull, September 17, 1938, PSF: Great Britain: Kennedy: M., *FDRL*; Kennedy to Hull, September 17, 1938, *FRUS, 1938*, I, 611–21; Bullitt to Hull, September 19, 1938, ibid., 621. For the Anglo-French talks of September 18–19, see *DBFP*, Third Series, II, 373–99. For the Anglo-French message to Prague, see Halifax to Newton, September 19, 1938, ibid., 405.

[48] Lindsay to Halifax, September 20, 1938, *DBFP*, Third Series, VII (London, 1954), 627–28.

of Europe's treaty structure. Bullitt shared Roosevelt's revulsion at the Anglo-French ultimatum to Czechoslovakia. The two governments, he wrote, "have acted like little boys doing dirty things behind the barn." Then he added, "If you have enough airplanes you don't have to go to Berchtesgaden." With the prospects for Europe discouraging, Bullitt advised the President that "the further we keep out of the mess the better."[49]

V

Count de Saint-Quentin, the French ambassador in Washington, called at the State Department to explain that military weakness alone had forced France's decision, a very painful one. The ambassador complained about the insulting editorials in the American press and the attacks on France in letters to the French embassy and the various French consulates.[50] The French ambassador did not exaggerate. The condemnation of the Anglo-French note to Czechoslovakia was widespread, if not universal. Editorials lamented the decline in the status of both Britain and France. *The New York Times* regarded the note as incredible, demanding an official explanation. *The Nation* revealed the extremes of anti-British and French sentiment: "Was there ever an occasion that so cried out for mass action, for thunderous denunciation, as this moment when the heads of the great European democracies have cast off the last shreds of political morality and elevated an obscene blackmailer to the dominance of a continent?"[51] Some saw danger in the immorality. *The New Republic* predicted that "the cession of Sudeten German territory to Hitler would not be a solution of anything, but an almost certain guarantee of future war." Similarly the *Christian Science Monitor* noted that "each day the pace of retreat is increasing."[52]

Czechoslovakia's capitulation to the Anglo-French ultimatum came hard. Beneš accused the two powers of abandoning his country. The German demands, he declared, were only the first that would terminate in Czechoslovakia's total destruction.[53] Phipps, in Paris, suggested "that the moment seemed to have come when we should inform M. Beneš that, unless his reply was an acceptance pure and simple, France and Britain would wash their hands of Czechoslovakia in the event of a German attack." In Prague, the British minister believed that a final ultimatum would give the Czech government the needed excuse to bow to superior power. Czech leaders must understand, he wrote, that if they failed to accept the Anglo-French proposals without reservation or delay, the British government would "take no further interest in

[49] Bullitt to Roosevelt, September 20, 1938, PSF: France: Bullitt: TS, *FDRL*.
[50] Memorandum of J. Pierrepont Moffat, September 20, 1938, PSF: State: TS, *FDRL*.
[51] *The New York Times*, September 19, 1938, 18; September 21, 1938, 6; *The Nation*, September 24, 1938, 282.
[52] *New Republic*, September 21, 1938, 172–73; *Christian Science Monitor*, September 22, 1938, 14.
[53] Newton to Halifax, September 19, 1938, *DBFP*, Third Series, II, 416–17.

the fate of the country."[54] As late as September 21, Czech leaders continued to resist, insisting that Britain and France had no right to desert them. In the end, the Prague government acknowledged its isolation, and on that day accepted the Anglo-French demand on the supposition that the two powers would do everything possible to safeguard Czechoslovakia's vital interests.[55]

Chamberlain now arranged to meet Hitler on September 22 at Godesberg, a quiet German city on the Rhine. Armed with the Czech acceptance of Hitler's demands, the Prime Minister could anticipate a pleasant and agreeable meeting. It proved to be stormy when Hitler turned down the British and French proposal flatly. He insisted that the Sudeten Germany territory be turned over at once, that there be a general plebiscite, and that all transferred territory be occupied by German troops. Such uncompromising demands left Chamberlain no apparent choice but war or diplomatic retreat. The British leader agreed to carry Hitler's demands to the Czech government, suggesting that he would support them. Again Hitler assured him that Germany would not invade Czechoslovakia while the negotiations continued.[56]

VI

In its outright rejection of the Godesberg memorandum, the Czech government closed off all further concessions to Germany. The Czech minister in London, Jan Masaryk, informed Halifax: "My Government wish me to declare in all solemnity that Herr Hitler's demands in their present form are absolutely and unconditionally unacceptable to my Government ... We rely upon the two great Western democracies, whose wishes we have followed much against our own judgment, to stand by us in our hour of trial."[57] Faced with such resistance, the British and French governments refused to recommend to Prague the acceptance of Hitler's latest demands. The Czech refusal to compromise beyond the post-Berchtesgaden agreement of September 21, a decision urged by Britain and France, created a new crisis.

Czech intransigence compelled Britain to confront Germany with a new proposal. Phipps reminded London that France lacked both the needed preparations for war and the will to fight.[58] At the Anglo-French talks in London on September 25 and 26, the French, under intensive British questioning, acknowledged their military weakness and agreed to another Chamberlain initiative. The Prime Minister announced that he was dispatching Sir Horace Wilson to Berlin to confer with Hitler. In his personal message, Chamberlain informed Hitler that Czech resistance now terminated all possibility of a

---

[54] Phipps to Halifax, September 20, 1938, ibid., 422–23; Newton to Halifax, September 20, 1938, ibid., 425.

[55] Ibid., 444–45.

[56] William L. Shirer, *"This is Berlin": Radio Broadcasts from Berlin* (Woodstock, 1999), 24.

[57] Masaryk to Halifax, September 25, 1938, *DBFP*, Third Series, II, 519.

[58] Kennedy to Hull, September 24, 1938, *FRUS, 1938*, I, 643; Phipps to Halifax, September 24, 1938, *DBFP*, Third Series, II, 510.

peaceful settlement purely on German terms. He asked Hitler to accept a Joint Commission, including German, Czech, and British representatives, to negotiate a new settlement. He reminded the German Chancellor that "the only difference between us lay in the method of carrying out an agreed principle."[59]

Wilson's meeting with Hitler on September 26 was scarcely promising. Chamberlain's message requested German concessions. Hitler read it and declared that the time for talking had ended. He had received the needed Czech concessions on September 21. Henderson, who was present, assured the German leader that the British government could still deliver the Sudetenland to Germany. With that, Wilson agreed. He hoped that Hitler would not close the door to further negotiations in his speech, scheduled for that evening.

On Monday September 26, Hitler addressed a mass meeting at Berlin's Sport Palace, with its 15,000 seats. He announced that Czechoslovakia would transfer the Sudetenland to Germany by the coming Saturday night, or suffer the consequences. The millions who gathered in every German town or village to hear the speech through loudspeakers, or listened quietly in their homes, could not doubt the significance of Hitler's words. "On the Sudeten problem," he declared, "my patience is at an end. And on October 1, Herr Benes will hand us over this territory." With the crowd cheering wildly, he warned: "Benes has now in his hand, war or peace. He can grant the Sudeten Germans their freedom, or we will take it for them." At this point, 15,000 people leaped to their feet, saluting and yelling their approval. "In this fateful hour," Hitler continued, "the whole German people are united behind me. We are determined. Herr Benes can choose." The warning was clear: the transfer of the Sudetenland by Saturday, or war.[60]

In their final session, on September 27, Hitler warned Wilson that if Czechoslovakia rejected his demands, he would smash that country. At the same time, he wondered why Czechoslovakia would pay such a heavy price for refusing to accept a memorandum "which meant nothing more than the fulfillment of pledges already made."[61] In his report, Wilson admonished Chamberlain to inform the Czechs how matters stood. Henderson warned Halifax that Britain now faced the choice between war and a resumption of pressure on Paris and Prague to find a solution. "It was not a question of what is reasonable or unreasonable," he wrote, "but of hard facts."[62]

[59] Bullitt to Hull, September 26, 1938, Bullitt, *For the President*, 290; Record of Anglo-French Conversations, September 26, 1938, *DBFP*, Third Series, II, 539–40; Chamberlain to Hitler, September 26, 1938, ibid., 541–42.

[60] Shirer, *"This is Berlin,"* 29–30.

[61] Notes of a conversation between Sir Horace Wilson and Hitler, Berlin, September 26, 1938, ibid., 554–57; conversation between Hitler and Wilson, September 27, 1938, ibid., 565; *Documents on German Foreign Policy* (hereafter *DGFP*), *1918–1945*, Series D, II (Washington, 1949), 964–65.

[62] Henderson to Halifax, September 27, 1938, *DBFP*, Third Series, II, 563; Henderson to Halifax, September 27, 1938, ibid., 574.

That evening, Chamberlain addressed the British people in a radio broadcast. "How horrible, fantastic, incredible, it is," he began, "that we should be digging trenches and trying on gas-masks here because of a quarrel in a faraway country between people of whom we know nothing!" The Prime Minister sympathized with the Czech reluctance to accept the German memorandum, but he reminded his listeners that Britain had offered Czechoslovakia a guarantee for the protection of its interests following a territorial settlement. For Chamberlain, the issue confronting Britain was no longer treaty revision, but war, and Britain had often sought to escape wars that might prove to be unproductive. "However much we may sympathize with a small nation confronted by a big and powerful neighbor," he acknowledged, "we cannot in all circumstances undertake to involve the whole British Empire in war simply on her account. If we have to fight it must be on larger issues than that." Chamberlain agreed that life in a world dominated by force would not be worth living, but, he added, "war is a fearful thing, and we must be very clear, before we embark on it, that it is really the great issues that are at stake."[63] For Chamberlain, nothing remained but an unwanted war or another journey to Germany.

Washington offered no response to the ever-deepening crisis. The President canceled two speaking engagements to remain near his office, but neither he nor Hull made any statement defining United States policy. Roosevelt avoided a press conference to prevent any possible misinterpretation of his remarks. *The New York Times* observed that the administration apparently intended to "make its policy conform to the views of the people who seemingly have become more isolationist than ever."[64] But not all Americans discounted the importance of the Czech issue to the United States. *The New York Times* reported a massive pro-Czech rally at Madison Square Garden, attended by some 20,000 people, that passed a resolution calling on the government of the United States, in case of war, to prohibit all traffic with Germany. One letter-writer protested:

> Yesterday afternoon I listened to the broadcast of a rally held at Madison Square Garden. I found myself bewildered and aghast; feebly wondering if the American people have gone completely mad. . . . I heard the Prime Minister of a great nation booed. I heard a man of debatable morality but of obvious significant efficiency referred to by implication as insane. I heard the fantastic suggestion put forth that we appeal over the head of this man to the army and to the people of Germany. Is there to be no end to this preposterous hysterical nonsense? . . . [Do the American people] not appreciate the absurdity of a national habit of protesting everything under the sun? If we are prepared to meet force with force, let us have more Garden rallies. If we are not, let us in the name of dignity and common sense, put an end to these exhibitions of unreasoning emotionalism.[65]

---

[63] *Documents on International Affairs, 1938*, 270–71.
[64] *The New York Times*, September 25, 1938, 3E.
[65] Ibid., September 26, 1938, 4; October 1, 1938, 16.

On September 25, while London, Paris, and Prague pondered Hitler's Godesberg demands, President Beneš asked Roosevelt to defend his country from another British and French sellout. Predictably, the President refused to intercede in the Sudeten affair.[66] Roosevelt followed the more expedient route of placing the burden of peace on the Europeans. On September 26, he broke his official silence with an appeal to Beneš, Hitler, Chamberlain, and Daladier, pointing to the danger of war and the unspeakable horrors that a rupture of the peace would bring to millions of people in every country of Europe. He reminded the four European leaders that their countries had assumed obligations, as had the United States, to peace and peaceful procedures by signing the Kellogg–Briand Pact. For Roosevelt, the specific issues in the Sudeten controversy mattered little. "I am persuaded," he wrote, "that there is no problem so difficult or so pressing for solution that it cannot be justly solved by the resort to reason rather than by resort to force."[67] The responsibility for finding the solution belonged to Europe, where the United States, the President added, had no political entanglements.

In his reply of September 27, Hitler agreed that war was unacceptable, but he argued that the Czech decision at Paris was a shameful betrayal of the German people. The Czech boundaries were drawn without regard to history or nationality. Thus, Germany was correct in demanding the application of Woodrow Wilson's principle of self-determination to the settlement of the Sudeten question. Inasmuch as the Czech government had agreed to the separation of the Sudetenland from Czechoslovakia before the Godesberg meeting, Germany's new proposals contemplated only the prompt fulfillment of the previous agreement. Prague could decide whether it wanted peace or war.[68]

Roosevelt responded to Hitler's argument with his own communication of September 27. Again the President focused on the price of war in the mutilation and death of millions. It was essential, therefore, that differences between the German and Czechoslovak governments be settled by pacific methods. A general war, he added, was unnecessary and unjustifiable. Therefore, negotiations should continue and resorts to force avoided. "Should you agree to a solution in this peaceful manner," Roosevelt admonished, "I am convinced that hundreds of millions throughout the world would recognize your action as an outstanding historic service to all humanity." Roosevelt then added: "The Government of the United States has no political involvement in Europe, and will assume no obligations in the conduct of the present negotiations. Yet in our own right we recognize our responsibilities as a part of a world of neighbors."[69] To elicit Italy's support, Roosevelt sent a special message to Benito Mussolini in Rome. Roosevelt's veiled warnings and appeals to principle combined his own and

---

[66] Carr to Hull, September 25, 1938, *FRUS, 1938*, 1, 649–50.
[67] Roosevelt to Hitler, September 26, 1938, *DGFP*, Series D, II, 959.
[68] Hitler to Roosevelt, September 27, 1938, ibid., 960–62.
[69] Roosevelt to Chancellor of Germany, September 27, 1938, Department of State, *Peace and War* (Washington, 1943), 428–29.

the State Department's thought on a proper American response to Hitler's Godesberg demands.

Chamberlain understood that the time for a negotiated settlement of the Sudeten issue had long passed. Hitler reinforced that reality when he informed Henderson that he would order German mobilization on September 28 unless Prague accepted his demands and made preparations to send representatives to settle the details before 2 o'clock on that day.[70] With time running out, Chamberlain, on the morning of September 28, inaugurated plans for his final conference with Hitler. He informed the Chancellor that he would return to Germany to discuss with him, and possibly with representatives from France and Italy also, the necessary arrangements for the transfer of the Sudetenland. London and Paris would guarantee full Czech compliance with any agreement. "I cannot believe," wrote Chamberlain, "that you will take the responsibility of starting a world war which may end civilization for the sake of a few days' delay in settling this long standing problem."[71] At the same time, the Prime Minister addressed a note to Mussolini, asking him to urge Hitler to accept the British overture and to inform the Chancellor that he would be willing to attend a meeting in Germany.[72]

Later that morning, the British ambassador in Rome took Chamberlain's message to Count Galeazzo Ciano, the Italian foreign minister. Ciano quickly conferred with Mussolini, who instructed Italian Ambassador Bernardo Atayalic in Berlin to convey Chamberlain's request to Hitler. Hitler agreed to postpone German mobilization for twenty-four hours and accepted the proposal for a four-power conference.[73] Late that afternoon, near the end of his speech before the House of Commons, Chamberlain received a note from Hitler inviting him to a conference at Munich on the following day. The Prime Minister's announcement of Hitler's message sent waves of approval through the House, expressing Parliament's deep aversion to war.

In accepting Hitler's invitation, Chamberlain reassured Prague that he would seek an accommodation between Germany and Czechoslovakia to achieve an orderly and equitable application of the agreement that it had already accepted.[74] Roosevelt sent Chamberlain a simple congratulation on his forthcoming trip to Munich: "Good man." Chamberlain, joined by Daladier and Mussolini, conferred with Hitler in two sessions during the afternoon of September 29. The Munich agreement, signed that evening, provided for the gradual Czech

---

[70] Henderson to Halifax, September 28, 1938, *DBFP*, Third Series, II, 598.

[71] Chamberlain to Hitler, September 28, 1938, PSF: Great Britain: CT, *FDRL*.

[72] Chamberlain to Mussolini, September 28, 1938, ibid.

[73] For an account of the events in Rome and Berlin on September 28, see Phillips to Roosevelt, September 29, 1938, PSF: Italy: Phillips: TS, *FDRL*; Record of conversation between the Earl of Perth and Phillips, September 28, 1938, *DBFP*, Third Series, II, 608; Perth to Halifax, September 30, 1938, ibid., 641–45; Hugh Wilson to Welles, October 21, 1938, PSF: State: Welles: M, *FDRL*; Roosevelt to Phillips, October 17,. 1938, PSF: Italy: Phillips: CT, *FDRL*.

[74] Halifax to Newton, September 28, 1938, *DBFP*, Third Series, II, 599.

evacuation of the Sudetenland between October 1 and October 10, and the German occupation of the region by stages during the same period, with no existing installations damaged or destroyed.[75] The German occupation of predominantly German territories along Czechoslovakia's periphery, divided into four regions, would also begin on October 1 and continue for seven days. As requested by Britain and France, the Munich settlement contained an international guarantee of Czech independence.[76] Chamberlain, with Daladier, agreed to carry the agreement to the Czech representative in Munich, who was waiting at his hotel. They presumed correctly that Prague would regard the document as an improvement over the Godesberg memorandum and would accept it. In a private meeting on September 30, Hitler and Chamberlain agreed to settle future questions that concerned their two countries through consultation.[77] For Chamberlain, the peace of Europe now appeared secure.

VII

Much of the post-Munich euphoria in both the United States and Europe centered on Roosevelt's second letter to Hitler. In that letter, as in the first, the President denied any U.S. responsibility for addressing the problems of Europe. It was not even clear exactly when Hitler read the second message.[78] Yet, for many observers, that letter confirmed the impression that Roosevelt had admonished Hitler sufficiently to spare Europe another major war. During succeeding days, Roosevelt received fulsome praise for maintaining peace in the Czech crisis.

London's financial community, wrote J. P. Morgan's Thomas Lamont, regarded Roosevelt's second letter to Hitler as essential for bringing about the Munich conference. Also, in London, Lord Halifax requested Ambassador Kennedy to convey to the President the thanks of the British government "for the help that [he] had given by his intervention during the last two or three days." Halifax added that he had no doubt whatever "that this had exercised a very powerful influence upon the course of events."[79] From Ambassador William Phillips in Rome came the same verdict. Bullitt lauded the President from Paris on September 28: "I was a great deal prouder of you today. Your second telegram to Hitler was a masterpiece."[80] Roosevelt himself, at a press conference on September 30, gave credit for Europe's peace to Hull, the State Department, and the United States diplomatic corps in Europe.[81]

---

[75] Munich agreement of September 29, 1938, ibid., 634–35.

[76] *The New York Times*, September 30, 1938.

[77] Chamberlain–Hitler agreement of September 30, 1938, *DBFP*, Third Series, II, 640.

[78] See Wilson to Welles, October 20, 21, 1938, PSF: State: Wells, M, *FDRL*.

[79] Thomas Lamont to Roosevelt, September 28, 1938, PPF 70: T; Halifax to Lindsay, September 29, 1938, *DBFP*, Third Series, II, 625.

[80] Phillips to Roosevelt, September 28, 1938, PSF: Italy, Phillips, TS; Bullitt to Roosevelt, September 28, 1938, PSF: France: Bullitt: TS, *FDRL*.

[81] Press Conference in the White House, September 30, 1938, President's Press Conferences: TS, *FDRL*.

Although the Munich settlement was scarcely a triumph for America's principle of peaceful change, Roosevelt continued to receive the plaudits of the American peace community. Irving Fisher, the noted Yale economist, congratulated the President for his contribution to world peace. "I suspect," he wrote on October 3, "that your part has been greater, and more influential, than reported in the press." Isolationist Oswald Garrison Villard thanked the President for his "friendly intervention in the European crisis.... I am sure," he added, "that there is no more brilliant chapter in our diplomatic history...."[82]

Members of the United States diplomatic corps in Europe voiced their own and Europe's gratitude for Roosevelt's efforts in the Munich crisis. Ambassador Franklin Mott Gunther addressed the President from Bucharest: "Your intervention with Hitler, Mussolini, and Benes was hailed here with deep admiration and relief. On all sides and from all quarters I heard your praises sung and it made me glow with pride."[83] Joseph E. Davies wrote from Brussels that Roosevelt's messages to Hitler, by placing the responsibility for peace directly on Germany, were more potent than any other thing in preventing war. "I find on all sides," wrote Davies, "the greatest enthusiasm here, not only because of the President's leadership but because of the clarity and power with which he analyzed the situation, swept aside the non-essentials and put the bee right on Hitler."[84] Foreign leaders were no less appreciative of Roosevelt's messages to Hitler. Chamberlain personally acknowledged his gratitude to Roosevelt for his messages to Hitler and his helpful attitude toward British policy both during and after the Munich crisis.

VIII

Throughout the Czech crisis, Chamberlain exploited rather than confronted his country's lack of preparedness and its apparent preference for peace at any price. At Berchtesgaden and Godesberg, under the growing threat of violence, Britain and France, with ample American support, shifted from the pursuit of an honorable settlement of the Sudeten question, with some recognition of the need for treaty revision, to the maintenance of peace at the cost of surrender to Hitler's threats of force.[85] What underlay the Munich settlement was the willingness of Britain and France to compel Czechoslovakia to pay the price for their escape from disaster. Chamberlain asked nothing of his country, of France, or of the United States in his response to the continuing disintegration of the Versailles order. Hitler confronted Chamberlain at Munich with

[82] Fisher to Roosevelt, October 3, 1938, PPF431: TS; Villard to Roosevelt, October 5, 1938, PPF2178: TS, *FDRL.*

[83] Gunther to Roosevelt, November 1, 1938, PSF: State: TS, *FDRL.*

[84] Davies to Roosevelt, November 3, 1938, OF1913: TS: Carr to Roosevelt, November 10, 1938, PSF: Czechoslovakia: TS, *FDRL.*

[85] H. R. Trevor-Roper, "The Dilemma of Munich Is Still with Us," *The New York Times Magazine,* September 15, 1968, 34–35, 72–76.

the disastrous choice of an ignominious peace or war. The Prime Minister ignored the choice by proclaiming the settlement a victory. He wrote to the Archbishop of Canterbury on October 2: "I am sure that some day the Czechs will see that what we did was to save them for a happier future. And I sincerely believe that we have at last opened the way to that general appeasement which alone can save the world from chaos."[86]

Munich destroyed the illusion of American isolation from the political affairs of Europe. The news of Hitler's dramatic annexations, especially in overseas radio reports, stirred the nation's consciousness. Selig Adler described the phenomenon in the following passage:

> ... Americans ... could hardly shut their ears to the blow-by-blow description of events. As putches, invasions, threats, surrenders, dramatic airplane flights of prime ministers followed one another seriatim, the dispensation of foreign news became increasingly efficient. Gifted on-the-spot radio correspondents broadcast round-ups that could be heard from four countries in one program. Never before had the Old World seemed so close....[87]

American writers and editors agreed overwhelmingly that the Munich settlement comprised a massive and dangerous collapse of Western leadership. Much of the press attributed this costly failure of collective security not to the force of German aggression but to the unnecessary weakness and vacillation in British and French diplomacy. Other editors, however, reminded the critics of Munich that their rebukes were totally illogical, if not dishonest. "No one who approves the course this country has pursued since 1920," cautioned the Richmond (Virginia) *Times-Dispatch*, "has a right to criticize those democracies for the course they have pursued. The United States has followed policies in the past 18 years which have not only helped to make the rise of the dictators inevitable, but which have made resistance by Britain and France to the dictators much more difficult." *The New York Times* challenged those who would condemn the British and the French nations:

> Let no man say that too high a price has been paid for peace in Europe until he has searched his soul and found himself willing to risk in war the lives of those who are nearest and dearest to him. Let no man say that it would have been better to resist, and to fight it out, "now rather than later," unless he himself would have sent young men marching into the dreary hell of war. Let no man say that the statesmen of Britain and France were out-traded in the bargain they have struck, until he has attempted to add the total of the price they might have to pay for another settlement than the one which they have taken.

Ultimately the press defended American isolationism by accepting the logic that the peace achieved at Munich, whatever the cost to others, was preferable to war. *The New York Times* praised Chamberlain unstintingly for his

---

[86] Feiling, *The Life of Neville Chamberlain*, 375.
[87] Selig Adler, *The Isolationist Impulse: Its Twentieth-Century Reaction* (London, 1957), 269.

immediate achievement of a settlement: "Whatever happens in Europe – and what happens now depends on how much sanity still prevails in the councils of Berlin – Mr. Chamberlain will emerge from the momentous events of the past fortnight as a heroic figure, with the respect and admiration of men of good-will the whole world over."[88]

Both Roosevelt and Hull saw in the Munich agreement not only a welcome peace but the possibilities for a more principled future. The President confided to Ambassador William Phillips in Rome: "I want you to know that I am not a bit upset over the final result." Hull, ignoring the role that threats and power had played in the Munich settlement, declared that "the forces which stand for principles governing peaceful and orderly international relations ... should not relax, but redouble, their efforts to maintain these principles of order under law...." Roosevelt wired Chamberlain: "Now that you have established personal contact with Chancellor Hitler, I know that you will be taking up with him from time to time many of the problems which must be resolved in order to bring about that new and better order."[89]

Some American officials shared the doubts of Chamberlain's critics in London that the Munich settlement had achieved anything notable. Assistant Secretary George S. Messersmith reminded Hull on September 29 that the four-powers meeting in Munich might well preserve the peace momentarily, but that the settlement would result less from pacific procedures than from Anglo-French concessions under the threat of force. Those concessions, he predicted, would result in either German mastery of Europe or war.[90] U.S. diplomats in Europe warned that Munich had destroyed what was left of Europe's equilibrium. Early in October, Ambassador Biddle reported from Warsaw that European leaders were reexamining the positions of their respective countries in the light of Hitler's triumph. That settlement reinforced the determination of the Oslo group of smaller states – Belgium, Holland, Switzerland, and the Scandinavian countries – to maintain their neutrality in the burgeoning European conflict. Ambassador Herbert C. Pell reminded Roosevelt from Lisbon, that Hitler at Munich had diminished British and French prestige almost beyond recall. In Portugal, he wrote, Italians and Germans viewed Munich "as a second Canossa, a great victory for the Dictators and a crushing defeat for England."[91] Pell predicted that Hitler would demand greater concessions within a year. Davies in Brussels, despite his fulsome praise of Roosevelt's letter-writing, agreed with Pell

---

[88] Richmond (Virginia) *Times Dispatch*, September 26, 1938, 8; *The New York Times*, September 28, 1938, 24; September 30, 1938, 20.

[89] Roosevelt to Phillips, October 17, 1938, in Elliott Roosevelt, *F.D.R.: His Personal Letters, 1928–1945* (New York, 1950), II, 817–18; Cordell Hull, *Memoirs* (London, 1948), I, 595; Department of State, *Press Releases* 19 (1938), 240.

[90] Messersmith to Hull, September 29, 1938, PSF: State TS, *FDRL*.

[91] Biddle to Roosevelt, October 6, 1938, PSF: Germany: TS; Biddle to Roosevelt, November 5, 1938, PSF: Poland: TS; Pell to Roosevelt, October 21, 1938, PSF: Portugal: TS, *FDRL*.

that Germany had emerged from Munich as Europe's most powerful and effective country.[92]

Such observations were remarkably accurate. Munich offered no guarantees for future peace. Indeed, Munich quickly emerged as the decade's major symbol of failure. The United States, acting under the assumption that the resolution of the Sudeten problem rested on European statesmanship, did little to prevent the outcome. Roosevelt's letter-writing and verbal interventions demonstrated that pleas for peaceful change, accompanied by mere condemnations of aggression, had little influence on international behavior. Britain had no historic interests in Central Europe that demanded the protection of Czechoslovakia. For some British leaders, especially the Churchill–Eden group, the Munich syndrome – the supposition that the failure to hold the line at Munich merely invoked further assaults and ultimately war – seemed to demonstrate the high price of military and diplomatic weakness. These critics assumed that firm opposition would have stopped Germany, whereas Hitler, it seems clear, actually desired a war over the Sudetenland to capitalize on his immediate advantages.[93]

Power is not the only factor in successful external relations. The objectives and timing of policy are equally so. Decisions for war, whatever the provocation, must presume the public's recognition of a clear threat to the nation's well-being and its preparations to make the sacrifice that war entails. In September 1938, the masses of Britain, France, and the United States were not ready for war, unless Germany engaged in outrages, both direct and inescapable. So profound was British, French, and U.S. isolationism that none of the three powers was prepared, physically or emotionally, to embark on war. Clearly, the Czech defense system, with the Sudetenland's impressive arsenal and thirty-five Czech army divisions, was stronger in 1938 than a year later, but no opponent of Hitler was then free to exercise its military option. Even the British Dominions announced their total objection to a war over the Sudetenland. Ultimately, Hitler alone could draw any of the three democracies into armed conflict. Europe and the United States paid a high price for the Munich settlement, but that did not mark September 1938 as a propitious, or even possible, moment to confront Hitler with war.

[92] Davies to Roosevelt, November 3, 1938, OF1913: TS, *FDRL*.
[93] For the argument that Hitler desired war in September 1938, see Gerhard L. Weinberg, "Munich after 50 Years," *Foreign Affairs*, 67 (Fall 1988), 168–73.

10

The Road to Prague

I

For Neville Chamberlain, Munich established a new international order that would bring peaceful reconciliation to the major powers of Europe. But realist critics of Munich denied the possibility of a satisfactory outcome. Among them was Winston Churchill, who had attacked British concessions before Munich and was among the first to condemn the Munich agreement itself. He unleashed his verbal attack in the House of Commons: "I shall begin by saying what everybody would like to ignore or forget but which must nevertheless be stated, namely, that we have sustained a total and unmitigated defeat...." In typical Churchillian style, he charged that all Chamberlain had gained for Czechoslovakia was the German dictator, who, "instead of snatching his victuals from the table, had been content to have them served to him course by course." In the end, he asserted that the British people were misled and not told that their defenses had been sacrificed – and without war. With the "equilibrium of Europe ... deranged," he concluded, the Western democracies were "weighed in the balance and found wanting."[1]

Perhaps the most devastating condemnation of Chamberlain's policy came from Third Secretary of the British Embassy in Berlin, Con O'Neill, who resigned in disagreement over what he defined as the disastrous appeasement at Munich. He wrote a lengthy final dispatch to Sir William Strang in the Foreign Office that he hoped would not be construed as presumptuous, coming from a Third Secretary. "But as my reasons for resigning are largely political," he continued, "I should like to explain why, and on what grounds of observation and anticipation in Germany, I think the policy his Majesty's Government have followed and, in October at least, seemed likely to continue to follow towards Germany, is mistaken."

[1] Robert Rhodes James, ed., *Winston S. Churchill: His Complete Speeches, 1897–1963*, IV, 1935–1942 (New York and London, 1974).

O'Neill hoped that he was not being inexcusably disloyal to his Ambassador, Nevile Henderson, and then proceeded to lay out the reasons his ambassador and the prime minister were grievously in error in the policy pursued at Munich. He thought the Munich agreement could be expressed in "deliberate but not outrageous exaggeration, as a defeat of the British Navy and the French Army.... Not to speak of the Czech fortifications and the Czech army." He charged that "the Czechs were ready to fight for us, scarcely less directly threatened by Germany than themselves, even if we were not ready to fight for them." He agreed with the military historians who, contrary to the Chamberlain argument, thought that the Czechs had defensible borders and, if military aid were forthcoming, could have held out long enough to put a large crimp in Hitler's plan of conquest.

Throughout September, O'Neill hoped that England would go to war to support the Czechs. He contended that there were several lost opportunities between April and the end of September to force German withdrawal from the Czech borders. Lest Strang think he wanted simply to defend Czechoslovakia, O'Neill argued that British interests were at stake and that there was no future time the British could be more readily united in support of their defense. This failure to act, he added, drove France into an inglorious accommodation with the Germans.[2]

In a direct assault on Chamberlain's naiveté, O'Neill expressed amazement that anyone who had dealt with the Nazis over a period of time could not see that "they can and will make and keep no compromise, in method or in aim.... If they will not compromise, then we must either do so ourselves or fight them, whether in the ideological or the military arena." He was afraid Britain was in danger of compromising. "I am writing all this," he added, "because I earnestly hope we shall not." He contended that there were many examples of concessions to the Nazis that produced no return. For him, the case against Germany was strong. "I marvel," he complained, "at our apparent readiness to throw it away." He returned to Anthony Eden's argument about what England really needed, "As in 1935 and for a moment this year," he noted, "the whole world – or should I say America? – would welcome a policy of resistance by us to an authoritarian regime: and today such a policy toward the Nazi regime ... would have little danger and some prospect of success."

O'Neill scored the Chamberlain group for not recognizing that a considerable element in Germany (the *Widerstand* – opposition) would, with some encouragement, willingly oppose Hitler. There was great danger, he warned, in isolating the Russians and driving them in the direction of Berlin. For him, there was one hope: "Above all we should continue to search for allies, and persist in the patient construction of coalitions.... We should see in every

[2] Con O'Neill to W. Strang, C.M.G., November 29, 1938, 1–5. Strang 4/2, Strang Papers, Churchill College, Cambridge.

enemy of Germany a friend of ours. We should make peace with Russia before Germany does so."[3]

There was much wishful thinking in the plans of the statesmen who defined British policy during and after Munich. This was especially true for Halifax and Chamberlain. Lord Halifax was convinced that Czechoslovakia was not worth defending and that Germany was destined to control Eastern Europe. He attempted, with reason, to provide a corrective to Churchill's rejection of Munich.

Clearly Chamberlain's and Halifax's hopes for continuing peace rested on the Munich agreements. When Churchill attacked the British decisions, Halifax argued that Britain could not have demanded more, given the state of unpreparedness in the British army and air force. Chamberlain discounted the advice he received from those who understood that Hitler could not be satisfied by any concessions that did not include German control of most of Europe, east of France, and that the French and Russians were willing to take action only with British support.

Roosevelt's private reaction to the Munich agreement was totally at odds with the acceptance he displayed at the time of its signing. When Chamberlain went to Munich, Roosevelt advised his cabinet privately that the British were about to sacrifice the Czechs on the altar of appeasement, perhaps bringing only a temporary peace, after which the British and French would "wash the blood from their Judas Iscariot hands."[4] FDR went even further in condemning Chamberlain's actions when he told his cabinet that Chamberlain was "slippery" and could not be trusted as he played the British game of "peace at any price," with the result that the Germans need not go to war because they got everything they wanted without it.[5] FDR might complain about the British actions and even resent them, but actually knew he could do nothing about it.

Relying on the image of power that the United States could exert in post-Munich Europe, Roosevelt focused not on Germany but on Italy. The President was perplexed by the Italians' failure to understand what it meant to ignore America's potential power. He lamented to Ambassador William Phillips in Italy that the Italians did not seem to understand the reality of American power. The Italians, he wrote, should understand that the whole of Italy would fit inside the boundaries of Texas, and they were incredibly outnumbered in both population and natural resources.[6] For Mussolini, America's potential was one thing, its commitment quite another. Hitler sat on the Italian border because of the annexation of Austria, England was pursuing a policy of appeasement, France was being emasculated by the British denial of support.

---

[3] Ibid., 10ff, 28.
[4] As quoted in Dallek, *Franklin D. Roosevelt and American Foreign Policy*, 164.
[5] Cited in Bennett, *Separated by a Common Language*, 205.
[6] Ibid., 204.

What Germany did or did not do was far more important for Mussolini than what the United States might do.

Peace rested on the Munich agreement and Hitler's commitment to it. German State Secretary Ernst von Weizsäcker was reassuring. He boasted in a circular to the German embassies on October 3 that the "historic conference" at Munich ensured the acceptance of Hitler's East European policy, including settlement of the Sudeten-German question. He contended that it was the first peaceful settlement of border revisions in history, accepted by "the four major European statesmen," plus the rest of Europe, including the Czechs. He chastised newsmen who contended that this was merely a first step in a German campaign of territorial expansion.[7]

II

In the aftermath of the Munich agreement, Czechoslovakia was unquestionably at the mercy of Adolf Hitler. Sir Nevile Henderson reported from Berlin that the problem of resistance to the Munich accords was about to be solved when Edouard Beneš resigned on September 30. For Henderson, this was a "hopeful sign that Czechoslovakia will now put her relations with her neighbors, particularly Germany, on a friendly footing." He reported to Halifax that relations between the Czechs and the Germans, working under the auspices of the International Commission, could not help but improve. In other words, the sellout of the Czechs had gone so smoothly that there would be no bloodshed.[8]

But in Prague, British Minister Basil Newton reported to Halifax that the representative from the Czech foreign office had already appealed to the British to live up to their obligation to prevent the final demise of the Czech republic. He concluded as early as October 6, "It remains of course to be seen whether those in control of German policy want to leave Czechoslovakia with ... [an] independent existence."[9]

Hitler, on October 21, 1938, provided an answer to this question. Three weeks after the Munich agreement, he gave the German Army a directive to prepare for what he called eventualities: "1. Securing the frontiers of the German Reich and protecting against surprise attacks; 2. liquidation of the remainder of the Czech state; 3. occupation of Memeland," the port on the Baltic Sea that had been taken from Germany in the Versailles settlement.[10] Occupation of the whole Czech state meant, for Hitler, what he knew would come later: his plans to control the whole of Eastern Europe and regain Danzig. In short, the economic and strategic value of the Czech republic

---

[7] Circular of the State Secretary, Berlin, October 3, 1938, *DGFP*, Series D, Vol. IV, 18–19.

[8] Bennett, *Separated by a Common Language*, 204.

[9] Basil Newton (Prague) to Viscount Halifax, October 6, 1938, PHHP, Churchill College, Cambridge, 108–09.

[10] Ian Kershaw, *Hitler, 1936–45: Nemesis* (New York, 1998), 163.

demanded its absorption by the German state. The Czechs realized that they
had little opportunity to resist, and tried in every way to accommodate Hitler's
demands on their rump nation.[11]

It did not take long for the Germans to assert that the Munich agreement clearly turned over not merely the government-owned and -operated
facilities in the Sudeten region, but also the privately owned public utilities.
Within one week, neighboring countries moved to extend the dismemberment. Hungary and Yugoslavia demanded Czech territory; the Ruthenians
asked to be joined to either Hungary or Poland. The Czechs hoped that either
Britain or Germany would prevent these annexationist movements, a vain
hope. German propaganda encouraged the complete detachment of Slovakia
and Ruthenia; then, according to Newton, the German plan seemed to "create
two separate and nominally independent states out of Bohemia and Slovakia,
both under its dominance, while Ruthenia could be divided between Poland
and Hungary...."[12]

Among British Tories there was little sympathy for the plight of the Czechs.
Sir Maurice Hankey wrote to a friend stationed in Poland, "I think you have
taken the Czech affair too much to heart. The Czechs had their chance after
the Treaty of Versailles [concerning the ethnic divisions in their territory] and
threw it away ...." If the Czechs had played the Sudeten's game, and granted
more autonomy to them earlier, he wrote, they never would have gotten into
such a mess. He concluded that the Czechs were not worth a world war, which,
in any case, could never have restored them to their old position.[13] Hankey was
one of those British officials who supported letting the Czech state sink into the
Nazi sea, without understanding what it meant for Britain. The degree to which
the British failed to see what a Czech abandonment might lead to was nowhere
more evident than in the Halifax–Phipps correspondence at the end of 1938.

Ambassador Sir Eric Phipps wrote to Halifax from Paris on October 24,
recounting what Bonnet had told him about François-Poncet's recent meeting
with Adolf Hitler at Berchtesgaden. He reported that Hitler complained bitterly that Munich had not produced an improvement in Franco-German relations. He recalled the debate[14] that took place in the House of Commons during
which, Hitler contended, Germany was insulted. He illustrated Poncet's wishful thinking when the Frenchman recorded that he was "deeply impressed"
with Hitler's "genuine desire for general pacification and anxiety to avoid a
European war." In this fashion, the French leaders indicated that they still
believed that an arrangement with Germany, sustaining the status quo, was
feasible, a position that Halifax and Phipps thought commendable. They

---

[11] Ibid., 163–66.

[12] Newton (Prague) to Viscount Halifax, October 7, 1938, ibid., 118.

[13] Sir Maurice Hankey, October 20, 1938. Hankey Papers, Churchill College, Cambridge.

[14] During a debate on Anglo-German relations in the House of Commons, Duff Cooper made
"rude insults" to Hitler that the speaker did not censure. See Herbert von Dirksen, *Moscow,
Tokyo, London: Twenty Years of German Foreign Policy* (Norman, 1952), 217–18.

failed to understand that Hitler's actions were not a response to Britain and France's failure to live up to the Munich accords; he intended from the outset to continue his thrust eastward. Hitler perceived that Britain and France, once they realized the game he was playing, would either give up their traditional relationship to East Europe, or fight, and he presumed that it would mean a military conflict – which he desired from the outset.

Some leaders in both France and Britain perceived Hitler's expansionist objective, but they were opposed by those in authority. Phipps recorded that any criticism forthcoming from French critics was no doubt backed by the French Bolsheviks. Phipps lamented the position taken by General Secretary of the French Foreign Office Alexis Saint-Léger, regarding events since Munich: "I saw him this afternoon and found him as convinced as ever that no arrangement could be reached between France and Germany or … Italy. In fact his point of view remains hopelessly sterile."[15]

Phipps then reported on November 8 that Bonnet told him a deal with Hitler was in the offing wherein they would mutually guarantee that no territorial questions separated them. They would undertake to settle all future disputes by consultation. He said that Bonnet kept the fact of this agreement on the status quo strictly limited in its distribution so that no leaks would torpedo it. How it would be implemented had not been decided. It could be by a visit by Bonnet to Germany, or Ribbentrop to Paris, or merely through signing a agreement. He hoped the second approach would be taken, so that it would not look as though he were running after Hitler. Phipps reported also that he had recently spoken to the German ambassador and anticipated a quick agreement.[16]

The central tragedy in late 1938 rested with the failure of Britain and France to stand firmly against the Nazi program to control all of Eastern Europe, despite guarantees to abide by existing borders. Inside Germany, the *Widerstand*[17] was prepared to overthrow the Nazi regime if there was a strong stand by the British and French against the dismemberment of Czechoslovakia. This response required overt British and French action. When there was none, the movement failed.[18]

---

[15] Phipps to Halifax, October 24, 1938, PHPP 2, Churchill College, Cambridge.

[16] Phipps to Halifax, November, 8, 1938, PHPP 1/21, Churchill College, Cambridge.

[17] Klemens von Klemperer, *German Resistance against Hitler: The Search for Allies Abroad, 1938–1945* (Oxford: 1992). This study provides the best accounting of the *Widerstand* (opposition movement) in Germany. He contended that the tragedy of this group was that the conspirators, motivated by either remorse for the sins of Nazism, or by genuine respect for their nation and its heritage, or even by religious motivation, sacrificed themselves, often to horrible deaths, only to be rejected by the only people who could do something to aid their effort to overthrow their despotic leader.

[18] Ibid., 106–07. Klemperer points out here that the problem in the failure of this effort was the dependence on external action to set off the revolt, when in fact if there had been internal action, it might have forced the hand of British and French leaders. There was plenty of blame available for the failure to act; partly it was the timidity of General Franz Halder, who wanted someone else to start the revolt and then he and his group would follow.

III

Newton's despatch from Prague on November 7 anticipated Czechoslovakia's
fate. Clearly the British and French guarantees of the remaining borders of
Czechoslovakia were of no value in preventing Germany's emasculation of the
remaining Czech state. France refused a loan, explaining that Czechoslovakia
was a German satellite, and for economic and geographical reasons must
maintain good relations with Germany. He reported that on the Czech Foreign
Minister's recent visit to Munich, Hitler threatened that if the Czechs irritated
him, "in 24 hours – no, in 8 hours – I will make an end (mache ich Schluss)
[to the Czech state]."[19]

How the British viewed the developments in Eastern Europe was related to
circumstances that proved both realistic in terms of what they wrought, and
illusory in terms of what the appeasers believed they had accomplished. The
British Military Attaché in Berlin, Colonel F. N. Mason-MacFarlane, thought
that there was a logical progression of events as the Sudeten question had
become a direct corollary to the Austrian Anschluss. Even before the occupation was completed, the Germans began to consider the German minority
in Czechoslovakia. Analyzing events before and through the Munich decisions, Mason-MacFarlane concluded that Hitler had moved from a wait-and-
see posture on the Sudetenland to a willingness to fight for it, strengthening
German defenses to guard the western frontier against possible action by the
French and the British.

Mason-MacFarlane thought that Hitler's determination to advance was
reenforced by Ribbentrop, Goebbels, and Himmler – who argued that Britain
would not fight. He contended that Hitler's meetings with Chamberlain at
Munich offered the Wehrmacht time to organize on the Czech border for
the assault that would follow when the order was given. It was apparent that
the people in Germany did not want war; the Berliners met the marching of
troops in Berlin with sullen silence. This did not mean the people would not
support Hitler in a war that went well. In the end, there was "satisfaction at
the success of Herr Hitler's 'Machtpolitik'...." Hitler had again successfully
bluffed the Western Powers.[20]

Halifax's own role in this fiasco may have prompted his defense of the
Munich policy. On November 1, 1938, he wrote to Phipps concerning the
rumor, coming from Paris, that German intrigue might be moving the French
to drift away from England. He doubted this because of French hostility to
Germany, but went on to contend that a chief difficulty in the past was "the
unreal position" that the French occupied in Central and Eastern Europe. He

---

[19] Newton (Prague) to Viscount Halifax (received November 7), No. 540, saving: telegraphic
   [C 13546/2319/12], PHPP, Churchill College, Cambridge, 222.
[20] Memorandum on military measures taken by Germany in connection with the Sudeten question from Sir G. Ogilvie-Forbes (Berlin) to Viscount Halifax, with an enclosure from Colonel
   F. N. Mason-MacFarlane, October 25, 1938. *DBFP*. Third Series, IV, 1938, Appendix III,
   622–26.

added that France claimed great influence [through its alliance system], but owing to the rising strength of Germany, and because of France's neglect of its own defenses, it could not render its claims effective. At the same time, such French designs continued to irritate Germany.

But Munich, Halifax added, had made possible a fresh start in Franco-German relations. He noted that German predominance in Central and Eastern Europe was inevitable. Britain's challenge was to prevent Germany from spreading westward. The real danger, he contended, was not that France would give up any claims in Eastern Europe to gain Germany's approval, but that France might "turn so defeatist as to give up the struggle of maintaining adequate defences even for the safety of metropolitan France." It was essential that England encourage France to rearm as quickly as possible so that Britain would not need, "to face alone the full weight of German military power in the West."[21]

IV

As the crisis mounted in Europe, the Americans and the Russians considered various ploys to deal with the disintegration of the Versailles settlement – without actually providing any concrete opposition to the Anglo-French appeasement. Roosevelt spoke out emphatically against the violations of Austrian and Czech sovereignty. Letters and telegrams poured into the White House, some vehemently opposing any U.S. move to become involved in Europe's problems, and venting an irrational spleen in a somewhat threatening mode against involvement. But most of these communications encouraged the president to become more bold. The editors of *The United States in World Affairs* had a better appreciation of where FDR was going than did Sumner Welles, who advised caution based on the president's support level. They surmised that his suggestions were receiving a cordial response even though "in his latest message Mr. Roosevelt definitely aligned the country on the side of one group of nations with an intimation that they might count on something more than moral support."[22]

George Messersmith, as early as September 1, 1938, advised Key Pittman, Chairman of the Senate Committee on Foreign Relations, that the situation in Europe was headed for disaster. He stated flatly that Hitler would not be satisfied with any settlement in Czechoslovakia short of annexation.[23] Pittman wrote a letter complaining to Assistant Secretary of State R. Walton Moore that there was too much pacifist-isolationist sentiment in the Congress and the public.[24] Pitman declared in the Senate in December that the United States opposed the governments of Germany and Japan and possessed the power to

---

[21] Halifax to Sir Eric Phipps, November 1, 1938. Churchill College, Cambridge.
[22] William H. Shepardson and William O. Scroggs, *The United States in World Affairs: An Account of American Foreign Relations, 1939* (New York, 1940), 6–7.
[23] Messersmith to Pittman, September 1, 1938, Committee Papers, SEN 75A-F9–1 (105H).
[24] Pittman to Moore, October 15, 1938, ibid., SEN 74A-F9–1 (105H).

confront them. But the United States would not use force "unless necessary."[25] This veiled threat came from a senator who, in 1936, had declared that the United States would not fight anybody for any reason, to enforce treaties or stop aggression. In his turn, Moore was no less of an isolationist, but in 1938 he wrote to his friend Ambassador William C. Bullitt, suggesting that it was time to speak out. He still opposed an American war, but sought some alternative to force to halt the totalitarian powers.[26] What the United States could do short of force remained a mystery.

FDR tried to persuade the British and French that a defensive war was in the offing and that he would provide all the help he could within the limits of American laws. He would, he added, bend them as far as he could. British Ambassador Sir Ronald Lindsay cabled Roosevelt's promise to London and noted the extremely strong support that he discovered in Washington that favored a U.S. stand against Hitler. Roosevelt told a French visitor that France could count on everything except loans and troops. Whatever supplies France desired were available. FDR surmised that if Britain and France unleashed a defensive war, the United States would eventually enter. Roosevelt warned that if Hitler succeeded in taking Czechoslovakia, it would not be the end: next would come Denmark, the Polish Corridor, and the economic or physical penetration of Rumania.[27]

One event of November 9, 1938, unleashed not only a strong American revulsion but also one throughout the non-Axis world. This was Kristallnacht [The Night of the Broken Glass]. The excuse for the attack on Jews and Jewish institutions, homes, and businesses was the assassination in France of the German Paris Embassy Counselor, Ernst vom Rath, by a young Jew named Herschel Grynszpan, who may have intended to assassinate the ambassador. Grynspzan could not find the ambassador, so he shot vom Rath instead.[28]

American reporters wanted FDR's reaction. President Roosevelt read to the reporters his statement concerning the German atrocities perpetrated against the Jews on Kristallnacht, when German Jews were beaten and killed, their property stolen or destroyed, synagogues burned and looted. FDR said he personally "could not believe such things could occur in a twentieth-century civilization."[29] These events, he told the reporters, deeply shocked American public opinion and resulted in FDR's calling Ambassador Hugh Wilson home from Berlin for consultations right after his last dispatch from Germany of November 16. There would not be full U.S. representation in Germany again till after the war.[30]

---

[25] Statement in the Senate, December 22, 1938, Pittman Papers, Box 162, Library of Congress.
[26] Moore to Bullitt, August 31, 1938, R. Walton Moore Papers, *FDRL*.
[27] See, for example, Lindsay to Halifax, No. 324 [C 9711/194/18], September 12, 1938, warning of the American reaction to a sellout.
[28] See Wikipedia under "Ernst vom Rath."
[29] Lindsay to Halifax, No. 500. November, 15, 1938, p. 227.
[30] Press Conferences of the President, vol. 12, 1938, July to December 31, no. 490, October 11, 1938, p. 154.

Kristallnacht was a specifically organized pogrom throughout Germany to incite Germans to attack and burn Jewish synagogues, shops, and residences, and to arrest and deport 25,000 to 30,000 young Jewish men. SS leader Reinhard Heydrich reported the destruction of 7,500 businesses and 267 synagogues, with 91 Jews killed.[31] The international reaction to these atrocities caused numerous nations to break relations with Germany. The anger in Great Britain filled the House of Commons, where members discussed what action should be taken.

The "Jewish problem," as the Nazis liked to refer to anything relating to Jews, spread across every area in which the Germans exercised influence or control. George Kennan even used the term when reporting in a despatch of February 17, 1939, from Prague. He listed the number of Jews in the country and the degree to which German influences after Kristallnacht crossed the border and systematically eliminated Jewish businesses as well as Jews from important educational, entertainment, or political positions. In his despatch, Kennan noted: "It is, of course, not surprising that in all Germanic institutions supported by the Czech state Jews are being eliminated completely." He enumerated the processes, and then stated: "This more or less exhausts the list of hardships which Jews, as far as the Legation is informed, have been and are being subjected at the hands of the Prague authorities." He added that local Germans objected to the "moderate" treatment of Jews by the government and the degree to which the government resisted further anti-Semitism. In Slovakia, Kennan reported, the treatment of Jews would be more severe, as the Slovaks always charged the Jews with supporting the Czechs in any conflict over the issues between the two ethnic groups. Kennan could see nothing but trouble for the Jews.[32]

V

By November, the Czechs were discovering how extreme had been their sacrifice at Munich. Halifax learned on November 14 that the German government had "submitted demands for ... further territory under the pretext of 'minor modifications' as contemplated in paragraph 6 of the Munich Agreement. [The] territory to be ceded was spread over a number of districts and comprised in all a considerable area." The region demanded was mostly mountainous, with a small population of about 40,000, but "practically all Czechs." The Czechs were not allowed to discuss this cession. They were told it was a reality, and they had forty-eight hours to accept the demand.[33] What was not revealed, however, was that this land was strategically significant and

[31] See Wikipedia under "Kristallnacht."

[32] George F. Kennan, *From Prague after Munich: Diplomatic Papers, 1938–1940* (Princeton, 1968). See Kennan's dispatch to the Department of State, February 17, 1939, 42–68.

[33] Troutbeck (Prague) to Viscount Halifax (received November 14, 7:30 p.m.), No. 1035, telegraphic [C 13891/11169/18], *DBFP*, 1938, 227.

contained mineral resources, again part of Hitler's reason for wanting all of Czechoslovakia.[34]

What happened at Munich has been judged by some observers as wholly a German plot from the outset, with the British and French caving in under pressure. There is another point of view to be considered. Willson Woodside, a contemporary observer, contended that Munich came not from Hitler's pressure but from Chamberlain's determination to surrender the Czechs to the Germans. He wanted Hitler to have the Sudetenland, in part under the influence of Lord Lothian, who argued that a united Germany was inevitable, so why not permit it immediately? Further, Woodside noted that Chamberlain's group called Czechoslovakia "an impossible state," with no reason to exist at all, so why defend it? The terrible failure of Munich, Woodside observed, had rendered Czechoslovakia "the last pillar in the foundations of the Versailles system." After that, the system was doomed.[35]

As German advances continued in Europe, President Roosevelt faced another problem. He discovered an alliance of the totalitarian powers in the offing. Sumner Welles reported to Roosevelt on December 5 that British sources revealed plans for an alliance among Germany, Italy, and Japan that would commit these countries to come to one another's aid if they became involved in a war.[36] If any of the three powers were threatened by another power, economic, political, and diplomatic support would be immediate. Welles thought it significant that in the anti-Comintern pact, Russia was singled out as the danger, but this pact included anyone who entered a war with a signatory. He was especially concerned that Japan wanted specifics relating to the nature of the support being offered, and wanted it to become effective immediately, while Italy wanted a year's delay and Germany was non-committal.[37]

Roosevelt, alarmed by the accelerating aggressiveness of Germany, wanted England to act more forcefully. He must have been surprised by the response of his old friend, Sir Arthur Murray, who had earlier told Roosevelt that England needed a firm commitment from the United States to confront mutual foes. Now he wrote that Chamberlain had obviously saved the peace at Munich. This was all the more astounding because Murray had met with FDR at Hyde Park, where the president had told him that he could inform Chamberlain that if Europe went to war, he would immediately "have the industrial resources of America behind him." Murray said that the prime minister was "gratified to have this information." He went further to assure Chamberlain that the raw materials essential to a warring nation would be guaranteed from the democratic nations. The United States would ensure delivery.[38]

[34] Kershaw, *Hitler*, 164–65.

[35] Willson Woodside, "The Road to Munich," *Harper's Monthly Magazine*, vol. 178 (January 1939), pp. 28–29, 30, 35, 37.

[36] This pact was signed in 1939, but Japan refused to join until it became the Axis Alliance Pact in 1940.

[37] Welles to FDR, December 5, 1938, PSF: Great Britain. *FDRL*.

[38] Murray to FDR, December 15, 1938, Schewe, *Roosevelt and Foreign Affairs*, III, 310 ff.

Amid all this, a British Cabinet meeting on November 12, 1938, discussed a guarantee for Czechoslovakia. In this curious document, the French and British considered guaranteeing the rump borders of the Czech state. According to this proposal, Britain and France would offer to the Czechs "an international guarantee of the new boundaries of the Czechoslovak state against unprovoked aggression." The intent would be to safeguard the independence of Czechoslovakia "by the substitution of a general guarantee against unprovoked aggression in place of existing treaties which involve reciprocal obligations of a military character."

When this was discussed in Parliament, a question was put to the government about whether Russia was consulted and was to be included. The Home Secretary Sir Samuel Hoare responded: "Let me say to the honorable gentleman opposite, who asked me a specific question that we do not in any way contemplate exclusion of Russia. I believe that the guarantee, coupled it may be, with pacts of non-aggression given by this country, France, Germany and Italy, with the minorities question settled in Czechoslovakia, will make the new [Czech] republic as safe as Switzerland has been for many generations in the past on the continent of Europe."

On October 5, the Chancellor of the Exchequer referred to this speech and added:

> It is our hope that Russia will be willing to join in the guarantee of Czechoslovakia. It is most important that she should do so. The Government have no intention whatever of excluding Russia or trying to exclude Russia from any future settlement in Europe. If outstanding differences are to be resolved, it must be on the basis of free consultation with all the European Powers.[39]

After this pledge, trust in the Chamberlain government began to decline when, piece by piece, Hitler annexed Czech territory against only verbal assaults by the British and French. Then, when the British ambassador in Germany, Sir Nevile Henderson, rationalized these actions as the fault of the Czechs, the prestige of the Chamberlain government dropped like mercury in winter.

In a memorandum to Halifax, the editor of the *Yorkshire Post* expressed some conclusions he reached after interviews with Chamberlain, Halifax, Churchill, Eden and numerous other members of the Conservative Party. Vansittart collected two memoranda from this editor, one prior to the Munch agreement and another afterward. In the former, the editor suggested that the appeasement policy was wrong-headed and based on faulty assumptions concerning the reliability of the dictators to keep their word. He wrote that Hitler strove to secure the "complacency of Great Britain ... through Englishmen who were brought to accept the view that Hitler had done great service to Europe by saving Germany from Communism, and by restoring the

---

[39] Cabinet Minute – British Guarantee for Czechoslovakia: Memorandum by the Secretary of State for Foreign Affairs, November 12, 1938, CAB 24/280/258.

self respect of the German people." These Englishmen concluded that because Germany had been unjustly treated by the Treaty of Versailles, its restitution had been earned. "Hitler would now become a good European."[40]

The *Yorkshire Post* editor was amazed that this notion was accepted so readily by British leaders. His supposition rested on a realistic appraisal of the dictator's character and stated objectives, clearly outlined in his memoir. "Hitler's character is ruthless and, like many German statesmen in the past, he uses duplicity as a natural means to his ends. The threat of war is to him an instrument of policy." The editor noted that Hitler had told Schussnigg when they met: "I shall always get my way because I am ready to run the risk of war, and my opponents are not." He charged that Chamberlain and his cohorts rejected Eden's realistic appraisal and "seem to have turned a blind eye to Hitler's actions and words." He then surmised, "Perhaps the most significant indication of Hitler's military intentions has been his treatment of the Jews, for he would not create in the world cells of hatred of Germany unless he were a megalomaniac, careless, in his obsession, of world opinion." Resulting British policy, the editor observed, had encouraged the dictators. Their hatred of Eden, Churchill, and the others who urged action against Hitler and Mussolini rested on realizing that if these critics of Chamberlain's policy won, Germany's easy conquests would end. "Mr. Chamberlain," he charged, "has declared more than once that he has no sympathy with Fascism and the Dictators, but how can the common people of this country reconcile this claim with the pursuit of a policy that seems consistently to encourage and assist the Fascist Powers?" He contended that those of Chamberlain's persuasion who said the policy saved the nation from war merely provided an encouragement to the dictators when it was time to stand up to them.[41]

After Munich, the editor wrote a second memorandum that charged Chamberlain with duplicity in the demise of the Czech republic. The charge was specific: "The Munich settlement being a humiliating surrender to force, was a further encouragement of aggression in circumstances most injurious to British prestige throughout the world." Instead of reassessing policy with foreign policy experts from the party, he charged, "the first thought of the Conservative party leaders seems to have been to make party capital out of Munich." Instead of saving the peace, as Chamberlain contended, "he brought the country to the verge of war.... Instead of a cornerstone of peace there has been laid a cornerstone of Nazi aggression in Europe." When critics of the newspaper said that the attacks on Chamberlain's policies betrayed the party in time of crisis, the editor contended: "This is asking us to acquiesce in perpetrating a state of dangers and at the same time [to be] incapable of uniting vigorously against them."[42]

---

[40] A PRE-MUNICH MEMORANDUM: Great Britain and the Dictators, December 15, 1938, Vansittart Papers, VNST II, 5/2, Churchill College, Cambridge.
[41] Ibid.
[42] See the Second Memorandum, ibid.

VI

Germany in the meantime edged closer to the total scrapping of any military limitations imposed by the Versailles Treaty. On December 10, 1938, Germany's Ambassador in London, Herbert von Dirksen, wrote a note to Halifax announcing the scrapping of the limitations on German heavy cruisers and their armaments. Von Dirksen observed that in the light of the fact that the Russians were arming their cruisers with heavy caliber weapons, the agreement signed with Great Britain limiting cruiser sizes in 1937 was no longer in force, and the new German cruisers would equal the Soviet cruisers.[43] Next came a German declaration that Berlin would no longer abide by the limitations placed on German submarine production at the Naval Conferences of 1935 and 1937. The British chargé in Berlin, Sir George Ogilvie-Forbes, reported that the German government responded to the British protest about submarine tonnage as follows: "Considerations contained in Foreign Office memorandum of December 28 were laid before German representatives who maintained that it was quite impossible for them to reconsider their decision to avail themselves of the right to build up to 100 per cent of our submarine tonnage."[44] The Germans ignored the British protest.

German pressure on the Czechs intensified. On December 11, Newton wrote from Prague that the Czech foreign minister requested that the British live up to their guarantees of the preservation of the Czech nation as promised in the Munich agreement. Newton explained to Minister Chvaldovsky that the Czech government "seemed hardly to have appreciated the importance of distinctions between an individual guarantee and various forms of collective guarantees."[45] Britain would not enforce any promises that might upset Hitler. The French reminded Berlin of the four-power guarantees that the new ambassador to Germany, Robert Coulandre, brought up to State Secretary Baron Ernst von Weizsäcker in a conversation of December 21, 1938. Weizsäcker informed Coulandre that Czechoslovakia belonged to those territories that "must be regarded as German domain." But Coulandre clung to the subject, and referred to the existing French, and also the English, promise of a guarantee, whereupon the German asserted that "although in fact the political situation was a new one and Czechoslovakia was quite dependent on Germany... my rejection of the idea of a French guarantee upset M. Coulandre, who obviously had instructions on the matter."[46] The French tried to represent Czech interests in the end, but the matter was already decided.

[43] The German Ambassador to Viscount Halifax (received December 13) [A 9348/55/45], *DBFP*, 3rd ser., II, 1938 (London, 1949), 422.

[44] Sir G. Ogilvie-Forbes (Berlin) to Viscount Halifax (received December 30, 12.20 p.m.), No. 780, telegraphic by telephone [A 9731/55/45], ibid., 455.

[45] Newton (Prague) to Viscount Halifax (received December 11), No. 1072, telegraphic [C 15333/11169/18], ibid., 423.

[46] Memorandum by the State Secretary, Berlin, December 21, 1938. *DGFP*, Series D, Vol. IV, 121/119509–10, 482.

Weizsäcker informed the Italian ambassador on March 14, 1939, that the Czech state was breaking up, and as the Beneš spirit of resistance to German control had "again showed its head, our patience is exhausted. Intrigues have been spun with our enemies in the west.... The Führer intends to lance the abscess.... The present event is useful preparation for a contest in another direction which will be necessary sooner or later and for the tasks which this will bring to the Axis Powers jointly."[47]

George Kennan was the chargé at the American legation and recorded the sad disintegration of the whole republic and the desperate plight of any Czechs who might be subject to the terror tactics of the Gestapo. These people besieged the legation seeking asylum, as Kennan recorded: "A stream of desperate persons was ... arriving at the legation and we had to post a man down at the gate to turn away those whom we did not know well. But even the others were too numerous."[48]

Willson Woodside responded to the Germans' contention that they opposed war. He acknowledged that most people he knew in Germany did not want a war – "they had enough the last time to do them for life." He thought German youth might want a skirmish or two to test their mettle, but not a general war. Even the Nazi leaders were not planning on a total European war because, Woodside thought, they were convinced they could get everything they wanted through a strong show of force or a well-timed coup. Despite this, he saw "powerful forces" sweeping Germany along a course that, unless the Nazi leadership should be deposed, could not help but lead to a general war. He assessed the reasons for this with deadly accuracy: It would be accountable to "Hitler's reckless foreign policy," accompanied by, "the boundless ambitions of the pan-Germans," all of which combined "to make up the 'dynamic' of the Nazi movement, the fervor into which the youth has been whipped, the elation over the great victory in Austria, the discontent which has been stirred up in the German border populations, and the gearing of the country's entire economy to war production...."

Added to this assessment was the wise observation that there were saner heads in Germany, appalled by what they foresaw as a road leading to disaster based on the public perception of the favorite old delusion that France was degenerate and disunited, British disinterested, Russia disorganized, the opposition likely to be put up by small countries of no consequence, and, most important, that Germany was invincible.

The real terror in the saner heads came as they were "aghast at the rapidly [growing] readiness among the Nazi and radical military circles to gamble everything should one of their startling coups land them into trouble on a Blitzkrieg or 'lightning war.'" This was epitomized by Goering's confident boast, "Give me 20,000 airplanes ... and I'll be master of Europe in a week!"

---

[47] Memorandum by the State Secretary, Berlin, March 14, 1939, No. 224, 140/76474, ibid., 261.
[48] Kennan, *From Prague after Munich*, 86.

In the long run, Woodside continued, sensible Germans knew they did not have the resources to win a long war, and the theory that they could capture the necessary resources was folly because they could not defend such a vast empire against the combined forces they would confront.[49]

There was no better assessment of German ambitions or the fate of Hitler's enterprise. Hitler provided the lamest of excuses for annexing the remainder of the Czech rump state. State Secretary Weizsäcker circularized the German embassies and legations with the fiction they were to present as a rationalization for Hitler's decision to annex the remainder of the Czech republic on March 15, 1939. "The events of the last few days have finally proved that the Government in Prague is neither willing or able to guarantee a state of lasting peace in the country on the basis of its previous constitution."

Weizsäcker cited "illegal measures" by Prague against autonomy in Slovakia, and actions in Carpatho-Ukraine, where the Hungarian army had to intercede to protect ethnic Hungarians, and finally: "From Czechia itself come constant and increasingly urgent appeals for help from the Volksdeutsche, who are persecuted by the Czechs. Confusion, unrest, and terror reign in all parts of the country." These conditions, he stated, led to an inescapable decision: "In this grave situation the Reich Government, conscious of its responsibility for insuring peace in central Europe and for ending the chaotic conditions on its eastern frontier, which are intolerable for the interests of the Reich, finds itself compelled to initiate the necessary measures." He added a supplement for the diplomatic mission that stated only that a further communication would be forthcoming, giving "the tenor of the Reich Government's assessment of the situation, to be given to the Government to which you are accredited, and the decisions thereby resulting for us."[50]

Ian Kershaw analyzed Hitler's real intent in swallowing all of the Czech republic. It rested on several objectives: "Part of the answer is doubtless to be found in Hitler's own personality and psychology. His Austrian background and dislike of the Czechs since his youth was most certainly a significant element." In addition, he felt, that he had been "cheated" of the glory of a real conquest. He complained, "That fellow Chamberlain has spoiled my entry into Prague." But beyond this were far more significant reasons. "The vast bulk of the industrial wealth and resources of the country lay in the old Czech heartlands of Bohemia and Moravia .... Not least the Skoda works produced locomotives and machinery as well as arms.... And a vast amount of equipment could be taken over and redeployed to the advantage of the German army." These amounted to enough arms to equip "20 divisions" of the Wehrmacht.

Also significant was the position this gave Germany in relation to pressure on Poland. Hitler noted that he regretted not taking all of the Czech state

[49] Willson Woodside, "What Would Germany Fight With?" *The American Chamber of Commerce Journal* (December 1938), 426ff.

[50] Circular of the State Secretary, Berlin, March 14, 1939, sent March 15, 5:45 a.m. *DGFP*, 262–63.

right after Munich, because "negotiations with the Poles over Danzig and the extra-territorial transit-route through the Corridor would then have been far more advantageous." The problem was that Hitler's original plan to deal with Poland and bring the Poles into the German orbit ran up against obstructions in Warsaw. A more aggressive posture toward Poland had become a necessity. Possession of all the Czech state played the dominant role in Hitler's future plans.[51]

George Kennan, who served as Secretary of Legation in Prague during the demise of the Czech republic, meticulously recorded the death knell of the Czech state as he recounted the final occupation of Prague by the Germans. Appropriately, he described the collapse of Czech authority on Thursday March 9, 1939, as "a raw and dark day." In the evening, he strolled past the Wallenstein Palace, where the Council of Ministers met with trays of "excellent Prague beer," and he thought it comforting that the delegates relaxing with this "conciliatory beverage [believed that] no fatal steps could be taken. I underestimated the Slovak ability to separate business and pleasure." He recalled that on March 13 he walked to his office: "The bad weather was holding on: a damp, nasty wind, low clouds, flurries of snow. The morning's news was as foreboding as the weather."

The reality of the demise of the Czech republic struck in the early morning hours of the next day. Kennan learned that the Germans were demanding the independence of Slovakia, a new cabinet, and "further guarantees for the treatment of German minorities in Bohemia. The last was a new and menacing note. The German minority had been living off the fat of the land for the last four months – in a peace and security that amounted to sheer extraterritoriality. The revival of the tales of its mistreatment could come only from ulterior motives." He said that it appeared certain that Slovakia was about to declare its independence, and this was true. Despite forebodings among his diplomatic colleagues, Kennan recorded that, amid the sequence of events, "no one understood ... that a trap was being prepared which was designed to bring about the end of Czechoslovakia."[52]

Kennan recorded a verified rumor of March 13 that German troops were massed on the border. With the announcement of Slovak independence came the breakup of the Czech republic as Ruthenia was lost as well as Slovakia, and "some sort of new order for Bohemia and Moravia." He concluded that it "was probable that the German-language islands in the bottleneck of Moravia would be taken over by Germany." This would provide a corridor between Austria and Silesia, with the territory east of them assigned to the Slovaks "as compensation for their treachery, and the mutilated remnants of Bohemia and Moravia left to preserve the fiction of an independent Czechoslovakia and serve as a source of foreign exchange and raw materials to Germany."[53]

[51] Kershaw, *Hitler.* 166–67.
[52] Kennan, *From Prague after Munich*, 80–83.
[53] Ibid., 83.

The final act occurred on Wednesday morning, March 15, as Kennan was awakened before dawn with the news that German troops had begun to occupy Bohemia and Moravia and would arrive in Prague in short order. He dressed and shaved so that German troops, when they reached the legation, would find everything and everyone in good order. Word came that German troops had reached the palace by 10 o'clock. Prague was occupied by the end of the day as a curfew went into effect and the streets of the capital were empty. Kennan continued: "Tomorrow, to be sure, they would fill with life again, but it would not be the same life that had filled them before; and we were all acutely conscious that in this case the curfew had indeed tolled the knell of a long and distinctly tragic day."[54] As Hitler and his legions marched into Prague, a newsreel cameraman scanned a sorrowful Czech crowd lining the streets, catching a particularly poignant photo of a man with tears running down his cheeks.

[54] Ibid., 87.

11

The Soviet Quest for Collective Security

I

Germany and the Soviet Union entered the post-Versailles world as pariah states. Both had been denied roles in the Paris decisions of 1919; both had been ostracized thereafter from the main currents of European economic and diplomatic affairs. Their partial reentry came with invitations to the Genoa Economic Conference of April–May 1922. The agenda demanded their presence. The conference quickly broke down over Russia's refusal to honor its pre-war debt to France. France, joined by Britain, rejected any further efforts at accommodation with the USSR. In response, Georgii Chicherin, the Soviet Commissar of Foreign Affairs, with the acquiescence of Deputy Commissar Maxim Litvinov, turned to Germany for support. The result was the Rapallo Treaty of April 16, 1922, in which both countries renounced reparations.[1]

Rapallo was ostensibly a trade pact between Russia and Germany, but actually constituted an arrangement for military cooperation whereby the German army would avoid the Versailles restrictions by training in the Soviet Union. Meanwhile, the Red Army would benefit from the military expertise of the German high command. Rapollo, however, was never a bond of friendship. For Joseph Stalin, friendship among nations was an impossibility. The only principle that guided the conduct of the USSR was self-interest.

It was quite easy to see justice in the point of view expressed by some other nation, but the Soviet Union was not interested in sacrificing its own security to obtain justice for someone else. Stalin, for example, had no sympathy for the hope of the former Allies to maintain intact the Treaty of Versailles at the expense of Germany. "It is not for us," he observed, "who have experienced the shame of the Treaty of Brest-Litovsk to praise the Treaty of Versailles." But neither was he willing to accept wholly German revisionism. He stated bluntly that Germany should not count on seeing the Soviet Union stand idly by while

---

[1] Hugh D. Phillips, *Between the Revolution and the West: A Political Biography of Maxim M. Litvinov* (Boulder, San Francisco, Oxford, 1992), 53–54.

Germany plunged the world into a war over the Versailles Treaty, and most certainly Russia would not make any new orientation toward the Germans that would permit this. Stalin contended that Russia was no more oriented toward Germany than toward Poland or France; instead, the Russians were interested in self-preservation, and in this regard would seek accommodation with whomever helped to serve that interest.[2]

By 1925, Germany, under the leadership of Gustav Stresemann, had managed to reenter the main currents of European politics and diplomacy. But the Soviet Union, with its Bolshevik government, experienced continuing diplomatic, political, and economic exclusion.

Russia faced its first, unanticipated post-war challenge in Hitler's rise in Germany. Driven by his hatred of socialists, Bolsheviks, and Jews, Hitler had never accepted the legitimacy of either the Versailles Treaty or the Weimar Republic. His troubling memoir, *Mein Kampf*, published in 1925, explained his total rejection of those responsible for both, as well as his disregard for the peoples of Eastern Europe. *Mein Kampf* ended with Hitler's ultimate territorial designs in the East, including vast regions of Russia. "Only a sufficiently extensive area on this globe," he wrote, "guarantees a nation freedom of existence."[3] Limited to its present territories, he continued, Germany was not a world power. The necessary territorial expansion to achieve that status would no longer encompass lands in the south and west, but in the east.[4] Having focused German territorial ambitions on Russia, he turned on its rulers:

> We must never forget that the regents of present day Russia are common bloodstained criminals; that here is the scum of humanity, which ... over-ran a great State, butchered and rooted out millions of its leading intellects with savage bloodthirstiness, and for nearly ten years has exercised the most frightful regime of tyranny of all time. Nor must we forget that these rulers belong to a nation which combines a rare mixture of bestial horror with an inconceivable gift of lying, and today more than ever before believes itself called upon to impose its bloody oppression on the whole world.[5]

In 1924 and the half decade that followed, neither Russia nor the world could take such political and territorial threats seriously. Not until 1929 did Russia, threatened by Hitler's declared ambitions, respond to its own industrial weakness and burgeoning insecurity with its first five-year plan, completing the plan in four years. Stalin acknowledged the plan's necessity in his famed address before the First All-Union Conference of Managers of Soviet Industry on February 4, 1931:

> [T]he history of old Russia is the history of defeats due to backwardness. She was beaten by the Mongol khans. She was beaten by the Turkish beys.

[2] Vladimir Potemkine et al., *Histoire de la Diplomatie, 1919–1939*, trans. from Russian by I. Levin, J. Tarr, and Boris Metzel, III (Paris, 1947), 501.

[3] Adolf Hitler, *Mein Kampf* (New York, 1940), 935.

[4] Ibid., 950.

[5] Ibid., 959.

> She was beaten by the Swedish feudal barons. She was beaten by the Polish-Lithuanian "squires." She was beaten by the Anglo-French capitalists. She was beaten by the Japanese barons. All beat her for her backwardness.... She was beaten because to beat her was profitable and could be done with impunity.... That is why we must no longer be backward.... We are 50–100 years behind the advanced countries. We must cover this distance in 10 years. Either we do this or they will crush us.[6]

By 1932, the USSR had made enormous strides toward catching up with the West industrially, but still had far to go. Not until 1934 did Soviet industrialization reveal itself in military preparation, but transportation deficiencies continued to limit the country's ability to mobilize. The USSR was growing slowly in international stature, but still needed time to achieve industrial development, international acceptance, security, and a status of equality in European affairs.

It was at this juncture that the chief spokesman for the old-line Communists and their perception of Soviet foreign policy, Karl Radek, wrote an article for *Foreign Affairs* in its first issue of 1934, setting forth for an American audience the foundations of Soviet foreign policy as understood by a practicing Communist. The article first appeared in *Izvestiia* in December 1933,[7] and to the Soviet readers it was presented both as a statement of policy and an article of faith. In the light of subsequent events, not the least of which was Radek's elimination as an official spokesman of the Soviet system during the purges,[8] his attempt to prove that there was no carryover from tsarist objectives in foreign policy is significant. He criticized writers who contended that the USSR carried on traditional Russian objectives. He stated: "Tsarism or any other bourgeois regime in Russia, would necessarily resume the struggle for conquest of Poland and ... the Baltic states...." The Soviet Union would ally with whomsoever served its interest. But he also noted that alliance and friendship were distinctly different, and allies should know that the only victor in any war would be the Soviet Union.[9]

With the Versailles victors in complete command of European politics, the Kremlin followed the flow of European diplomacy carefully, noting the combinations and alignments that might touch Soviet interests. The persistent changes and insecurities in Europe's political climate produced a transformation in the official Kremlin view of the Versailles Treaty. Earlier, the Soviets had joined the Germans in condemning the territorial and political decisions

---

[6] Joseph Stalin, *Leninism (New York, 1933)*, 423–24.

[7] Karl Radek, "The Bases of the Foreign Policy of the Soviet Union," *Izvestiia*, December 16, 1933.

[8] Radek was purged in 1937 for being a "Trotskyite Internationalist," though he was not shot because he turned state's evidence. For details of this event, see George Von Rauch, *A History of Soviet Russia*, (New York, 1957), 241–42, 244.

[9] Radek, "The Bases of the Foreign Policy of the Soviet Union," *Izvestiia*, December 16, 1933.

in Paris. Now they viewed the Versailles settlement, with its recognition of Russia's territorial and political integrity, as the foundation of their security – no less than Europe's peace and stability. The League of Nations became their country's first line of defense, receiving Soviet support and leadership on every issue that challenged Europe's peace and stability.

Maxim Litvinov emerged as Russia's primary advocate of international agreements to solidify the peace with appeals to collective security. No longer, he argued, could the USSR isolate itself from Europe's international conflicts. "One can scarcely doubt," he advised, "that, given current international relations, no war, on any continent whatever ... can be localized, and that practically no country can be assured that it will not be drawn into a war which it has not started." Fearful that the USSR could not escape another war, Litvinov, in his response to every crisis, was concerned with preserving not only his nation's peaceful relations with other states, but also the peace of the world.[10]

Military weakness in an unstable world dictated the pervasive Soviet interest in disarmament, or at least a reduction of armaments. Recognizing this necessity, Soviet leaders welcomed the League of Nations Security Council's decision of early 1931 to call a disarmament conference. What mattered for the Soviets was the assurance of equality among the participants. This required a neutral environment. But Geneva, the designated site for the conference, with its intensely anti-Soviet press, was scarcely neutral. The Soviet delegation to the preparatory commission complained that the decisions, as well as the conduct of the chairman, Arthur Henderson, leader of the British Labour Party, whose country had never recognized the Soviet Union, revealed an anti-Soviet bias. The Soviets argued that the conference required a meeting place that maintained normal relations with all states represented at the conference.[11] They complained in vain.

Meanwhile, Russia continued to face persistent economic, political, and diplomatic discrimination. Litvinov responded with the observation that the world was still divided between the "victors and the vanquished" of the Great War. On matters of foreign trade, he charged, the Soviet Union desired to expand its commercial relations but that "certain hostile capitalist groups ... are conducting a campaign for the severance of economic relations with our Union. Their efforts appear to be directed chiefly at our exports, but in fact they are against our entire foreign trade...."[12]

In May 1931, Litvinov introduced a measure against economic aggression at the League of Nations. The obligations under this protocol, he declared,

[10] Jonathan Haslam, *The Soviet Union and the Struggle for Collective Security in Europe, 1933–39* (London, 1984), 1–2.

[11] Statement to the Governments of ... members of the Council of the League of Nations, on the Calling of the Disarmament Conference, January 12, 1931, Jane Degras, ed., *Soviet Documents on Foreign Policy* (London, New York, Toronto, 1951–1953), II, 468–69.

[12] Phillips, *Between the Revolution and the West*, 112.

"amount to the abstention from hostile measures in the economic sphere against any country or group of countries from political or other motives – in other words, to declare economic war illegal." The measure would not deprive any country of the right to conclude commercial treaties based on mutual concessions and privileges, but would prevent economic discrimination – the singling out of one or more countries with hostile legislative or administrative measures that were not applied to other countries. This protocol, he continued, "has a special bearing upon the relationship between the Soviet Union and the rest of European countries." Nothing less, he added, would permit peaceful coexistence between two economic systems. The commercial policy of every country, he agreed, must be based on mutuality, and the mutuality would be assured for all by the protocol.[13] Again the League failed to respond to a Soviet concern.

II

In the absence of any international support in matters of economic or political security, Litvinov looked to Rapallo. His faith in Germany was not totally misplaced. During a trip to the Ukraine in the spring of 1935, Gustav Hilger of the German embassy in Moscow was surprised at the pro-German views expressed openly by local officials. While in Kiev, he reported, the German consul gave a reception in his honor. A number of high Soviet officials accepted the invitation. Some described the strained state of German-Russian relations as highly unnatural, noting that Russia harbored no evil intentions against Germany, and that Germany enjoyed the highest esteem among all elements in the Russian population. They agreed that Germany was only trying to liberate itself from the oppressive fetters of Versailles. They insisted that Litvinov's burgeoning anti-German policies had no mass following and that history would soon forget the Soviet leader.[14] Opposition to Litvinov and his pursuit of alliances also dominated the views of fundamentalists in the Soviet Communist Party who opposed collective security. Not even Stalin, a Bolshevik nationalist, revealed much interest in collective security, convinced that the country's safety, in an undifferentiated hostile world, rested in its geography and other domestic sources of power.

Hitler launched his crusade against Soviet Communism in *Mein Kampf*, but not until February 1933 did he assault the German Communist Party (KPD) when he denied it the right to hold open air demonstrations, and then ordered the occupation and ransacking of the Party's headquarters. The Reichstag fire of February 27, attributed to the Communists, set the stage for the final German suppression of the KPD. For the moment, the Soviets, still bound to Rapallo, refused to condemn the German action. But almost immediately, a

---

[13] Statement by Litvinov on the Soviet Draft for a Pact of Economic Non-Aggression, May 21, 1931, Degras, *Soviet Documents on Foreign Policy*, II, 500–01.
[14] Haslam, *The Struggle for Collective Security*, 3.

united European front against German Fascism began to emerge. Moscow refused to respond, revealing the continuing Soviet attachment to Rapallo. Although an Anglophile, Litvinov made no effort to draw Britain into an anti-German pact, or address France's continuing animosity toward the USSR.

Whatever Moscow's attachment to Rapallo, the pact could not survive. At the World Economic Conference in London during June 1933, Alfred Hugenberg, leader of the German National Party and Minister of the Economy, declared that Germany required additional living space. Litvinov responded to this potential threat with appeals for an economic non-aggression pact. *Izvestiia* demanded a clarification from Berlin and sent a formal protest to the German government. Moscow acknowledged publicly for the first time its concern for the fallen KPD in Germany. On June 26, 1933, the German military attaché at the Moscow embassy received formal notification that all agreements on military cooperation between the two countries were henceforth rescinded. Rapallo ceased to exist. Despite this though, Stalin was willing to let Litvinov try for collaboration with the democracies because, as Stalin noted in a 1931 speech, he had forced Russia into collectivization because Russia was decades behind the industrial powers. If the Soviet Union did not catch up, the enemy states would crush the Russians, and the only one that had made threats was Nazi Germany. And if that policy failed, there was always a possible return to Rapollo.

What this meant essentially was that if Litvinov's plan for collective security failed, there was a position to fall back upon where collaboration with Germany could again become possible for purely national objectives. This was something the Chamberlain people failed to realize despite warnings from the Soviet experts in the British Foreign Office, not to mention hints from Ambassador Maisky and Litvinov. There were many similarities between Stalin and Hitler – both were shrewd analysts of personal and national objectives, and both were totally ruthless in pursuit of their aims. If opponents underestimated them for any reason, they did so at their peril.

III

Germany's departure from the League of Nations in October 1933 opened a new era of European insecurity, one that registered heavily in France and the USSR. During November, French Foreign Minister Joseph Paul-Boncour opened Franco-Soviet talks on a mutual assistance agreement. In December, the Soviet Politburo passed a resolution favoring such collective security. The alliance proposals favored a multilateral assistance pact that included not only the USSR, France, and Poland, but also Bulgaria, Czechoslovakia, and the Baltic states. Some Soviets resisted the inclusion of such broad obligations to defend much of Central Europe against Germany. Moreover, many Soviet leaders anticipated a return to Rapallo. But Litvinov refused to retreat. For him, Russian security against Germany required nothing less than an alliance with France. Now elevated to the Soviet Central Committee, Litvinov enjoyed

Stalin's confidence. But in his devotion to a French alliance, he overreached. France succeeded in obtaining Soviet membership in the League of Nations, but thereafter many French leaders lost interest in an alliance with Russia.[15] Pierre Laval, who became President of France in October 1934, favored Germany, convinced that European peace required a Franco-German agreement.[16] Litvinov's Franco-Soviet design for a security pact now faced a powerful antagonist in Paris.

Hitler's announcement of German compulsory military service on March 16, 1935, further alarmed the Russians. But Moscow took comfort in the possibility that Hitler's insensitivity to Western concerns enhanced Russia's diplomatic position in dealing with France. For the following month, with some promise of improved Soviet-German relations, the Soviets pushed hard for the desired Franco-Soviet pact. Laval,[17] encouraged by London, continued to avoid any commitment to the defense of Russia. Laval's decision to attend the Stresa Conference of Italy, Britain, and France on April 11–14 annoyed the Russians. But the prospect of a united front against Russia prompted the Germans to improve their relations with Moscow with a five-year 200 million Deutschmark credit. This shift toward Germany was reassuring, but it undermined Litvinov's quest for a pact with France. The German agreement enhanced his bargaining position with Paris, but it also threatened to undermine his quest for collective security.

When the League of Nations, took up the issue of German conscription in April, the Soviet Politburo instructed Litvinov not to vote with the French in condemning Germany's clear defiance of the Versailles Treaty. Litvinov held his ground in supporting the League action against Germany because it advanced the idea of a regional security pact. At Litvinov's insistence, the Politburo gave way. But now Laval lost interest in a security pact with the USSR. He rejected Litvinov's proposals for immediate assistance prior to a decision of the League Council, on the grounds that it infringed on the Locarno Treaty. It would, he argued, provide the German government with an excuse to renounce Locarno, thus terminating the security system that had governed Western Europe since 1925.

What remained was not the alliance the Russians had sought, but Litvinov still regarded it of value to the Soviet Union. It would, he concluded, hinder close ties between France and Germany. But not all disagreements with France were settled. The French had diluted the obligation of mutual assistance in the text. Litvinov insisted that the French maintain the original wording. Laval defended the changes as purely formal. The entire affair was becoming a fiasco. Laval to the end refused to concede on the issue of obligation. In the final compromise, mutual assistance was subordinated to a decision of the League, but

[15] Ibid., 43.
[16] Ibid., 44.
[17] Laval, who later signed the ill-fated Hoare–Laval agreement, was staunchly committed to a deal with Hitler, and was charged by later critics with actually being pro-German.

both parties were obligated to hasten the process. The Franco-Soviet pact was signed on May 2, 1935. The sense of achievement was diminished by the long and trying negotiations. Soviet officials noted the many unsettled disagreements. For many, the pact was no substitute for Rapallo. Stalin did not trust the French, and harbored no illusions about future cooperation with the Paris government.

The Franco-Soviet pact undoubtedly placed the USSR in a stronger international position, but not by much. The manner in which Laval had treated the Soviet negotiators, the severe limitations he imposed on the agreements, and his declared determination to use the pact in bargaining with Germany reinforced the conviction in Moscow that the pact should be seen as a prelude to Soviet negotiations with Berlin. Germany's continuing economic depression, the Kremlin understood, created immense economic and diplomatic possibilities for Russia. By 1932, the USSR had become one of the most important markets for German manufactured goods. But that trade had declined as Soviet industry expanded. The Nazi harassment of Soviet trade negotiators hastened the decline. By 1934, German officials had recognized the error of their ways and began to encourage Russian imports with ample credit. Russia, however, resisted the German incentives, convinced that German proposals threatened the progress toward collective security. Not until the Franco-Soviet pact of May 1935 was concluded were the Russians prepared to turn to Berlin.

Litvinov now sought a non-aggression pact with Germany to diminish the negative impact of the Franco-Soviet alliance, and to improve relations between the two powers. Predictably, Hitler revealed his animosity toward Russia by ignoring the proposal. But Litvinov had exposed the continuing anti-Soviet aggressiveness in German intentions. Hitler underscored that animosity when on May 21, 1935, he delivered a Reichstag speech in which he assured the powers of his peaceful intentions. He pointedly ignored Russia.[18] At the same time, the Soviets had little remaining reason to trust the French. During subsequent months, renewed Soviet disputes with Germany were matched by Laval's efforts to secure an understanding with Berlin, as well as his indefinitely delayed ratification of the Franco-Soviet pact. By the autumn of 1935, the Russians were troubled by the growing frequency of meetings between the French ambassador and Nazi leaders in Berlin.[19]

Again the declining Soviet confidence in France turned the Russians toward Germany. In late October 1935, the Soviet Deputy Commissar of Military Affairs reminded the German military attaché in Moscow that the Red Army still harbored great respect for the Reichswehr. He expressed his regret that the two countries were not cooperating. Germany and the Soviet Union, he added, complemented one another and had no territorial issues in dispute. He added: "If Germany and the Soviet Union still had the same friendly relations they used to have, they would now be in a position to dictate peace to the

---

[18] Haslam, *The Struggle for Collective Security*, 82.
[19] Ibid., 89.

world."[20] German officials were not prepared to take such sentiments seriously. They were equally suspicious of similar statements from Litvinov. Soviet relations with France were no more promising. In early November 1935, the Soviet Commissar was convinced that Laval had "decided in so far as it depends on him, that whatever happens he will wreck Franco-Soviet co-operation and join the German anti-Soviet bloc."[21]

Against the background of growing suspicions regarding France, the Soviet embassy in Berlin examined German opinion. The Soviet ambassador, Jacob Surits, reported to Litvinov on November 28: "All my contacts with the Germans merely reinforced the conviction I already held that the course against us taken by Hitler remains unchanged and that one cannot expect any serious changes whatever in the immediate future. Everyone I spoke to was unanimous in this.... [Hitler's] hostility towards the USSR stems not only from his ideological position vis-à-vis Communism, but [also] forms the basis for his tactical line in the field of foreign policy."[22]

Soviet officials in Berlin continued to lobby their German counterparts with no substantial success. Surits acknowledged that Russian-German relations were under discussion, but concluded that "there is no doubt that Hitler and his immediate entourage stand firmly by their primitive anti-Soviet positions."[23] Soviet efforts at collective security had apparently reached a dead end. Yet Soviet insecurity demanded that the pursuit continue.

IV

Early in 1936, the Rhineland crisis brought new concerns to Litvinov regarding Hitler's plans. Remilitarization of the Rhineland violated both the Treaties of Versailles and Locarno. Litvinov appealed to the League to act in opposition to Germany's violations. According to a despatch from the American embassy in Moscow, the Soviets received information that members of the German General Staff opposed the move into the Rhineland. This convinced Moscow that any move to stop Hitler was sure to succeed.[24] In his assault on the Versailles Treaty's restrictions, Hitler took a calculated risk; Litvinov asked the former allied powers to join him and stop the downward spiral toward war. No answer was forthcoming from London or Paris. Hitler was emboldened to make his next thrust, and this moved the Soviet Union to inaugurate a serious reexamination of Soviet policy.

Litvinov decided to present his defense of the Versailles security system directly to the League, where he argued that the entire peace structure depended on whether the League defended Versailles and Locarno against

---

[20] Ibid., 90.
[21] Ibid., 90.
[22] Ibid., 91.
[23] Ibid., 92.
[24] Despatch of February 17, 1936, DSF 711.61/594.

such German violations. To prove his point, he cited *Mein Kampf*, wherein Hitler had stated that the first step in the subduing of the European continent to German domination was remilitarization of the Rhineland. This was a promising chance to alter the future of the European peace.[25] Again, no one in authority, would heed Litvinov's warning.

During 1936, Litvinov's efforts at collective security through the League of Nations failed to prevent wars in Abyssinia and Spain. When, Italy threatened in 1935 to invade Abyssinia, Litvinov pressed the League to impose sanctions if Italy attacked. He assured Moscow that League sanctions would warn Germany as well. With no support from Britain and France, the League refused to act. On October 2, Italy launched its invasion of Abyssinian, Moscow informed the League that it favored sanctions against Italy on condition that other members of the League followed. But none chose to do so. To the end, Litvinov sought to defend the sanctity of the League Covenant, but Britain rendered that impossible. With Abyssinian leader Haile Selassie's departure into exile on May 4, 1936, Litvinov could only hope that the Italian conquest of Abyssinia would remind League members of the high price of inaction, thereby enhancing the cause of collective security.[26]

In July 1936, war came to Spain when Spanish generals sympathetic to Fascism, led by Francisco Franco, launched a rebellion against Spain's Popular Front government. That month, Fascist Italy and Germany began to supply Franco's forces. Spanish officials turned to France for arms and munitions. For the Soviet Union, the involvement of France created a dilemma. Under the Franco-Soviet pact, Moscow owed some support to France and, with it, some defense of the Spanish government. Soviet sympathies, moreover, flowed naturally to Spain's anti-Fascist cause. Litvinov favored the defense of the established order, with or without collective security. France soon withdrew from the conflict, leaving the USSR as the sole defender of the Spanish regime. Moscow's full commitment to the Spanish cause came on August 3 with a demonstration in Red Square. As Germany and Italy poured men and aircraft into the fight, the USSR met the challenge head-on with shipments of soldiers and equipment. The Spanish government had no choice but to rely on the Soviets for its survival. Litvinov in Geneva pressed the League for collective action, but Anglo-French neutrality rendered the quest hopeless. As the months of heavy fighting continued, the combined German-Italian military superiority, especially in aircraft, assured a rebel victory – which came finally in 1939. It was a defeat for collective security and the Soviet Union.

V

Maxim Litvinov understood very well that his tenure as Foreign Minister rested on the degree to which his support for collective security succeeded.

[25] *The New York Times*, March 18, 1936.
[26] For the Abyssinian War, see Haslam, *The Soviet Union and the Struggle for Collective Security*, 60–79.

He understood not only the precariousness of his position vis-à-vis Stalin, but also the Soviet Union's dangerous situation if the Russians had to face either Hitler alone or both Germany and Japan in a pincer movement. Early in 1936, he thought his problem was solved with the encirclement of Germany and the resultant easing of Soviet-German relations, but toward the end of the year, his concern over an aggressive Germany was reinvigorated by Hitler's Nuremberg speech, in which he made a clear threat to Soviet territory.[27] This moved Litvinov to make another appeal to the League, where he asked, in fact demanded, that German membership in the League of Nations be declared incompatible with League principles, and called for the League to reform itself by strengthening its coercive machinery. That his concerns had a real foundation was illustrated in a conversation Hitler had with the Hungarian Minister of the Interior on December 15, 1936. Hitler said that in a decade, Russia would be formidable and aggressive, adding, "If we do not want to be swallowed up by this danger, we must, while concentrating our whole strength, appreciate it clearly and must confine ourselves to what is necessary and possible."[28]

Clarence Streit wrote in *The New York Times* that Litvinov's League speech was a counter to German policy and assumed for Russia "the role of leader and protector of the Slavic countries of Central and Eastern Europe ... who fear they are being abandoned now to Germany and Italy." Litvinov charged that there was only one way to deal with Hitler and Germany, and that was to promote a policy no less firm, with a cold calculation of the relative strength of forces.[29]

Litvinov's warning about the threat of an aggressive war seemed prescient when, on November 26, Germany and Japan signed the Anti-Comintern Treaty, which clearly carried military clauses, negotiated as it was by Major General Hiroshi Oshima, the Japanese military attaché in Berlin. The Japanese Foreign Office was neither involved nor even aware it was being done. Ambassador Joseph C. Grew was convinced that not even the German Foreign Office knew about it.[30] Litvinov faced the Central Executive Committee with a frank admission that while the Soviet Union was urging collective security and military preparedness, others facing the aggressors were not following suit. He warned that some governments apparently thought the aggressors could be appeased; too late they were learning that their freedom of choice in avoiding war was being abridged. They were now faced with only two choices: join the collective security program advanced by Russia or seek a rapprochement with Germany and face being gobbled up one bit at a time.[31] Litvinov told

[27] "Speech of Hitler – Threat of a Madman," *Pravda*, September 18, 1936.
[28] Memo of a conversation between Hitler and the Hungarian Minister, December 15, 1936. U.S. Department of State, *Documents on German Foreign Policy*, Series C, VI, 191.
[29] Clarence K. Streit, "Speedy Reform Urged on the League," *The New York Times*, September 29, 1936.
[30] Joseph C. Grew, *Ten Years in Japan* (New York, 1944), 191.
[31] "Litvinov's Speech to the Central Executive Committee," *Izvestiia*, November 11, 1936.

his audience that the Soviet Union could afford to wait because Russia had prepared for any eventuality by readying itself to meet force with force if necessary. "If the other nations really want to organize peace, to guarantee collective security, and oppose the forces of aggression, they cannot do it without the Soviet Union."[32]

Robert Coulandre, the French ambassador in Moscow, concluded in February 1937 that Litvinov was in serious trouble and would soon be dismissed. What the commissar faced, however, was not the official demise of collective security but Stalin's emerging reign of terror that soon encompassed many foreigners and those involved in Germany's external affairs. For historian Jonathan Haslam, the terror soon "enveloped the country in a macabre web of suspicion, denunciation, imprisonment, torture, confession and execution, more medieval than modern."[33] The repression rested in large measure on the supposition of Soviet isolation in a hostile world of alleged enemies of the state. Stalin's speech to the Central Committee plenum on March 3, 1937, set the tone for the unfolding campaign of terror. Stalin attributed the alleged sabotage and espionage against the USSR to foreign agents who had played an active role in Soviet economic, administrative, and Party organizations. He charged that leading comrades had often failed to discern the "wreckers, saboteurs, spies and murderers, but ... frequently facilitated the advancement of agents of foreign states to some responsible [Soviet] post or other."[34]

Stalin's early climate of suspicion centered on anyone in contact with foreigners, especially cosmopolitan pro-Western and liberal elements. These included Jews, many of whom were foreigners and prime targets for police persecution. Stalin's new favorite, Zhdanov, an established opponent of Litvinov's, declared on March 15, 1937: "Many have forgotten ... that Soviet power has so far triumphed on only one-sixth of the earth's surface, while on the remaining five-sixths the bourgeoisie still rules. Capitalist encirclement sends us plenty of spies, snoopers, and saboteurs...." International capitalism, he continued, was "galvanizing the remnants of the classes in the USSR hostile to us...."[35] All those involved in external affairs had to cover their tracks.

The terror's full force began in June 1937, when it focused on the Red Army. From the outset, the purging of the armed forces was merely an extension of the assault on the Party and state apparatus. But because of the preeminence of the fighting forces as the country's most powerful element, the terror directed at them assumed a more dramatic form. Stalin had little interest in the military, but Hitler's rise to power after 1933 led to a vast expansion of the Soviet military establishment. By the end of 1936, the army alone boasted some 1.3 million men. Concessions to the military included the restoration of some Tsarist ranks, including that of Marshal, a more

[32] Ibid.
[33] Haslam, *The Struggle for Collective* Security, 128.
[34] Ibid., 130.
[35] Ibid., 131.

autonomous military role, and the establishment of a publishing house to meet the demands of military education.

This enormous expansion of the military coincided with the purging of Party ranks to eliminate the disaffected and corrupt, producing a decline in army membership along with a reduction in the size of the Party itself in the army. By the end of 1936, there were only some 150,000 Communists in the armed forces out of a total of 4.2 million under arms. Stalin demanded blind political conformity; to obtain it, he was willing to sacrifice military efficiency. For him, the threat of war was far less immediate than the danger to his own supremacy.[36] The execution of much of the Red Army's high command was followed by the liquidation of a significant proportion of their subordinates. The purge eliminated the experienced far more than the untried. This massive purge created a gaping hole in the walls of fortress Russia, crippling the Red Army's fighting power as well as the country's standing among Europe's leading states. It also weakened the USSR's credibility as a potential partner in a coalition against Nazi Germany. This provided a ready alibi for those Western governments that for ideological reasons had no intention of becoming allied with the USSR. It undermined the position of those such as Winston Churchill who, for security reasons, favored a Soviet alliance against German militarism.

For many European military analysts, the fighting capacity of the USSR had been doubtful even before the purges. The terror merely confirmed such professional evaluations. High-ranking European officers who attended the September 1936 Russian maneuvers were not impressed. One concluded: "The Soviet army, appears strong, equipped with abundant and modern material, prompted by a will to win, at least at officer level, but insufficiently prepared for a war against a European Great Power." For the French, such judgments of Soviet preparedness provided a convenient excuse to avoid staff level talks with the Soviet Union. The conclusion that such contacts would alienate Germany, Poland, Romania, Yugoslavia, and England encouraged French skepticism beyond what the negative judgments of Soviet power warranted.[37] The resulting French dismissal of the Russian alliance paralleled France's continuing reliance on Britain.

Soviet officials who survived the purge addressed foreigners with declining openness and cordiality. This unpleasantness did not terminate the Soviet interest in collective security, but it undermined Litvinov's efforts to win support in the West. Throughout the summer of 1937, the Russians took shelter from the outside world. What soon reversed the withdrawal and a reassertion of Litvinovian values was the fear that wars in China and Spain could not be localized. The Soviet shipments of planes, tanks, armored cars, machine guns, rifles, shells, and ammunition to Spain had been prodigious, but much was lost at sea because of the shortage of Soviet naval power. By August 1937, the shipping losses placed the Soviet commitment to the Spanish government in

---

[36] Ibid., 135–36.
[37] Ibid., 140–41.

doubt. The continuing Russian terror amplified the accumulating limitations on both Soviet action and the Soviet pursuit of collective security.

By the end of 1937, Litvinov was in a bitter and despondent mood. His quest for collective security continued to face its chief impediments in Britain and France. France was dependent on Britain. Without Britain there could be no successful coalition against Germany. Lacking needed support, the USSR withdrew from its role as leader of the anti-Fascist vanguard. The Soviets had withdrawn from the outside world, but events in Spain soon drove them back onto the world stage. And so heavy were their losses to Italian submarines that Moscow ceased to send supplies to the Spanish front. Between October 1936 and July 1937, the Soviets lost almost a hundred vessels to capture or sinking. Such losses placed in doubt any further Russian commitment to the survival of the Spanish Republic, and, with that retreat, their commitment to collective security.

What underwrote this continuing disinterest in collective security was largely the absence of British support. France was too dependent on Britain to exercise any independence in external affairs. Chamberlain still took comfort in his belief that he could talk Hitler out of any aggression. How long Britain would accept the continuing failures and indignities it faced, in its denial of any international responsibility, remained unclear. On June 29, 1937, Chamberlain assured Soviet Anglophile Ivan Maisky that if he, Chamberlain, could have a quiet conversation with Hitler, he would discover the limits of German demands and frame the necessary responses. That, he concluded, was what the challenges of 1937 required. Litvinov responded to Chamberlain's naiveté in a Leningrad address of November 27, 1937. There were nations, he acknowledged, that were content with their acquisitions. But there were three states, he added, "which show no restraint in publicly, loudly, day in and day out proclaiming their resolve to respect no international laws, nor any international treaties, even those they themselves have signed." Instead, they showed, "their resolve to annex other people's territory, wherever they can, and therefore they reject any collective co-operation in the organization of peace...." Despite the clearly aggressive stance of these nations, "nonetheless there are states which do not believe their statements about their aggressive designs and devote all their diplomacy to obtaining confirmation and clarification of these completely unambiguous statements."[38]

Litvinov's caustic caricature of British and French policy was prompted by Lord Halifax's conversations with Hitler between November 17 and November 21, 1937, and Chamberlain's attempt to revive the notion of a Four Power Pact in response to the burgeoning European crisis. This continuing dismissal of Litvinov's appeal for collective action rendered his position in Moscow increasingly precarious.

For Litvinov, collective security was becoming a dead letter. He observed that Germany had rendered the Versailles victors powerless without firing

[38] Ibid., 151.

a shot. In five years, he noted, they had offered no resistance to Germany's aggressive actions, thereby placing that country in a better position for war than it possessed in 1914.[39] The coming conflict, he predicted, with each side again in pursuit of total victory, would result in another massive slaughter.[40] If Britain would not act, and France followed Britain, the USSR of necessity would reconcile itself with Germany.[41] Safe behind its borders, it would observe the German conquest of Central and Southern Europe. Hitler, he concluded with remarkable insight, would then turn on the British, but not before he had come to terms with the USSR.[42]

Meanwhile, the Soviet feeling of betrayal by the West encouraged a full-scale retreat to fortress Russia. If that played to Germany's advantage, it was a decision that the West deserved. On December 25, Litvinov saw the *Le Temps* correspondent in Moscow, who asked him whether the Soviet position was one of isolation. Litvinov responded: "Obviously, since at the moment no one wants anything to do with us. We will carry on waiting ... and then we'll see."[43] The costly worsening of Russia's political and diplomatic standing emanating from the terror, added to its concomitant isolation imposed by an ideologically hostile world, was again taking its toll on Litvinovian internationalism. Hitler alarmed the Western powers, but not sufficiently to counter their underestimation of the USSR as a potential partner to Nazi Germany or to themselves.[44]

VI

Litvinov's perennial pursuit of collective security never included the United States. The reason did not lie in American indifference. Events in Europe, especially when they erupted into crises, flooded much of the American press and national radio. Overwhelmingly, the U.S. public accepted the supposition that American interests lay in peace, and the major threat to peace, for them, lay in the expansionism of Hitler's Germany. Nowhere was the concern over German behavior stronger than in the administration of President Roosevelt. Frances Perkins, his secretary of labor, observed that the President began to apprise the Cabinet of the dangers to peace as early as 1935. In 1936, Perkins recalled, "he began nagging about them, and a year later he was nagging about them all the time."[45] Nagging, for Perkins, was educating, and by 1937, she recalled, the President "was determined to educate the American people on the seriousness of the threat that Hitler posed."[46]

[39] Phillips, *Between the Revolution and the West*, 164.
[40] Degras, *Soviet Documents*, III, 282–94.
[41] Coulandre to Bonnet, May 1, 1938, Phillips, *Between the Revolution and the West*, 164.
[42] Coulandre to Bonnet, October 18, 1938, ibid., 165.
[43] Haslam, *The Struggle for Collective Security*, 153.
[44] Ibid., 156–57.
[45] Edward Bennett, interview with Frances Perkins, University of Illinois, Spring 1958.
[46] Ibid.

Edwin L. James, columnist of *The New York Times*, wrote that Roosevelt's concerns over threats to American security were genuine. He wondered, however, what that conviction could achieve within the framework of U.S. foreign policy. In a world that spoke of peace while it armed at a frantic pace, James advised the nation, foreign policy based on moral sanctions achieved nothing. He argued that Roosevelt and Hull, in facing Europe, should be more alert to the reality of what the national interest demanded. But he did not blame them for not following that course; American public opinion, he knew, would not permit it.[47]

American isolationism was so all-pervasive that Roosevelt refused to unleash a verbal and policy war against it. It was a war that he could not win, and he knew it. He refused, therefore, to sacrifice the public support he required to achieve his domestic program. Moreover, he dared not assume responsibilities in Europe without the public support to underwrite them. For many isolationists, Hitler's violations of the Versailles Treaty were none of America's business. They added the advice that Hitler was a threat to the United States only if the country interfered in matters that did not concern it.[48] Countless Americans feared and opposed Hitler, but not sufficiently to advocate any defense against Germany that required more than a verbal commitment to collective security.

The USSR emerged as Europe's chief proponent of an American presence in a European system of collective security. It presumed that the United States, also isolated from the main currents of European politics, was equally devoted to the Versailles peace structure. The USSR, moreover, was more isolated from potential allies than were the other European powers. Finally, the Soviets were convinced that the Americans understood their country's mutual interests with the USSR, and regarded their security needs close enough to Russia's to make genuine cooperation a reality. For the Soviets, that mutual interest in protecting the Versailles structure was lacking in Britain and France. Such realities, they presumed, would motivate the United States to give more than lip service to collective security. The Soviet press gave full coverage to every Washington pronouncement that indicated a stiffening of American attitudes.[49] But the Soviets were reading what they wished into American news. The United States, they discovered, had no foreign policy.

VII

Hitler's continuing assault on the Versailles settlement came with his demands of September 1938 on Czechoslovakia's Sudetenland. In the emerging Munich

[47] Edwin L. James, "Again We Sermonize on Brotherly Love," *The New York Times*, September 20, 1936.

[48] *New York Herald Tribune*, March 18, 1935; *New York Post*, March 25, 1935.

[49] *Pravda*, on January 7, 1936, gave full coverage to the maneuvers of the American fleet as evidence that the United States was preparing to play a larger role in world affairs.

crisis, the Soviets, like the British and French, sought to escape any commitment to the defense of Czechoslovakia. Litvinov, distrustful of both the French and the British, charged that the Versailles powers were responsible for the crisis by refusing to confront Hitler in previous German assaults on the Versailles structure. The French, equally determined to avoid involvement, moved to assign responsibility for confronting Germany to the Soviet Union. Bonnet favored sufficient Russian involvement in the crisis to discourage a Soviet-German rapprochement, but no more. Litvinov, however, suggested a conference of Britain, France, and Russia to warn Hitler against another German assault. France would not move unless Britain moved, and Britain would not move. The Soviets, totally distrustful of the British and French, refused to assume the lead in framing a response, cautioned by the prospect of confronting Germany alone. Thereupon the French proclaimed that Soviet hesitation was evidence that the USSR was not prepared to act. This permitted the French to abjure any commitment to collective security in defense of Czechoslovakia. The French capitulation was executed without any consultation with the Soviets.[50]

Litvinov turned to the League, without effect. Amid the subsequent British retreats, he attempted to keep his policy of collective action afloat. When Chamberlain's September 1938 talks with Hitler achieved nothing, the British sought out the Soviet position. On September 23, Litvinov reported to Moscow: "I pointed out to them that up to now, despite the fact that the fate of Europe is at stake, … they have ignored us and now want to receive a reply from us without giving us any information."[51] Moscow officials knew that any support from Britain and France was doubtful; the two countries, throughout the Munich crisis, had ignored the Soviet Union. Chamberlain, in favoring appeasement, opposed the presence of any Soviet forces in Central Europe. On September 30, the Czechs, having received the Anglo-French ultimatum to cede the Sudetenland, sought Soviet support. Before the Soviets could reply, the Czechs capitulated.

Jonathan Haslam passed critical judgment on Anglo-French behavior, especially its total exclusion of the USSR in the Czech crisis:

> The Munich settlement completely disoriented the Soviet regime. The rickety platform of collective security so assiduously assembled by Litvinov with whatever lay to hand – and building materials were in hopelessly short supply while Britain steadfastly refused to help – crumpled into an undignified heap as the British, aided and abetted by the French, wrenched out the main pillars of support from underneath.[52]

On October 4, the Soviet sense of betrayal pierced the post-Munich silence with an editorial in *Izvestiia* entitled: "The Policy of Awarding Prizes to the Aggressor." The paper agreed that Munich was not the first time that Europe

---

[50] Haslam, *The Soviet Union and the Struggle for Collective Security*, 178–80.
[51] Ibid., 187.
[52] Ibid., 195.

confronted Nazi aggression, but it was the first time that Germany's seizure of another country's territory was termed "a triumph or victory for peace." Amid the rapturous acclaim of the Munich settlement, Chamberlain addressed a special message to Daladier in which he praised the "boldness and dignity" with which the French leader had represented France at Munich.[53]

Europe, in praising the Munich settlement as a triumph for peace, had apparently come to terms with Germany. In that Europe, collective security had no role. The popular supposition that cooperation with Hitler was now possible isolated Litvinov from those in Moscow who had long asserted that collective security had no future. The grave deterioration of the USSR's international standing, as well as its exclusion from the Great Power Concert, ruled out any new or significant departures in Soviet foreign policy.[54] From Moscow the British ambassador reported that Litvinov was scarcely visible, his future in doubt.[55]

What brought momentary relief to Moscow was the supposition that Hitler's ambitions, as revealed in *Le Journal de Moscow*, had shifted toward Britain and France, again driving the two powers toward capitulation. Moscow pressed its advantage, based on the supposition that Britain and France had no choice but to "make a supreme effort and gather together at least to discuss collective action." For the Soviets, the pendulum was swinging in their direction. It proved to be a mere interval. It eased Litvinov's position, but did not silence his critics, who regarded collective security as an impossible dream. For them, Litvinov continued to play into the hands of London and Paris as they encouraged Hitler to turn eastward.

By December 1938, rumors spread across Europe that the Ukraine had become Hitler's primary target.[56] The burgeoning Ukraine problem encouraged the Soviets, in December, to respond favorably to a German move to renew German-Soviet trade relations. On January 10, 1939, the two countries agreed to commence negotiations in Moscow on trade credits, broken off at the time of the Austrian Anschluss. Mikoyan, Soviet Commissar of Foreign Trade, was to conduct the negotiations. Litvinov, who still distrusted the Nazis, opposed the arrangement. In the end, Hitler vetoed the meeting – which promised to be the first hesitant step toward a German-Soviet entente.

On February 1, 1939, *Izvestiia* published an article that suggested a new Soviet-German rapprochement. The report ended: "It would be extremely imprudent to suggest that disagreements now current in Moscow and Berlin will of necessity remain an unchanging factor in international politics." On February 14, an article in *Bol'shevik* suggested that "the Rappallo agreement between the USSR and Germany still exists. Does that not mean that it is being kept in reserve for any eventuality?" What encouraged this trend was the obvious weakness and unreliability of Britain and France.

[53] Ibid., 195.
[54] Ibid., 196–97.
[55] Phillips, *Between the Revolution and the West*, 165.
[56] Haslam, *The Soviet Union and the Struggle for Collective Security*, 201.

Amid the movement toward a Soviet-German alignment came Stalin's noted speech of March 10, 1939, to the XVIIIth Party Congress. Stalin quickly made clear that he had not reached a decision on where Soviet interests lay. He attacked Britain and France for rejecting collective security, giving away Austria and then sacrificing the Sudetenland, leaving Czechoslovakia defenseless against further Nazi aggression. Having reneged on every obligation, he continued, the Versailles victors had emphasized the weakness of the Soviet army, as they encouraged the Germans to turn eastward and engage the Soviets in war. Finally, Stalin admonished his country to "observe caution and not let [the USSR] be drawn into conflicts by war mongers urging others to take the chestnuts out of the fire."[57]

Stalin's indecision on Soviet policy left the external affairs department of *Izvestiia* confused. It concluded that Stalin's speech left unchanged Soviet relations with Britain and France, which deliberately excluded the Soviet Union from European affairs. Nor for the moment did any improvement in relations with Germany seem possible. The Germans were more perceptive as they detected the possibility of coming to terms with the USSR. As the British and French revealed no concern, the German invasion of Czechoslovakia on March 15, 1939, challenged their indifference.

Stalin's response to the invasion, although it measured the ultimate collapse of collective security, was cautious. Instead of an outburst of rage and a conference call, as in the Soviet response to the Austrian Anschluss, Stalin, on March 18, resorted to a sharply worded note to Berlin, a note of no obvious significance. Litvinov, expecting more, was not impressed. A subsequent scare over a Nazi assault on Romania prompted the British to ask the Soviets to call a conference. When the Soviets agreed to the request, the British ignored their effort, undermining what little credibility they still possessed in Moscow.

Litvinov's perennial quest for collective security was now living on borrowed time. Recalling the failure of his relations with Britain, he summarized his own and his country's fading distrust of the Western powers. He assigned responsibility for future efforts at collective action to them:

> For five years in the foreign policy field we have been making suggestions and proposals for the organization of peace and collective security, but the Powers have been ignoring them and acting in defiance of them. If England and France are really changing their line, let them either make known their views on our previously advanced proposals or else make their own proposals. The initiative must be left to them.[58]

Soviet isolation still demanded a collective defense. Kremlin leaders were again prepared to accept the only available solution for Russian insecurity: a joint declaration of Britain, France, Poland, and the USSR on the indivisibility of peace. Poland, terrified of provoking Hitler and fearful of the USSR,

[57] Ibid., 204–05.
[58] Ibid., 206.

refused to enter any security arrangement. This provided Chamberlain with another escape from both collective security or an entente with the Soviet Union – a country he continued to fear and despise. It mattered little; any Soviet security agreement with Britain and France would be unequal, for the two Western nations would not be committed to anything. Thus, with the fall of Czechoslovakia, the two European Versailles victors – Britain and France – confronted two, still isolated, Versailles losers – Germany and the Soviet Union – both in command of far greater military power, with implications of predictable disaster that the victors could not recognize.

What finally turned the Soviet Union away from collective security and toward an approach to Hitler? According to the historian John F. Thompson, two events of 1938 determined the failure of Litvinov's long struggle to promote collective security. First, the armed clashes along the Soviet-Manchukuo border, though they were clearly won by the Soviet forces, made Stalin think of the problem Russia would face with Japan if a war with Germany ensued. Second, and probably most importantly, was the Czech crisis and what the British and French policy led to when France in particular was wedded to the defense of Czechoslovakia. Thompson argued that the essential point for Stalin was this: "When Hitler brazenly threatened an important ally of both the Soviet Union and the Western powers, the latter reneged on their treaty obligations, backed down, and meekly handed Czechoslovakia on a silver platter to Hitler at the Munich Conference in September 1938." Stalin had to ask: "What sort of collective security was this? What did this say about the reliability of the Western powers as allies against Hitler?" Stalin decided that this suggested a very disturbing possibility, "That they hoped to get the Soviet Union embroiled with Germany and then stand aside."[59] Munich was decisive in Stalin's decision to dump Litvinov and collective security.

---

[59] John M. Thompson, *Russia and the Soviet Union: An Historical Introduction* (New York, 1986), 238.

12

The Coming of War: 1939

I

Germany's seizure of Czechoslovakia in March 1939 inaugurated the final crisis in the disintegration of the Versailles peace structure and the march toward war. Again, Britain, France, and the United States – the makers of the Versailles Treaty – had failed to relieve Europe's burgeoning tensions by modifying their treaty or defending it through an effective display of force. Even after the Munich settlement of the previous September, British leaders assumed that some form of accommodation would produce a general European settlement and forestall a German continental hegemony. But in the fall of Prague they detected a new and inescapable threat to Europe's future. What troubled European observers was not merely the ruthlessness of the German occupation but, even more alarming, the revelation of a German expansionism without visible limit. On no grounds, and certainly not self-determination, could anyone justify such aggression. "The utter cynicism and immorality of the whole performance," wrote British Ambassador Sir Nevile Henderson from Berlin, "defies description. Nazism has definitely crossed the rubicon of purity of race and German unity...."[1]

With that judgment, U.S. officials agreed. "The Czech annexation," wrote the American consul in Geneva, "... can not be justified on racial or other reasonable grounds and starkly reflects a determination to extend German expansion to such an extent that this ambition can only be checked by force." From Paris, U.S. Ambassador William C. Bullitt reported that all hope for a successful accommodation with Hitler's Germany had vanished.[2] American chargé Raymond H. Geist explained from Berlin that further concessions would simply compel the German government to find new pretexts to justify its territorial gains.[3] "No one here," observed Assistant Secretary of State

[1] Henderson to Halifax, March 16, 1939, *DBFP*, Third Series, IV (London, 1951), 278.
[2] Consul at Geneva to Hull, March 18, 1939, FRUS, *1939*, I (Washington, 1956), 53; Bullitt to Hull, March 17, 1939, ibid., 48.
[3] Geist to Hull, April 3, 1939, ibid., 109.

Adolf A. Berle in Washington, "has any illusions that the German Napoleonic machine will not extend itself almost indefinitely; and I suppose this is the year. It looks to me like a hot summer ahead." Berle predicted war in four months.[4] Berle added the warning that any war involving Britain, France, and Germany would leave Russia the dominant power in Europe. If the American reaction was violent, it was also impersonal; the United States had no traditional stake in Czechoslovakia.

President Franklin D. Roosevelt understood Hitler and harbored no illusions that Europe could escape further trouble. He had attempted to modify German behavior through public statements and even personal messages to Hitler. He had failed (1) to influence Hitler perceptibly, (2) to encourage London and Paris to stand together in effective alliance, or (3) to break the hold of isolationism on American-European relations. Unable to ignore Hitler's aggressions, yet barred from formulating any positive responses by a deeply engrained American tradition of non-involvement in Europe's political and military affairs, Roosevelt and his Secretary of State, Cordell Hull, again retreated to the principle of peaceful change – the embodiment of American internationalism. This enabled the administration to involve the United States verbally, morally, and even emotionally, in Europe's burgeoning crisis without creating a national commitment to defend anything. Washington's official pronouncement on Hitler's annihilation of the Czech state scarcely differed from Hull's response a year earlier to the German annexation of Austria:

> This government ... cannot refrain from making known this country's condemnation of the acts which have resulted in the temporary extinguishment of the liberties of a free and independent people.... The position of the government of the United States has been made consistently clear. It has emphasized the need for respect for the sanctity of treaties and the pledged word, and for non-intervention by any nation in the domestic affairs of other nations; and it has ... expressed its condemnation of a policy of military aggression.[5]

The principle that change, to be legitimate and thereby acceptable, must also be peaceful, defined Britain's responses to Hitler's demands on the Versailles settlement no less than those of the United States. Such responses created an image of retaliation as well as concern for Europe's peace, but they were totally irrelevant to the existing conditions in international affairs.

Roosevelt preferred that Britain and France, as in former times, take responsibility for their own and Europe's defense. At the same time, he kept open the possibility that Washington might reward their firmness with material aid. What troubled the President was an underlying spirit of desperation in English society. In late January 1939, Harvard historian Roger B. Merriman sent Roosevelt a letter written by the noted British historian, George

4 Bernice Bishop Berle and Travis Beal Jacobs, eds., *Navigating The Rapids, 1918–1971: From the Papers of Adolf A. Berle* (New York, 1973), 201–08.
5 Department of State, *Press Releases*, xx (1939), 199–200; *FRUS, 1939*, 49–50.

M. Trevelyan. For Trevelyan, British and French prospects were black indeed. With the Soviet Union and the United States out of the European equation, Britain and France, he wrote, could not repeat their success against Germany in the Great War, especially since Germany now had the support of Japan and Italy. Trevelyan suggested that the United States, faced with the loss of Europe and Africa, reconsider its isolationist policy before it became isolated.[6] At the same time, Lord Lothian, then in Washington, reminded Roosevelt: "Britain has defended civilization for a thousand years. Now the spear is falling from her hand and it is up to you to take it and carry on."[7] Roosevelt, presuming that the United States had no direct responsibility for Europe's Versailles order, turned on Trevelyan and Lothian in a burst of outrage. "I got mad clean through," he confessed to Merriman in mid-February, "and told [Lothian] that just as long as he or Britishers like him took that attitude of complete despair, the British would not be worth saving anyway. What the British need today is a good stiff grog, inducing not only the desire to save civilization but the continued belief that they can do it."[8]

Roosevelt continued to urge a more vigorous British policy in Europe. On March 26, he asked Sir Arthur Willert, the distinguished British journalist:

> Why did we [the British] not have conscription? Why did we let Germany have a monopoly of intimidation? Why did we not build more bombers or at least say that we were building more? Why did we not let stories leak out about the tremendous preparation on foot to bomb Germany? He believed the German home front was pretty weak anyhow. Such stories (even if they were not true) would weaken it still more.

That most Americans in 1939 desired Britain to pursue a more determined policy of confrontation in Europe implied not an American readiness to follow the British lead, but the hope that British firmness would eliminate the need for U.S. intervention. Unfortunately, Britain, no more than the United States, was prepared for the role that Roosevelt assigned it.[9]

II

Hitler introduced Poland to his continuing assault on the Versailles settlement when, following the German occupation of Prague, he demanded the return of Danzig to the status of a German city, as well as the creation of an

[6] Merriman to Roosevelt, January 28, 1939, President's Secretary's File (PSF): Great Britain, *FDRL*.
[7] Lothian to Roosevelt, January 29, 1939, in *Ickes*, II: *The Inside Struggle*, 591.
[8] Roosevelt to Merriman, February 15, 1939, PSF: Great Britain, *FDRL*. For French views that only the United States could save Europe, see Bullitt to Hull, March 15, 1939, *FRUS, 1939*, I, 42. For a full discussion of Roosevelt's attitude toward the British, see David Reynolds, "FDR on the British: A Postscript," *Proceedings of the Massachusetts Historical Society*, 90 (1978), 106–10.
[9] For British military weakness, see M. Howard, *The Continental Commitment* (London, 1972); B. Bond, *British Military Policy between the Two World Wars* (Oxford, 1980).

extra-territorial railway and other major communications between the Reich and German-held East Prussia. Following the peaceful settlement with Lithuania, Hitler, on March 23, welcomed Memel into the Reich, addressing the Memel Germans from the balcony of the Municipal Theater. The Chancellor appealed to his listeners to express their devotion, faith, and loyalty to their new country.[10] Hitler then returned to the issue of Poland.

German demands on Poland did not challenge any historic British interests in Central Europe; indeed, London officials recognized some legitimacy in Hitler's claims to Danzig. Britain, moreover, possessed no power to defend Poland. But by March 1939, Hitler's repeated assaults on the Versailles edifice had shaken Europe's confidence and stability. "Unless some new stabilizing factor could be introduced into Europe," Prime Minister Neville Chamberlain informed the House of Commons, "the dissolution of a large part of Europe might be imminent." U.S. Ambassador Joseph P. Kennedy, in London, observed that if Europe succeeded in building an effective international front against Germany, "Great Britain and France will have to assume burdens of incalculable responsibility."[11] To preserve what remained of European stability, the Prime Minister, supported by an increasingly anxious British public, resolved to deny Hitler another easy triumph. On March 31, he addressed the House of Commons:

> I now have to inform the House that ... in the event of any action which clearly threatens Polish independence, and in which the Polish Government accordingly considers it vital to resist with their national forces, His Majesty's Government will feel themselves bound at once to lend the Polish Government all support in their power. They have given the Polish Government an assurance to this effect. I may say that the French Government have authorized me to make it plain that they stand on the same ground in this matter as do His Majesty's Government.[12]

Chamberlain, in his reversal of British policy, believed that he could dissuade Hitler from attacking Poland, and that Poland, as a nation more powerful than Russia, was a worthy ally.[13] France, already committed to Poland's defense, was relieved. But Englishmen with a strategic vision were appalled. They had no greater confidence in Poland's leader, Josef Beck, than in the Polish army. Military expert Basil Liddell Hart declared the Polish guarantee "foolish, futile, and provocative ... an ill-considered gesture" that "placed Britain's destiny in the hands of Poland's rulers, men of very dubious and unstable judgment." Hart promptly resigned as military correspondent of *The Times* (London). David Lloyd George asked in the House whether the General

---

[10] Baynes, ed., *The Speeches of Adolf Hitler*, II, 1587–89.

[11] Kennedy to Hull, March 22, 1939.

[12] William Manchester, *The Last Lion: Winston Spencer Churchill* (Boston, 1983), 406.

[13] For an evaluation of Chamberlain's statement of March 31 as a futile effort at deterrence, see Alan Alexandroff and Richard Rosecrance, "Deterrence in 1939," *World Politics*, 29 (1977), 404–24.

Staff agreed to defend Poland, which they could not reach militarily under any conceivable circumstances. Duff Cooper confided in his diary: "Never before in our history have we left in the hands of one of the smaller powers the decision whether or not Britain goes to war." Winston Churchill, long clamoring for British action, was delighted to know that Chamberlain was willing to fight for something, but within a week began to question the wisdom of the Polish guarantee.[14]

Beck arrived in London on April 3 to negotiate the details of Britain's pledge of military aid to Poland. British spokesmen expected a Polish guarantee of Rumania's frontiers, but to their dismay, Beck refused to commit Poland to anything. When Beck declared that Poland supplied guns to Britain, Chamberlain, who knew what Britain imported, recalled that Polish arms were not on the list. Chamberlain, with other London officials, began to understand why Beck was a legend; they had been had.[15] Following the Italian annexation of Albania on April 7, London and Paris offered guarantees to Rumania without making the commitment dependent on Polish action. Soon, Britain added Greece and Turkey to its Eastern peace front.[16] With Britain carrying the risk, the British guarantee to Poland evoked a favorable response in the United States. The Washington correspondent of *The Times* (London) observed: "When the American people see European nations – and especially those nations, Britain and France – which have their sympathy – courageously taking the leadership which they strongly feel must not be American, their disquiet gives way to unstinted approval."[17]

Standing before the Rathaus in Wilhelmshaven on April 1, Hitler condemned the uncompromising adherence of Britain and France to the Versailles treaty structure. He again termed the League of Nations the guarantor "of the basest 'Diktat' that had ever been devised by men." In response to London officials who continued to demand that all problems be settled by conversation and negotiation, Hitler retorted that Britain had had fifteen years for that. For fifteen years, he continued, he had sought to resolve differences through negotiation, and had been rejected every time.[18] All empires, including the British Empire, he asserted, had been built and sustained through force. He had sought to restore only what had been taken from Germany at Paris. "Not only was the German Reich destroyed and Austria split ... by the criminals of Versailles," he declared, "but Germans were also forbidden to acknowledge that community which they had confessed for more than a thousand years."[19]

[14] Manchester, *The Last Lion*, 406–07.
[15] Ibid., 408–09.
[16] Bullitt to Hull, April 13, 1939, *FRUS, 1939*, I, 129.
[17] For the reference to *The Times* and the Willert letter, the original of which is in the Public Record Office (London), Norman Graebner is indebted to Alexander E. Campbell.
[18] Baynes, *Speeches of Adolf Hitler*, II, 1592, 1594–95.
[19] Ibid., 1606, 1609.

III

On April 14, 1939, Roosevelt reminded Hitler that his repeated aggressions were subjecting the world to the constant dread of another war.[20] "Plainly," he wrote, "the world is moving toward the moment when the situation must end in catastrophe unless a more rational way of guiding events is found." Even a war confined to other countries, the President warned, would bear heavily on the people of the United States. Again he reminded Hitler that international problems could and should be solved at the council table. Committed to U.S. non-involvement in European challenges, the President attempted to bind Hitler to the status quo by asking him to enter into reciprocal guarantees against aggression with all the countries of Europe. Specifically, Roosevelt demanded assurances that German armies would not invade some thirty countries that the President listed. Thereafter, the United States would join any discussions designed to bring relief from armaments and restrictive international trade barriers.[21] On the following day, Roosevelt informed newsmen that "we in this country should leave no stone unturned to prevent war."[22] On April 25, Secretary of State Cordell Hull repeated the supposition, before the Red Cross convention in Washington, that "there could be no controversies between nations impossible of settlement by peaceful processes of friendly adjustment."[23]

On April 20, Berlin celebrated Hitler's fiftieth birthday with a huge military parade. Observer William L. Shirer acknowledged that he had witnessed some big parades in France and Italy, but this exhibition of the new German army, he observed, "must certainly have been the greatest display of military power that modern Europe has ever seen." Among the street decorations along the line of march were thirty-foot banners hanging from specially erected posts, representing the regions of the Reich. Three banners carried the inscription of Danzig. Shirer described the action:

> From 11:25 this morning until 3:25 this afternoon I stood in the press stand by the side of the place Herr Hitler ... took the salute. All the time, for four hours, we saw these steel-helmeted troops, moving with the precision of a mighty machine, goose-step by. They didn't all goose-step, of course, because a large part of an army nowadays moves on wheels. And overhead, at the beginning, we saw a sample – a pretty good-sized sample – of that deadly new weapon, the air force.

Hitler took the salute standing on a platform under a canopy in front of the Technical High School. Dressed in his brown Nazi party uniform, he saluted

---

[20] For Roosevelt's message of April 14, 1939, see *FRUS*, *1939*, I, 130–33. The origin and drafting of the message are discussed in Cordell Hull, *The Memoirs of Cordell Hull* (New York, 1948), I, 620. That day, Roosevelt sent a similar message to Mussolini.

[21] Ibid, Hull.

[22] White House news conference, April 15, 1939, President's Press Conferences, *FDRL*.

[23] U.S. Department of State, *Peace and War: United States Foreign Policy, 1931–1941* (Washington, 1942), 63.

literally every platoon, tank, and truck. To Shirer, the multitudes who viewed the parade seemed proud over the country's triumphs and advances since Hitler proclaimed conscription in 1935. Yet that display of German military dominance scarcely touched the unfolding drift toward war.[24] Hitler's celebration offered a powerful warning to Poland, as well as to Britain and France. Poland alone could not withstand a Nazi onslaught; its Western allies could not reach Poland, much less defend it from an overpowering German invasion. Such realities were not governing the ongoing diplomacy.

Hitler answered Roosevelt's message of April 14 in a two-hour Reichstag speech on April 28. If the United States had any interest in peace, he averred, it could long have challenged the human and historic derangements of the Versailles Treaty, for which it carried a heavy responsibility. Woodrow Wilson, he reminded Roosevelt, had promised self-determination at Paris, and then distributed Germany's colonial possessions to others.[25] Hitler challenged the President to name one country that believed itself threatened by Germany.[26]

In more telling passages, Hitler aimed at the heart of the matter – the inability of councils and conferences to settle international disputes peacefully. The United States itself had demonstrated its skepticism toward conference procedures when it refused to join the League of Nations. In almost twenty years, Hitler added, the League, the greatest conference in history, had failed "to solve one single decisive international problem." Hitler explained that failure to Roosevelt: "At a conference there is no accused and no prosecutor, but only two contending parties. And if their own good sense does not bring about a settlement …, they will never surrender themselves to disinterested foreign Powers."[27] Clearly the necessary revisions in the Versailles Treaty required negotiations between the parties directly concerned, a procedure rendered impossible by the Western adherence to the principle of peaceful change, which, in effect, meant no change at all. From Washington, German Chargé d'Affaires Hans Thomsen discerned that Roosevelt and Hull, in their appeals for peaceful change, were acting as sponsors of the Versailles settlement, thereby intervening dangerously in the affairs of Europe.[28]

In an international environment where compromise had become synonymous with sellout and potential disaster, the achievement of capitulation through moral suasion constituted the only alternative to war. As Bullitt reminded Hull in May, it was the allied refusal to negotiate over Danzig that protected what remained of Europe's equilibrium.[29] It was not surprising, therefore, that Roosevelt's letter-writing, with its veiled demand of capitulation, received the

[24] William L. Shirer, *"This is Berlin"* (Woodstock, 1999), 39–41.
[25] Baynes, *Speeches of Adolf Hitler*, II, 1653.
[26] Ibid., 1647.
[27] Ibid., 1644.
[28] Thomsen to the Foreign Ministry, April 22, 24, 1939, *Documents on German Foreign Policy (DGFP), 1918–1945*, Series D, VI (London, 1956), 304, 318.
[29] *FRUS, 1939*, I, 182.

plaudits of grateful observers everywhere in Europe. Britain's Lord Hankey thanked Roosevelt for his apparent effort to rehabilitate the concept of balance of power. Prime Minister Chamberlain concurred: "I think the appeal is very skillfully framed and has put H. and M. into a tight corner. I have no doubt they will refuse to play.... But world opinion and particularly American opinion will have been further consolidated against them."[30]

Roosevelt's English friend Arthur Murray found even greater power in Roosevelt's words. "What a sigh of profound thankfulness and gratitude to you went up from us all," he wrote, "as we became apprised of the courageous message and watched its beneficent results." With more subdued enthusiasm, British author Arthur Ransome declared that Roosevelt had "done three quarters of a magnificent piece of work on behalf of humanity as a whole." What remained was the President's need to assure the Germans that he "has at heart not only our interests but theirs, and is not committed to the maintenance of a status quo that includes the injustices that make them sore.... [The Germans] must be made to feel that he is not a man of Versailles, but a man looking for a Europe that has a chance of staying out and not one that leaves Germany with a grievance of a kind that we ourselves, for example, would not tolerate for a moment."[31]

Ransome advocated American neutrality as the necessary precursor to the negotiation of essential changes in the Versailles Treaty structure as the only means of preventing war. European leaders as well as American internationalists, for whom the *sine qua non* of Western policy was the defense, not the modification, of the status quo, argued that the United States could influence events in Europe only by deserting its official neutrality, permitting at last the creation of a policy that conformed to national sentiment. Former Secretary of State Henry L. Stimson asserted in a letter to *The New York Times* of March 6, 1939, that the United States could do nothing to stop aggression until it dropped every semblance of impartiality. He reminded his readers that the country, to "keep alive the American faith in its principles must discriminate between right and wrong, between an aggressor and its victim, between an upholder of law and a violator thereof...."[32] Similarly, in a radio broadcast of March 29, Under Secretary of State Sumner Welles admonished the American people to accept the repeal of the neutrality legislation, permitting

---

[30] Lord Hankey to J. B. Bickersteth, April 29, 1939, Lord Hankey Papers, Roskill Library, Churchill College, Cambridge; Chamberlain to Hilda Chamberlain, April 15, 1939, NC 18/1/1094, Neville Chamberlain Papers, University of Birmingham.

[31] Murray to Roosevelt, May 20, 1939, PSF: Great Britain; Murray; Francis W. Hirst to Roosevelt, May 3, 1939, President's Personal File (PPF) 1147; Arthur Ransome to Hirst, May 2, 1939, ibid., Franklin D. Roosevelt Library, Hyde Park (*FDRL*). For similar messages from American diplomats and Roosevelt's friends, see William Phillips to Roosevelt, May 26, 1939, PSF: Phillips; Thomas Lamont to Miss LeHand, April 28, 1939, PPF 70, *FDRL*; Bullitt to Hull, April 15, 1939, *FRUS, 1939*, I, 134; Consul in Geneva to Hull, April 17, 1939, ibid., 137.

[32] Letter to *The New York Times*, March 6, 1939.

the United States to sell the materials of war to the potential victims of aggression. Nothing less would enable the United States to uphold its conception of a world order built on law, justice, and reason.[33]

Congressional isolationists had anchored their anti-war program to the neutrality acts and were determined to keep the policy of enforced neutrality in operation. During May, Senator Key Pittman, the administration's spokesman in Congress, prepared a modified neutrality bill that would extend the principle of cash-and-carry beyond the May 1, 1939, deadline, and make no distinction in its application between arms and raw materials such as steel, copper, oil, and scrap metal. A significant number of witnesses appeared before the Senate Foreign Relations Committee to attack the neutrality laws. Stimson hoped that Pittman would "strike the shackles off the foreign policy of the American government."[34] Ambassador William Bullitt warned from Paris that the neutrality legislation would permit Germany to risk war with impunity.[35] But so strong was the opposition that Pittman would not bring his measure out of committee.

Still, Roosevelt refused to retreat on the neutrality issue. On May 19, he reminded Democratic leaders at the White House that with the expiration of cash-and-carry, the United States could make none of its industrial potential available to Britain and France in the event of war. His arguments failed to move the isolationists. On July 11, Pittman's Foreign Relations Committee finally rejected the new neutrality measure. The President responded bitterly that the administration should "introduce a bill for statues of [Senators] Austin, Vandenberg, Lodge, and Taft ... to be erected in Berlin...."[36] Three days later, Roosevelt sent another appeal to Congress, and on July 15 he called leading senators to the White House to remind them of the probability of a European war. "Our decision," he said, "may well affect not only the people of our own country, but also the people of the world." He warned the senators: "I've fired my last shot. I think I should have another round in my belt." Isolationist Senator William Borah insisted that his own information was more reliable than that received at the State Department; it assured him that Europe was in no danger of war.[37] At last the administration gave in. Vice-President John Nance Garner informed the President that "you haven't got the votes and that's all there is to it."[38]

[33] Welles draft, March 29, 1939, PSF: State: Welles, *FDRL*.

[34] Stimson to Pittman, April 25, 1939, Committee Papers, SEN 76S-F9 (141), Neutrality Hearings Folder.

[35] Memorandum, Bullitt to Roosevelt, May 19, 1939, PSF Neutrality, Box 33, *FDRL*.

[36] Quoted in Robert Dallek, *Franklin D. Roosevelt and American Foreign Policy* (New York, 1979), 191.

[37] Press Conferences of FDR, 14, No. 564, July 21, 1939, 34.

[38] For superb analyses of the neutrality issue in 1939, see Robert A. Divine, *The Illusion of Neutrality* (Chicago, 1962), 236–81; Dallek, *Franklin D. Roosevelt and American Foreign Policy*, 179–92.

IV

With Poland powerless to escape the mounting German pressures on Danzig, the surest guarantee against a German invasion appeared to lay in resurrection of the Triple Entente comprising Britain, France, and Russia. On April 2, Joseph E. Davies, American Ambassador to Belgium, advised Britain's David Lloyd George that his country could avoid a war over Poland only by entering a firm military arrangement with the Soviet Union.[39] Such an agreement, Foreign Office officials agreed, would compel Hitler to fight a two-front war and permit Britain to avoid the necessity of dealing with a towering Soviet presence in Europe after a war that left Britain, France, and Germany in ruins. French Premier Edouard Daladier, and much of the French Foreign Office as well, accepted the necessity of a military alliance with the USSR.[40] In mid-April, Britain and France offered the Soviet Union a security agreement that quickly exposed the suspicions and conflicting interests of the three countries.

Chamberlain hoped to limit Britain's obligations in Eastern Europe to Poland and Rumania, avoiding a direct commitment to the Soviet Union. He needed, however, some formula that would enable the Kremlin to aid Poland and Rumania despite the refusal of both countries to tolerate any Soviet forces within their borders. London proposed that the Soviet government announce that it would offer help to the two countries should they suffer an invasion and seek Soviet support. But Britain's unalterable commitment to Poland ruled out any Anglo-Soviet action.[41]

Soviet intentions emerged with equal clarity. British Ambassador Sir Ronald Lindsay informed Welles that the Soviet government, like its Tsarist predecessors, desired to keep the rest of Europe at a distance under the assumption that the USSR was invulnerable as long as it fought defensively and limited its commitments to bordering regions. Thus the Kremlin would avoid obligations outside Eastern Europe while it attempted to strengthen its borderland defenses against Germany. The basic Soviet proposal of April 18 demanded a three-power agreement covering both mutual assistance and the protection of all states lying along the Soviet Union's western frontier between the Baltic and Black Seas. Finally, the Kremlin requested a convention to arrange matters of military cooperation.[42]

Not until May 9 did the London government reply to the Soviet overtures, and for good reason. British and Soviet objectives were irreconcilable: Britain sought help from the Soviet Union, whereas Poland and Rumania were determined to prevent any Soviet presence on their territory. The Soviet proposal

[39] Davies to Lloyd George, April 2, 1939, PSF: Belgium, *FDRL*.

[40] Sir Eric Phipps to Halifax, June 8, 1939, Eric Phipps Papers, Roskill Library, Churchill College, Cambridge.

[41] Bullitt to Hull, April 15, 18, 1939, *FRUS*, 1939, I, 233, 237.

[42] Memorandum of conversation by Welles, June 23, 1939, ibid., 274; Kennedy to Hull, April 18, 1939, ibid., 235; Bullitt to Hull, April 18, 19, 21, 1939, ibid., 237–38.

suggested that Poland and Rumania would receive Soviet assistance whether they desired it or not. The reply to the Soviet government, along with a reluctant French acquiescence, declared that the time had not arrived for an arrangement as comprehensive as the Soviet proposal. Instead, the British government returned to an earlier formula whereby the Soviets, should Britain and France become involved in hostilities in fulfillment of their Eastern European obligations, would provide assistance in accordance with terms determined in advance. This formula offered the Soviet government some assurance of common action, but it did not satisfy the Soviet officials.[43] The Soviet reply, on May 15, came from Vyacheslav Molotov, who had replaced Litvinov as Commissar for Foreign Affairs. This change brought the conduct of Soviet foreign affairs into the governing inner circle, foreshadowing a possible shift in policy away from a front against Germany.

Following a month of diplomatic maneuvering, the British government, on May 25, submitted a counterproposal. If Britain, France, or the Soviet Union became involved in war directly, or as the result of aggression against another European state that offered resistance, the three countries would enter into consultation under the League Covenant's Article XVI. This arrangement would remove the appearance of a Soviet threat to Poland and Rumania while it avoided reciprocal guarantees to the USSR.[44] French diplomats acknowledged that the British proposal offered little security to the Soviets. Clearly, Anglo-Soviet differences were profound. Nevertheless, on May 27, the British and French governments, under intense public pressure, opened political discussions with the Soviet Union through their ambassadors in Moscow.[45]

During June and July, the two Western powers sparred with the Soviets over the issue of possible indirect German aggression – the exertion of influence in the Baltic states especially through threats of violence. Any Baltic concessions would permit the Germans to reach the Soviet frontier without facing any resistance. In early June, Soviet Ambassador Ivan Maisky in London informed Foreign Minister Lord Halifax that the problem of the Baltic states was crucial for his country; either the powers would reach an agreement on that or there would be no agreement at all.[46] For American officials in Europe and Washington, the Soviet price for an agreement seemed excessive. Interior Secretary Harold Ickes recorded his reactions in his diary on June 17:

> The latest terms that Russia has demanded would give her the right to go into any of the Baltic States on the Russian frontier, not only to meet a military invasion but to meet an economic or propaganda invasion, and France and Great Britain would have to stand by even though the decision as to whether

[43] Baron William Strang, *Home and Abroad* (London, 1956), 164–65.
[44] Kennedy to Hull, May 25, 1939, ibid., 262–63.
[45] Bullitt to Hull, May 30, 1939, Strang, 265.
[46] Halifax to Sir William Seeds, June 12, 1939, *DBFP*, Third Series, VI (London, 1953), 50–51.

Russia should go in would be Russia's alone. Bill [Bullitt] said that such terms were absurd and that even the French would not agree to them.[47]

In Paris, Foreign Minister Georges Bonnet complained to Bullitt that the Soviet right to counter Germany's indirect aggression "would make it possible for the Soviet Union to invade any of the Baltic states at any minute on any flimsy pretext with the armed support of France and England. It is obvious that neither France nor England could accept such a proposal."[48] Loy Henderson, U.S. Assistant Chief of the Division of European Affairs, expressed the doubts of many when he warned Washington officials against underestimating Soviet expansionism. "The present rulers of Russia," he wrote, "are still dominated by a spirit of aggressiveness, that is, they have not departed from the ultimate aim to ... include under the Soviet system additional peoples and territories."[49]

British leaders had long ceased to take the Soviets seriously. During June, Chamberlain admitted to Kennedy that except for the psychological importance that many Londoners attached to a Soviet pact, the Cabinet would terminate the conversations in Moscow.[50] The lingering suspicion of Soviet intentions among Britain's ruling classes diminished the possibility of any genuine cooperation from the beginning. Both Chamberlain and Halifax refused to visit Moscow.[51] London officials distrusted Soviet power no less than Soviet purpose. The notorious purge trials of 1936–1938 had eliminated much of the Soviet Union's top civilian and military leadership; thereafter, the USSR appeared too weak to be of any consequence in an anti-German coalition. Chamberlain and much of the Foreign Office regarded Poland as more powerful than the USSR; they preferred to rely on Poland and Rumania as allies. "If bringing Russia in meant their running out," Chamberlain wrote in May, "I should think the change a very disastrous one."[52] By July, the British disillusionment with the Kremlin was complete. Halifax informed Kennedy on July 19 that if the Soviets continued to insist on their definition of indirect aggression, the British were "going to call the whole deal off." Chamberlain complained to Kennedy that "he was sick and disgusted with the Russians

[47] Ickes, *Secret Diary*, II, 652.
[48] Bullitt to Hull, July 7, 1939, *FRUS, 1939*, I, 284.
[49] Henderson memorandum, July 22, 1939, *Foreign Relations of the United States: The Soviet Union, 1933–1939* (Washington, 1952), 773.
[50] Kennedy to Hull, June 27, 1939, *FRUS, 1939*, I, 276.
[51] Chamberlain expressed his opposition to the USSR freely in letters to his sisters. See, for example, Chamberlain to Ida Chamberlain, March 26, 1939, NC 18/1/1091; Chamberlain to Hilda Chamberlain, April 29, 1939, NC 18/1/1096; Chamberlain to Ida Chamberlain, May 21, 1939, NC 18/1/1100; Chamberlain to Hilda Chamberlain, May 28, 1939, NC 18/1/1101, Neville Chamberlain Papers.
[52] The assumption of Poland's military superiority underlay British policy toward Poland and the USSR throughout the period from Munich to the final crisis of August 1939. These views were held generally by Foreign Office and military officials.

and while he believes the Russians are willing to continue talking without accomplishing anything his patience is exhausted."[53]

To American critics, the British were attempting to exercise choices they did not have. They saw clearly that Moscow, not London, was dealing from strength; ultimately, they predicted, not even Hitler would dare to make a move without considering Soviet power and intent. They doubted that Britain and France could really offer the Kremlin an attractive alliance; both countries were totally unprepared to fight in Eastern Europe – or effectively anywhere. "My private hunch," noted Assistant Secretary Berle on June 1, "is that the Russians will not sign any alliance but will keep the British and French dangling, meanwhile dickering a little with the Germans behind the curtain somewhere....The danger is that in one of their comings apart the Germans may decide the time has come to move."[54] Similarly, Poland's Josef Beck suggested to Ambassador Anthony J. Drexel Biddle Jr. that the Soviets, anticipating a long war, planned to enter at a later stage, "swing the balance," and gain a position to dictate the terms of peace. With good reason, Joseph Davies continued to plead for a London-Paris-Moscow axis, wondering why the British government refused to take the power of the Soviet regime and army seriously despite the overwhelming evidence it possessed. He expressed his fears to Roosevelt: "Chamberlain will soon have to make up his mind or the old Bear will get tired of being cuffed around and make peace on his own terms possibly with Germany. If that happens, Europe will be in the hollow of Hitler's hand."[55] Whatever their concern for the immediate or more distant future, such observers understood that it did not necessarily belong to Britain and France.

As the political discussions continued aimlessly, the British government, on July 27, agreed to send a military mission to Moscow. The American chargé in London informed Hull that the British mission would attempt to prolong the military discussions at least until October, with the discussions of "indirect aggression" proceeding simultaneously.[56] The mission left London on August 5, and after a slow trip by boat, arrived in Moscow on August 11 without authority to negotiate. On the day preceding the arrival of the British delegation, fourteen Soviet leaders, under the direction of Marshal Kliment Voroshilov, Soviet Commissar of Defense, gathered in the Kremlin to determine the guidelines for the talks with the Anglo-French mission. Voroshilov, in his prepared paper, began with a scathing attack on the vagueness and incompetence of the Anglo-French delegation. His earlier meeting with the French delegates reinforced his accumulating doubts. He agreed to offer the Anglo-French mission the traditional Russian hospitality, but he wanted

---

[53] Kennedy to Hull, July 19, 20, 1939, *FRUS, 1939*, I, 286–87.

[54] Beatrice Bishop Berle and Travis Beal Jacobs, eds., *Navigating the Rapids, 1918–1971: From the Papers of Adolf A. Berle* (New York, 1973), 225.

[55] Biddle to Hull, June 17, 1939, PSF: Poland; Davies to Roosevelt, June 8, 1939, PSF: Belgium, FDRL.

[56] The American chargé in London to Hull, August 8, 1939, *FRUS, 1939*, I, 294.

guidance on how seriously he should pursue the negotiations. What underlay the Soviet mood of confidence was the gratifying knowledge that Russia was no longer a leper in the international community, but a country now asked to name its price.[57]

When Russian Ambassador Constantine Oumansky returned to Moscow early in August, he carried with him a letter that conveyed Roosevelt's concern for the burgeoning crisis in Europe. The President reminded Soviet leaders that the United States, like the USSR, would be materially affected by the outbreak of war. Whereas the United States could take no responsibility for the negotiations in Moscow, the President believed that "a satisfactory agreement against aggression on the part of the other European powers ... would prove to have a decidedly stabilizing effect in the interest of world peace...."[58] During U.S. Ambassador Laurence Steinhardt's interview with Foreign Minister Molotov on August 16, the Soviet leader lauded Roosevelt's concern for peace, but informed Steinhardt that the USSR demanded of Britain a definition of the specific conditions for mutual responses to counter aggression. Moscow alone, Molotov asserted, was not responsible for the delay in reaching agreement; the future of negotiations depended on others quite as much as on the USSR.[59]

Hitler's ever-increasing pressures on Danzig in no way modified Poland's attitude toward the Soviet Union. On August 16, Voroshilov insisted, finally, that any military agreement must include Polish permission for Soviet troops to enter Poland through Vilna and Lwow to meet the German armies should Poland become involved in war. As late as August 18, Poland refused to accept any Russian aid unless Britain and France guaranteed the subsequent Soviet evacuation of Polish territory. Suddenly, the long Soviet-Western quest for political and military agreement ground to a halt, for Germany had entered the bidding.[60]

V

For Hitler, the Moscow negotiations left Germany with few good choices. His territorial ambitions required an invasion of Poland, but he could not attack Poland without risking a war with Britain and France. The two Western allies, however, could not fight Germany successfully without Russian support. German policy, therefore, required Russia's neutralization. Somehow, the Moscow deliberations had to be thwarted. A successful negotiation would not only neutralize Russia, keeping it from the conflict, but also eliminate

---

[57] Anthony Reed and David Fisher, *The Deadly Embrace: Hitler, Stalin, and the Nazi-Soviet Pact, 1939–1941* (New York, 1988), 184–85.

[58] Welles to Steinhardt, August 4, 1939, ibid., 293–94.

[59] Steinhardt to Hull, August 16, 1939, *Foreign Relations: The Soviet Union*, 775; Steinhardt to Welles, August 16, 1939, *FRUS*, *1939*, I, 296–98.

[60] Bullitt to Hull, August 16, 18, 1939, *FRUS*, 226, 295. For the official American view of Soviet-German relations leading up to the Nazi–Soviet Pact, see ibid., 312–44.

the danger of a war against Britain and France – which alone dared not fight Germany. Stalin thus became the key to German planning.

Hitler personally admired Stalin, but he harbored a deep loathing for Russian Communism. Stalin, meanwhile, sensing the coming of a final crisis, with Hitler striking somewhere, was determined to purchase Russian security by playing his cards with consummate skill. The Soviet leader, in a Moscow speech of March 10, had declared that he had no intention of pulling any nation's chestnuts out of the fire – a clear statement that he was not going to fight for Britain and France. Still, Stalin made no approach to Berlin until he appointed Molotov, a member of the Soviet Politbureau, as head of the Foreign Affairs Ministry. He continued the Anglo-French negotiations in Moscow to keep the Germans on edge. Meanwhile, with a showdown over Poland approaching, Hitler was ready to open his critical negotiations with Stalin. He had already made his decision for war, and launched preparations for an attack on Poland at the end of August.

At the outset, it was clear that both Berlin and Moscow shared a deep mutual interest in the success of their coming negotiations. On July 26, meeting privately in a Berlin restaurant, Russian and German representatives quickly addressed the basic issues. The Germans made it clear that they were willing to pay for Russian neutrality in the burgeoning crisis by consigning large areas of Eastern Europe to the USSR. Armed with this knowledge, Stalin and Molotov increased the pressure on the British and French negotiators in Moscow to resolve the issue of indirect aggression. Not realizing that they were facing serious competition, the Anglo-French negotiators continued to temporize. They desired Russian help against Germany, but they were not prepared to buy it by sacrificing their Polish allies or the Baltic states. Hitler faced no such inhibitions; he could compensate the Soviets amply with territorial concessions. On July 14, Shirer reported the possibility of a Russo-German alignment, viewed by many as "Europe's Secret Nightmare." The two giants complemented each other economically, politically, even diplomatically, as joint enemies of the British Empire. Such a partnership, he noted, could dominate Europe, if not the world.[61]

Hitler was ready to force the issue. On August 15, he informed the Soviet government that he was prepared to send Foreign Minister Ribbentrop to Moscow to lay the foundations for better German-Soviet relations.[62] With the mutuality of interests so well established, the negotiations, conducted largely in Moscow, moved rapidly toward their conclusion. In the Molotov–Ribbentrop Pact, signed on August 24, the German government, in a secret protocol that Ambassador Steinhardt detailed for Washington that day, granted the USSR the freedom to refashion its relations with its small European neighbors, including Poland, Finland, Latvia, Estonia, Rumania, and soon Lithuania.[63]

[61] Shirer, "This Is Berlin," 51.
[62] George F. Kennan, *Russia and the West under Lenin and Stalin* (Boston, 1961), 325–27.
[63] Steinhardt to Hull, August 24, 1939.

Recognizing his isolation from the West, Stalin sought time to improve his defenses. Hitler, having neutralized Russia for ten years, was free to venture elsewhere. Thereafter, no Western action could prevent Central and Eastern Europe from slipping totally into Soviet and German hands.

For Berliners, the news of the pact was exceedingly welcome. Berlin's Nazi mouthpiece, *Angriff*, proclaimed the revival of the traditional friendship between the Russian and German peoples. "The world," it concluded, "stands before a towering fact: two peoples have placed themselves on the basis of a common foreign policy which during a long and traditional friendship produced a policy of common understanding." The nightmare of German encirclement had ended. The elimination of an enemy on its eastern front freed Berlin of all constraints in its confrontation with Poland.[64]

On August 25, Voroshilov terminated the Anglo-French military mission to Moscow, attributing the failure of the negotiations to Polish intransigence.[65] For too long, some American officials and editors countered, Britain had haggled with the Soviets under the assumption that it might secure a more desirable agreement from Germany. What mattered in the end was Germany's capacity and willingness to satisfy the Kremlin's immediate security needs.[66] But for Chamberlain, Russia remained too weak and morally unfit for admittance into a Western alliance. He characterized a well-placed minority in Britain that feared Russia more than Germany. Chamberlain's feeling of repugnance toward Stalin's purge trials and convictions of Russia's military ineffectiveness were widespread. The tales of Bolshevik horrors confirmed the conviction that the more Britain avoided ties to Russia, the safer it would be. On September 1, 1939, the *Daily Telegraph* published a letter from Lord Alfred Douglas that rejoiced over Hitler's "success in saving Britain from the 'odious predicament' of an alliance with Russia...."[67]

VI

With the signing of the Nazi–Soviet Pact, Alexis Léger, Secretary General of the French Ministry of Foreign Affairs, advised Bullitt that war over Poland was now inevitable. In Washington, Berle observed: "It seems to me that the British and French now have to fight, whether they like it or not."[68] In anticipation of this new threat to peace, Daladier appealed to Roosevelt on August

[64] Shirer, "This is Berlin," 56–57.
[65] Steinhardt to Hull, August 25, 1939, 309; Steinhardt to Hull, August 27, 1939, 311.
[66] Ickes argued this view in *Secret Diary*, II, 705. In a long analysis of the three-power negotiations, Alice Teichova concluded that the British government never wanted a treaty with Russia, hoping rather to obtain one with Germany. See her "Great Britain in European Affairs, March 15 to August 21, 1939, *Historica*, III (Prague, 1961), 239–311.
[67] Christopher G. Thorne, *Approach of War* (London, 1967), 15.
[68] Bullitt to Hull, August 24, 1939, *FRUS, 1939*, I, 309; Berle's diary, August 24, 1939, Berle and Jacobs, *Navigating the Rapids*, 242.

22, asking him to summon "all the nations of the earth to send delegates immediately to Washington to try to work out a pacific solution of the present situation." The French leader informed Bullitt that Germany would probably reject the conference proposal, but the President, in any event, would have clarified the moral issue and done his utmost "to prevent a horrible catastrophe for the entire human race."[69] Instead, Roosevelt addressed a message to King Victor Emmanuel of Italy on August 23. After reminding the king of his (Roosevelt's) April 14 appeal to Hitler and Mussolini, he invited the Italian government to frame specific proposals for a solution of the crisis. The United States, he added, would happily enter any peaceful discussions. "The unheard voices of countless millions of human beings," he pleaded, "ask that they shall not be vainly sacrificed again."[70]

That day, Chamberlain warned Hitler that Britain would come to the defense of Poland, but expressed the hope that Germany and Poland could avert a general European war. This time, Britain would not, unlike its action at Munich, urge Poland to give up Danzig in the interest of a peaceful settlement. But London, Kennedy reported, reacted badly to the President's message to the Italian king, and would have preferred a strong message to Poland, urging that country to make some concessions to Germany. "If the President is contemplating any action for peace," Kennedy concluded, "it seems to me that the place to work is on Beck in Poland .... I see no other possibility."[71] Berle wondered how Washington might word a strong message to Poland; the Nazi–Soviet Pact granted western Poland to Germany and eastern Poland to Russia, with Russia obtaining other bordering regions as well. The message, wrote Berle, would need to begin: "In view of the fact that your suicide is required, kindly oblige etc." Britain, Washington assumed, wanted the United States to do what it could not do. "As we saw it here," Assistant Secretary Jay Pierrepont Moffat recalled, "it merely meant that they wanted us to assume the responsibility of a new Munich and to do their dirty work for them."[72] Roosevelt refused to arrange what might have led to the sellout of another country.

On August 24, Roosevelt responded to the deepening crisis by addressing messages to Hitler and President Ignacy Mościcki of Poland. He reminded Hitler that the German government had never responded to his appeal of April 14. Now he urged the leaders of Germany and Poland to refrain from active hostilities and settle their differences through negotiation, arbitration, or conciliation. No nation had the right to pursue its ends through force. Roosevelt argued that any just and reasonable objective could be "satisfied through processes of peaceful negotiation or by resort to judicial arbitration."[73] For

[69] Bullitt to Hull, August 22, 1939, *FRUS, 1939*, I, 350.

[70] Welles (Roosevelt) to Phillips, August 23, 1939, ibid., 352; Welles to Roosevelt, August 22, 1939, OF200XXX, *FDRL*.

[71] Kennedy to Hull, August 23, 1939, *FRUS, 1939*, I, 356.

[72] Berle and Jacobs, *Navigating the Rapids*, 243; Hooker, ed., *The Moffat Papers*, 253.

[73] Roosevelt to Hitler, August 24, 1939, *FRUS, 1939*, I, 360–61; Roosevelt to Mościcki, August 24, 1939, ibid., 351–62.

unreasonable objectives, Roosevelt had no answer. Daladier expressed his gratitude for Roosevelt's messages and asserted that the President "had done more than any other man had done or could have done to avert war."

Daladier's statement revealed the extent to which traditional diplomacy had given way to simple demands for German capitulation under the assumption that nothing less than capitulation was diplomatically or morally acceptable. As Daladier confided to Bullitt, "There was no further question of policy to be settled."[74] Berle recognized the futility in the President's effort. "These messages," he recorded in his diary, "will have about the same effect as a valentine sent to somebody's mother-in-law out of season, and they have all that quality of naiveté which is the prerogative alone of the United States. Nevertheless, they ought to be sent. The one certain thing in this business is that no one will be blamed for making any attempt, however desperate, at preserving peace."[75] One day later, Mościcki expressed his hope for direct negotiations with Hitler; Berlin never responded. Berle found Hitler's refusal to reply shattering. "I have a horrible feeling," he noted, "of seeing the breaking of a civilization dying even before its actual death."[76]

Central to the accumulating pressures against peace after August 25 was the failure of the Nazi–Soviet Pact, with its momentary destruction of the balance of power in Eastern Europe, to affect the confrontation over Poland. The pact rendered Poland especially vulnerable by wiping out the Anglo-French defense program in the East and opening the way for a German invasion. Pursuing his advantage, Hitler repeated his minimum objectives in Poland: Germany's acquisition of Danzig and a passage through the Corridor to connect East Prussia with the Reich.[77] Poland accepted the reality of its weakened position without tempering its refusal to deal with Hitler, convinced that any hint of compromise would break the anti-German coalition. Beck professed delight that the Soviets, in their pact with Germany, had clarified their intentions; no longer need Poland face the endless necessity of denying the Kremlin the right to place Soviet troops on Polish territory.[78] Polish leader Ignace Paderewski assured Roosevelt that Poland was resolved to defend its national honor and independence.[79]

Revisionism was still in the air, and many were prepared to accept another successful assault on the Versailles Treaty, convinced that the treaty's

---

[74] Bullitt to Hull, August 25, 1939, ibid., 365; Bullitt to Roosevelt, August 27, 1939, Bullitt, ed., *For the President, Personal and Secret*, 360.

[75] Berle and Jacobs, *Navigating the Rapids*, 243.

[76] Biddle to Hull, August 25, 1939, *FRUS, 1939*, I, 364; Mościcki to Roosevelt, August 25, 1939, ibid., 368; Roosevelt to Hitler, August 25, 1939, ibid., 368–69; Berle and Jacobs, *Navigating the Rapids*, 244.

[77] Bullitt to Hull, August 22, 1939, 740.00/2106, Reel M982–8, National Archives, Washington, DC; Bullitt to Hull, August 26, 1939, *FRUS, 1939*, I, 373.

[78] Welles to Roosevelt, August 23, 1939, OF200XXX, *FDRL*; Bullitt to Hull, August 22, 1939, 740.000/2106, Reel M982–8, National Archives.

[79] Paderewski to Roosevelt, August 27, 1939, PPF 881, *FDRL*.

arrangements regarding Danzig were the least defensible of all.[80] But whatever the predictable cost to themselves, if not to Europe, Britain and France
chose to sustain their commitment to Poland on purely Polish terms. Daladier
acknowledged to Bullitt France's desire to avoid war, but also its determination to fulfill its promises to Poland.[81] On August 26, Léger again informed
Bullitt that Britain and France would support Poland, even at the price of
war.[82] Hitler complained to French Ambassador Robert Coulondre that Britain
and France were aggravating the European crisis by granting carte blanche to
Poland, encouraging that country to behave toward Germany in a manner
no self-respecting nation would endure. Hitler, on August 23, explained to
Henderson in Berlin his refusal to reestablish direct contact with the Polish
government; British and French support rendered any negotiation with Poland
impossible.[83]

Through time, that uncompromising support of Poland enabled the Warsaw
government not only to defy Germany and the USSR, Europe's two most powerful nations, but also to drag Britain and France into war without adequate
preparation or an alliance that promised some measure of success. On August
25, Hitler reminded Henderson that the conflict over Poland rested on Danzig
and the Corridor, and on those issues Poland offered nothing.[84] Diplomacy
mattered, and there was none.

Ignoring Poland's intransigence on the Danzig issue, Henderson assured
Hitler that Britain objected only to Germany's acceptance of force. Hitler
asked "whether England had ever found a solution for any of the idiocies of
Versailles by way of negotiation." The burden of revising Versailles, Hitler
continued, rested not with Germany, but "with those who, since the crime
committed by the Versailles (Diktat), have stubbornly and consistently
opposed any peaceful revision." On August 26, Roosevelt again informed
Hitler that no issue between Germany and Poland transcended the possibilities of peaceful negotiation. Hitler found Roosevelt's appeal so meaningless
that he refused to answer it. That day, Daladier sent Hitler a letter requesting that he make another direct effort to seek a peaceful agreement with
Poland.[85]

On August 27, in a long letter to Daladier, Hitler complained that he had
sought from France a return of the Saar district as a final revision of the
Versailles Treaty in the West. But he advised Daladier that such a settlement

---

[80] For the role of appeasement in the coming of war, see Paul Kennedy, "Appeasement," in
     Martel Gordon, ed., *The Origins of the Second World War Reconsidered: The A. J. P. Taylor
     Debate after Twenty-five Years* (Tiptree, 1966), 140–61.
[81] Bullitt to Hull, August 25, 1939, PSF: France, Bullitt; Bullitt to Hull, August 26, 1939, ibid.,
     FDRL; Bullitt to Hull, August 26, 1939, *FRUS, 1939*, I, 372–73; Bullitt to Hull, August 26,
     1939, ibid., 375–76.
[82] Bullitt to Hull, August 26, 1939, ibid., 373.
[83] Baynes, *Speeches of Adolf Hitler*, II, 1979–80.
[84] Ibid., 1689.
[85] Daladier to Hitler, August 26, 1939, ibid., 1693.

would not constitute acceptance of the Versailles territorial decisions in other spheres. "I have," Hitler continued, "tried year after year by the way of negotiation to effect a revision of at least the most impossible and most intolerable provisions of this 'Diktat.' This proved impossible." Revision had to come: "The 'Diktat' of Versailles was intolerable. No honorable Frenchman not even yourself, Monsieur Daladier, would ... have acted otherwise than I have done." His offer to Poland, he declared, had shocked the German people; he would not repeat it.[86]

Had Britain counseled Poland to be reasonable, Hitler averred, Europe would have enjoyed a lasting peace. It was the British and French assurance that they would fight for Poland, he charged, that sustained the "ludicrous insanity" in Polish behavior. Any acceptable settlement required the return of Danzig and the Corridor to Germany. "I see no way here," Hitler concluded, "by which I can induce Poland, which now under the protection of its guarantees, feels itself invulnerable, to adopt a peaceful solution." Europe approached its ultimate crisis on August 28, as Nevile Henderson arrived in Berlin to confer with Hitler on the status of Germany's relations with Poland. To the British offer of peace, based on a freely negotiated Polish solution, Hitler replied that he was prepared to negotiate with any reasonable Warsaw government, but Britain, he added, was incapable of inducing Poland to be reasonable.[87]

As the situation in Europe disintegrated, Washington focused its attention on London, hoping that Britain might still avert war by negotiating a Danzig settlement. "There really is not much for us do to other than wait." Moffat observed on August 28. "What trumps we had were long since played."[88] Chamberlain, Kennedy reported, doubted that Danzig was worth a war and hoped that Poland might compromise, but he would not encourage its government to do so. It mattered little. The pressures against another Munich were intense and overpowering. No Polish officials would follow the footsteps of Austrian or Czech leaders to their destruction. Britain and France supported Poland to the end. Bullitt explained their reluctance to accept the Italian appeal of August 31 for another four-nation conference. For Daladier, it promised to be another Munich in which the butchers would "dismember Poland in the absence of Poland." French opinion, Bullitt continued, was that "if Poland should be disintegrated by Germany, similar demands against Rumania would follow within a few weeks, to be followed in turn by similar demands against Yugoslavia, Hungary, and other states and finally by similar demands against France and England and in the end Italy."[89] Poland had become the test of whether the West could perpetuate the Versailles order

---

[86] Ibid., 1693–95.

[87] Ibid., 1697–98.

[88] Hooker, *The Moffat Papers*, 257.

[89] Kennedy to Hull, August 30, 1939, *FRUS, 1939*, I, 392; Biddle to Hull, August 30, 1939, ibid., 388; Bullitt to Hull, August 31, 1939, ibid., 388; Bullitt to Hull, August 31, 1939, ibid., 398–99.

as well as the international status of the powers that made it. Not without reason, Harry Hopkins feared that another Munich would be fatal to the democracies.[90] For him, as for others, the real issue of August 1939 was not Poland but the future of Europe. Germany's invasion of Poland, on September 1, assigned Versailles's entire territorial, legal, and moral order, not merely Poland, to the vagaries of war.

Whether a peaceful settlement of the Danzig issue would have eliminated war was doubtful. Hitler's territorial ambitions included Germany's eastward expansion. But from the beginning of his rise to power over Germany and his threatening role in European politics, Hitler and much of his country shared the single determination to consign the territorial and military clauses of the Versailles Treaty to history. That settlement, to achieve longevity, required the full recognition of the established interests of all, including those of Germany. Now Europe would pay the full price of the 1919 Paris decisions that failed to pass this essential test.

Throughout the August crisis, Roosevelt avoided any commitments to Europe's contestants. Europe would fight its own war. Fundamentally, Roosevelt and his advisers viewed the events of August from afar as well-informed spectators. Hull described the flow of communications from the country's diplomats as the crisis deepened after August 26: "Cables from all the major capitals of Europe were now streaming to my desk. Ambassadors Kennedy and Bullitt were frequently on the trans-Atlantic telephone to the White House and the State Department. We followed with minute care and tenseness each development...."[91] Bullitt's reporting was exceptional, enhanced by his close relations with Daladier. "I have seen Daladier constantly and intimately through this crisis." Bullitt explained to Roosevelt on August 29. "I do not telegraph half what he says to me for the simple reason that there is nothing he doesn't say and some of his remarks would raise hell if they should be known."[92]

In the end, Roosevelt's internationalism embraced everything and came to grips with nothing. Hull's very claims that the United States had done all in its power to prevent war explained why the country, in its studied avoidance of commitment, failed to achieve anything. Hull recalled in his memoirs:

> Six years and six months after I came to the State Department war came to Europe.... During those six and a half years the President and I never halted our efforts to prevent the war from coming. We took numerous steps to bolster and encourage the European and Asiatic nations still devoted to peace, and the League of Nations. We took other steps to discourage the aggressor nations from their plans of conquest, and to lay before them an alternative program for peace. When I entered the office of the Secretary of State I had a definite set of guiding principles on which foreign affairs should be

[90] Hopkins to Roosevelt, August 31, 1939, PSF: Hopkins, *FDRL*.
[91] Hull, *Memoirs of Cordell Hull*, I, 663.
[92] Bullitt to Roosevelt, August 29, 1939, Bullitt, *For the President*, 361.

conducted. We never varied from these principles, but sought by every means possible to induce other nations to embrace and follow them.[93]

Unfortunately, such reliance on principles became, for Hull, the means to avoid study and action in response to the concrete issues that troubled other nations.

VII

What underlay the disaster of war was the decision of the Paris Peace Conference to entrust the Versailles decisions to the military preponderance of the victors, as embodied in the principle of collective security. That decision presumed a permanent capitulation to the will and the design of the victors, ruling out the necessity of any diplomatic or military response. Facing no collective opposition, Hitler and Mussolini revised the Paris decisions in Africa, Austria, the Sudetenland, and Czechoslovakia, and threatened what remained of the Versailles structure of Poland. Their successes in treaty revision were not the result of diplomacy to address specific challenges to the Versailles structure, but of threatened or actual resorts to force.

What the forceful changes from Manchuria to Danzig demonstrated was the repeated failure of collective security as the ultimate defense of the Versailles Treaty structure. For some scholars, the assaults on the treaty's territorial decisions did not demand a response, arguing that the Versailles Treaty assigned no special merit to the post-war order. James T. Shotwell, the noted historian of Columbia University, observed that the central problem confronting international relations was "the need for a more flexible structure than that which identifies justice with the status quo." It was better to permit change, even through force, echoed Yale's Edwin M. Borchard, than to "endow the existing status quo with moral sanctity." To uphold a decaying status quo, he noted, might be "anything but constructive."[94] Edwin DeWitt Dickinson, professor of international law at the University of California, warned that the organization of effective sanctions dared not take precedence over "the development of procedures for orderly modification of the *status quo*." Professor Clyde Eagleton of New York University observed that the community of nations would never prevent war until it provided individual states with peaceful procedures to remedy injustices. He predicted: "[I]f force is used merely to maintain the

[93] Hull, *Memoirs of Cordell Hull*, I, 665. To foreign criticisms that Roosevelt's messages comprised little but inexpensive and risk-free ways for the United States to sustain a treaty structure beneficial to the Western democracies, Hull responded that the country was doing all in its power to convert its principles into practical results by discouraging governments from taking any action that might endanger the peace. See Hull to Kiichiro Hiranuma, Prime Minister of Japan, May 18, 1939, PSF: Japan, *FDRL*.

[94] Shotwell quoted in Current, "The United States and 'Collective Security,'" 21, 46; Edwin M. Borchard, "Neutrality," in Frank P. Davidson and George S. Viereck Jr., eds., *Before America Decides: Foresight in Foreign Affairs* (Cambridge, MA, 1938), 222, 226.

status quo, to preserve for the *beati possidentes* their happy situation, the system is bound to fail."⁹⁵

Strangely, those who advocated collective security almost invariably regarded it as a substitute for power politics. They assumed that the preponderance of nations, dedicated to preserving the status quo, could prevent aggression without war. Sir Alfred Zimmern, the noted British publicist and professor of international relations at Oxford, defined collective security as "the safety of all by all." Fortunately for him, the free, constitutional, and democratic states that he trusted controlled the bulk of the world's resources; through cooperative economic policies they could defend their universe against aggression without compromise or war. Denna Frank Fleming of Vanderbilt University, writing in November 1937, insisted that the United States take its place at the center of a collective security system, whether the commitment be to the League or to an alliance, but he denied that collective security would lead to war. "No collective action taken by a preponderance of the nations against an aggressor," he averred, "can hereafter be legally called war, nor be morally considered as war." He agreed with Zimmern that preponderant economic power, if used effectively, would prevent aggression without the danger of war.⁹⁶ Eagleton, in a speech at Harvard University in December 1937, agreed that collective action did not mean war. "Collective security," he explained, "means the combination *omnium contra unum* – of the community against a lawbreaker, whoever he may be." Such a combination of all countries would render aggression futile; thereafter, Eagleton wrote, "no state would have to demand the blood of its mothers' sons.... [A]n international police force recruited by volunteer efforts would be sufficient."⁹⁷

For Fleming, the League's collective security would not commit the United States or even the European powers to the protection of peace everywhere. Geographical safety permitted a graduated responsibility. Those most directly endangered by aggression would carry the major responsibility for opposing it. More distant countries would fulfill their obligations by applying economic sanctions. It was not strange that critics of collective security, such as Borchard, predicted that the system would always fail. "In practice," he wrote, "the collectivists do not remain collected and ... the divergence of their interests is disclosed as soon as they are asked to act." Nations, he suggested, would never defend interests other than their own.⁹⁸

---

⁹⁵ Edwin DeWitt Dickinson, "The United States and Collective Security," in Quincy Wright, ed., *Neutrality and Collective Security* (Chicago, 1936), 158, 163; Clyde Eagleton, "Collective Security," in Davidson and Viereck, *Before America Decides*, 212–13.

⁹⁶ Alfred Zimmern, "The Problem of Collective Security," in Wright, *Neutrality and Collective Security*, 4, 23, 55, 72–73 (emphasis in original); Denna F. Fleming, *The United States and World Organization, 1920–33* (New York, 1938), 536–37.

⁹⁷ Eagleton, "Collective Security," in Davidson and Viereck, *Before America Decides*, 191–92, 204–05, 211.

⁹⁸ James T. Shotwell, *On the Rim of the Abyss* (New York, 1936), 353; Dickinson, "The United States and Collective Security," in Wright, *Neutrality and Collective Security*, 179–80, 182;

After 1919, the utopia embodied in the Versailles Treaty and supported by the League of Nations, was without substance. It could not command the future; by the mid-1930s, it had collapsed. It was no longer possible to rationalize international relations by pretending that what was good for the designers of the Versailles Treaty could, without revision, be rendered acceptable to its victims. Unfortunately, the Versailles arrangements did not serve all nations equally. The endless efforts of the satisfied powers to maintain the status quo with appeals to peaceful change confronted the dissatisfied nations with the extreme choice of accepting existing conditions or defying them without benefit of negotiations or compromise. In the burgeoning conflicts of the 1930s, moreover, the powers of Europe, as in earlier times, did not face the defenseless peoples of the Afro-Asian world, who had no choice but to accept their fate as the price of progress. They now faced Germany and Italy, which defended their ambitions with rationalizations based on the Versailles decisions and the possession of superior power. No longer comforted by the illusion of a global harmony of interest, the Western democracies sought to construct a new international morality, not on the rights of the stronger, but on the rights of possession. This new utopia became the ultimate defense of the world's vested interests and the bulwark of the status quo. British historian Edward H. Carr, writing in 1939, passed judgment on those who had sought to institutionalize change:

> It is a moot point whether the politicians and publicists of the satisfied Powers, who attempted to identify international morality with security, law and order and other time-honored slogans of privileged groups, do not bear their share of responsibility for the disaster as well as the politicians and publicists of the dissatisfied Powers, who brutally denied the validity of an international morality so constituted.[99]

In the absence of a harmony of interests, the world could manage change to the maximum benefit of all, as had always been true, through wise, unflinching judgments of power, interests, and morality.

In contrast to the realities of world politics, Western leaders, no less than students of international relations, defined proper external policies not in terms of the world that existed, but in terms of the world they thought *should exist* – one that could, through rules of proper international conduct, resolve the conflicting purposes between the satisfied and dissatisfied powers peacefully and without change. Tragically, the realities of European politics were different; the choices confronting the democracies were limited, immediate, uncomfortable. Europe's arbitrary boundaries, no less than Europe's peace, rested on strength of arms. The makers of Versailles had either to revise those boundaries as time passed through diplomatic procedures, or keep potential

Fleming, *World Organization*, 543; Borchard, "Neutrality," in Davidson and Viereck, *Before America Decides*, 225.

[99] Edward Hallett Carr, *The Twenty Years' Crisis, 1919–1939*, 224–25 (New York, 1996).

aggressors weak by force. They did neither, preferring instead to assume that they could protect their privileged positions without either sacrificing their freedom in binding defensive guarantees or accepting a new European order of power. Having abjured the historical courses available to them, they would now defend what remained of their universe through the very alliances and destruction they sought to avoid.

Bibliography

Archives and Manuscript Collections

Churchill College, Cambridge University
Cabinet Document
Franklin Delano Roosevelt Library Hyde Park, New York
President's Personal File
President's Secretary's File
Speech File
Press Conferences
Official File
R. Walton Moore Papers
Library of Congress
Committee Papers, Senate Committee on Foreign Relations, *Cong. Record*, 64th
    Congress, 2nd Session, February 1, 1917.
  65th Congress, 3rd Session, February 21, 1918; December 21, 1918; February 21,
    1919.
  66th Congress, 1st Session, August 20, 1919.
  67th Congress, Special Session, Warren G. Harding's Inaugural Address, March 4,
    1921.
  69th Congress, 1st Session, December 18, 1925.
Congressional Digest, May 1923; February 1926.
Key Pittman Papers
National Archives
Microfilm Records, Diplomatic Correspondence Reel M982–8
U.S. Government Captured German Documents, Record Group 59
Public Record Office, London
Cabinet Minutes (CAB)
Roskill Library, Churchill College, Cambridge University
Malcolm Christie Papers
Lord Halifax Papers
Maurice Hankey Papers
Sir Eric Phipps Papers
William Strang Papers
Robert Vansittart Papers

University of Birmingham
Neville Chamberlain Papers

Government Publications

Public Record Office, London
Documents on German Foreign Policy (DGFP), 1918–1945.
DGFP, Series D, II, London, 1949.
Medlicott, W. N., Douglas Deakin, and Gillian Bennett, eds., *Documents on British Foreign Policy (DBFP)*, *1919–1939, Second Ser., XVIII–XIX*, London, 1980.
Woodward, E. L., and Rohan Butler, eds., *Documents on British Foreign Policy (DBFP)*, *1919–1939*, Third Series, 1938, I and II, 1949: IV, London, 1950.
U.S. Department of State, *Papers Relating to the Foreign Relations of the United States (FRUS): The Lansing Papers, 1914–1920*. 2 vols. Washington, 1939–1940.
  The Paris Peace Conference. 13 vols. Washington, 1942–1947; *The Soviet Union, 1933–1939*, Washington, 1952.
  1914, Supplement, 1928.
  1915, Supplement, 1928.
  1915, 1928.
  1917, 1926.
  1919, 2 vols, 1934.
  1922, 1938.
  1931, 1946.
  1932, 1948.
  1933, General, 1950.
  1936, 1953.
  1938, vol. 1, 1954.
  1939, vol. 1, General, 1956.
U.S. Department of State, *Peace and War: United States Foreign Policy, 1931–1941*, Washington, 1942.
  Documents on German Foreign Policy, 1918–1945, Series D, II, IV, Washington, 1949.

Published Documents and Memoirs

Baker, Ray Stannard, and William E. Dodd, eds., *Papers of Woodrow Wilson: College and State*, New York, 1925.
Bullitt, Orville H. ed., *For the President: Personal and Secret*, Boston, 1972.
Carnegie Endowment for International Peace, *The Imperial Japanese Mission*, Washington, 1918.
  The Sino-Japanese Negotiations of 1915: Japanese and Chinese Documents, Washington, 1921.
Curtis, Monica, *Documents on International Affairs, 1938*, London, 1943.
Degras, Jane, ed., *Soviet Documents on Foreign Policy, II, III*, New York, London, Toronto, 1951–1953.
Grayson, Cary T., *Woodrow Wilson: An Intimate Memoir*, New York, 1960.
Gwynn, Stephen, ed., *The Letters and Friendships of Sir Cecil Spring-Rice: A Record*, London, 1929.
Lansing, Robert, *War Memoirs of Robert Lansing*, Indianapolis, 1935.

Link, Arthur S., *The Papers of Woodrow Wilson* (69 vols.), Princeton, 1966–1994. Vols. 41, 44, 45, 46, 51, 53, 54, 55, 56, 63.

Lloyd George, David, *Memoirs of the Peace Conference*, 2 vols. New Haven, 1939.

Montoux, Paul (trans. and ed. Arthur S. Link with the assistance of Manfred F. Boemeke), *The Deliberations of the Council of Four, March 24-June 28, 1919*, Princeton, 1992.

Nixon, Edgar B., *Franklin D. Roosevelt and Foreign Affairs*. Vol. 2. Cambridge, MA, 1969.

Rosenman, Samuel I., *The Public Papers and Addresses of Franklin D. Roosevelt*. Vol. 6. *The Constitution Prevails*. New York, 1938.

Schewe, Donald B., ed. *Franklin D. Roosevelt and Foreign Affairs*. Vol 3. New York, 1979.
    Franklin D. Roosevelt and Foreign Affairs. Vol. 8. New York. 1979.

Seymour, Charles, ed., *The Intimate Papers of Colonel House*, 4 vols. (Vol. 3), Boston, 1928.

Starr-Myers, William, ed., *The State Papers and Other Writings of Herbert Hoover*, Garden City, 1934.

Interviews

Perkins, Frances. University of Illinois, Urbana. Spring 1958.

Roosevelt, Eleanor. Hyde Park, New York. Summer 1959.

Books

Adams, D. K. *FDR, The New Deal, and Europe*. Keele (England), 1979.

Adler, Selig. *The Isolationist Impulse: Its Twentieth Century Reaction*. New York, 1957.

Albrecht-Carrie, René. *Italy and the Paris Peace Conference*. New York, 1938.

Ambrosius, Lloyd W. *Woodrow Wilson and the American Diplomatic Tradition*. New York, 1987.

Bailey, Thomas A. *Woodrow Wilson and the Lost Peace*. Chicago, 1963.

Baker, Ray Stannard. *Woodrow Wilson and the World Settlement*, vol. 2. Garden City, New York, 1922.

Baker, Ray Stannard, and William E. Dodd, eds. *The Public Papers of Woodrow Wilson*, vol. 1. *The New Democracy*. New York, 1925.
    The Public Papers of Woodrow Wilson, vol. 2, *College and State*. New York, 1925.

Bartlett, Ruhl J. *The League to Enforce Peace*. Chapel Hill, 1944.

Baynes, Norman, ed. *The Speeches of Adolf Hitler*, vol. 2. New York, 1969.

Bennett, Edward M. *Separated by a Common Language: Franklin Delano Roosevelt and Anglo-American Relations, 1933–1939: The Roosevelt-Chamberlain Rivalry*. Lincoln, 2002.

Berle, Bernice Bishop, and Travis Beale Jacobs, eds. *Navigating the Rapids, 1918–1971: From the Papers of Adolph A. Berle*. New York, 1973.

Beveridge, Albert J. *The State of the Union*. Indianapolis, 1924.

Blakey, George T. *Historians on the Home Front: American Propagandists for the Great War*. Lexington, 1970.

Bolloten, Burnett. *The Spanish Civil War: Revolution and Counter Revolution*. Chapel Hill, 1991.

Bond, B. *British Military Policy between the Two World Wars.* Oxford, 1980.

Bonsal, Stephen. *Unfinished Business.* Garden City, 1944.

Borg, Dorothy. *The United States and the Far Eastern Crisis of 1933–1938.* Cambridge, MA, 1964.

Blum, John Morton, ed. *From the Morgenthau Diaries: Years of Crisis, 1928–1938,* vol. 1. Boston, 1959.

Bowers, Claude. *My Mission to Spain: Watching the Rehearsal for World War II.* New York, 1954.

Brune, Lester. *Chronological History of the United States Foreign Relations, 1776 to January 20, 1981,* vol. 2. New York, 1985.

Buitenhuis, Peter. *The Great War of Words: British, American, and Canadian Propaganda and Fiction, 1914–1933.* Vancouver, BC, 1987.

Bull, Hedley. *The Anarchical Society.* London, 1977.

Bullitt, Orville H. ed. *For the President, Personal and Secret: Correspondence between Franklin D. Roosevelt and William C. Bullitt.* Boston, 1972.

Bullock, Alan. *Hitler: A Study in Tyranny.* New York, 1962.

Bulow, General Otto von. *Memoirs.* New York, 1930.

Burns, Richard Dean, and Edward M. Bennett, eds. *Diplomats in Crisis: U.S., Chinese, Japanese Relations, 1919–1941.* Santa Barbara, 1974.

Butler, Michael. *Cautious Visionary: Cordell Hull and Trade Reform.* Kent, 1998.

Cantril, Hadley, ed. *Public Opinion.* Princeton, 1951.

Carr, Edward Hallett. *The Twenty Years' Crisis, 1919–1939.* New York, 1966.

Chamberlain, Neville. *In Search of Peace: Speeches, 1937–1938.* London, 1938.

Chapman, George. *A Passionate Prodigality.* New York, 1933.

Churchill, Winston S. *Step by Step: 1936–1939.* London, 1939, 1975.

  The Gathering Storm. Boston, 1948.

  While England Slept: A Survey of World Affairs, 1932–1938. New York, 1938.

Cole, Wayne S. *Senator Gerald P. Nye and American Foreign Relations.* Minneapolis, 1962.

Coogan, John W. *The End of Neutrality: The United States, Britain, and Maritime Rights, 1899–1915.* Ithaca, 1981.

Cooper, Duff. *Old Men Forget.* New York, 1954.

Cooper, John Milton Jr. *Breaking the Heart of the World: Woodrow Wilson and the Fight for the League of Nations.* New York, 2001.

  The Warrior and the Priest: Woodrow Wilson and Theodore Roosevelt. Cambridge, MA, 1983.

Craig, Gordon A., and Felix Gilbert, eds. *The Diplomats, 1919–1939,* vol. 2. New York, 1963.

Crozier, W. T. *Off the Record: Political Interviews, 1933–1943.* London, 1973.

Curtis, Monica, ed. *Documents on International Affairs, 1938.* London, 1943.

Dallek, Robert. *Franklin D. Roosevelt and American Foreign Policy, 1932–1945.* New York, 1979.

Davidson, Frank P., and George S. Vierick Jr. eds. *Before America Decides: Foresight in Foreign Affairs.* Cambridge, MA, 1938.

Dennis, A. L. P. *The Anglo-Japanese Alliance.* Berkeley, 1923.

Dilks, David, ed. *The Diaries of Sir Alexander Cadogan, 1938–1945.* London, 1971.

Dirksen, Herbert von, *Moscow, Tokyo, London: Twenty Years of German Foreign Policy.* Norman, 1952.

Divine, Robert. *The Illusion of Neutrality.* Chicago, 1962.

Doughty, Robert A. *Pyrrhic Victory: French Strategy and Operations in the Great War*. Cambridge, 2005.

Eden, Anthony. *Memoirs: Facing the Dictators*. London, Boston, 1962.

Edwards, Sir James E. *A Short History of World War I*. New York, 1968.

Einstein, Lewis. *A Prophecy of the War*. New York, 1918.

Eisenhower, John S. D., and Joanne Thompson Eisenhower, *Yanks: The Epic Story of the American Army in World War I*. New York, 2001.

Ellis, George D. ed. *Platforms of the Two Great Political Parties*. Washington, 1932.

Fay, Sidney Bradshaw. *The Origins of the World War*. New York, 1928.

Feiling, Keith. *The Life of Neville Chamberlain*. New York, 1946, 1970.

Ferrell, Robert H. *The Origins of the Kellogg-Briand Pact*. New Haven, 1952.

ed. *The Twentieth Century: An Almanac*. New York, 1984.

Fisher, Irving. *League or War*. New York, 1923.

America's Interest in World Peace. New York, 1924.

Fite, Gilbert C., and Norman A. Graebner. *Recent United States History*. New York, 1972.

Fleming, D. F. *The United States and the League of Nations*. New York, 1932.

Fleming, Denna F. *The United States and the World Court*. New York, 1945.

The United States and the World Organization, 1920–1933. New York, 1938.

Florinsky, Michael T. *Russia: A History and an Interpretation*. New York, 1958.

Foley, Robert T. *German Strategy and the Path to Verdun: Eric von Falkenhayn and the Development of Attrition, 1870–1916*. New York, 2005.

Fromkin, David. *A Peace to End All Peace: The Fall of the Ottoman Empire and the Creation of the Modern Middle East*. New York, 1989.

Gardner, Lloyd C. *Safe for Democracy: The Anglo-American Response to Revolution, 1913–1923*. New York, 1984.

Gelfand, Lawrence E. *The Inquiry: American Preparation for Peace, 1917–1919*. New Haven, 1963.

Gilbert, Martin, ed. *Britain and Germany between the Wars*. London, 1964.

Winston S. Churchill: Companion to the Coming of War, 1936–1939, vol. 5. Boston, 1983.

Gordon, Martel, ed. *The Origins of the Second World War Reconsidered: The A. J. P. Taylor Debates After Twenty-Five Years*. Tiptree, 1966.

Grayson, Gary Traverse. *Woodrow Wilson: An Intimate Memoir*. New York, 1960.

Grew, Joseph C. *Ten Years in Japan*. New York, 1944.

Graebner, Norman A. *Ideas and Diplomacy: Readings in the Intellectual Tradition of American Foreign Policy*. Oxford, 1964.

Gruber, Carol S. *Mars and Minerva: World War I and the Uses of Higher Learning in America*. Baton Rouge, 1975.

Gwynn, Stephen, ed. *The Letters and Friendships of Sir Cecil Spring-Rice: A Record*, vol. 1. London, 1929.

Halifax, Lord. *Fullness of Days*. New York, 1957.

Fullness of Time. London, 1965.

Halle, Louis J. *Men and Nations*. Princeton, 1962.

Harley, John Eugene. *The League of Nations and the New International Order*. New York, 1921.

Harrod, Roy Forbes. *The Life of John Maynard Keynes*. New York, 1969.

Hart, B. H. Liddell. *The Road to War, 1914–1918*. New York, 1968.

Harvey, John. *The Diplomatic Journals of Oliver Harvey 1937–1940.* London, 1970.

Haslam, Jonathan. *The Soviet Union and the Struggle for Collective Security in Europe, 1933–1939.* London, 1984.

Headlam-Morley, Sir James. *Studies in Diplomatic History.* London, 1930.

Hitler, Adolf. *Mein Kampf.* New York, 1940.

    Mein Kampf. trans. Ralph Manheim, Boston, 1971.

Holborn, Hajo. *The Political Collapse of Europe.* New York, 1951.

Hooker, Nancy Harvison, ed. *The Moffat Papers: Selections from the Diplomatic Journals of Jay Pierrepont Moffat, 1919–1943.* Cambridge, MA, 1956.

Hoover, Herbert. *The Memoirs of Herbert Hoover.* New York, 1951–52, 2 vols.

Hornbeck, Stanley K. *The United States and the Far East.* Boston, 1942.

Hull, Cordell. *Fundamental Principles of International Policy.* Washington, 1937.

    Memoirs. vol. 1, London, New York, 1948.

Ickes, Harold L. *The Secret Diary of Harold L. Ickes: The Inside Struggle, 1936–1939,* vol. 2. London, 1955.

Ishii, Kikuijiro. *Diplomatic Commentaries,* trans. William R. Langdon. Baltimore, 1936.

James, Robert Rhodes, ed. *Winston S. Churchill: His Complete Speeches, 1897–1963,* vol. 4 1935–1942. New York and London, 1974.

Jonas, Manfred. *Isolationism in America.* Ithaca, New York, 1966.

Keegan, Sir John. *The First World War.* New York, 1999.

Kennan, George F. *From Prague after Munich: Diplomatic Papers, 1938–1940.* Princeton, 1968.

    Russia and the West under Lenin and Stalin. Boston, 1961.

    The Fateful Alliance: France, Russia, and the Coming of the First World War. New York, 1984.

Kershaw, Ian. *Hitler 1889–1936: Hubris.* New York, 1999.

    Hitler 1936–1945: Nemesis. London, 2000.

    Making Friends With Hitler: Lord Londonderry and Britain's Road to War. London, 2004.

King, Wuntz. *Woodrow Wilson, Wellington Koo, and the Chinese Question at the Paris Peace Conference.* London, 1959.

Klemperer, Klements von. *German Resistance against Hitler: The Search for Allies Abroad, 1938–1945.* Oxford, 1992.

Knock, Thomas J. *To End All Wars: Woodrow Wilson and the Quest for a New World Order.* New York, 1992.

Lansing, Robert. *The Peace Negotiations: A Personal Narrative.* Boston, 1921.

Link, Arthur S. *The Papers of Woodrow Wilson* (69 vols.). Princeton, 1966.

    The Struggle for Neutrality, 1914–1915. Princeton, 1960.

Lippmann, Walter. *The Public Philosophy.* Boston, 1955.

Livermore, Stewart W. *Politics Is Adjourned: Woodrow Wilson and the War Congress, 1916–1918.* Middletown, 1966.

Lloyd George, David. *Memories of the Peace Conference.* New York, 1939. 2 vols.

Lodge, Henry Cabot. *The Senate and the League of Nations.* New York, 1925.

Loewenheim, Francis L. *Peace or Appeasement? Hitler, Chamberlain, and the Munich Crisis.* Boston, 1965.

Luebke, Frederich. *Bonds of Loyalty.* De Kalb, 1974.

Lutz, Herman. *German-French Unity: Basis for European Peace.* Chicago, 1957.

Macdonald, Lyn. *1915 The Death of Innocence*. New York, 2004.

Manchester, William. *The Arms of Krupp, 1587–1968*. Boston, 1968.

The Last Lion: Winston Spencer Churchill, Alone, 1932–1940. Boston, 1988.

Mantoux, Paul. *The Deliberations of the Council of Four (March 24-June 28, 1919)*. trans. and ed. Arthur S. Link, with the assistance of Manfred F. Boemeke, Princeton, 1992, 2 vols.

Marbury, Theodore, and Horace E. Flack, eds. *William Howard Taft: Taft Papers on the League of Nations*. New York, 1920.

Marks, Frederick W. *Wind Over Sand: The Diplomacy of Franklin Roosevelt*. Athens, 1988, vols. 2 and 3.

Marks, Sally. *International Relations in Europe, 1918–1933*. New York, 1976.

Mayer, Arno J. *Politics and Diplomacy of Peace-Making*. New York, 1967.

Miller, David Hunter. *The Pact of Paris: A Study of the Briand-Kellogg Treaty*. New York, 1928.

My Diary: At the Conference of Paris. New York, 1924.

May, Ernest R. *The World War and American Isolation, 1914–1917*. Chicago, 1966.

McMillan, Margaret. *Paris 1919: Six Months that Changed the World*. New York, 2002.

The Drafting of the Covenant. New York, 1928, 2 vols.

Morgenthau, Hans. *Politics Among Nations*. New York, 1949.

Morison, Elting E. *The Letters of Theodore Roosevelt*. Cambridge, MA, 1951.

Morley, Felix. *The Society of Nations*. Washington, 1932.

Morton, Frederick. *Thunder at Twilight: Vienna 1913/1914*. New York, 1928.

Moses, John A., and Christopher Pugsley. *The German Empire of Britain's Pacific Dominions, 1871–1919: Essays on the Role of Australia and New Zealand in World Politics in the Age of Imperialism*. Claremont, 2000.

Murphy, James W. ed. *Speeches and Addresses of Warren G. Harding, President of the United States*. Washington, 1923.

Nevins, Allen. *Henry White: Thirty Years of American Diplomacy*. New York, 1930.

Nicolson, Harold. *Peacemaking, 1919*. London, 1933.

Nixon, Edgar B., ed. *Roosevelt and Foreign Affairs*. Cambridge, MA, 1969, 3 vols.

Noble, George Barnard. *Policies and Opinions at Paris, 1919*. New York, 1935.

Nolan, Cathal J., ed. *Notable U.S. Ambassadors Since 1775: Michael Polley, "William E. Dodd."* Westport, 1997.

Paasen, Prince van. *Days of Our Years*. New York, 1939.

Palmer, Frederick. *Bliss, Peacemaker: The Life and Letters of General Tasker Howard Bliss*. New York, 1934.

Payne, Howard C., Edward M. Bennett, and Raymond Callahan. *As the Storm Clouds Gathered: European Perceptions of American Foreign Policy in the 1930s*. Republished by Regina Books, Claremont, n.d.

Peterson, H. C. *Propaganda for War*. Norman, 1939.

Phelps, Hugh D. *Between the Revolution and the West: A Political Biography of Maxim M. Litvinov*. Boulder, San Francisco, Oxford, 1992.

Pool, James. *Hitler and His Secret Partners: Contributions, Lost and Rewards, 1933–1945*. New York, 1997.

Potemkine, Vladimir et. al. *Histoire de la Diplomatie, 1919–1939*. trans. I. Levin, J. Tarr, and Boris Metzel. Paris, 1947, vol. 3.

Rauch, Georg von. *A History of Soviet Russia*. New York, 1957. trans. Peter and Annette Jacobsohn.

Reed, Anthony, and David Fisher. *The Deadly Embrace: Hitler, Stalin and the Nazi-Soviet Pact, 1939–1941*. New York, 1988.

Remarque, Erich Maria. *All Quiet on the Western Front*. Greewich, 1967.

Roosevelt, Elliott. *FDR: His Personal Letters, 1928–1945*. London, 1952, 3 vols, vol. 2.

Root, Elihu. *Men and Policies*. eds. Robert Bacon and James Brown Scott. Cambridge, MA, 1924.

Rumbold, Sir Horace. *The War Crisis in Berlin, July-August 1914*. London, 1940.

Salvemini, Gaetano. *Prelude to World War II*. London, 1953.

Sanders, Michael. *British Propaganda during the First World War*. London, 1932.

Schriftgiesser, Karl. *This Was Normalcy*. Boston, 1948.

Schulte-Nordholt, Jan Wilhelm. *A Life for Peace*. Berkeley, 1991.

Scott, William Evans. *Alliance Against Hitler*. Durham, 1962.

Shepardson, William H., and William O. Scroggs. *The United States in World Affairs, 1939*. New York, 1940.

Shirer, William L. *The Rise and Fall of the Third Reich*. New York, 1960.
    "This is Berlin": Radio Broadcasts from Berlin. Woodstock, 1999.
    This is Berlin: Journals of a Foreign Correspondent, 1934–1941. New York, 2001.
    Berlin Diary: The Journal of a Foreign Correspondent, 1933–1941. London, 1941.

Shotwell, James T. *At the Paris Peace Conference*. New York, 1937.
    On the Rim of the Abyss. New York, 1936.

Simonds, Frank H. *American Foreign Policy in the Post-War Years: The Albert Shaw Lectures in Diplomatic History*. Baltimore, 1979.

Sonnenfeldt, Richard W. *Witness to Nuremberg*. New York, 2006.

Stalin, Joseph. *Leninism*. New York, 1933.

Stiller, James H. *George S. Messersmith: Diplomat of Democracy*. Chapel Hill, 1987.

Stimson, Henry L. *Far Eastern Crisis: Recollections and Observations*. New York, 1939.

Stimson, Henry L. and McGeorge Bundy. *On Active Service in Peace and War*. New York, 1948.

Strachey, John. *The Menace of Fascism*. London, 1933.

Strang, Baron William. *Home and Abroad*. London, 1956.

Takeuchi, Tatsuji. *War and Diplomacy in the Japanese Empire*. New York, 1935.

Tardieu, Andre. *The Truth About the Treaty*. Indianapolis, 1921.

Taylor, A. J. P. *Origins of the Second World War*. New York, 1962.

Templewood, Viscount. *Nine Troubled Years*. London, 1941.

Thayer, Charles W. *Diplomat*. Westport, 1974.

Thompson, John M. *Russia and the Soviet Union: An Historical Introduction*. New York, 1986.

Thorne, Christopher. *The Approach of War, 1938–1939*. London, 1968.

Toland, John. *Adolf Hitler*. New York, 1976.

Trask, David F. *The Supreme War Council*. Middletown, 1961.
    General Tasker Howard Bliss and the "Sessions of the World" 1919. American Philosophical Society, 1966.

The AEF and Coalition Warfare, 1917–1918. Lawrence, 1993.

Trevelyan, George M. *Grey of Fallodon.* Boston, 1937.

Tuchman, Barbara. *The Zimmermann Telegram.* New York, 1958.

Tumulty, Joseph P. *Woodrow Wilson as I Knew Him.* Garden City, 1921.

Unterberger, Betty Miller, *Intervention against Communism: Did the United States Try to Overthrow the Soviet Government, 1918–1920?* Texas A&M Lecture Series, 1986.

Van Alstyne, Richard W. *American Diplomacy in Action.* Stanford, 1947.

Vansittart, Robert. *The Mist Procession.* London, 1958.

Walworth, Arthur. *Wilson and the Peacemakers: American Diplomacy at the Paris Peace Conference, 1919.* New York, 1986.

Weinberg, Gerhard L. *The Foreign Policy of Hitler's Germany: Diplomatic Revolution in Europe.* Chicago, 1970.

Hitler and World War II. New York, 1955.

White, William Allen. *The Autobiography of William Allen White.* New York, 1946.

Widenor, William C. *Henry Cabot Lodge and the Search for an American Foreign Policy.* Berkeley, 1980.

Wikipedia on "Herschel Grynszpan."

Wilson, A. N. *After the Victories.* New York, 2005.

Wilson, Edith Boling. *My Memoirs.* Indianapolis, 1938.

Wilson, Hugh R. *Diplomat Between Wars.* New York, 1941.

Wright, Dwight, ed. *Neutrality and Collective Security.* Chicago, 1936.

Yates, Louis. *United States and French Security.* New York, 1957.

Articles in Journals and Magazines

Ambrosius, Lloyd, "Wilson's League of Nations," *Maryland Historical Magazine,* 65 (Winter 1970), 370–93.

Beveridge, Alfred J., " George Washington and Present American Problems," *American Monthly,* 13 (April 1921), 46.

Boothe, Leon, "Lord Grey, the United States, and the Political Effort for a League of Nations, 1914–1920," *Maryland Historical Magazine,* 65 (Spring 1970), 36–39, 50–51.

"A Fettered Envoy: Lord Grey's Special Mission to the United States, 1919–1920," *The Review of Politics,* 33 January 1971), 78–94.

Borah, William E. "Disarmament," *Nations Business,* ix (September 1921), 7–8.

"Opinion Outlaws War," *Independent,* 113 (September 13, 1924) 147–49.

Chamberlain, Joseph F., Proceedings of the Society of International Law (1929), 93.

Claude, Inis, "The Collective Theme in International Relations," *International Journal of Canadian Institute of International Affairs,* 24, no. 4 (Autumn 1969), 639–50.

Cooper, John Milton, "The Shock of Recognition: The Impact of World War I on America," *The Virginia Quarterly Review,* 79 (Autumn 2000), 577.

Current, Richard N., "The Stimson Doctrine," *The American Historical Review,* LIX. No. 3 (April 1954), 516–517, 518, 519, 529, 534, 537, 541–42.

Dewar, George A. B., "Peace or Truce: After the Signature," *The Nineteenth Century* (July 1919), 29.

Dickinson, G. Lowes, "Can These Bones Live?" *New Republic,* 36 (October 24, 1923), 229–30.

Donnelly, J. B., "An Empty Chair in Paris: Dawes, Sweetser, and the Manchurian Crisis," *A Journal of the Liberal Arts*, no. 19, Washington and Jefferson College (Spring 1970), 37–49.

Einstein, Lewis, "Our Still Dubious Foreign Policy," *North American Review*, 232 (September 1931), 210–18.

Featherstone, Steve, "The Line is Hot: A History of the Machine Gun, Shot," *Harper's Magazine*, 311 (December 2005), 59–66.

Fosdick, Raymond B., "The League of Nations after Two Years," *Atlantic Monthly*, 130 (August 1922), 262.

"Will the League Stop Wars," *New York Times Book Review and Magazine* (October 17, 1920), 1.

Freeman, Edward A., "Danger to the Peace of Europe," *Forum*, 12 (November 1891), 301.

Friedlander, Robert A., "New Light on the Anglo-American Reaction to the Ethiopian War, 1935–1936," *Mid America*, XLV (April 1963), 115–25.

Gardner, William Howard, "A Naval View of the Conference," *Atlantic Monthly*, 129 (April 1922), 522–39.

Grey, Viscount of Fallodon, "Viscount Grey on the League of Nations," *Survey*, 40 (July 8, 1918), 401.

Hackett, Francis, "The League at Half Stage," *Survey*, 52 (July 1, 1924), 388.

Housley, John Eugene, "The World Court of Justice," *Journal of Applied Sociology*, 7 (May-June 1923), 245.

Howley, Charles, "Hot Topics in Germany: Aggression in World War I," *Christian Science Monitor* (August 2004), 6–7.

Holt, Hamilton, "The Successful League of Nations," *Independent*, 104 (October 23, 1920), 124.

Hudson, Manley O., "The Permanent Court of International Justice – An Indispensable First Step," *Annals of the American Academy*, 108 (July 1923), 188–90.

James, Edwin L., "Our World Power and Moral Influence," *International Digest*, I (October 1930), 21–24.

Josephson, Harold, "Outlawing War: Internationalism and the Pact of Paris," *Diplomatic History*, 3 (Fall 1979), 377–90.

Killen, Linda, "Self Determination vs. Territorial Integrity: Conflict within the American Delegation at Paris toward the Russian Borderlands," *Nationalities Papers: The Association for the Studies of the Nationalities (USSR and East Europe)*, Spring 1982, X, no. 1, 6578.

Lauren, Paul G., "Human Rights in History: Diplomacy and Racial Equality at the Paris Peace Conference," *Diplomatic History*, 26 (Summer 1978), 265.

Lauzanne, Stephanie, "France and the Treaty," *North American Review*, 210 (November 1919), 604–12.

Lowell, A. Lawrence, "A League to Enforce Peace," *North American Review*, 205 (January 1917), 29.

"A League to Enforce Peace," *Independent*, 82 (June 28, 1915), 533.

"A League to Enforce Peace," *World's Work*, 30 (October 1915), 720.

Madariaga, Salvador de, "Disarmament – American Plan," *Atlantic Monthly*, 143 (April 1929), 537–38.

Marshall, Alfred, "The Social Possibilities of Economic Chivalry," *Economic Journal*, 17 (March 1907), 16n.

Morris, Roland S., *Proceedings of the Society of International Law* (1930), 90.

Peffer, Nathaniel, "Manchuria: A Warning to America," *Harper's Magazine*, CLXVI (February 1933), 301–08.

Powers, H. H., "After Five Years," *Atlantic Monthly*, 133 (May 1924), 694–95.

Schmitt, Harris A., "Hitler: Obsession without End," *The Sewanee Review*, XCVI, no. 1 (January 1988), 158–59.

"The Treaty of Versailles: Mirror of Europe's Postwar Agony," *The Treaty of Versailles: The Shaping of the Modern World, Proceedings of the Virginia Humanities Conference April 7–8, 1989* (Center for Programs in the Humanities, Virginia Technical University), 1989.

Selassie, Haile, "Appeal to the League of Nations" (June 30, 1936).

Shotwell, James T., "The Pact of Paris: With Historical Commentary," *International Conciliation*, 243 (October 1928), 453, 458.

Stillman, W. J., "Italy and the Triple Allliance," *Nation*, 51 (October 30, 1890), 340.

Stimson, Henry L., "The Pact of Paris: Three Years of Development," *Foreign Affairs*, XI (October, 1932), Supplement.

Stracham, Hew, "The End of All Wars? Lessons of World War I Revisited," *Foreign Affairs*, 82 (January-February 2003), 148–49.

Stromberg, Roland, "Uncertainties and Obscurities about the League of Nations," *Journal of the History of Ideas*, 33 (January-March 1972), 139.

Taft, William Howard, "From Battle and Murder, and From Sudden Death," *The Nation's Business*, V (February 1917), 19.

Teichova, Alice, "Great Britain in Europe's Affairs, March 15 to August 21, 1939," *Historica*, III (Prague, 1961), 239–311.

"The League on its Merits," *Independent*, 109 (April 14, 1923).

"The Strange Case of Karl and Adolf," *The Economist*, 352 (September 11, 1999), 8.

Thompson, Dorothy, "National Socialism: Theory and Practice," *Foreign Affairs*, XIII (July 1935), 573.

Thompson, J. A., "Woodrow Wilson and World War I: A Reappraisal," *Journal of American Studies*, 19, (1981), 309–30.

Toth, Charles W., "Isolationism and the Emergence of Borah: An Appeal to American Tradition," *Western Political Science Quarterly*, 14 (June 1961).

"Versailles Revisited," *U.S. News & World Report* (December 2, 2002), 44–45.

Villard, Oswald Garrison, "Briand's Failure," *The Nation*, CXIII (December 7, 1921), 641–42.

Vinson, J. Chal, "The Imperial Conference of 1921 and the Anglo-Japanese Alliance," *Pacific Historical Review*, XXXI (August 1962), 258, 261.

Weinberg, Gerald L., "Munich After 50 Years," *Foreign Affairs*, 67 (Fall 1988), 168–73.

"We Must Kill to Save," *North American Review*, 207 (February 1918), 165.

"What They're Ending in Germany," *Time*, October 11, 2010, 15.

"Wilson's Great Utterance," *New Republic*, 17 (June 5, 1916), 103.

Woodside, Willson, "The Road to Munich," *Harper's Monthly Magazine*, 178 (January 1939), 28–30, 35, 37.

"What Would Germany Fight With," *Chamber of Commerce Journal* (December 1938), 426 ff.

Newspapers

Alexandria (Virginia) *Gazette*, October 14, 1937

Detroit Free Press, February 2, 1919

Izvestiia, Radek, Karl, "The Bases of the Foreign Policy of the Soviet Union," December 16, 1933

  "Litvinov's Speech to the Central Committee," November 11, 1936

New York Herald Tribune March 18, 1935

New York Post, March 25, 1935

The New York Times, January 16, 1919; August 13, 1920; October 24, October 29, 1924; January 28, 1929; January 30, 1933; March 8, September 29, 1936; September 15, 19, 21, 1938; September 25-October 1, 1938; March 6, 1939; January 30, 1983

Philadelphia Bulletin, February 3, 1919

Pravda, January 7, 1936; "Speech of Hitler: Threat of a Madman," September 18, 1936

Richmond (Virginia) *Times Dispatch*, September 26, 1938

Index

DATE DUE

Made in the USA
San Bernardino, CA
10 January 2017